MARRAKESH
FEZ & RABAT

*'...like the desert palm, though it is rooted in Africa, it is watered by
Islam and rustled by the winds of Europe...'*

Barnaby Rogerson

About the Guide

The **full-colour introduction** gives the author's overview of the region, together with suggested **itineraries** plus a regional **'where to go' map** and **feature** to help you plan your trip.

Illuminating and entertaining **cultural chapters** on local history, art, architecture, music and wildlife give you a rich flavour of the region.

Planning Your Trip starts with the basics of when to go, getting there and getting around, coupled with other useful information, including a section for disabled travellers. The **Practical A–Z** deals with all the **essential information** and **contact details** that you may need while you are away.

Each of the three **city chapters** are arranged in a loose touring order, with plenty of practical information on how to get around, where to eat and stay, as well as suggestions for day trips. The author's top **'Don't Miss'** ⭐ **sights** are highlighted at the start of each chapter.

Although everything we list in this guide is **personally recommended**, our authors inevitably have their own favourite places to eat and stay. Whenever you see this **Author's Choice** ⭐ icon beside a listing, you will know that it is a little bit out of the ordinary.

Hotel Price Guide (*see also* p.79)

Luxury	€€€€€	over €200
Expensive	€€€€	€100–€200
Moderate	€€	€50–€100
Inexpensive	€	€20–€50
Cheap	€	under €20

Restaurant Price Guide (*see also* p.84)

Expensive	€€€	over €30
Moderate	€€	€15–30
Inexpensive	€	under €15

About the Author

Barnaby Rogerson first fell in love with the idea of Morocco aged nine, standing before Delacroix's *Arab Tax* in Washington D.C.'s National Gallery. He first visited Morocco when he was 16, on an errand from Gibraltar to buy fresh vegetables in the souk in Tetouan. He has been going back ever since, but has also found time to lay pebble floors in grottoes and write a history of North Africa.

2nd edition published 2010

INTRODUCING MARRAKESH FEZ & RABBAT

01

Top: Koutoubia mosque at sunset, Marrakesh

Above: Mint tea in a street market, Marrakesh

Morocco has been likened to both an island and a palm tree. For it is all but surrounded by three seas – the Atlantic, the Mediterranean and the sand sea of the Sahara – and, like the desert palm, though rooted in Africa, it is watered by Islam and rustled by the winds of Europe. The country has an exoticism all its own, created by these conflicting influences washing against its shore.

Whatever your experience of the Latin temper of southern Europeans, the heady lifestyle of Morocco is more dramatic. From the moment you land, adventure assails you. In simple transactions, such as buying a kilo of oranges, there is unexpected drama, humour and competitive gamesmanship. The sun is always shining somewhere in Morocco, and from March to October it is difficult to avoid. Travelling is cheap and easy. You can fly, drive, take the train, or share the tempo of local life by packing into a communal taxi or bus.

It is not only the sights of Morocco but also the everyday way of life that lingers in the memory: breakfasts of aromatic coffee, croissants and freshly squeezed orange juice, the heady odour of virgin olive oil. In the markets stand shiny pyramids of fruit, vegetables, olives, dates and nuts, so fresh and pure they seem like a new species altogether.

This guide concentrates on the chief glory of Morocco – the vast storehouse of architecture, culture, history, cuisine and craftsmanship preserved in the Imperial Cities. Morocco's grandest cities are proof in mud, stone, wood and tile of both its Muslim heart and of its several influences: Berber, Roman, Byzantine, Arab, Iberian, even French.

The sunbaked walls, gardens, covered markets and magical open square of **Marrakesh** have become worldwide icons of exotic elegance. The city, fringed with palm, orange and olive groves, sits beneath the snow-capped peaks of the High Atlas. At its heart lies a complex spider's web of narrow alleys, down which lie hidden markets, museums and palatial restaurants, as well as stunning mosques, *medersas* and tombs. Marrakesh is the city which gave Morocco its name, and the music, foods, dances and people that fill its main square, the Jemaa el Fna, capture the country's cultural breadth and energy like nowhere else. Immediately south of the city, half a dozen valleys allow access into the mountains, either for a cool lunch or a visit to an ancient mosque or kasbah.

Fez, just a day's drive north across the Tadla Plain, is bewitchingly different. While Marrakesh is a recognizably African city, particularly in terms of space and colour, Fez is a triumphant citadel of Arabic and Islamic culture. It is one of the world's miraculous survivals, an almost complete medieval city which still maintains its ancient guild system of craftsmen. To walk its narrow streets, to smell, to taste and feel your way through the tanneries, shrines, theological courtyards and bazaars is as close to time travel as a mortal can get.

Below: Main gateway, to the souks of the old medina, Fez

Opposite: Jemaa el Fna square, Marrakesh

Cupped in a bowl of low hills, this labyrinthine city has been likened to an ossified prayer. Fez's gems are often hidden behind high walls, or glimpsed through tiny windows, yet Morocco's old capital is the country's spiritual and cultural guide.

Meknès, which sits on the western side of the fertile plain of Saiss, just an hour away from Fez, was turned into an Imperial capital in the 17th century, and the vast gates, cisterns, stables and walls of the Imperial City evoke its former grandeur. To the northeast of Meknès lie the extensive ruins of **Volubulis**, the inland capital of Morocco during the Roman Empire, with its mosaic floors and the Arch of Caracalla still intact.

Rabat lies on the coast overlooking the Bou Regreg river. It is a city of multiple identities – 12th-century gates and towers, an

elegant 17th-century old town, a modern political capital – not to mention its medieval walled neighbour, **Salé**, on the other bank of the river. The tempo of life in Rabat is calmer than in the other, frenetic Imperial Cities, though it is just as rich in cultural monuments as Fez, Meknès and Marrakesh.

The great commercial 20th-century city of **Casablanca**, an hour's journey from Rabat, has never been a cultural centre, though the late king did his best to reverse this with the construction of the monumental Grand Mosque of Hassan II, one of the eight wonders of the modern world.

Although the history, environment and architecture of Morocco's great cities are extraordinarily diverse, ultimately it is their people that prove most fascinating. In any one Moroccan there may lurk a turbulent and diverse ancestry: of slaves brought across the Saharan wastes to serve as concubines or warriors, of Andalucian refugees from the ancient Moorish cities of southern Spain, and of Bedouin Arabs from the tribes that fought their way west along the North African shore. All these people have mingled with the indigenous Berbers, who have continuously occupied the land since the Stone Age. The ruler of Morocco, King Mohammed VI, shares these influences, as well as being a direct descendant of the Prophet Mohammed.

Where to Go

The guide begins at **Marrakesh**, launching directly into the mayhem of Morocco's great market city. Despite their nomadic heritage, the Berbers, who founded the city in 1062, chose the location well. Marrakesh's proximity to the mountains protects it from the fierce Saharan winds and provides it with fresh water and snowmelt, once brought to the city by aqueduct. Marrakesh's past is dominated by the Almoravid and Almohad dynasties. The Almohads launched Morocco's architectural Golden Age but more substantial remains survive from the Almoravid era, including the magnificent ramparts. Beyond the ramparts, the peaks and valleys of the High Atlas offer solace from the city, while **Essaouira** is a charming seaside retreat.

From here, we head 150 miles northeast to the upper edge of the Middle Atlas and the city of **Fez**, long the key to holding power in Morocco. Almohad Fez was reportedly home to 785 mosques, close to 10,000 shops and nearly 100,000 homes. The city was the factory of Moroccan social mores and of much purist Sunni theology as well as a haven for craftsmen. Its mosques and *medersas*, as inward-looking as the city itself, are quiet testament to its sublime artistic vision. Nearby **Meknès** and **Volubilis** offer distinctly Berber and Roman foils to Sunni, Arab Fez.

The guide then turns west to **Rabat**, the modern capital, with its colonial architecture and cliff-top views. Morocco's soul may face Mecca, but Rabat embodies its Mediterranean dealings, links with the Phoenicians, the Romans, the Spanish and the French. Across the estuary, **Salé** was the area's medieval capital and its quiet, pious character sits comfortably with the scattering of exceptional Merinid monuments. Ending with Morocco's most modern and international offering, the guide closes 60 miles down the coast with the metropolis of **Casablanca**.

Above: Roman ruins at Volubilis

Below: King Hassan II mosque, Casablanca

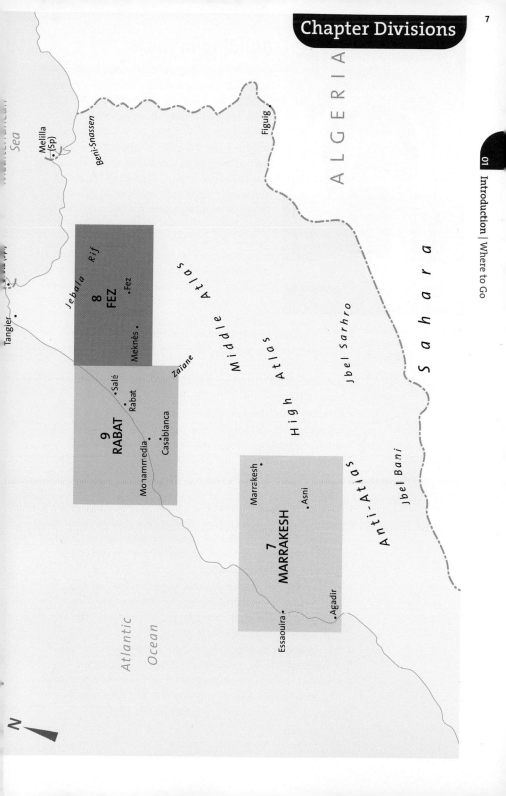

Chapter Divisions

Building in Faith

The Almohad dynasty, which reached its zenith around 1200, launched Morocco into a new age of grand architecture, one which the Merinids (1258–1554) continued. Buildings stamped visible signs of authority on the country while declaring the dynasty's allegiance to Islam. They also acted as the driving force behind the rise of the great imperial cities of Fez and Marrakesh. Late medieval Morocco was a centre of learning where the latest discoveries in geometry could be literally set in stone or mosaic. Some of the greatest late-medieval minds travelled to study in its colleges, such as the Andalucian genius Averroes. The legacy of mosques and *medersas* are among the finest Islamic monuments in the world; the following is a selection.

Above: Courtyard in the Ben Youssef Medersa, Marrakesh

Opposite: The minaret of Koutoubia mosque, Marrakesh

- The **Koutoubia Mosque** is the largest place of worship in Marrakesh, with a capacity for 25,000 people. It was named by the booksellers who used to work from booths that surrounded it, and, today, its fabulous African minaret has become the emblem of the city, p.103
- **Karaouiyne University** in Fez has been an intellectual and cultural centre for more than a millennium, and may be the world's longest-running university. The honeycomb vaulting in the mosque is a particularly North African detail, while its horseshoe arches reflect the influence of Muslim Córdoba in Spain, p.199
- The **Tinmal Mosque**, in the High Atlas outside Marrakesh, is a rare example of an Almohad mosque that is accessible to non-Muslims. This 12th-century mosque has only the sky for a roof and boasts fabulously carved arches and a minaret you can climb for excellent views, p.155
- The **Ben Youssef Medersa** in Marrakesh, restored by the Saadians in the 16th century, is now a museum. Among its highlights are the tranquil courtyard with mosaics, and the marble-columned prayer-hall, p.113
- The **Koubba el Baadiyin**, built in 1117, is the only surviving Almoravid building in Marrakesh. It bears magnificent testament to Almoravid craft and vision, from its dignified horseshoe arches and astonishing cupola, to the play of silhouettes created by the window arches, p.115

Markets: Food, Spices and Handicrafts

Markets are the life and zest of Morocco's city streets. Farmers tend to sell their own exceptional produce in the souks of their nearest town, and local craftsmanship abounds. Around the large cities much buying and selling still operates on a medieval model, with markets of tiny stalls dominating. Morocco's food and crafts markets are one of the country's most beguiling experiences, a rage of colour and commerce.

Above: Colourful tagine pots, Marrakesh

Opposite Top: Pyramids of spices, Marrakesh

Opposite Bottom: The Tanneries District, Fez

- The **Jemaa el Fna** is the central square of the Marrakesh medina and the country's most boisterous forum for petty trade, musicians, snake charmers, pickpockets and clowns. After dusk, rural Berbers settle down to eat and groups of musicians explore religion through their melodies as their loitering admirers smoke after-dinner pipes. Eat your Marrakesh dinner here at least once, p.106

- The **medina souks** of Marrakesh lie north of the Jemaa el Fna and here the business of trade is more serious. Its warren of streets profile Morocco's great tradition of arts and crafts, although dealers predominate here, p.108

- Fez's **Kissaria** is a disfigured chessboard of alleyways, squares and miniature shops which thrives off local goods and shuns tourist gimmicks. For cloth, jewellery or blankets, the Kissaria is given over to the best kind of Moroccan shopping, p.196

- The **Dyers' Souk** is proof that medieval crafts continue in time-honoured fashion in Fez. Some men rake rubbish out of the stream's current, others crush seeds and minerals at the mill, while still more dunk cloth into large vats before hanging it out to dry on nearby walls, p.200

- The **Henna Souk** in Fez sells only henna paste and leaves, antimony, rhassoul and kohl as its stock in trade, but the dried skins of snakes lizards and lie alongside caged hedgehogs and aphrodisiacs, p.194
- The **Tanneries district** of Fez lies just inside the city's northern wall. From the higher streets you can just about peer into the tanneries themselves, often vivid with the colours of the dyes. The nearby shops are the best place to buy leather goods in Morocco, p.201
- For **food markets**, wander through Rabat's medina, the Souk el Kheir and Bab Doukkala in Marrakesh (buying your tagine cooking pot at the latter) and Fez's markets close to the main gate of Bab Bou Jeloud (just east of the Kasbah An-Nour), where the street food is enticing and affordable.

Exotic Gardens

In spring and autumn, Morocco comes into bloom. Gladioli, the Barbary nut iris and juniper emerge on the slopes of the High Atlas – but you need not leave the cities to find sanctuary amid groves and flowers. Moorish gardens were traditionally enclosed by walls, perhaps of a palace or a harem, to provide shelter and escape. Laurel, cypress or olive trees provided shade, the soothing sound of trickling water filled the air, and flowers were often planted only for their scent. Here are ten of the best classical gardens:

- The **Aguedal Gardens** in Marrakesh are enormous and evocative. First built in the 12th century, the present version dates to the 19th century, when pavilions were built, including one for the harem of Moulay Hassan, p.135
- The **Saadian Tombs** in Marrakesh date from the sixteenth century, adding grandeur to the surrounding cemetery gardens, where trees, rosemary bushes and mosaic graves lie nestled between protective walls, p.122
- Marrakesh's most famous tower, piercing the skyline from the **Koutoubia Mosque**, is set among roses and orange blossom. This garden is at its best in the late afternoon, p.104
- The **El Badi Palace** in Marrakesh was once a 16th-century wonder, but today is no more than a ruin. For enthusiasts, the layout of a formal, royal Moroccan garden remains, but they also make for an atmospheric stroll, p.125
- Marrakesh's royal **Menara Gardens** are home to olive groves and 19th-century pavilions and look onto the Atlas Mountains, which glow at sunset, p.136
- The **Chellah** outside Rabat boasts an endearing and restful garden, offset by romantic ruins, p.265
- Through Rabat's magnificent Bab Oudaïa, or Gate of the Oudaïa, the Andalucian Garden fills the southern corner of the **Oudaïa Kasbah**, offering flowers, shade, rest – and tea, p.259
- The **Andalucian Gardens of Fez** are found in the Palace of Dar Batha, where mellow walls frame a lush and shaded retreat, p.188
- The 10th-century **Boujeloud (Jnan Sbil)** gardens in Fez make an ideal stop on your walk through the medina, p.187
- Marrakesh's **Majorelle Garden**, with its museum of Islamic art, was given to the city by Yves St Laurent. The garden was designed and planted in the 1920s by French artists Louis and Jacques Majorelle and blaze with the colours of more than 300 species, p.136

Right: A tranquil fountain in Majorelle Garden, Marrakesh

Below: Waterside pavilion in the Menara Gardens, Marrakesh

Itinerary 1: A Week In and Around Marrakesh

Marrakesh has married Morocco to sub-Saharan Africa for centuries, thanks to its strategic position at the end of one of the two most important medieval trade routes, which carried gold and slaves northwards from Africa's heartlands. Today, Marrakesh remains a local crossroads, the ideal launch pad from which to explore both the High Atlas and parts of the Atlantic coastline.

Day 1 Spend the morning at the **Koutoubia Mosque** and climb its talismanic minaret. Wander through the **Jemaa el Fna** and up through one or two of the **medina souks**, buying lunch on your way. In the afternoon, continue north to see the **Ben Youssef Medersa** and, if time allows, the nearby **Koubba el Ba'Adiyn**.

Day 2 In the morning, explore Marrakesh's **Saadian tombs** and the nearby **El Badi Palace**, both in the southern limb of the old medina and home to atmospheric gardens. If you feel energetic, return to the medina souks just north of Jemaa el Fna. When you've had enough, take a taxi northwest to Yves St Laurent's vibrant but peaceful **Jardin Majorelle**.

Day 3–4 Hire a car to take you to the **Toubkal region** of the High Atlas, about 2 hours' drive from Marrakesh. In November to May you should only aim to trek the lower valleys, but in season you have a choice. Either follow part of the 7-day **Toukbal Circuit**, a fabulous way to explore Berber rural culture, or head for the **Zat Valley** and hike up to the Tizi-n-Tichka peak. The Zat Valley offers local village hostels to stay in while trekkers on the Toubkal Circuit can eat in local villages but will need camping gear, although minor detours will take you to accommodation.

Day 5 Return to Marrakesh in the morning by bus or taxi and take a two-and-a-half hour bus ride (use CTM buses if ordinary buses are full) along the desert road to **Essaouira** on the Atlantic coast. In the afternoon and evening, wander through Essaouira's walled medina, a UNESCO World Heritage Site, enjoy the clifftop views and explore the old harbour.

Day 6 Eat a hearty breakfast before wandering down to the **beach** for surfing and windsurfing or organize a **horse trek** in the region – perhaps head south to **Diabat** for the latter. Buy wood carvings and spices in Essaouira itself and finish your day with dinner overlooking the ramparts.

Day 7 There is plenty left in Marrakesh you'll be desperate to see, but the **Musée de Marrakesh**, one of the **hammams** and a few local **riads** would make for a pleasurable final day. Pick out your own tagine cooking pot at the **Bab Doukkala market**.

Below: The Saadien tombs, Marrakesh

Opposite Top: El Badi Palace, Marrakesh

Opposite Bottom: Port of Essaouira

Itinerary 2: A Tale of Two Cities: Morocco Old and New

'Al-Magreb' is the term used to describe the full breadth of North Africa. It means 'land of the setting sun', a reflection of the region's Arab, Islamic history and orientation. The medieval origins of this identity can be glimpsed again in Fez. But Morocco has an Atlantic face too as the most modern and liberal Muslim state in the world. To see both its European heritage and its contemporary face, you should head a hundred miles west to Rabat.

Above: Bou Inania Medersa, Meknes

Below: Tiled niche in Meknes and the Hassan tower, Rabat

Day 1 Begin by finding nearby vantage points from which to peer into the **Karaouiyne complex** in Fez (entrance is forbidden to non-Muslims). Next put your map in your pocket and while away a few hours in the labyrinthine, evocative streets and alleyways of the medina, but aim west. When you finally emerge, the Bou Inania Medersa and minaret are restored wonders and open to all.

Day 2 Head to craft museums in the morning: **Fondouq Nejjarine, Dar Batha** and the **Belghazi Museum**. In the afternoon, visit a **hammam** then explore the attractive **Mellah** (Jewish quarter), especially its cemetery and synagogue.

Day 3 Spend a day in nearby **Meknès**, far less trumpeted but almost as enticing as Fez, and encircled by lush farmland.

Day 4 From Fez or Meknès, head for **Rabat** but stop off at **Salé** for lunch and a stroll (and see the fine 12th-century mosque) before taking a ferry to Rabat and entering the old Mellah. Next, the medina, the Grand Mosque and Mosque of Sultan Moulay all beckon.

Day 5 A morning should be given to the **Oudaïa Kasbah** in the northeast corner of the medina, a Moorish masterpiece, with lunch at its pretty café. Later, explore the **markets** of the old city that the Kasbah overlooks to buy carpets, belts, hats, carvings and wool. End by climbing the **Hassan Tower** to look over the expansive ruins of the old mosque and the mausoleum of Mohammed V.

Day 6 Visit the magnificent remains of **Chellah** and perhaps the neighbouring Roman ruins of **Sala Colonia**. In the afternoon, walk down **Avenue Mohammed V** to take in some of the old French government buildings and their syncretistic architectural styles.

Day 7 Local pottery at the **Complexe des Potiers** in the morning and later the sandy **Temara Plage** (beach) for swimming, surfing and sunbathing to end your journey in modern style.

CONTENTS

Contents

History

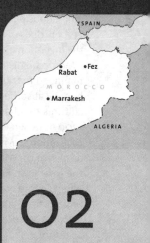

02

History

Morocco was long known in the Muslim world as *Maghreb el Aksa*, the land of the farthest west. It was literally considered to be on the edge of the world, a place notorious for its powerful magicians and demon-like *jinn*. It is a country with an intense, almost insular, awareness of itself. In a sense it is an island, encircled by the seas of the Atlantic, the Mediterranean and the sand-sea of the Sahara. The land is further defended by four great mountain ranges (the Rif, Middle Atlas, High Atlas and Anti-Atlas) that run like vast ramparts across its breadth, breaking up the area's geographical unity and providing a secure mountainous refuge for the indigenous people, the Berbers, against both invaders and any central power. The Berber tribes of the mountains have remained in occupation of the land ever since the invention of agriculture.

Moroccan history is essentially the tale of a conservative society which has managed to triumph against all attempts at conquest. At the same time it has happily absorbed technical and spiritual innovations from the various foreign cultures that have tried to dominate the country. The first great change was from 1000 BC, when Phoenician traders brought settled agriculture and urban civilization to Morocco. The second came in the 8th century AD, when the cavalry armies of the Muslim Caliphate brought Islam, Arabic and the advanced culture of the Near East. Aristotle was being translated in the court of the rulers of Morocco when Oxford was still a muddy unlettered village. Arab military rule lasted only a few decades, but the spiritual and social message took deep root. All subsequent rulers of Morocco were legitimate only for as long as they championed Islam, either as reformers or as military protectors.

The third great revolution was in the 20th century, when the French, albeit for the selfish motives of a European power, implanted the scientific and medical advances of the Industrial Revolution in Morocco. Morocco's identity has been likened to the desert palm: rooted in Africa, watered by Islam and rustled by the winds of Europe.

Before *c.* 150 BC
Berber Roots

Evidence of the camp fires and tool-making of the wandering bands of *Homo erectus*, who first crossed the Sahara to North Africa about a million years ago, have been discovered in the coastal sand dunes around Rabat and Casablanca. It was not until 10,000 BC that the melt waters of the last Ice Age separated North Africa from southern Europe, and the original inhabitants of both shores are of similar racial stock. The Neolithic Revolution, with the invention of both agriculture and stock breeding, reached the inhabitants of Morocco by about 3000 BC. It transformed the small bands of hunter-gatherers living in the area into communities of agriculturalists or nomads, and vastly increased the population. Stone circles in northern Morocco, such as that at M'Soura dating from around 1800 BC, prove that local tribes had strong contacts with the Megalithic culture of the Atlantic coast of Europe. There is also evidence of an ivory trade between the Tangier region and Spain.

At about this time we can begin to speak of the indigenous population of North Africa as **Berber** (from the Greek for 'barbarian'). They spoke a language of the Hamitic family related to ancient Egyptian. The men were devoted to war, polygamous, and allowed their women to do most of the agricultural labour. The horse, first bred in North Africa in this period, and the donkey were greatly prized, while in the savannah plains the chariot became a dominant element in war. A brief wet period allowed the Berber tribes to expand into the Sahara, an event recorded in cave paintings showing dreadlocked cattle-herders fleeing before conquering charioteers.

The Berbers enter the written history of the Mediterranean world via the trading settlements of the **Phoenicians**. By about 1100 BC these merchants from the coast of Syria had established a network of harbours along the North African shore which allowed them access to Cornish tin, Spanish silver and Saharan gold. The Phoenicians had a good eye for a harbour, and the shore of Morocco is dotted with their trading stations, such as Rusaadir (Melilla), Tingis (Tangier), Lixus (Larache), Sala Colonia (Rabat), Tit (Moulay-Abdallah) and Mogador (Essaouira). As well as their lucrative trade in metals and precious oils, the Phoenicians developed a more humdrum 'country trade' in corn, oil, fish, dyes, timber and ivory. These trading colonies were responsible for the diffusion of new skills to the tribes of the North African coast. The pottery wheel, an alphabet, improved weaving techniques, the art of masonry, new crops, arboriculture, iron and metal work were all Phoenician gifts to the Berbers of Morocco.

C. 150 BC–AD 429
Roman Influence

Effective dominion over the Phoenician colonies passed in the 5th century BC to Carthage, and with the defeat of Carthage in the 2nd century BC to Rome. The Romans exercised a loose protectorate over the extensive kingdom of Mauretania, which covered both Morocco and eastern Algeria. Mauretania remained an area of Phoenician culture (recalled by the Libyo-Berber script that can be seen carved on stones in the sub-Saharan region) and was ruled from the two capitals of Volubilis (in central Morocco) and Cherchel (in the centre of Algeria). Roman influence increased from 25 BC under Juba II, a Mauretanian prince who had been educated in the household of the Caesars in Rome.

The gradual absorption of Mauretania into the Empire was reversed by a widespread revolt in AD 42 which it took an army of four legions over three years to subdue. In AD 44 the Emperor Claudius officially annexed Mauretania, but the fierce resistance of the tribes left the Moroccan portion of the old kingdom much reduced in size. The frontier of Roman Morocco, known as the province of Mauretania Tingitania, extended just south of Sala Colonia (Rabat) and just east of Volubilis. There was no secure road east to Roman Algeria, whose western frontier reached Oujda and the river Moulouya.

The Romans' authority was continuously challenged by the Berber tribes, but within their frontiers they built upon the trade and settlement patterns of the Phoenician period to create a small but prosperous and civilized province. In addition to the magnificent ruins of the capital, Volubilis, their achievement is witnessed by lesser sites such as Lixus, Cotta, Banasa, Thamusida, Sala Colonia and Tamuda. As part of the reorganization of the Empire in the reign of Emperor Diocletian (285–305) the frontier was withdrawn to a defensive line between Tamuda (Tetouan) and Lixus (Larache). Volubilis was abandoned, but the two port cities of Tangier and Ceuta were protected. These remained under Roman rule until 429.

429–704
Vandals and Byzantines

An army of the Germanic Vandals, led by Gesneric, invaded North Africa from Spain in 429, landing at Tangier. Although they were relatively few in number, their rule in North Africa lasted a century, until their defeat in 535 by the Byzantine general Belisarius. The Byzantines installed governors at Ceuta and Tangier, who remained dominant figures in local politics until the Arab invasion two centuries later.

704–40
The Arab Conquest

The Arab conquest brought Islam to Morocco: a religion, a social code, a system of law and a new language that were to provide the central identity of all future Moroccan states. Islam's introduction was due not to peaceful missionaries but to Arab cavalry armies despatched by the caliphs, the political heirs of the Prophet. Within 25 years of Mohammed's death the first three caliphs had conquered an empire that stretched across Syria, Mesopotamia, Persia, Egypt and Libya.

The Arab advance along the North African coast was delayed by a succession dispute, but in 682 **Uqba ben Nafi** made his famous raid. Partly a dazzling conquest, partly a missionary voyage of discovery, this is a cherished episode in Moroccan history, but the facts have long since been wrapped up in legend. The tale records that Uqba defeated a joint Berber and Byzantine army, was welcomed by Count Julian into Tangier, accepted the submission of Volubilis and went on to conquer the Haouz, the Drâa and the Sous Valleys. Arriving at the Atlantic, he rode deep into the surf declaring, 'O God, I take you to witness that there is no ford here. If there was I would cross it.' This was all to no avail, for on his return east Uqba was ambushed and killed by an old adversary.

The Arab conquest of Morocco did not begin in earnest until 704, when **Musa ben Nasser** arrived at Kairouan in Tunisia to take up his appointment as commander of the western Arab army. Between 705 and 710 he advanced rapidly westwards, content to accept the nominal conversion of towns and tribes, which he enforced by establishing garrisons, notably at Tangier, Tlemcen and Sijilmassa. His aim was to secure Morocco in order to be able to proceed with the conquest of Spain. The prospect of an invasion of rich, plunderable Spanish provinces brought thousands of Berber warriors flocking to the Arab banners. In 711 an advance guard of 7,000 under the command of the governor of Tangier, **Tariq**, crossed the Straits, first landing at what came to be known as Jbel Tariq, or Gibraltar. He was welcomed by many among the Christian and Jewish population of Spain as a deliverer from the harsh rule of the Germanic Visigoths. In one day's work at the Battle of the Barbate River, Tariq destroyed the Visigothic army. Muslim armies quickly occupied Spain, and the Arab advance into Western Europe was not checked until Charles Martel stood firm at Poitiers in 732.

In 740 a mutiny among the Berbers in the Arab garrison at Tangier lit a chain of rebellions that swept right through North Africa. Though the caliphate sent a succession of Arab armies, these were only able to reconquer Tunisia. Morocco, having absorbed the message of Islam, returned to its customary independence.

740–1042
The Spread of Islam

For a while, northwestern Morocco found unity under **Moulay Idriss**, a kinsman of the Prophet who had fled civil war in Arabia. The tribes of central Morocco accepted him as a holy man and arbitrator. His son **Idriss II** established a unitary state based around a small army and the new settlement of Fez, which Moulay Idriss had founded in 799. Within a few decades it had grown into an influential city, filled with skilled craftsmen and noble Arab warriors who fled there from civil war in Spain and revolution in Tunisia. Fez became the cultural, political and economic centre of Morocco, from where Arabic language, religious knowledge and technical innovations spread into the rest of the country.

The political authority of Idriss II was lost when his kingdom was divided between nine sons on his death in 828. The various Idrissid princes soon fell under the influence of powerful neighbouring dynasties, such as the Shiite Fatimids of Tunisia and the Omayyads of Spain, who controlled many of the chief ports and towns of Morocco throughout the 10th and 11th centuries. This period also witnessed the gradual conversion of the Berber tribes of the interior by missionaries and warriors, many of whom claimed descent from the Idrissid princes. Idrissid ancestry is still a mark of prestige in Morocco, while the process of conversion is remembered in hundreds of different local folk tales that recall trials of power between Muslim holy men and diabolic magicians.

1042–1147
The Almoravids

In the middle of the 11th century there was no Morocco, just a confused patchwork of half-converted Berber tribes, Arab trading cities, foreign garrisons and petty principalities. The Almoravids created Morocco. Their conquests welded the civilized northwest of the country to a vast Berber and Saharan hinterland and created a common identity. The Almoravid Empire marks a historical threshold, just as the Norman Conquest, which occurred in the same period, does for England.

The Almoravids were not a foreign power but a simple confederation of Berber tribes from the Western Sahara who had been united by **Ibn Yaasin**, a charismatic holy man from the Sous Valley. Determined to impose a pure Islamic state, he launched his crusade from the desert in 1042. A generation later, in 1070, the young Almoravid general **Youssef ben Tachfine** established Marrakesh as their advance northern base and principal city. By the 1080s he controlled central Morocco and Fez. In 1086 he landed in Spain at the invitation of the embattled Muslim states. He promptly defeated the Christians, but then proceeded to absorb the 26 principalities of Spain into his empire. At its height the Almoravid Empire stretched from Spain to West Africa and from the Atlantic to eastern Algeria.

The empire sought to be the ideal Islamic state. The ruling class of princes and tribal emirs were deposed, and all taxes not sanctioned in the Koran were abolished. Islamic law according to the Malekite tradition was imposed upon society. Almoravid generals subdued even the remotest hill tribes, built stone castles on the summits of mountains to enforce their authority and encircled cities in protective walls.

After the conquest of Spain, skilled craftsmen were brought over to build and decorate mosques, fountains and public bathhouses. Talented Andalucian secretaries, employed in the court, brought increased literacy and the Maghrebi script to the country. The Almoravid sultans also made a practice of consulting the doctors of Islamic law before making any major decision, even in matters of war. This council, the *ulema*, remained a central feature of the Moroccan state. The sultans sought recognition from the caliphs of Baghdad for their title, *Amir al Muslimin* (Commander of the Muslims), which aptly expresses their championship of orthodox Islam. But there was a dark side to Almoravid rule. The great flowering of Andalucian mysticism, poetry and intellectual enquiry seen in the previous two centuries was suppressed. Their insistence on collecting only Koranic taxes left them short of revenue, made up for by extortion. Their narrow puritanism led to the persecution of Jewish communities and the extermination of the last Christians in Morocco.

Ali ben Youssef succeeded in 1107. He completed the conquest of Muslim Spain and his generals advanced the frontier by adding Lisbon and the Balearics to the Empire. Ali reigned for 37 years and was responsible for the great building projects of the Almoravids: the grand mosque of Tlemcen (in Algeria), the Karaouiyne Mosque in Fez, and the Ben Youssef Mosque and Koubba Ba'Adiyn in Marrakesh. His sons, though, lost control to a rival Berber dynasty, the Almohads, who stormed Marrakesh in 1147 and killed Ishaq, the last Almoravid sultan.

1147–1248
The Almohads

Medieval Morocco reached its zenith of confidence and achievement under the Almohad Empire, whose rule extended over Spain, Morocco, Algeria and western Libya. The Almohads had much in common with the Almoravids. They too were a confederation of Berber tribes (though from the High Atlas not the Western Sahara) that had been united by the zeal of a charismatic holy man, **Ibn Tumert**, and led to final victory by his more pragmatically minded successor, **Abdel Moumen**, whose descendants inherited the empire. An Almohad fleet dominated the waters of the western Mediterranean, and the monumental architecture of this period still dominates the cities of Morocco, such as the Hassan Tower and Bab Oudaïa in Rabat, and the Bab Agnaou and Koutoubia minaret in their major centre, Marrakesh. The regional capitals at Taza, Tlemcen, Tunis and Seville were also adorned, and great philosophers such as Averroes enjoyed the friendship of the sultan.

The empire's first important reverse came in 1212, when the Spanish Christians inflicted a crushing defeat on it at Las Navas de Tolosa. It was a blow from which Muslim interests in Spain never fully recovered. Ferdinand III of Castile captured Córdoba in 1235 and Seville in 1248, leaving only the mountainous kingdom of Granada under its own independent Nasrid dynasty. Remorselessly, the empire contracted.

In Tunisia, an Almohad governor established the Hafsid dynasty, whilst western Algeria fell to a Berber tribe, the Ziyanids, who ruled from Tlemcen. In 1248 an Almohad sultan died whilst on campaign against the Ziyanids. His leaderless army was betrayed and then massacred on the eastern plains of Morocco by the Beni-Merin tribe. The Beni-Merin chieftain then promptly seized control of Fez (the chief city of the north) and founded the Merenid dynasty. However, it was not until 1276, when the last Almohad sultan was killed in the High Atlas, that the Merenids controlled the south of the country as well, and could feel secure on the throne of Morocco.

1248–1554
The Merenids

The rule of the Merenid sultans is recalled by a series of dazzling architectural compositions. The ruins of the Chellah necropolis at Rabat, the sumptuous *medersas* that can be seen in Fez, Salé and Meknès, as well as numerous mosques, fountains and *fondouqs* scattered throughout the towns and cities of Morocco reveal the exquisite taste and wealth of this period. Merenid power and creativity was at its glorious peak during the reign of **Abou Hassan** (1331–51) and his son **Abou Inan** (1351–8). A series of ambitious campaigns seemed on the point of recovering the old territory of the Almohad Empire in North Africa, while the glittering new *medersas* (university colleges) helped train a generation of loyal officials to serve in Fez Jdid (New Fez), the separate and defensible royal city that they founded to the west of old Fez. Literary figures such as the great historian Ibn Khaldoun and Ibn Batuta (the Muslim Marco Polo) received the enlightened patronage of the court.

By the beginning of the 15th century it was a very different story. The Merenid state fell into the hands of a corrupt cabal of viziers, financiers and generals. Against a background of economic decline, the Portuguese and Spanish gradually seized control of most of the Moroccan ports, starting with the sack of Ceuta in 1419. By the mid-16th century the Portuguese cavalry controlled the Atlantic coast and had begun to penetrate deep into the interior. Marrakesh and Fez were defended only with the military assistance of the Ottoman Turks, who had already seized control of Tunisia and Algeria.

1554–1668
The Saadians and the Battle of the Three Kings

From this point of apparent hopelessness Morocco unexpectedly recovered. The Saadians, an influential family from the Drâa oasis valley, led the fight against the Portuguese and made themselves rulers of southern Morocco in the process. By 1542 their success in expelling the Portuguese from Agadir, Safi and Azemmour had brought them the support necessary to dethrone the old dynasty which, surrounded by Turkish guards, hung on to power in Fez.

The true turning-point in Saadian power came in 1578, when they destroyed a Portuguese invasion led by the youthful King Sebastian at the battle of Ksar-el-Kebir. This is also known as the Battle of the Three Kings, since the reigning sultan, Sebastian and his treacherous Moroccan royal ally all died during the battle.

The throne passed to **Ahmed el Mansour**, 'the victorious' (1578–1603), who further increased his prestige and wealth by seizing control of the gold fields of West Africa. Ahmed el Mansour remodelled the state along the lines of Ottoman Turkey. External trade was encouraged and with the revenue from customs duties he was able to fund a professional army, recruited from Andalucian exiles, Christian renegades and Turks, that was untarnished by tribal loyalties. He gave audiences from behind a screen, introduced the scarlet parasol that is still a distinguishing mark of a Moroccan sultan's sovereignty, and built the palace of El Badi in Marrakesh to be the magnificent ceremonial heart of his court. Provincial leaders were enticed away from local politics to the glittering life of the capital. His rule was that of an enlightened despot: in the words of the chroniclers, 'he sweetened his absolute power with much clemency'. In Marrakesh the magnificent ruins of El Badi, the serene elegance of the Ben Youssef Medersa and the glittering opulence of the Saadian Tombs survive to give a suggestion of this near-fabulous period of history.

In 1603, a vicious war of succession between the Saadian princes shattered the prosperity of the state. For much of the 17th century the Saadian sultans were mere shadows locked in their Marrakesh palaces while real authority was exercised by a jumble of petty powers that included the pirate republic of Rabat-Salé and four rival dynasties of sheikhs who controlled the Berber tribes in the western Rif, Middle Atlas, High Atlas and Anti-Atlas.

1668–1727
The First Alaouite Sultans: Moulay Rachid and Moulay Ismaïl

The Alaouite prince **Moulay Rachid**, from an Arab holy family long resident in the oasis of Tafilalt, succeeded in seizing the throne in 1668. His family still holds it to this day.

During the 54-year reign of his younger brother, **Moulay Ismaïl** (1672–1727), the Portuguese were expelled from their fortresses on the Atlantic coast, the English were driven out of Tangier, and the Turks pushed back on the eastern frontier to the line of the present border with Algeria. Morocco is filled with evidence of the constructive nature of Moulay Ismaïl's reign. He founded towns, built bridges, ports and forts, and secured the safety of roads. He encouraged trade and reformed religious life, purging unorthodox cults but restoring shrines and mosques.

Moulay Ismaïl deliberately neglected the existing capitals of Fez and Marrakesh with their rebellious citizens and built up Meknès to be the new administrative and ceremonial centre of the nation. Meknès was also the headquarters of the sultan's black slave army of 150,000 men, which functioned as both a corps of engineers and the brutal instrument of his authoritarian regime. There were a number of bloody campaigns against the mountain tribes and frequent instances of despotic tyranny. The sultan's proudest boast was that he had made Morocco safe enough for a woman or a Jew laden down with jewellery to travel across the breadth of the country without being troubled.

1727–1822
Decline and Isolationism

A vicious period of civil war followed Moulay Ismaïl's death as the slave regiments championed a swift-changing variety of his heirs. None of his descendants could hope to equal his power. They ruled as much by consensus and arbitration as by decree. The authority of the government was restricted to the fertile coast, river valleys and towns – the Bled el Makhzen, the 'land of government'. The dry plains and mountains were known as the Bled-es-Siba, the 'land of dissidence', where the tribes respected only the spiritual authority of the sultan and had no time for his tax-gatherers and ministers.

Sidi Mohammed (1757–90) was one of the most astute sultans of the period, beloved by the towns for his firm but fair rule and by the nation at large for his expulsion of the Portuguese from El-Jadida. He maximized government revenue by concentrating the export trade at Essaouira, which he built up into the elegant town it is today. He also played a clever game with the European nations and kept their influence at a minimum by a quick-footed policy of encouraging competition between them. His son, **Moulay Sliman** (1792–1822), changed to the ultimately disastrous policy of isolationism, attempting to seal Muslim Morocco from any contact with Europe. His foreign policy was dominated by suspicion of all the Christian powers and a particular loathing for the French Revolution. Despite being offered Ceuta and Melilla he refused to recognize the upstart Bonaparte as king of Spain. All exports were banned, a 50 per cent duty imposed on imports, and European consuls were confined to Tangier in an attempt to keep outside influence firmly at bay.

1822–1904
The Growth of European Influence

Moulay Sliman ignored the claims of his inadequate sons and nominated his nephew, **Abder Rahman** (1822–59), to succeed him on the throne. It was during his reign that Morocco felt the full force of the growing power of France. The sultan had provided some support for the Algerian tribes during the French invasion of Algeria, but this policy was shattered in 1843 when a Moroccan army was destroyed at the Battle of Isly (outside Oujda) and the ports of Tangier and Essaouira were bombarded. The tribes' reaction to these humiliating national defeats was to rise in widespread revolt against the sultan.

Suddenly aware of his nation's military vulnerability, the sultan played on the strong and traditional Anglo-French rivalry. He made approaches to the British, who were interested in opening up Morocco to their traders and obsessed by keeping the Straits of Gibraltar open for their shipping. As a corollary of British diplomatic support against the French, the 1856 Treaty of Tangier removed all the sultan's restrictions on trade except his monopoly on tobacco and arms. It instituted a flat 10 per cent customs rate and introduced consular courts and privileges which soon deprived the sultan of any control over his nation's trade. Spain as well as France soon became envious of British influence. In 1859, as the sultan lay dying, a Spanish army advanced from Ceuta to defeat a tribal army and occupy the city of Tetouan. The tribes rose again in revolt against their defeated government, and British protection was revealed to be a false and illusory hope.

Abder Rahman's son Sidi Mohammed (**Mohammed IV**, 1859–73) was faced with a problematic inheritance. The Spanish demanded a crippling indemnity of 100 million pesetas before they would leave Tetouan; a pretender to the throne appeared in the Rif; and the Rehamna tribe pillaged Marrakesh. The Spanish left Tetouan in 1862, paid off by a British loan which required the surrender of customs revenue and its administration by the British and Spanish. Internal dissidence was subdued by 1864.

The unhappy start to the reign was followed by a remorseless growth in European influence. By 1900 there were over 10,000 European residents in the country. Foreign consuls in the ports of Tangier and Casablanca organized lighthouses, port works, sanitary services and a national postal service, increasingly supplanting the sultan's sovereignty. The consular privileges of the treaty of 1856 put European merchants and their many Moroccan agents beyond the law of the sultan. As a graphic illustration of this trend, between 1844 and 1873 the national currency lost 90 per cent of its value. Trade was conducted in the French five-franc coin.

Sultan **Moulay Hassan** (1873–94) attempted the almost impossible task of modernizing Morocco while keeping the nation's independence. On his accession in 1873, he began a programme of reform. Whilst instituting this, however, he still had to maintain central authority through the traditional system of annual military campaigns. The students he dispatched to Europe to learn the latest medical and engineering skills returned unable to cope with the political realities of their homeland.

The sultan attempted to stabilize the currency by minting the Koranically approved *riyal* in Paris, but it was of such quality that it was hoarded or smuggled abroad. At the Conference of Madrid in 1880 he attempted to limit the ruinous extent of consular privileges, and a limit was set of two agents per country in each port; but no European power except Britain respected these terms. Military reforms proved just as difficult. When the European powers blocked his schemes, he wisely balanced their influence: there was a French military mission, a British chief of staff ('*Caid*' Maclean), the German Krupp firm was given contracts for coastal defence, and the Italians built and ran a munitions factory at Fez. Moulay Hassan exhausted himself in the service of his country, reasserting order and personally dispensing justice in regions that had not seen an official of the sultan for a hundred years. He died while on campaign in 1894.

His two sons presided over the last stormy decade of Moroccan independence. Useless Western products were enthusiastically acquired, their purchase financed through ruinous foreign loans. **Abdul Aziz** (1894–1908), surrounded by a court composed of European adventurers, unscrupulous salesmen and doctors, became alienated from his traditional advisers and political realities. Meanwhile, the tribal chiefs and *caids* (magistrates) appointed by Moulay Hassan, notably in the High Atlas mountains, expanded their power in the vacuum created by the disordered central government.

1904–21
The Imposition of French Rule

It is doubtful whether any ruler could have successfully resisted the anarchy created by the advance of French power in Morocco at this time. In exchange for a free hand in Morocco the French had begun to negotiate a series of bargains with the other colonial powers: Spain was offered territory in northern and southern Morocco, Italy a free hand over Libya, while the French agreed to recognize Britain's rule over Cyprus, Egypt and the Sudan, with the additional promise that Tangier would remain a demilitarized zone.

French control was tightened in 1904 when Abdul Aziz accepted a loan of 50 million francs from a consortium of French banks. In 1906 the Conference of Algeciras ratified the various secret negotiations that had been taking place between the Europeans over the future of Morocco. The French army had slowly been occupying oases on the eastern frontier since 1900, but in 1907 the lynching of a few Europeans in Marrakesh and Casablanca gave them the excuse for direct intervention. Oujda was occupied in the east, and 3,000 French troops were promptly landed at Casablanca. The 'Moroccan Crises' of 1905 and 1911, when Imperial Germany sought to gain influence in Morocco, only spurred the French into more aggressive action, to deny access to the country to their greatest rival.

Sultan **Moulay Hafid** (1908–12), faced with simultaneous French and Spanish invasions and internal rebellions, accepted the inevitable and signed the Treaty of Fez (1912), which established colonial rule over Morocco. The nation was carved up into Spanish and French spheres of influence: the French took everything of value, leaving only bare bones for their rivals. The Spanish protectorate consisted of Ifni (an enclave in the Anti-Atlas), a stretch of desert south of the Drâa Valley, and the mountainous Rif coast of northern Morocco.

The French takeover of Morocco was not entirely unopposed. Two weeks after the Treaty of Fez was signed, revolution broke out in Fez, eighty Europeans were lynched and the walls were manned. In the south, El Hiba, 'the Blue Sultan', raised the black banners of revolt and marched up from the Sahara with a tribal force of 12,000. French artillery and machine guns, though, did for them both, and by September Marrakesh had been occupied.

The colonial regime soon became critically short of manpower, as the storm clouds of the First World War became apparent. Deals were struck with the Glaoui brothers, a pair of ex-government ministers from the Berber High Atlas, who were armed and encouraged to build up a private army to secure the south. Taroudannt was taken in May 1913 without the use of a single French soldier, and the first French resident general, Marshal Lyautey, was able to hold central Morocco with a skeleton military presence. However, the Rif, Middle Atlas and the areas south of the High Atlas remained beyond his control until reinforcements in 1921 allowed the conquest to proceed. It was not completed until 1936.

It was in the rugged eastern Rif, in the Spanish zone, that the colonial powers encountered the most serious military resistance. The rebel leader **Abdel Krim** defeated a Spanish army in July 1921. It took several years and a full-scale combined Franco-Spanish campaign under the command of Marshal Pétain to subdue him.

Tangier was left as a demilitarized zone. A constitution in 1923 provided the international city of Tangier with a ruling council of consuls, a small house of representatives and the *mendoub*, the representative of the sultan. In practice, French and Spanish officials dominated the administration, the Italians gave the best parties, and the British created some beautiful gardens.

1921–56
The Achievements of the French Protectorate and the Struggle for Independence

Peace, with the end of tribal pillage and administrative extortion, led to a rapid growth in population and trade. In 1921 Morocco had a population of three million. After only thirty years of French rule this had risen to eight million.

The Second World War

Morocco was involved in the events of the Second World War as a Protectorate of France. After the conquest of France by Nazi Germany in 1940, her overseas possessions passed under the control of Marshal Pétain's Vichy regime. Pétain strove to maintain a degree of neutrality, but a series of British and Free-French attacks soon pushed Vichy into a tacit alliance with Germany. After the entry of the USA into the war many of Pétain's generals in North Africa began to enter into covert discussions with the Allies, and in November 1942 a British-American force stumbled ashore in the Casablanca landings that 'liberated' Morocco.

It was a near farce: the soldiers were all horribly seasick and the whole thing had been arranged in advance by secret negotiations. Morocco was promptly placed under the Free-French administration of De Gaulle, and in January 1943 Roosevelt and Churchill met in the country for the Casablanca Conference. In a meeting with Sultan Mohammed V, the American president gave private encouragement that the post-war era would bring a return of sovereignty to Morocco.

By the end of the war there were 300,000 Moroccans under arms. They formed a very substantial portion of the French forces that fought alongside the Allies in Italy and then in France itself after the collapse of the Pétain regime in 1942. It was the Moroccan 4th Mountain Division that in May 1944 broke the Gustav Line. The Moroccan 2nd Division captured Monte Pantano in 1943 and, transferred to France, also won great respect for crossing the Rhine under heavy fire on 31 March 1945.

Apart from military conquest and administration the Protectorate's chief concern was to develop Morocco's agricultural and mineral wealth. French banks financed major public works, and the government attracted capitalist investment into mining and agriculture by a tempting package of low taxes, cheap labour and land. By 1953, irrigation, expropriation and purchase had created one million hectares of cultivable land under French ownership concentrated in the fertile coastal zones. In 1951 there were 325,000 Europeans in the country, including a rich controlling minority of 5000 and a sub-class of 80,000 'poor whites'. An impressive infrastructure of roads, railways, ports, administrative centres and dams was developed to provide water and power for the settlers and facilitate the economic exploitation of the country. Hospitals, schools and hotels were also built for the use of settlers and a tiny minority of the traditional Moroccan ruling class of *caids*, merchants and sheikhs. Even by Independence in 1956 less than 15 per cent of the Moroccan population had received any sort of education.

Independence

Though there was no immediate political evidence for it, the Second World War saw a transformation in the relationship between France and Morocco. France had been humiliated, whilst Moroccan forces had contributed to the liberation of Europe. The European colonial powers had been replaced by the anti-colonial world leadership of America and Russia. India and Egypt, which both rapidly achieved independence at the end of the war, pointed the way for Morocco.

Mohammed V had been chosen by the French in 1927 to succeed his father for his apparent docility. He proved to have an unexpectedly strong character and enjoyed the moral high ground against a series of unimaginative generals who served as Residents. The sultan resisted all of Vichy France's anti-Semitic measures and refused to receive a single German officer, and, while 200,000 French Jews died in

Nazi concentration camps, he protected all 300,000 of his Jewish subjects. By 1953 the sultan was so clearly identified with the popular demand for independence that the French authorities deposed him and exiled him to Madagascar. By the summer of 1955 the campaign of civil disobedience for the sultan's return had escalated into widespread violence and the French were threatened by an incipient armed rebellion. The situation in Algeria, where the FLN revolt had erupted in 1954, helped concentrate their minds. The French decided to quit Morocco (and Tunisia) with good grace in order to concentrate on holding on to Algeria. The Spanish and the 'international protectors' of Tangier were forced to follow suit. In November 1955 Mohammed V returned to a tumultous popular reception, and by March 1956 the French had formally recognized Moroccan independence.

1956–61
King Mohammed V

Upon independence the sultan restyled himself as King Mohammed V to emphasize his position as a modern constitutional monarch removed from the practices of the pre-1912 regime. In the euphoric first years of independence a national government established schools, universities and newspapers, and elected regional assemblies. The Sufi brotherhoods – many of which had become involved in pro-French politics – were reformed; orthodoxy and public morality were reaffirmed; and massive public work schemes were launched. In the early burst of nationalist enthusiasm labour battalions absorbed unemployment and created some lasting monuments, such as the Route de l'Unité road across the Rif, which joined the road systems of the hitherto-separate French and Spanish Protectorates.

For all this wave of modernization Mohammed V was quietly determined that the monarchy should always remain the controlling force in national politics. The Istqlal, the sole national party, which had played a central role in the struggle for independence, was seen to pose a potential threat. It dominated the first cabinet, although Mohammed V insisted on retaining control over the army and the Ministry of the Interior. By 1959 the left wing of the Istqlal under Ben Barka had broken away to form the UNFP (*Union Nationale des Forces Populaires*) and ranged themselves in a socialist alliance with the UMT labour union; the centrist rump of Istaqlal then established their own union, the UGTM. The rural Berber hinterland, meanwhile, remained suspicious of the urban Istqlal, and with discreet support from the king a new and conservative party, the Mouvement Populaire, was formed.

Crown Prince Hassan was given the task of creating a royal army. Units of the Liberation Army were absorbed within this new force, which, by recruiting experienced veterans of French service, soon rose to 30,000 men. In 1958 and 1959 rebellions in the Rif, the Saharan oases and the Middle Atlas tested the army's discipline and efficiency. The more radical and militant members of the Liberation Army were meanwhile directed south to the unofficial siege of the Spanish enclave of Ifni and the struggle to gain control over the western Sahara.

1961–75
The Early Years of King Hassan II, the 'Great Survivor'

In February 1961, at the height of his powers, King Mohammed V died during a routine operation on his nose. He was succeeded by his 32-year-old son, **Hassan II**, who foreign observers did not expect to last more than a few years. In fact he would rule Morocco for 38 years with an iron fist. Much of this success was due to his political adaptability. He freely confessed that at least 40 per cent of his decisions had been wrong, but he never once relaxed his control over the realities of power: the army, the police and the local governors.

The new king excluded the socalist UNFP from government by forming a cabinet from the Mouvement Populaire and Istqlal in June 1961. In December 1962 a referendum was held to give popular approval to Morocco's **first democratic constitution**. The UNFP called for a boycott, but this failed due to lack of support from the labour unions. The new king, having won the referendum, no longer felt the need for Istqlal support, and sacked its members from his cabinet.

The first parliamentary elections were held in March 1963. The Ministries of Agriculture and the Interior assisted the electoral victory of the FDIC, a royal coalition headed by the Mouvement Populaire. Istqlal was strongest in the older cities and successful farming areas such as Tadla, Doukkala and the Rharb; UNFP in the new cities of the coast – Rabat, Casablanca and Agadir – and throughout the Sous Valley; the Mouvement Populaire's greatest support came from Marrakesh and the Berber hinterland as well as Oujda, Taza and Nador.

The socialist UNFP increasingly identified itself with the Arab republics of Egypt and Algeria, which its supporters publicly cited as role models for Morocco. The local elections of July 1963, and the conspicuous but fixed FDIC victory of an 85 per cent vote, encouraged the UNFP to think in terms of revolutionary change. The king responded by arresting over 130 UNFP militants on treason charges later in the month. Ben Barka, the leader of the UNFP, fled to Paris and widened the political breach by calling on the Moroccan army not to resist Algeria in the border war fought in the Sahara during the winter of 1963.

The first parliament was a failure. In two years of existence, it passed only three minor bills. A three-year plan drawn up in 1964 was aborted as the planners had failed to consult the Finance Ministry. A short-lived liberal party was formed around disgruntled technocrats appalled by the jobbery and factional intrigue that dominated the parliament. The student and worker riots of Casablanca in March 1965 encouraged the king to dissolve parliament in June and rule directly, though he retained most of the parliamentary cabinet. Ben Barka was assassinated in Paris that August, in a plot that was traced back to the Moroccan Ministry of the Interior. The king, in an adroit political move, then borrowed a popular UNFP issue and initiated the nationalization of foreign businesses and farms.

By August 1970 a new constitution was prepared and approved in a national referendum that gave the king increased influence over parliament. Istqlal and the UNFP boycotted the elections, with the result that the parliament was made up of loyalist placemen. As a result of this narrowing of the field of power there were two *coups d'état*. A group of senior army officers had grown disgusted at the scale of corruption in government and the extent of patronage and client networks. In the Coup of Skhirate in July 1971 they attempted to purge the king of his existing advisers, who were to be replaced by a puritanical reforming military council. In 1972 there was another failed coup when the king's aeroplane was ambushed by Air Force jets but was saved by a quick-talking pilot. Investigations traced the plot back to General Oufkir, the widely feared Minister of the Interior. The following year, in March 1973, bands of armed men crossed the border from Algeria in the hope of sparking off a popular rising. It never got off the ground, but the public trial was used to accuse some of the left-wing opposition of treasonable rebellion.

1975–99
The Later Years of King Hassan II, the 'Unifier'

If the first 14 years of King Hassan's reign earned him the nickname of the 'Great Survivor', his later period of rule allows him to be considered the 'Unifier'. In 1975 the king orchestrated a march of 350,000 civilians south to reintegrate the Spanish colony of Rio de Oro (western Sahara) into greater Morocco. This 'Green March' buried the political problems of the past in a surge of nationalism. It was a brilliantly timed political gamble which caught the Spanish government paralysed by the lingering death of General Franco. The resulting war against a group of the Saharan tribes, united under the Polisario movement for independence in the western Sahara, prolonged the mood of national unity. Libya and Algeria supported the Polisario, but this 'revolutionary' alliance led to firm backing for Morocco from both Saudi Arabia and the United States.

After a shaky start the war was won militarily. A methodical system of well-patrolled sand walls, begun in 1981 and completed in 1987, excluded the Polisario fighters from all but the frontier fringes of the province. This policy of practical action was matched by a 'hearts and minds' programme that sought to win over the Saharan population with new housing and development schemes. The enhanced pay, equipment and prestige afforded to the army kept it loyal to the king. Meanwhile, the Polisario, locked up in their refugee camps around the Algerian town of Tindouf, gradually lost the support of their hosts. In 1989 a UN-sponsored ceasefire was agreed and King Hassan met with Polisario leaders for talks in Marrakesh. His hand was further strengthened in 1992 when the foreign minister of the Polisario defected to Morocco, and the Algerian government seemed to renounce the idea of an independent western Sahara. Ever since the ceasefire there has been talk of a UN-monitored referendum, but the question of who is eligible to vote will be decisive. Further talks were held between the two sides in 2007 after a US- and French-backed Moroccan proposal to create an autonomous region. The talks failed. The UN mission still officially supports the staging of a referendum to help determine the region's future.

The enormous cost of the war, an estimated US$1 billion a year, added to Morocco's already grave economic problems. Strikes in 1979 led to the arrest of activists, but wages were increased to keep abreast of the annual 10 per cent inflation rate. The political temper was heated by these strikes, and later that year teachers and students demonstrated against the presence of the deposed Shah of Iran, who had sought refuge with the king.

By June 1981 the situation had been aggravated by a succession of bad harvests that increased basic food prices just when the International Monetary Fund (IMF) insisted that the state subsidy on food must be reduced. A day-long demonstration against the IMF cuts degenerated into looting and rioting. The police restored order after many casualties, and some of the organizers of the original demonstration were prosecuted. Local elections were held in June 1983, but the scale of the royalist victory suggested heavy-handed electoral influence. Parliamentary elections were subsequently cancelled and the king assumed emergency powers in October, though again he skilfully checked criticism by assembling a cabinet from a broad spectrum of political parties. In January 1984, the events of 1981 were repeated as the IMF insisted on further heavy cuts in subsidies in exchange for vital loans. Riots broke out throughout Morocco. The king withdrew the cuts in question, but at the same time heavy police action against rioters and political dissidents put 2,000 men behind bars.

The state of emergency lasted only six months, and by the summer of 1984 a new parliament had been elected which produced a moderate government committed to economic reform. There was much work to be done. The internal tax situation was in an anarchic state, with all the big earners such as tourism, agriculture and property speculation enjoying an official tax holiday. The state phosphate industry that bestrides the domestic economy ran at a paper 'loss', while a flourishing black market, covering much the same ground, turned over an estimated US$5 billion a year.

The IMF provided the new reforming administration of Morocco with a series of loans to restructure its industry and gradually create something approaching a free market. Though there is still much to be done, a bold start has been made in creating an open stock exchange, statutory accounting for businesses, VAT, independent management, cuts in the top heavy civil service, and some accountability in the state phosphate monopoly. A policy of privatization, initiated in 1989, has already disposed of some of the enormous state sector, although, as in many such schemes elsewhere, it is the small profitable concerns that are easy to sell off while the monolithic loss-makers remain. These reforms have attracted an increasing amount of foreign investment and there are now over 1,000 foreign companies in operation, mostly concentrated around the tourist, part-assembly and textile trades, which look to the EU as their natural market.

Though the man in the street is much more concerned with Morocco's relations with the rest of the Arab world, it is the European Union that is the country's vital trading partner. The rejection of the 'Muslim applications' of both Morocco and Turkey to join the EU during the 1990s has allowed a more pragmatic spirit to be introduced into later negotiations for a free-trade agreement between Morocco and the Union. Morocco arguably now enjoys the best of all possible worlds, since it has free trade agreements with the EU and US but is not a member of the EU (and is therefore not subject to its laws). Officially the country remains in negotiations to join the union but a change to the status quo is unlikely for some time.

Of the EU countries, relations with the old colonial powers of France and Spain remain dominant. Over 40 per cent of Morocco's imports come from France and Spain, and also the bulk of her invisible earnings through tourism and guest workers. Both countries have proved generous suppliers of government loans, technical assistance and arms. Despite the nationalization of foreign-owned land and businesses in the 1970s, both France and Spain have a substantial stake in the Moroccan economy, for French and Spanish banks hold influential shareholdings in Morocco's own chain of commercial banks. The Spanish territories of Ceuta and Melilla are not yet a major issue of confrontation, although it is easy to imagine they could become a tempting nationalist diversion in any future period of popular unrest.

The connection with France remains very strong. Thousands of young Moroccans finish their education in a French university, and there are still thousands of skilled French technicians, teachers and governmental experts employed by the government of Morocco. French and Moroccan troops have even performed joint operations, such as the 'policing' of Zaire in 1979. US support and aid throughout the Polisario war has drawn Morocco quite firmly into the Western camp.

In June 1988 several decades of mutual hostility between Morocco and Algeria were ended with the restoration of full diplomatic ties. This was followed in the spring of 1989 by the Maghrebi Union Treaty between all the countries of northwestern Africa – Libya, Tunisia, Algeria, Morocco and Mauritania. This surprising turn of events had as much to do with the economic difficulties of Algeria and Libya, and mutual anxiety at the growth of an isolationist Europe, as the common culture of the Maghreb. This block of nations is known as UMA (*Union de Maghreb Arabe*); it has pleasing associations with the Arabic word *umma*, which refers to the wider community of Islam. The alliance did not have any dramatic consequences, but for a time allowed an easing of border controls that permitted Morocco and Tunisia to sell food to new importers such as Libya and Algeria. However, the demise of Algeria's peace in 1992 meant ferocious violence between the established FLN regime and army and the Islamic fundamentalists of the FIS. This led the Moroccan government once again to seal the Algerian border in 1994 (it remains closed at the time of writing), undoubtedly motivated to a considerable extent by concern to head off any contagion of fundamentalism within its own territory.

For all his authoritarianism at home Hassan II made one crucial decision in the early 90s, which was to launch a Royal Council for Human Rights. This came on the heels of pressure from various rights groups beyond Morocco as well as activists within the country, and it opened inquiries into much of the politically-motivated torture and injustice that had taken place in the previous two decades.

There was no display of Maghreb unity during the Gulf War of 1991. King Hassan rode the conflict with consummate skill. His early pledge to send Moroccan troops to join the Alliance forces put him in good standing with all those powers – the USA, Saudi Arabia, the Gulf States and Western Europe – on whom Morocco is dependent for loans and investment. Faced with massive popular demonstrations in favour of Saddam Hussein he was forced to back down from his original strong pro-Alliance stance, but in the aftermath of the war Morocco did not suffer the sudden withdrawal of aid that affected so many Arab states.

The 1993 elections to parliament produced few surprises and confirmed the king's control of the political life of the country through the offices of his feared Minister of the Interior, **Si Basri**, the successor to Oufkir. In 1994, seemingly at the height of his powers, he hosted a Middle East Economic Summit at Casablanca attended by both the Israeli prime minister, Yitzhak Rabin, and Yasser Arafat, president of the PLO. The next year he knew he was dying, whilst his regime was hit by criticism of Morocco's human rights record and a withering World Bank report which attacked corruption and administrative lethargy.

Nothing in his life would quite match the shrewdness with which he prepared for his death. Political prisoners were released and a new constitution drafted to create a bicameral parliament, the 325 members of the lower house to be elected, the upper house – a 270-seat Chamber of Advisers – to be filled by old office-holders and an indirectly elected assortment of the great and the good. The 1997 elections seemed to be (for once) free of the manipulations of the government, although plenty of complaints followed. A centre-left coalition won a majority and in 1998 the old king appointed his first socialist prime minister, the 75-year-old **Aberrahmane Youssoufi**. A quiet spirit of optimism prepared the country for Hassan II's death on Friday 23 July 1999, when the nation was swept by a spontaneous explosion of grief.

1999–Present
King Mohammed VI

Hassan's 36-year-old eldest son ascended the throne as Mohammed VI, and quickly distanced himself from his father's henchmen. In a series of public tours to such forgotten and depressed corners of the regime as the eastern plains and the Rif mountains he revealed a compassionate interest in the plight of the poor and unprotected. On 9 November he sacked the deeply unpopular Minister of the Interior, Si Basri, but awarded him the Medallion of the Throne (the kingdom's highest honour) in acknowledgment of 30 years of loyal service to the late king. Only the release of his father's most significant opponent, **Abdessalam Yassine**, ranked alongside Si Basri's sacking in its political significance, Mohammed granted amnesty to more than 45,000 prisoners and closed the palace harem. At the same time restrictions on the press were lifted and a current of critical journalism began to gain ground.

Old exiles were welcomed back (such as Abraham Serfaty and the family of Mehdi Ben Barka), while the young king's friends began to be placed in key positions of power. But there were soon problems too, as the king's expensive foreign trips began to be increasingly noted. The king's initial government had been formed by the Socialist Party and relations between monarch and government were good. The country's 2002 elections were described by international observers as Morocco's first free elections.

Morocco's proud image of a nation of tolerant Islam with Western political values suffered in 2003 as suicide bombers attacked foreign and Jewish targets in Casablanca, killing 45 people. The Madrid bombings of spring the following year, which killed 191, had their origins in Morocco too. Nevertheless, Morocco took a costly decision to commemorate the victims of 9/11 by holding a memorial service – and received criticism for doing so.

In 2007 **Istiqlal** (Independence), a monarchist, conservative party, won a general election and formed a new government.

No one can be certain of the future. From the past you learn that Islam, anarchy, regional loyalties and nationalism are consistent if contradictory features of Moroccan history. But it seems clear that only a strong man can rule a nation of such triumphant individualists.

The Moroccan Economy

Farming was long the most important element in the economy in terms of jobs but accounts for less than a sixth of the economy. Despite its rapidly growing population, Morocco remains almost self-sufficient after a good harvest, when the land yields about 4 million tons of wheat and 3 million tons of barley. Rainfall is still an absolute barometer of the national mood: good rainfalls led to a growth of over 20% in the agricultural sector in 2009. Almost half the population works on the land, producing cereals and root crops, as well as grazing animals over a vastly more extensive area. Excluding beasts of burden such as mules, donkeys, horses and camels, the nation's livestock numbers 18 million sheep, 6 million goats and 3.5 million cattle. Exportable agricultural goods such as sugar, citrus fruits, early vegetables and potatoes are principally produced by a few large well-irrigated estates established by the French in the Haouz Plain around Marrakesh and the Rharb. These are in the hands of a wealthy minority, while the masses survive on a pittance: average earnings are $12, or 107 dirhams, a day.

Industry is concentrated on the Atlantic coast around Casablanca, Rabat and Kénitra. The urban work force is estimated at at least 5 million, of whom 1 million are unemployed – this in a country without any welfare support. Industry employs about 20 per cent of the population and is principally involved with the processing of the country's enormous phosphate deposits and its agricultural products (such as olive oil, flour, milk, fish, fruit and vegetables). A second tier of industry includes cement works, tyre and textile factories. Traditional crafts, such as hand-weaving, leatherwork, metalwork, pottery and carpet-making are still broadly distributed among traditional towns and cities. Mining and construction employ another 15 per cent of the population but the former in particular was dramatically hit by the global financial crisis. Increasing numbers of workers are absorbed by the tourist industry, utilities and government services. Tourism has also boosted the construction sector, due in large part to a surge in investment from abroad.

Customs duties provide the bulk of state revenue through most of Morocco's history but this is increasingly shared with VAT revenues, especially as EU-Morocco trade borders become ever more open.

Foreign exchange comes from three major sources: US$1bn in receipts from between one and two million migrant workers, $610m from tourism, and $480m from phosphates. These figures help fill the $2500 million gap in the balance of trade. The export of fruit and vegetables to Europe is a lesser earner and this market has been severely threatened since the entry of the similar Mediterranean agricultural economies of Spain, Portugal and Greece into the EU in the 1980s. Fishing, though still a small earner of foreign cash, has been an area of continuous growth for several years. Morocco now lands over 500,000 tonnes a year, largely composed of the world's largest sardine catch.

An unlikely but valuable national resource is the king's friendship with the royal families of Saudi Arabia and the Gulf States. Generous loans, help in rescheduling debts, a daily 'allowance' of 50,000 barrels of oil, and outright gifts have propped up the Moroccan economy on numerous occasions. In 1985, for instance, $250m suddenly appeared in the ledgers of the foreign currency reserves when all other sources were known to be exhausted. Over-ambitious central planning, government waste, inefficient tax collection, a bungled attempt to quadruple the world phosphate price and the desert war have pushed the load of foreign debt perilously high. Twenty-five per cent of all government expenditure goes to service the interest of this debt, whilst 50 per cent is pledged to official salaries. The room for political manoeuvre is not large.

In 2008, Morocco's 2000 deal with the EU graduated to 'advanced status', granting the country still greater access to the free trade advantages generally limited to EU members. Thanks in part to good harvests, Moroccan GDP grew by 5.1% in 2009, a remarkable hike given the parlous state of Europe, its main export market, during the same period. Trade with the USA has been increasingly important ever since a free trade agreement between the two countries came into force in 2006.

Problems

The particular challenges facing Morocco today are to reduce the wealth disparity and to provide jobs in industry and services, as the country makes the transition from an agricultural economy to a more modernized one. If that is to work, it will need to invest in education and, as the literate middle class grows, to cut corruption too. The rule of law remains a particularly acute challenge, meaning many of the country's intellectuals and entrepreneurs experience the glass ceiling that comes with poor political connections. That same system allows influential merchants and industrialists undue freedom from the law and an appropriate level of taxes. This is unlikely to change soon since the man with the largest business interests in the country is the king himself but the tax system will need to become more equitable if the government is to make the necessary investments in education and social services.

The population is phenomenally young and it continues to grow quickly, having risen by four million through the the first decade of the 21st century, and is now approaching 32 million. The young population is also finding opportunities abroad, especially in Europe, and remittances have become a large part of the Moroccan economy as a result. That at least provides some slack for a system unwilling to encourage contraception but faced with a growing population which it is as yet unable to educate to literacy in sufficient measure. Only a little over half of those over the age of 15 can read and write.

The king remains Commander of the Faithful and it falls to him above all to ensure that Morocco can placate most of its important Muslim figures while also pressing ahead with key reforms. Morocco has never witnessed a split between the *ulema*, the Islamic hierarchy, and a determinedly secular government, as so many other Arab states have. The daily TV weather report provides an example of the natural religious conservatism of Morocco and the opportunities for consensus. The predictions of the weather were at first considered impious by the *ulema*, but once the announcer started to add enough *insha'Allah*'s (if God wills it) there was no further complaint.

Major progress has been made in recent years, most especially in 2004 with the introduction of the Moudawana legal code, which defends the right of women to divorce, enjoy custody of children, own property and receive child support. The fate of women in Morocco may yet be the best barometer of the country's tailwinds. My abiding image of Morocco is of a lady covered head-to-toe in black, with only a tiny eye-slit through her *niqab*. But she was riding a scooter, riding alone and at great speed through the small medina streets of Marrakesh. Such are the possibilities of Morocco.

Topics

SPAIN

Rabat •Fez

M O R O C C O
•Marrakesh

ALGERIA

03

Moroccan Architecture

As Muslims and Christians approach books from different ends, so do they architecture. This is less of a philosophical division and more to do with a difference in climate. Islamic architecture aims to enclose space, to create a sheltered garden from a wilderness. Architectural decoration, of pavilions, fountains, raised paths and pools, is reserved for the interior of this enclosure. European traditions are the complete reverse: gardens emanate from outside the house, decoration is reserved for the exterior of a structure, and the interior has more to do with a collection of rooms isolated from the environment than any feeling of a defined space.

In architectural detail both Christendom and Islam share the same classical influences, though Islam has more fully identified itself with the domes and arches of Christian Byzantium. Muslim architects in North Africa rejected horizontal beams early on and began experimenting with horseshoe arches. This was developed into a pervading, almost obsessive regional theme. The tracery of the interlocking arch is ubiquitous: rising from walls to support domes, or in serried ranks to support the roof of every major mosque, and defining the lowest tier of every interior courtyard. The squinches, the awkward corners left by a dome, are filled by *muqurnas*, which can appear like disordered dripping stalactites, though in their origin they are highly ordered tiers of arches. The surface of the arch itself is next adorned, with circular half lobes, tracery and *muqurnas*. By the 19th century the style had become debased; to see it with its early confidence and elegance you must visit the monuments of the Almoravids, Almohads and Merenids.

North African architects also moved away from using columns as a central structure and developed rectangular piers to support their arches. Columns that freely borrowed their capitals from classical, Egyptian and Persian styles were increasingly used as mere decoration. Often combined in pairs, they flank a window frame or define the edge of a horseshoe arch, or appear so ornate and thin as to be almost freestanding beside the load-bearing pier of an arch. In short, the column becomes vestigial.

The construction of the port town of Essaouira (which is accessible as a day trip from Marrakesh) in the late 18th century by a Christian architect in the service of the Moroccan Sultan provides a first taste of the Neo-Moorish style of architecture. This became widespread only in the late 1920s, when the French colonial administration began to construct a whole new infrastructure of post offices, railway stations, judicial and administrative offices. The Neo-Moorish style took elements of Morocco's medieval heritage and used them, totally divorced from their structural relevance, as mere decorative details and façades for otherwise entirely Western buildings. It was an inversion of the whole historical development of Islamic architecture, yet seems to work well. So far the style remains largely restricted to public buildings and hotels, though some newer housing developments are beginning to incorporate its repertoire.

Kasbahs

A Moroccan kasbah (or *qasaba*) can be a fortified manor house, the citadel of a city, an isolated government garrison or a tribal fort. A key to its definition is not so much its scale as its purpose, for a kasbah should be the domain of a ruler, be he sultan, governor or just a tribal chieftain. Most of the ancient cities of Morocco retain a large portion of their outer walls, but the kasbah (the government citadel containing palace, barracks, prison, arsenal and treasury) has too often decayed beyond recognition. Rabat provides an honourable and accessible exception. The walls of Essaouira are in even better condition, for they were built on the best European principles in the 18th century. Such fortifications are not always described as a kasbah, for there is a parallel military terminology which uses names such as *mahalla* (a fortified marching camp); *rabat* (or *r'bat*), meaning both a castle and a fortified base for the holy war; *hisn*, 'stronghold'; and *bordj* (or *burj*), a 'tower'.

The rise in power of the High Atlas *caids*, and particularly the Glaoui tribe, has left the southern region of Morocco studded with decaying kasbahs from which they administered their feudal domain. A Glaoui kasbah can still be seen at Telouèt, which can be visited from Marrakesh. At their best these kasbahs fuse the dazzling variety of traditional Berber battlemented exteriors with finely proportioned interiors that drew on Andalucían palaces for their inspiration. The Berber hill tribes were more capable of defending themselves than oasis- or valley-dwellers. They could afford to live in smaller family units, but stored their corn in communal stone-built hilltop fortresses which are known as an *agadir* (plural *igoudar*), *igherm* or *tighremt*, depending on which Berber dialect region they are in.

Marabouts and Koubbas

Throughout the cities, towns, villages and countryside of Morocco you will observe the *koubbas*, the domed tombs of *marabouts* – Muslim holy men. They are a striking feature of the Moroccan landscape and can range from a simple whitewashed, earth-walled hut to an opulent chamber covered by a green-tiled pyramid roof. The *marabout*'s tomb may be obscure, half-ruined and forgotten, or stand at the centre of a great city surrounded by a maze of outer courtyards around which stand dependent mosques, markets, *hammams*, schools and charitable institutions. As well as the size of the shrine, the nature of the holy man can vary. The venerated *Lalla* or *Sidi* could be a reforming sultan, a fearless warrior of the jihad, a Sufi master, the near-legendary ancestor of a tribe, the founder of a city, a pious protector of the poor, a learned arbitrator, or an Islamic identity for an old pagan deity of the mountain, river, forest or field. The one thing they have in common is *baraka*, which means both an enhanced spiritual standing and the power to benefit a pilgrim with a blessing.

The *koubba* is often the centre of spiritual life for the women of the area, as well as functioning as an asylum and a charitable centre. In the countryside it may also be the site of a weekly market or an annual *moussem*. These *moussems* may officially be held in honour of the saint but also function as exuberant secular festivals, popular social events, trade fairs and marriage markets.

Medersas

The earliest residential religious college in the Islamic world, or *medersa*, was built in Persia in the 9th century. *Medersas* were not built in Morocco until the 13th century, under the patronage of the Merenid sultans. Until then teaching took place in the courts of a mosque or in the houses of learned men. The earliest surviving Moroccan *medersa*, the Seffarine in Fez (1280), clearly shows the origin of this religious college in the town house of a lecturer. Later *medersas* drew more heavily on Andalucian decoration and the architectural developments of Cairo, though the basic plan of an open-air court surrounded by an upper storey of student lodgings and leading to a prayer-hall remains consistent. Marrakesh, Salé and Meknès each have a *medersa* that is open to the public, and Fez has three.

Mosques

Unlike Turkey and Egypt, Morocco does not allow those of other faiths to enter a mosque, nor in many cases Muslim cemeteries or the tombs of holy men. There are exceptions, most important of which are the Tin-Mal Mosque in the High Atlas south of Marrakesh, the Grand Mosque of Hassan II at Casablanca, and the tomb of Sultan Moulay Ismaïl in Meknès. There is no doctrinal basis for this exclusion, which seems to date from the period of the French Protectorate. The colonial authorities wished to avoid confrontation, and also believed that it would be useful for Moroccans, everywhere faced by the reality of European power, to have somewhere which was beyond the influence of foreigners. There was also an older tradition (born from a thousand years of warfare) of excluding Christians from even entering within the walls of a city; the sanctuary of Moulay Idriss, near Fez, remained inviolate until the 20th century. However, allowing non-Muslims to meet an intelligent and sympathetic believer who can dispel centuries of European obscurantism is something that is worth extending even further.

Although most mosques in Morocco are closed to non-Muslims, you are of course free to admire the exterior details such as gates and minarets. 'Mosque' literally means the place of prostration. At its simplest it can be an open-air space with a small niche, the *mihrab*, that indicates the direction of prayer towards Mecca. These mosques are known as *msalla* and can be seen outside the walls of Marrakesh and Fez, where they are used during festivals. The next stage in the development of the mosque can still be seen in use in poorer rural areas: a wall is built to enclose the prayer area and the *mihrab* extrudes, to appear like a white sugar loaf. It is only a small further development to roof over the prayer-hall, leaving an open-air court, the *sahn*, exposed at the opposite end to the prayer niche. The *sahn* or an adjoining building could be equipped with basins or a fountain for the ritual washing enjoined in the Koran.

Byzantine influence from Syria was strong in the construction of the cathedrals of Islam, the first grand mosques. The tendency to embellish the central aisle of the mosque with arches, pillars and domes strongly echoes the nave of a church. That characteristic Islamic feature, the minaret, was initially developed from the short towers that used to define a Byzantine churchyard. The first Muslim architects also borrowed from previous religious practice and elaborated the *mihrab* into a cave-like half-dome, upon which the two declarations of faith were carved, whilst the exterior of the niche was covered by an arch and flanked by two columns.

The walls and floors of Moroccan mosques are kept free of architectural decoration. The white pillars and arches may carry some simple carving, but there is seldom any colour beyond the hip-height reed matting pinned along the walls, and the carpets on the floor. Decoration is reserved for elaborate chandeliers and the pulpit-like *minbar*. The original *minbar*, used by the Prophet for his lectures at Medina, had six steps. He used a lower step in order to leave the throne symbolically empty. More steps were added by his successors to allow them to sit further from the throne, and so make clear their lesser spiritual authority.

The only substantial traditional mosque that a non-Muslim may enter in Morocco is also one of the oldest. The half-ruined Tin-Mal Mosque in the High Atlas was built by the Almohads in the 12th century. It is contemporary with the great achievements of Moroccan architecture: the Koutoubia Mosque of Marrakesh and the Hassan Tower of Rabat. The minarets of the Koutoubia and Hassan led to the creation of a characteristic style. Moroccan mosques all echo these two tall, square towers, which should be capped with a lantern that is exactly a fifth the size of the tower.

Palaces

The Roman ruins of Volubilis, near Fez, contain a number of palatial houses that are similar in design to the lesser palaces of later Muslim rulers. Moroccan palaces have an inconspicuous exterior and a covered hall that leads to a central open-air court. Around the walls of this court are arranged four public reception rooms or pavilions. The women's quarters are secluded from this male preserve and were known as 'the forbidden', the *harem* court. This arrangement of courts could be endlessly repeated or expanded in scale. The entire complex was known as the *dar* and a suite of rooms around a court a *buyt*. The *méchouar* was a space outside the immediate palace confines but within the outer walls where a ruler could review military parades or receive selected portions of the populace.

The oldest accessible palace in Morocco is the ruined 16th-century El Badi in Marrakesh. Of the palaces built in the 17th century by Sultan Moulay Ismaïl, the Oudaïa in Rabat is well preserved and open to the public. Meknès, for all its past glory, gives little insight into palace architecture. Of the royal palaces built in the 19th century, only the Dar Batha in Fez is accessible. There are, however, a number of lesser viziers' palaces that have survived from this period and are open to the public: the Palais Jamaï Hotel in Fez, the Dar Jamaï Museum in Meknès, the Bahia and the Dar Si Saïd in Marrakesh.

Flowers, Trees and Gardens

The Prophet said: '*If the end of the world happens while one of you is holding a palm tree that you are about to plant, do not get up before having planted it, if possible*'. Such an appreciation of the value of plants, so gently put, informs the Moroccan attitude towards the care and cultivation of their own plots, and the land is filled with the exuberance and beauty of plants which flourish under the clear skies of the Maghreb.

The progression from a Mediterranean to a desert ecology occurs in a diagonal belt across the country. Water supply rather than latitude is the key to plant identification. To the east the desert virtually reaches the Mediterranean, whilst in the south, around Marrakesh, irrigation allows groves of olive, orange and cypress trees to flourish. Plant growth ceases from June to August and begins properly with the rains in October. Some species flower throughout the winter but most perennials peak in March and April.

The real beauty of Moroccan flowers and trees lies not within the courtyards of the *harems*, but all around you, and all year round, even on city streets. Flowering trees along the boulevards, almost all imported from South America, decorate the streets from January onwards. The early yellow pom-poms of mimosas give way in April to the delicate blossoms of the coral tree (*Erythrina caffra*) and the pink calodendrum. May sees the jacaranda trees reveal their flowers of indescribable blue, and in June the delicate tracery of Jerusalem thorn (*Parkinsonia*) is lit up by an eruption of yellow flowers. The handsome evergreen leaves of figs and magnolias provide shade during the summer months. In December the extraordinary *Montanoa bipinnitifida* blazes with huge white daisies. Over the walls of the swanky out-of-town villas tumble hedges of bougainvillea, jasmine, passion flower, podranea, solanum, honeysuckle and roses, with the powerful fragrance of *Cestrum parqui*, charmingly known as *galant de nuit* in French, filling the June night air. And everywhere, of course, are palm trees, stretching up to the sky, providing a vertical counterpoint to the horizontalism of much of the urban architecture.

The clear blue flowers of larkspur, used in the ceremonial garlands of Egyptian mummies and undimmed 3000 years later when the tombs were opened, still overcome the dust of Moroccan roads and roundabouts in early summer. The sickly fragrance of *Datura* (angels' trumpets) is everywhere in villages and towns. It has been used as a (dangerous) hallucinogen since ancient times. The Greek doctor Theophrastus prescribed: '*If 3/20 of an ounce is given, the patient becomes sportive and thinks himself a fine fellow...four times the dose, he is killed*'.

In the souks the musty smell of boxes and bowls turned from thuja wood from the Atlas fills every woodworker's shop. An ancient tree, esteemed by classical writers from Homer to St John, thuja is still much sought-after. Its convoluted grain patterns of knots, spirals and veins are identified as tiger-, panther- and peacock-eyes by the cognoscenti, who prefer wood the colour of wine mixed with honey. Cicero paid one million *sesterces* for a thuja table, and Pliny mentioned the tree, '*which has given rise to the mania for fine tables, an extravagance with which women reproach the men when they complain of their vast outlay upon pearls*'.

Roses figure heavily in Moroccan agriculture and horticulture. Rose bushes surround the *pisé* walls of Marrakesh, and the mass production of roses for export is big business, providing the florists of Paris with fine long-stemmed, sweet-smelling blooms. The ancient damask rose *trigintipetala* is grown on a massive scale in Dadès, and is known as *beldi* in Arabic and *rose de M'Gouna* in French. Cultivated for the distillation of rose water and used as a handwash by Muslims, it is grown in hedgerow-like strips.

Traditional enclosed Moorish gardens aim to create a harmony of audible flowing water and restful shade thrown from elegant trees, typically laurel, cypress and olive. Roses, violets, jasmine, hollyhocks and blossoming fruit trees were traditionally planted chiefly for their scent. Modern gardens borrow some of these themes but are often dominated by 19th-century imports such as Australian mimosa, Brazilian bougainvillea and the 'boulevard palm' from the Canary Isles. A tour of traditional gardens in Morocco would include the Chellah and the Kasbah in Rabat, the Dar Batha, Bou Jeloud (Jnan Sbil) and Palais Jamaï Hotel in Fez, the Dar Jamaï Museum in Meknès, and conclude with the Mamounia Hotel, the Menara Gardens and the vast Aguedal Gardens in Marrakesh. The latter, more agriculture than horticulture, are still a living exponent of the tradition. The rhythm of the walks radiating from the massive central basins through acre upon acre of olive and orange grove lends a calm, reflective solitude all the more striking in its proximity to the bustling streets of the city.

Of the botanical gardens, Yves St-Laurent's celebrated haven, the Majorelle Garden in Marrakesh, is a collection of spiky plants rather than a garden, and its tranquillity may be shattered by hordes of tourists. The Jardins Exotiques at Bouknadel outside Rabat are much more extensive and overgrown, and less visited.

Islam

Allah is a noun which can be translated as 'the divinity' or 'the only and true God'. Islam literally means 'submission' or obedience to the divinity. Koran means 'the recitation' – the announcement of the word of God to Mohammed via the archangel Gabriel. This at its simplest is the Muslim religion: recognition of and obedience to the single divinity whose will is clearly stated in the Koran.

The Prophet Mohammed is not considered divine but a mere human mouthpiece for divine will. There is no veneration for a single historical act in the life of Mohammed, in contrast to Christianity, in which the moral teaching of Christ can be obscured by his miraculous birth, crucifixion and resurrection. Nor does Islam encourage any hopeless if heroic attempt to imitate the perfect life of a Christ figure. Instead it establishes a moral code that it is possible for the entire community to follow, and which assures salvation for those who honestly attempt to obey and damnation for those who ignore it or fail. It is acknowledged that man is deeply flawed, but great trust and hope is placed in the all-compassionate and merciful God.

Islam is not considered a new religion but a reformation of the ancient monotheistic worship of Abraham. The teachings of Mohammed presented an opportunity for the squabbling Christian and Jewish sects to unite on the common basics of belief. Moses, St John the Baptist and Christ are honoured in the Koran as prophets, but, although Christ's birth is seen as miraculous, he is not considered to be the son of God. Such a subdivision of divine power is regarded as impossible in monotheistic Islam, although a kind carpet-seller sympathetically suggested to me that if Christians could believe that Christ was filled with the breath of God rather than being his son there would be little disagreement between the two faiths. Towards the end of his life Mohammed realized the impossibility of converting all Christians and Jews. The direction of prayer was changed from Jerusalem to Mecca, and while he still instructed his followers to respect the 'peoples of the book' his views hardened. From the tolerant words of his early teaching, *'Will you dispute with us about God? When he is our Lord and your Lord! We have our words and you have your words but we are sincerely his'*, the Prophet progresses to, *'O believers! Take not the Jews or Christians as friends.'*

The Prophet Mohammed

Born in Mecca in 570, the young Mohammed was left an orphan and brought up by a succession of relatives from the influential Quraysh clan. As a young man he served as agent for Khadija, a wealthy widow 15 years his senior, whom he later married. Mecca was the centre of pagan Arab spiritual life, and Mohammed and his wife joined the circle of Hanyfs, puritanical seekers after enlightenment. The Hanyf venerated the religion of Abraham and were familiar with Jewish, Christian and Persian doctrines. These influences are repeatedly acknowledged in the Koran: *'Nothing has been said to thee which has not been said of old by apostles before'* and *'Every people has had its own apostle'*. Mohammed received his first revelation in 610, 15 years after his marriage, when he was 40 years old. The archangel Gabriel appeared to him in a cave outside Mecca that he used frequently for prayer and meditation. He was at first doubtful about the revelations but, encouraged by his wife, risked ridicule and shared the word of God. His ardent monotheism and criticism of the pagan worship centred on Mecca won some followers but even more enemies. Eventually the protection of his clan proved inadequate and, to avoid assassination, he fled to the city of Medina on 15 June 622, which is taken as the start of the **Hegira**, the Muslim era.

Mohammed was welcomed to the oasis of Yathrib (thereafter known as Medina el Nabi, or 'city of the Prophet') and invited to become its arbitrator, the learned figure who decided disputes within the community. There he established a theocratic state, and ironed out practical moral and legal codes for his community as well as the practice of prayer. From Medina he waged a defensive war on the Meccans and gradually subdued the surrounding Jewish and pagan tribes. By 630, two years before his death, his authority extended over all Arabia, and he proved magnanimous in victory. His enemies were pardoned and loaded with gifts, while the Prophet returned to his simple house built from palm trunks and canes.

The divisions within the Muslim world originated over the succession to the Prophet's leadership. Shiites believe in the claims of Ali (his cousin) to have succeeded Mohammed, while the Sunni accept the legitimacy of the first three caliphs. Sects such as the Ismailis, Druze and Kharijites all have their own beliefs on what the rightful succession should have been.

The Koran (Qur'an)

'The recitation' was first dictated to the illiterate Mohammed by the archangel Gabriel in his cave above Mecca. More verses were revealed to the Prophet in succeeding years, and were memorized and then written down by his followers. The Caliph Othman established the first written version 18 years after the death of Mohammed, in 650. Its 114 unequal chapters, the *suras*, containing 6,211 verses, were assembled carefully but in order of length, which has given the Koran a chronologically haphazard order. The *suras* have names, but these – 'The Cow', 'The Bee', 'The Ant' – have no significance other than as a memory aid. There are four main themes: the worship of Allah, the Day of Judgement with the division between heaven and hell, stories of earlier prophets, and proclamations and social laws. A collection of the Prophet's sayings and traditions remembered by his companions was also assembled, but despite great efforts there is no definitive edition of this **Hadith**. In Morocco the *caids* follow the Malekite tradition, one of the four schools of orthodox Islamic law.

The Five Pillars of Islam

The Prophet codified the religious life of his community into the five pillars of Islam: daily prayer, the pilgrimage to Mecca, the fast of Ramadan, the giving of alms, and acceptance that there is no other divinity but God. There were originally only three daily prayers, but some time after the Prophet's death this was increased to five. The first is known as *Moghreb* and is said four minutes after sunset; *Eshe* is said when it is dark; *Soobh Fegr* at dawn; *Dooh* at noon, just after the sun has passed its zenith; and *Asr* midway between noon and sunset. At each mosque a *muezzin* announces prayers by calling, *'God is great. I testify that there is no God but God. I testify that Mohammed is his prophet. Come to prayer, come to security. God is great.'* For *Soobh Fegr*, the dawn prayer, an extra inducement, *'Prayer is better than sleep'*, is added.

Alone or in a mosque the believer ritually purifies himself by washing with water or sand (this ritual purification was standard practice in all religions of the Near East, including early Christianity). Then, turning to Mecca, the believer stands with hands held up and open to proclaim that Allah is great. He then lowers his hands and recites the *fatiha* prayer still standing: *'Praise be to God, Lord of the worlds, the compassionate, the merciful, king of the day of judgement, thee do we worship and your aid do we seek. Guide us on the straight path, the path of those on whom you have bestowed your grace, not the path of those who incur thy anger nor of those who have gone astray.'* The believer bows with hands on knees and completes a full prostration. Kneeling up again, he recites the *chahada*, a prayer for the Prophet. The three positions of prayer have a symbolic meaning: standing distinguishes the rational man from an animal, bowing represents the act of a servant to his master, and prostration abandonment to the will of God. On Fridays the noon prayer is recited only in the grand or licensed mosque. This is followed by a sermon, the *khutba*, given from the steps of the pulpit-like *minbar* (with the throne and higher steps left symbolically empty).

In some of the grand mosques there are specific doors for the use of women. These lead to areas screened off from the sight of men, often at the side or the back of the prayer-hall. This is, however, the exception. In most of Morocco the mosque is a completely male preserve, and women pray at home or in the prayer-halls that surround *koubbas*, the shrines of the saints (see *'Marabouts* and *Koubbas'*, p.43).

The pilgrimage to Mecca was an annual month-long event centuries before the Islamic era. Mohammed acknowledged the Kaaba shrine as the ancient altar built by the son of Abraham, and a specific Islamic calendar of events was imposed on a cleaned-up version of the old rituals in 630. For a poor man it could be the journey of a lifetime, and in the past it was restricted to the healthy and wealthy, who granted their marriage partners a temporary divorce in case they should never return from the hazards of the journey. On their return they were greeted with the proud title of *hajji*. The distance of Mecca from Morocco (750 days by caravan for the complete trip) increased the attraction of local shrines. Towns such as Moulay Idriss, near Fez, claimed that five pilgrimages there equalled the trip to Mecca.

The fast of Ramadan, during the daylight hours of the ninth month of the Muslim year, commemorates Mohammed's spiritual practices before the Koran was first revealed to him. The night of the 26th day of the fast, which commemorates the first recitation, is known as 'the night of power', and Is filled with processions while the heavens are opened to hear the prayers of the faithful. It is a night apart, *'better than a thousand months...peace until the rising of the dawn'*. Although the 26th is widely celebrated, it is not known for sure that this is the correct date, for it could be any of the last ten days of Ramadan. This leads to some regional variations and anxious scholarly debate. Ramadan was specifically based on existing Arabian custom and Christian and Jewish spiritual practices such as Lent.

The giving of alms is a continual duty for the Muslim. The *zahir*, or 'fortieth', tax originated out of this obligation and was the foundation of all direct taxation in the Islamic world.

Jewish Morocco

The last decades have witnessed a minor renaissance in Jewish Morocco, as Moroccan Jews who emigrated *en masse* to Israel have begun to return to visit the land of their forefathers. On a mountain road I was told by a Jewish pilgrim that there are two great holy places in the world where heaven and earth are in the closest and most occasionally violent proximity. First is the land of Palestine, but after that there is only Morocco. Tombs, cemeteries and synagogues have been restored on the back of this growing pilgrimage trade, which coincides with a new assertiveness by the Sephardic community within Israel.

Jews first came to Morocco in the ships of the Phoenicians, for they provided a skilled labour force experienced in the working of inland mines. Initially they were concentrated in southern Spain, but gradually became a ubiquitous presence in all the ports established by the Phoenician traders along the North African coast. A tradition records that this scattered community sent tribute to King Solomon to assist in the construction of the first temple. Archaeological evidence is scant, though Hebrew gravestones have been found in the excavations of the Romano-Punic capital of Volubilis, near Fez. The community was greatly strengthened by refugees fleeing the destruction of Judaea in the reign of the Emperor Vespasian (69–79) and again in Hadrian's time (113–38), as well as following the failed Jewish revolt in Cyrenaica, in the east of present-day Libya.

The 'Dark Ages' following the fall of Rome are the unchronicled golden period of Jewish activity in Morocco, when missionaries converted whole Berber tribes and communities were established in every corner of the country. When Moulay Idriss first reached Morocco in the 8th century, the Jewish-dominated city of Sefrou, in alliance with the Meknassa tribe, was a key political force. As Islam triumphed, Jews were marginalized from political life, but established a key position in trade, metalwork, jewellery and similar crafts. In the 11th century, two rabbis, the philosopher-physician Maimonides and Yitzhak al Fasi, brought their intellectual culture to a golden flowering. During the Merenid period the first walled ghettoes (the Mellah) evolved out of the traditional Jewish quarters of cities to facilitate the protection, self-government and efficient taxation of this wealthy community. In the cities Jews were ruled by their own *caids* and judged and taxed by their own officials, while in the countryside Jewish villages placed themselves under the protection of the local military power. A second great wave of Jewish settlement occurred after the fall of Granada in 1492, when the sophisticated urban Jews of Andalucía were expelled from Spain and settled in such cities as Fez, Tetouan, Azzemour and Rabat. In music, speech, dress, cuisine and architecture these refugees had much more in common with their fellow Moors (Muslim Andalucians) than with the so-called Berber Jews, and this division remains today.

Jews were seen as a vital resource of the state and often held the most important financial posts in the administration, although when the Merenid Sultan Abdul Haqq tried to appoint a Jewish grand vizier he met widespread popular resistance. The ongoing distrust between Muslim Moroccans and the Christian Europeans, fomented by centuries of war and piracy, also meant that the Jews were in constant demand as middlemen by both antagonists. The Alaouite sultans in particular leant heavily on Jewish expertise. It was they who established the large and important Jewish community in Tangier, mostly recruited from the old community in nearby Tetouan, as well as those in Essaouira and Casablanca, most of whom were originally from Azzemour.

In the period of French dominance, European-based Jewish charities were quick to pour funds into Morocco for the education of the community. This effort was so successful that the native Moroccan Jews began to be co-opted into the settler community, though this never reached the level of assimilation (mixed with outbursts of anti-Semitism from the French *pieds noirs*) seen in Algeria and Tunisia.

During the Second World War, King Mohammed V protected the 300,000 Moroccan Jews from the horrors that overtook their brethren in France and the rest of Europe. Nevertheless, although the Moroccan Jews had always enjoyed royal favour and formed one of the world's oldest-established Jewish communities, they remained apart from the majority community, and with the rise of nationalism under the Protectorate they were frequently regarded by other Moroccans as a privileged, semi-Europeanized group who had identified themselves too closely with the French and Spanish colonizers. The events of the Holocaust followed by the establishment of the State of Israel in 1948 galvanized attitudes and Jewish opinion. Emigration to Israel began immediately after the state's foundation, and the trickle of the late 1940s turned into a flood after the Suez Crisis of 1956 led to a wave of anti-Jewish feeling throughout the Arab world. By 1967 this mass migration was all but complete, although the thread has not been completely broken. Around 6,000 Jews remain in Morocco today, and Moroccan Jews, even after they have settled in Israel, are allowed to keep their Moroccan passports. In May 2003, suicide bombers attacked several Jewish targets including a mosque in Casablanca: it was Shabbat, and the buildings were largely empty, but, tragically, 29 Muslims were killed. The attacks were widely decried and King Mohammed VI showed his support for the Jewish community by touring the sites where the attacks had been carried out. One of the King's most influential advisors, André Azoulay, is Jewish (unthinkable in much of the Arab world), and currently heads the Anna Lindh Euro-Mediterranean Foundation for the Dialogue Between Cultures as well as playing a prominent role in the pursuit of peace in the troubled waters of the Middle East.

Throughout this guide you will find information on accessible Jewish cemeteries and the location of the old Mellah quarters.

Moorish Decorative Arts

Morocco has an active tradition of decorative art which was first developed in Moorish Spain. This rich heritage combines geometric, floral and calligraphic themes in a distinctive style that also remains true to the mainstream traditions of Islam. Throughout the country you will find dazzling examples of decorative art carved into stone, cedar and plaster; painted on tiles, furniture, ceilings and ceramics; or assembled in tile mosaics.

Islamic art draws attention away from the real world to one of pure form. Titus Burkhardt defined Islamic art as the way to ennoble matter by means of geometric and floral patterns which, united by calligraphic forms, embody the word of God as revealed in the Koran. Of these forms of decoration only the calligraphic can be considered an Islamic invention, though the way all are combined is distinctively Islamic. Decorative themes from architecture provide many of the motifs for the lesser arts of ceramics, cabinet-making, embroidery and carpet-making.

Geometric decoration presents a direct analogy to spiritual truths, for both direct attention away from the confusing patterns of the world to find hidden cores of meaning. From the muddled three dimensions of the physical world, geometry creates a clearly defined two-dimensional order. But beyond the ordered geometric patterns a single hidden point rules the kaleidoscopic images of the surface. Thus all relates to the one, just as on the Day of Judgement all that has been created will return to the single entity of the Creator. Time, space, angles, planes, lines will collapse in on themselves and the physical universe will return to the One. There is no God but the one God.

Islam also inherited earlier Semitic religious traditions that saw sacred art as having an essentially geometric and mathematical nature. Many familiar Islamic geometric patterns were borrowed from Egypt and Syria. Representational art was a dangerous distraction that could degenerate into graven images and paganism, but numbers and figures were seen as symbols that defined a perfect world, created by the single Creator. Islam also absorbed the Platonic and Pythagorean respect for the divine harmony of geometry and mathematics. Numbers and shapes in the Pythagorean and Cabbalistic tradition were connected to mystical properties: a pyramid with its six sides represented fire; a tetrahedron air; a cube earth; and an icosahedron water. The result was a detailed symbolic vocabulary which allowed hidden abstractions to be built into a pattern. The infinite repetition of geometrical patterns, the lattices, interlaces, overlays and borders, is also the perfect aesthetic accompaniment to the human ritual of Islam, the endless chanting of single phrases, the recurring ritual of daily prayer and the repetitious nature of the Koranic verses themselves.

According to the Koran every artist on the Day of Judgement will be challenged to breathe life into his work and on failing will be condemned. The floral art of Persia and Rome was not considered to fall under this interdict, and was eagerly borrowed by the first Muslim conquerors. Floral motifs – acanthus, peonies, tulips, roses, pine cones, vine leaves, pomegranates and palmettes – are also a constant reminder to the faithful of the rewards of paradise, for the Koran is full of references to the overhanging trees and fruits in heaven. The symmetry of flowers and seed pods also reveals the geometric hand of the Creator.

Many Muslims believe that Arabic is the divine language and that their language did not exist before the Prophet Mohammed received the first verses of the Koran. Archaeological evidence, though, shows that written Arabic developed from the Nabato-Aramaic script, which was itself a successor to Phoenician. The earliest Arabic inscription was found near Aleppo and has been dated to AD 512. There appear to have been four distinct Arabic scripts before the Islamic era. A reform by the Caliph Abdel Malik (685–705) established the two schools of calligraphy that exist today. These are kufic, an angular, solid, hieratic script, suitable for carving and ornamental texts, and cursive, a rounded flowing script (sometimes referred to as *Nashki*), suitable for everyday use.

This reform did not check the continual development of scripts, which continued evolving until the spread of printing. Among the more characteristic is the graceful Persian *Taliq*; the variant cursive of *Rihani*; *Tughra*, the cryptic Tartar lettering; the thick, stout *Riqa* script of the Turks; *Sayaqit*, the secret script of the Seljuk clerks; and the opulent *Diwani* of the Ottoman court. *Ghober* script allowed for letters to be carried by pigeon post and could be read only with a magnifying glass, whilst the different tones of *Manachir* could indicate reprimand or satisfaction before even the first letter had been read.

Up to the 12th century, Morocco remained dominated by the old cursive script of Kairouan, in Tunisia. This was replaced by the distinctive Maghrebi script which had been developed in Andalucía, and preserved an ancient synthesis of kufic and cursive. Abdelkebir Khatabi and Mohammed Sigilmassa in *The Splendours of Islamic Calligraphy* (see Further Reading, p.306) describe it as '*Virile and generous with angular outlines, both horizontal and vertical well emphasized and accompanied by large cursives open at the top*'. Maghrebi script was written in black with ink prepared from scorched wool taken from a sheep's stomach. The official standard pen was composed of 24 donkey hairs, though dried reed was a common substitute. A red copper pen was used for marriage documents, a silver or stork-beak pen for a special friend, and a pomegranate sliver was used for an enemy.

Cursive and Maghrebi can be found in architectural decoration, though a plain kufic or floral kufic are much more common. Beyond their own attraction, horizontal bands of script are often used to bind together different sections of materials and decoration, as the Koran binds the community of Islam.

Music

The cry of the *muezzin*, summoning the faithful to prayer, is the most distinctive, universal and haunting sound in Morocco. In a large city such as Fez or Marrakesh the principal mosque has the honour of initiating the call, which is then picked up and echoed by dozens of lesser mosques. It is most impressive in the comparative quiet and diffused light of the early morning and evening, when it mocks the daytime bustle of the secular world.

Travelling through Morocco you will automatically be exposed to the music of the country as you sit scrunched up in a grand taxi or bus. Few cafés would feel complete without the sound of a radio, cassette player or television, while at markets, festivals and urban squares such as the Jemaa el Fna in Marrakesh there is always live music. No market, however small, is complete without at least one stall selling a colourful assortment of their own 45-minute recordings. These barrows carry a broad selection, ranging from Egyptian singers such as the great Ulm Khaltoum, West Indian reggae and some major Western bands, to the home-grown stars of *chaabi*, Moroccan popular music.

The centre for today's Moroccan music industry is Casablanca, where the main contemporary pop influence – Algerian Raï music – is most common. Moroccan Raï stars, such as Cheb Khader and Chaba Zahounia, and their Algerian counterparts create the most prominent sounds on today's urban soundtrack. In most cases they replace traditional instruments with electric and digitalized equivalents, but in their inspiration still draw heavily on a rich seam of Arab and indigenous musical traditions. You will win instant street kudos by asking for a CD by any of the big Moroccan names such as Haim, Hanino, El Hussein Slaoui, Lafkih Laomri, Nass el Ghiwane, Abselam Cherkaoui, Lhaj Amar Ouahraouch, Lem Chaleb, Jil Jalala or Muluk el Hwa.

Berber Music

The music of the Berber people is of ancient origin and inextricably linked with movement and dance. It is an astonishing example of the tenacity of an oral heritage which preserves a combination of dance, poetry and drama that could almost come from pre-Homeric Greece. There are musical differences between the three main dialect regions of Berber speech: the Tariffit of northern Morocco, the Tamazight of the Middle Atlas and the Tashelhit, or Chleuh, of the south. There is also a division between the music of the villagers and that produced by travelling musicians.

In village music (variously known as *ahaidous*, *ahidus* or *ahouach*) flutes, drums, rhythmic hand-clapping and large choruses predominate. The choruses, composed of long lines or circles of men and women, dance around the musicians as they perform. Soloists, known as *inshaden*, sometimes supported by two accompanists or by the sound of their own violin, improvise lyrics within the basic framework of these distinctive choral chants. As well as there being a difference in dialect, the music of southern Morocco is quite distinct as it is based on the pentatonic scale (like that of West Africa), while the other two regions use seven notes. Until the 20th century, traditional village music remained largely unknown to a wider audience, as it was considered improper to perform outside the tribal region or to seek any financial gain. Fortunately, folk festivals and recordings have changed this.

Traditionally, travelling musicians, usually groups of four, were led by a singer-poet, supported by a violin, tambourine and flute. He sang of heroic qualities, such as martial bravery and impossible love, into which he skilfully wove gossip and topical references to local politics, as well as flattering or chiding his hosts for their hospitality. These troupes bore a striking resemblance to the bards of Celtic Europe and the medieval troubadours of France. At the start of the 20th century they began to add female vocalists to the line-up, whose job was to echo the poetic refrain and to dance. These groups were increasingly based in the new urban centres of the coast, and replaced the older tribal tradition. Today's professional performers (male *shioukh*, female *shikat*) form a near-hereditary guild, and enjoy the kind of celebrity and notoriety that touring actors in the West experienced a hundred years ago. The groups are known as *urneziaren*, though in southern Morocco they can be referred to as *rwais*.

Two groups of particular eminence are the Jajouka and Daqqa. The Jajouka are known for their 1969 recordings with the Rolling Stones. They are a unique caste of musicians from the Jebala foothills in the western Rif. They perform on *ghaita*, *lira*, *guenbri* and drums to create a pagan ritual music that invokes the gods of fecundity and energies in a way similar to the ancient rites of Pan. The Daqqa of Marrakesh perform a ritual dance for the religious festival of Achura, accompanied by percussionists playing the *tar* drums and *n'far* trumpeters.

Further listening: *Brian Jones Presents the Pan Pipers of Jajouka* (Rolling Stone, London); *Berberes du Maroc* – from the far south (Le Chant du Monde, Paris); *Anthologie des Rwâyes* (4-CD Sous Berber collection, La Maison des Cultures du Monde); *Najat Aatabou: Goul el Hak el Mout Kayna* (Blue Silver); *Najat Aatabou: The Voice of the Atlas* (GlobeStyle); *Master Musicians of Jajouka: Apocalypse Across the Sky* (Axiom); *Bachir Attar: The Next Dream* (CMP); *Medium Atlas Range: Sacred and Profane Music* (Ocora); *Marrakesh Festival* (Playasound); *Maroc: Chants et Danses* (Chants du Monde); *Mohamed Rouicha: Ellil Ellil* (Sonodisc); *Mohamed Rouicha: Ch'hal Bkit Ala Alli Habit* (Sonodisc); *Festival de Marrakesh, Folklore National du Maroc* in 2 vols; *Rais Lhaj Aomar Ouahrouch: Musique Tachelait* (Ocora). Lyrichord, *http://lyrichord.com*, publishes a good selection, including Rwais from the High Atlas and a collection of Sufi music.

Al-Ala: the Classical Music of Andalus

The classical music of all the Maghreb countries is firmly based on the heritage of Moorish Spain. It is a lyrical and instrumental repertoire that has been elaborated over the last 200 years from verses written during the 700-year Muslim occupation of Spain, but which in turn had their origins in ancient Baghdad. The original reconstruction of these venerable verses was made in Morocco towards the end of the 18th century by Al-Hayek, under the enthusiastic patronage of two sultans, Mohammed ben Abdellah and Moulay Sliman. He completed his work in 1799, and the resulting manuscript provided the basis for the three collections of the modern repertoire, each based on a particular oral history and dynastic memory.

Of the original repertoire of 24 symphonies, or *nuba*, only eleven have even partly survived, though even this fragment takes some 90 hours to be sung right through. Each *nuba* is based on a specific mode that reflected one of the hours of the day, and is divided into five main rhythmic phases: the prelude (*mizan*), broad (*muwassa*), increased (*mahzuz*), quick (*inshad*) and fast (*insiraf*). Each *nuba* simultaneously passes through five tempo changes: *al bacit, al qaim wa nsif, btayhi, darj* and *quddam*. The sung poetry in the *nuba* is based on a corpus of classical Andalucian verse and later additions in similar tone and style.

Al-Ala is associated with the urban middle class, particularly from those cities that benefited from Andalucian refugees. In Morocco it is performed by extensive orchestras that use the lute, two-string viol, tambourine, vertically played European violin, and clay- and skin-drums. As well as the three big orchestras in Casablanca, Rabat and Fez, there are others from Tetouan, Tangier and Oujda. The latter follows the traditions of Algeria and performs the *gharnati*, believed to be the specific heritage of Granada. Going even farther east, other variations include *malouf*, played in Constantine, Tunisia and Libya, while a distant cousin called *moshahat Andalucía* can be found in Egypt, Syria and the Lebanon. A further offshoot of Andalus is preserved by the Sephardic Jews of Morocco, who added liturgical singing to the common tradition in the form of psalmodies and responsorial anthems.

These days Al-Ala is in healthy condition. There are conservatories in all the major cities; the complete *nuba* are available on a number of recordings; academics are currently notating all the varieties; and the Moroccan Royal Academy has commissioned a definitive edition of Al-Hayek's original manuscript.

Further listening: The complete *nuba* repertoire has been recorded and is being issued in several CDs (over several years) by La Maison des Cultures du Monde, Paris. For other recordings of Andalucian music, see also *Fez Orchestra: Classical Music of the Andalucian Magreb* (Ocora); *Ustad Massano Tazi: Classical Andalucian Music from Fez* (Ocora); *Orchestre de Meknès: Musique Andalouse Marocaine* (Sonodisc); *Orchestre de Fez: Irabbi Lward* (Sonodisc); and for a crossover between the music of Muslim Andalus and the flamenco of Spanish Andalucía, *El Lebrijano and Orquesta Andalusi de Tanger, Encuentros* (GlobeStyle).

Gnaoua

The word 'Gnaoua' refers to both a spiritual brotherhood (originally based around communities of black slaves), a musical troupe and a style of music closely related to that produced in West African countries such as Mali and Senegal. It is strikingly distinctive, whether you concentrate on the music (usually produced by drums, castanets and a distinctive long-necked flute), the characteristically African beat or the cowrie-shell caps of the whirling Gnaoua dancers. It is a confirmed favourite with tourists, whether in their hotels or the Jemaa el Fna square in Marrakesh. It has always had a public aspect, for the Gnaoua were employed to exorcize evil spirits and built up a variety of acts that include *l'fraja*, the show, designed to entertain crowds. Gnaoua is at its most impressive at a *lila*, an all-night ritual held on religious feast days where the great Islamic saints and prophets as well as the spirit world are invoked, while dancers take turns to swirl to the point of exhaustion and possession. In such trances they will bang their heads on the stone flagging, eat glass and cut themselves with knives, all without apparently inflicting damage. The instruments used are iron castanets, a big *t'bal* drum and a large bass *gimbri* lute with a camel-neck skin stretched over a walnut body. The enormously popular Gnaoua Festival (*www.festival-gnaoua.com*), held annually in Essaouira (*see* p.166), has brought the genre to a much wider audience over the past few years.

Further listening (Gnaoua and Sufi): *Mustafa Baqbou* (World Circuit); *Hadra of the Gnawa of Essaouira* (Ocora); *Gnawa Music of Marrakesh: Night Spirit Masters* (Axiom).

Arabic Song: *Guedra, B'Sat* and *Melhun*

In the Saharan provinces south of the Anti-Atlas Mountains, the Hassani Arabic dialect became dominant in the 13th century. The most famous musical song-dance of this region is *guedra*, the erotic, swaying dance of the Saharan women, performed on their knees. It shares many of the West African influences of Gnaoua spirit music. There is also the more light-hearted tradition of *b'sat*. This developed as an annual festival of popular theatre, one in which music and lyrics were inextricably mixed into the farcical shows of the actor-storytellers. These shows are very popular in festivals such as Aid el Kebir, and can often be seen at the Jemaa el Fna in Marrakesh. As well as for their musical background, they are being examined with renewed interest as a source of indigenous drama for local television and theatre.

Melhun represents a much more polished and literate tradition, as indicated by alternative names for the style which translate as 'the gift' or 'the inspiration'. It is believed to have derived from the pure Arabic poetry of Andalucía, which was first converted into a popular strophic verse some time in the 12th century, before being transformed into a rhythmic formula at the time of Merenid rule. Each song would begin with an instrumental prelude that was then followed by short, sung verses marked by choral and instrumental refrains; a gradual, accelerated rhythm marked the end. The songs' subject matter was the many themes made familiar in the Sufi-inspired medieval poetry of Andalucía – images and ideas such as the beloved, wine, gardens, sunset and night – and could be taken at a popular level or understood as metaphors for a spiritual quest. There was also a tradition of satire (known as *lahjou, ashaht* or *addaq*) which could be combined with prophecy (*jofriat*) to bring a strong political content to the songs.

Sufi Music

All Morocco's rich musical heritage was used by the Sufi brotherhoods in the composition of ritual chants and dances. These have a spiritual goal which is directed at the performers, not the audience, and may extend over many hours before reaching their sudden conclusion. It is a form of music that is inaccessible to the non-initiate, let alone a non-Muslim, but remains a vital force and influence in the lives of many of Morocco's leading musicians. The Derkaoua, Hamadasha and Aïssoua are three of the most influential brotherhoods, though their influence has necessarily taken a second place to that of the Gnaoua. Instruments generally used are a simple oboe and cymbals as well as a variety of clay and skin drums.

Musical Instruments

Percussion instruments: *bendir* – round wooden-frame drum sometimes with snare; *deff* – square wooden frame drum; *t'bal* – large wooden round drum played with sticks and hung round the neck; *daadouh, guedra, harazi, durbouka, goual, taarija, tbila* – clay and skin drums in descending order of size; *karkabus/qarqaba* – iron castanets; *naqus, nuiqsat* and *handqa* – iron castanets; *tar* – tambourine.

Stringed instruments: *ud* – lute, usually the six-course Egyptian-style, round-backed version; *kamanja* – the Western violin, but played vertically on the knee; *rbab* – the two-string viol, with a bow that is a short iron arc holding strands of horsehair; *guenbri/gimbri* – the most popular lute, a sound box made of the shell of a turtle, covered with goat skin with one or three strings along its neck (the body of a treble *guenbri* is customarily pear-shaped, the bass rectangular, and that with a round-backed body with six or three strings is known as a *lotar* or a *soussi guenbri* and used to be limited to southern Morocco); *hajouj* or *sentir* – large bass *guenbri* with a rectangular walnut body covered with camel-neck skin and goat-gut strings; *swisdi* – small two-string lute; *kanum* – Arabic zither or psaltery with 26 triple courses.

Wind instruments: *awwadat* – metal pipe, played like a straight flute; *lira/gasba* – flutes; *nai/nira* – Arab bamboo flute; *rita/ghaita* – super oboe-like flute with double-reeded mouthpiece, used by snake charmers; *n'far* – one-note processional trumpet, made of copper.

Sufi Brotherhoods

Alongside the formal practice of Islam there has always been a parallel tradition of Sufi mysticism. A Sufi attempts to go beyond mere obedience to Islamic law and reach for experience of God in this life. Ali, cousin and son-in-law of the Prophet and the militant hero of early Islam, is considered to be the originator of this mystical approach to Islam and the first Sufi. Traditions record that Ali received the secrets of the mystical life, which were considered too dangerous to be written down and revealed to the unprepared mass of mankind. The secrets are reserved for initiates who must first make themselves capable and prove themselves worthy of receiving this body of inherited oral instruction. The mystical discipline has been passed down through the generations in a human chain of masters, each of whom trained his disciples to succeed him. Sufi brotherhoods arose as aspirants gathered around a celebrated mystic who evolved into the master, or sheikh, of the community. Branches obedient to the teaching of a popular master might be formed throughout the Muslim world; as new brotherhoods formed they were all proud to be links in this one chain of spiritual succession.

The first Moroccan Sufi master was Sidi Harazem of Fez, whose name now features on a popular brand of mineral water. He was succeeded in the tradition by two great scholars of the 12th century. Abu Medyan of Tlemcen, who died in 1198, and Abdessalam ben Mchich, who died in 1228, are central to the brotherhoods of northwest Africa (the latter is also known as the master of Jbel Alam, and is the patron saint of the Jebala region of Morocco). These influential masters combined the teaching of Sidi Harazem with that of the great Eastern masters, Al Jilani of

Baghdad and Al Ghazzali. The life of a Sufi was not always easy or safe: the 12th-century Almoravid Sultan Ali ben Youssef burnt all Al Ghazzali's books and sentenced to death any Muslim found reading them.

Despite the fervent opposition of the 'fundamentalist' Almoravid and Almohad dynasties, the brotherhoods survived underground. Their spiritual heir was Abou el Hassan Ali ech Chadhili, who died in 1258 and from whose teachings arose 15 separate Sufi brotherhoods, many of which survive today. Al Jazuli in Fez, who taught and wrote *The Manifest Proofs of Piety*, was a continuation of this tradition. After his death in 1465 there was another explosion of brotherhoods, who all considered themselves his heirs.

The Sufi brotherhoods, whatever the exact pattern of their spiritual regime, all owe total obedience to a sheikh, their master. Most brotherhoods practise asceticism, and include charitable works and teaching among their activities. Initiates use spiritual tools in their search for *wajd*, ecstatic experience of the divine, including *hizb* – recitation, *dikr* – prolonged recitation, *sama* – music, *raqs* and *hadra* – dancing, and *tamzig* – the tearing of clothes. For an outsider the most common Sufi trait is indifference to the concerns of the world. This trend was developed by the Aïssoua and Hamadasha brotherhoods into self-mutilation to show indifference to pain, while the more off-beat practised the prolonged contemplation of a beautiful young man, an ephebe, who was believed to embody the divine.

Wildlife

Even the most distant and desolate wilderness landscape is likely to be a seasonal grazing ground for a village or nomadic herd. By day you are more likely to find herds of goat, sheep and camel than wild beasts, but it is possible, even without entering the guarded sporting and forestry reserves of the Administration des Eaux et Forêts, to spot wild boar, Barbary apes, a range of mountain cats, the ubiquitous red fox and the smaller desert fox with its bat-like ears. Most of these can be seen only at dawn, dusk or briefly caught in a car's headlights by night.

If you sleep anywhere near water you will be serenaded by a chorus of frogs and toads. In the daytime their identity can usually be patched together from squashed bodies on the roadside. They may include the Berber toad, green toad, green frog, western marsh frog and Mauritanian toad. Without even moving from a café chair it is possible to spot and photograph a variety of insect-hunting lizards. The Moorish gecko, Spanish wall lizard and chameleon all seem particularly tolerant of the presence of humans. The species of the mountains and deserts are harder to spot, although patches of sand will often be dotted with the winding tracks of the spiny-tailed sand lizard, the Algerian sand lizard and the Berber skink, or 'sandfish'.

The mouflon or wild mountain sheep, from which all the world's varieties of sheep derive, is indigenous to North Africa. Early Moroccan rock carvings of a sun placed between the twin horns of a sheep, and Egyptian records, hint that the cult of Amon, the horned-god of the sun and the herds, originated in the Maghreb. The people of this area may also have first perfected the practice of nomadic herding. Dominant tribes sometimes maintained sacred herds that acted as their standard or totem. The horse was a late arrival to Morocco (from c.1600 BC), while the Arabian camel was not successfully bred in the Moroccan Sahara until about AD 600. Nomads and herdsmen still recognize the sacred animals of a herd, such as the *Saiba* – the chief mother, the *Bahira* – the eleventh calf, and the *Ilami* – the senior stallion. In a widespread custom that extends throughout Africa and Arabia, a sacrificial calf is designated from birth and left free to graze over any field or boundary. Dedicated to a saint or spirit, it is sacrificed at their shrine and then consumed at the communal feast.

Birdlife

Birds are easily the most impressive of Morocco's wildlife. There is a large number of resident species, as well as dazzling and vastly varied concentrations of migrant flocks, which generally come to Africa for the mild winter from October to March and fly across the Mediterranean for the European summer.

The swift, swallow and crag martin are respected as birds inspired by Allah to protect the harvest and remove noxious insects and reptiles. They can be seen in showy evening flights above the rooftops of cities such as Fez and Marrakesh. The stork is Morocco's other great holy bird, and there are numerous legends to explain their constant attitude of prayer and symbolic prostration whenever they rest. Hospitals were established in Fez and Marrakesh to care for injured birds, where they could recover or die peacefully in protected enclosures.

The striped hoopoe is conspicuous during its migration, but is trapped by Moroccans, for its heart and feathers are powerful charms against evil spirits. The barn owl, a permanent resident, is recognized to be the clairvoyant ally of the Devil. The owl cries out the name of a fore-doomed individual who can only escape by cursing the owl with its own hidden name. Even a normal owl cry has the power to kill a child unless there is someone to spit and curse as they fly overhead. The Tangier raven is also viewed with suspicion, and always lays its eggs on 21 April. Killing a raven soothes the evil eye, whilst a raven's liver, tongue, brain and heart are made into useful antidotes.

Take a moment to look more closely at the Moroccan versions of familiar birds. Sparrows turn out to be mainly of the Spanish race (with rich chestnut heads and a pronounced black bib) and occasionally rock sparrows (with smartly striped heads). Chaffinches are most exotic with slate-blue heads, olive-green backs and salmon-pink underparts. The starling is not *vulgaris* but *unicolor*, which is to say spotless. Magpies sport a neat tear-shaped mark behind the eye in brilliant turquoise blue.

Crested larks are common along roadsides; buntings (corn, cirl, rock and house) are easily seen on top of walls and telephone wires; pigeons turn out to be turtle doves or rock doves with bright white rumps; glorious blue rollers and smart ginger, black and white hoopoes are widespread summer visitors; summer evenings are filled with the screeching and aerial displays of swifts and pallid swifts; herds of cattle are invariably accompanied by a few white cattle egrets; and common bulbuls sing delightfully from every bush in gardens and parks. Certain bird species now so rare as to be threatened with extinction, but still appearing in Morocco are the bald ibis, the slender-billed curlew, and bustards (Houbara, Arabian and great).

Food and Drink

04

Morocco has a distinctive, varied and very attractive national cuisine, with a wide range of dishes from simple to sophisticated that make great and imaginative use of Mediterranean produce. Whatever your budget, try to eat in a good Moroccan restaurant at least once during your stay and accept any genuine invitation to share in a family meal.

Eating, for all but the rich, French-influenced merchant class, is a home-based family affair. In a country of high unemployment the shared family meal of couscous, usually enlivened by a few chunks of steamed meat and vegetables, is the one great source of sustenance for the day.

Where to Eat

Exceptions aside, there are four basic categories of public eating-places: the **café**, the **café-restaurant**, the *ville nouvelle* **(New Town) restaurant** and the **Moorish palace**.

Cafés

All the more conspicuous cafés are male social centres that might serve a cake or croissant with mint tea or coffee, but seldom anything more substantial. It is usually quite acceptable to consume something from a nearby *pâtisserie* at a café table. The smarter *pâtisseries* may have their own tables, and serve fruit juices, ice creams and delicious cakes. They are some of the few places where you will regularly see the two sexes happily mix in public. Rural cafés serve *tagines* on market days, and can usually be persuaded to run up an omelette and salad.

Café-restaurants

Café-restaurants serve the freshest and by far the cheapest food in town. There will usually be a choice of salads, vegetables, soups, grilled meats and cold puddings. Their clients are principally travellers and workers away from home who are deprived of their customary meal.

Café-restaurants usually do not have a licence to serve alcoholic drinks and are fairly functional, and in short are not places to dawdle away an evening with wine and chatter. However, they are easy to sniff out and are excellent for a quickly consumed lunch or supper, eaten while perched on a shared bench. They are often clustered in a row along a street in such a way that it is useless to make distinctions, or suggest an exact address or telephone number.

Ville Nouvelle (New Town) Restaurants

For a neat tablecloth, wine, a menu and regular opening hours you will usually have to go to a French-, Spanish- or Italian-influenced restaurant in the modern port or *ville nouvelle* areas of a city. On the Atlantic coast of Morocco (where they attract the local business and adminstrative class and serve freshly caught seafood) these restaurants can be very good and yet remain reasonably priced. Inland, unless you go very expensive they tend to become increasingly dependent on the tourist trade and frequently suffer from a corresponding blandness.

Moorish Palaces

There are a number of 19th-century merchant palaces in the medinas of Fez, Meknès and Marrakesh that have been converted into restaurants. Traditional Moroccan cooking is served in a sumptuous Moorish interior, and most have drinks licences. It is rare to have this kind of evening without hearing local music or suffering some belly-dancing entertainment, and you won't be surprised to find that such places are almost entirely filled by tourists. Nevertheless, even though they are often expensive and boisterous, they are some of the few places where you can sample the more sophisticated and opulent dishes of Moroccan cuisine. If you are saving up for one grand meal, make it in Marrakesh, which is where the best and most genuinely opulent examples of this kind of restaurant are to be found.

Moroccan Specialities

One of the most striking features of Moroccan cooking is the quality and freshness of the ingredients. Produce comes from a land light on pesticides, chemicals, hormones and preservatives. Animals are slaughtered just hours before they are eaten. The meat you are offered will generally be mutton, not lamb. Market vegetables will have been gathered that morning. Spices, herbs, fresh fruit, nuts and dried fruit have an invigorating vitality completely removed from the packaged and imported products available in much of Europe and North America.

Morocco has many mainstream traditional dishes worth trying. To encourage you, here are explanations of some of the most common and popular dishes (for details of Arabic and French pronunciation, see Language, p.308):

Harira: a thick soup of chick peas, lentils and haricot beans often flavoured with mutton or chicken, lemon and tarragon.

Brochettes: Grilled kebabs of mutton, liver and fat.

Kefta: Spicy meatballs made of minced mutton and offal, often served in a rich egg sauce.

Pastilla/bastilla: A pie made up of multiple layers of flaky pastry filled with finely chopped pigeon meat, eggs, almonds and spices. Chicken or fish may be used instead of pigeon.

Tagine: Along with couscous, this is the most universal of Moroccan dishes – a slowly simmered stew, cooked in its own juices in an earthenware bowl with a distinctive conical lid. The *tagine* provides the foundation for using a whole spectrum of ingredients, spices and styles. The most popular variants found on most menus across Morocco are: *tagine de viande* (mutton stew cooked with vegetables or served alone with prunes); *tagine de poisson* (bream or sardine stew cooked with tomatoes and herbs); *tagine de lapin* (rabbit stew); and *tagine de poulet aux olives et citron* (a delicious chicken stew cooked with lemon and olives). The lemon gives a delicious zest to the meat.

Mechoui: Lamb roasted whole on a spit or baked in a special oven. This delicate and fragrant meat, far removed from the usual mutton, is generally eaten with bread. It is, however, an elaborate luxury which is often only available only if ordered well in advance.

Couscous: This dish is made from half-baked flour which is then ground into semolina-like grains. A perfectly prepared couscous is laboriously cooked in a succession of steamings and oilings that allow each grain to cook while retaining a distinct granular texture. Couscous served outside of a home or a good restaurant is unlikely to be found at its best. It is usually accompanied by *sept légumes* (seven steamed vegetables) with the odd lump of mutton. It can also be served as a pudding with sugar, cinnamon and rich, warm goat's milk.

Cornes de gazelle: Croissant-like pastries filled with honey and almonds.

Mezze: Fresh salads flavoured with pumpkin, aubergine dip and caramelized onion.

Drink

Mint tea is Morocco's liquid staple. This is green or gunpowder tea flavoured with a few sprigs of mint and saturated with sugar. It is almost repulsively sweet when you first taste it. You will be offered glasses of mint tea in every house or shop you visit, and it is expected that a guest drinks at least three glasses of tea before departing. Enjoying mint tea becomes a vital social grace and, with luck, before long you may begin to appreciate this invigorating and thirst-quenching drink. Tea was first brought to Morocco by British merchants in the 19th century who then invented the distinctive Moroccan teapot, first manufactured in Manchester, by giving the Yemeni coffee pot a fat bottom. Before tea, Moroccans enjoyed hot infusions of sweet mint, verbena and wormwood and these are still occasionally added to green tea.

Muslims are not permitted to drink **alcohol** in Morocco but non-Muslims are, although the medinas are usually dry areas. Since the Koran mentions only wine, Moroccans tend to consume grain-based drinks such as '*spéciale flag*' beer, *anis* or whisky, but seldom touch wine in public. Away from the big cities or principal tourist destinations, drinking is confined to the bars of just a few hotels. Ordering a small dish makes drinking acceptable although a conspiratorial whisper might help too. But never drink in sight of a mosque.

Beer is a varied brew in Morocco, but you might try the locally made Casa, Stork and Flag. Heineken is a common import.

You can order **Moroccan wine** to drink with your meal in licensed restaurants. Wine for lunchtime picnics can be bought from a few selected grocery shops in larger towns and cities. Despite Islamic prohibitions, wine is produced in Morocco in three regions: Berkane, Meknès and Boulâouane. Some of these areas were first making wine after the Phoenicians arrived 3,000 years ago.

You might find the **Moroccan reds** rather strong and heavy to drink without something to nibble at: they are at their best when accompanying a rich spiced meat *tagine*. Due to the problem of keeping a white or a rosé cool while travelling, reds are also much better suited for picnics, and don't seem to mind being shaken around in the boot of a car or bus for several hundred kilometres. The principal reds are Toulal, Rabbi Jacob (a kosher wine produced in a Muslim country), Beni Snassen,

Le Châtelain, Père Antoine, Valpierre, Les Trois Domaines, Amazir Beni M'Tir and Cabernet Président. If you have a choice, you might try the last two or even an Alain Graillot Syrah. The only wine chateau in Morocco produces the Guerrouane label.

The best of the **Moroccan whites** is Special Coquillages, and after that Valpierre Blanc de Blanc, which is dry and not too astringent. They are at their best when accompanying fish or a plate of shellfish at a meal on the coast.

The **rosé wines**, Gris de Boulâouane and Oustalet, are delightful at any time of the day, especially when chilled, and provide one of the basic sensory backdrops to a Moroccan holiday.

When it comes to **spirits**, these are increasingly available in Morocco and it is worth trying cocktails in Morocco too, where *mojitos* (with local mint) have already won a following.

The universal colas are naturally available throughout the country, but a recommended **non-alcoholic choice** is freshly squeezed orange juice (*orange pressé*), which is often served enlivened with a little grapefruit or lemon. This is available in hotels and cafés in most towns.

As for **tap water**, it is generally safe to drink in the north but not around the Sahara – but even the northern water has minerals which can upset delicate western stomachs.

Useful Phrases for Eating Out (French / Arabic)

At a Restaurant
What do you have?
  Qu'est-ce que vous avez?
  Ashnoo kane?
...to eat?/to drink? *...à manger?/à boire?*
  ...f'l-makla?/ f'l-musharoubat?
What is this? *Qu'est ce que c'est?* / *Shnoo hada?*
I would like... *Je voudrais...* / *B'gheena...*
I don't eat meat *Je ne mange pas de viande* / *makankoolsh lhem*
This is delicious *C'est délicieux* / *hada bnin*
breakfast *petit déjeuner* / *nfetru*
lunch *déjeuner* / *nteghddaw*
dinner *dîner* / *ntshaw*
big *grand* / *kbir*
small *petit* / *sghrir*
glass *verre* / *kess*
plate *assiette* / *t'b-sil*
knife *couteau* / *moos*
fork *fourchette* / *forsheta*
spoon *cuillère* / *malka*
salt *sel* / *l'melha*
pepper *poivre* / *lebzar*
sugar *sucre* / *azoukar*
the bill, please *L'addition, s'il vous plaît* / *L'h'seb, minfadlik*

Basic French-Arabic Menu Reader
almonds *amandes* / *louze*
apricots *abricots* / *mishmash*
artichoke *artichaut* / *kuk*
bananas *bananes* / *banane*
beef *bœuf* / *l'houli*
bread *pain* / *l'hobs*
butter *buerre* / *zebda*
chicken *poulet* / *djaj*
dates *dattes* / *tmer*
eggs *œufs* / *beda*
figs *figues* / *kermus*
fish *poisson* / *l'habra*
fruit *fruits* / *fekiha*
garlic *ail* / *tooma*
grapes *raisins* / *l'a'arib*
meat *viande* / *l'hem*
mixed salad *salade marocaine* / *chalada*
mutton *mouton* / *kabch*
olives *olives* / *zitoun*
onions *oignons* / *l'basla*
oranges *oranges* / *leetcheen*
peaches *pêches* / *l'khoukh*
potatoes (chips) *pommes de terre (frites)* / *btata (btata mklya)*
poultry *volaille* / *l'hout*
rice *riz* / *rouz*
salads *salades* / *chalada*
sardines *sardines* / *sardile*
tomatoes *tomates* / *matesha*
vegetables *légumes* / *ikhoudra*

French Menu Reader

Hors-d'œuvre et Soupes
(Starters and Soups)

amuse-bouche appetizer
bisque shellfish soup
charcuterie mixed cold meats, salami, ham, etc.
consommé clear soup

Poissons et Coquillages (Crustacés)
(Fish and Shellfish)

anchois anchovies
bar or *loup (de mer)* sea bass
cabillaud cod
calmar squid
coquillages shellfish
coquille St-Jacques scallop
crabe crab
daurade sea bream
écrevisse freshwater crayfish
escargot snail
friture deep-fried fish
fruits de mer seafood
homard lobster
huître oyster
langouste spiny Mediterranean lobster
lotte monkfish
moules mussels
poulpe octopus
St-Pierre John Dory
saumon salmon
thon tuna
truite trout

Viandes et Volailles
(Meat and Poultry)

agneau lamb
bœuf beef
brochette meat (or fish) on a skewer
chevreau kid
chorizo spicy Spanish sausage
côte, côtelette chop, cutlet
dinde, dindon turkey
faux-filet sirloin
foie liver
gigot leg of lamb
grillade grilled meat, often a
   mixed grill
jambon ham
lapin rabbit
lard (lardons) bacon (diced bacon)
maigret/magret (de canard) breast (of duck)
porc pork
pot au feu meat and vegetables cooked
   in stock
poulet chicken
veau veal

Légumes, Herbes, etc.
(Vegetables, Herbs, etc.)

ail garlic
artichaut artichoke
asperge asparagus
aubergine aubergine (eggplant)
avocat avocado
cannelle cinnamon
champignon mushroom
chou cabbage
chou-fleur cauliflower
clou de girofle clove
cœur de palmier heart of palm
concombre cucumber
cornichon gherkin
courgette courgette (zucchini)
échalote shallot
endive chicory (endive)
épinards spinach
fève broad (fava) bean
frites chips (French fries)
haricot vert green (French) bean
jardinière mixed vegetables
laitue lettuce
laurier bay leaf
lentilles lentils
maïs (épis de) sweetcorn (on the cob)
menthe mint
oignon onion
petits pois peas
pois chiches chickpeas
poivron sweet pepper (capsicum)
pomme de terre potato
potiron pumpkin
riz rice
safran saffron

Fruits et Noix (Fruit and Nuts)

ananas pineapple
brugnon nectarine
citron lemon
citron vert lime
coco (noix de) coconut
dattes dates
figue (de Barbarie) fig (prickly pear)
fraise (des bois) strawberry (wild)
framboise raspberry
grenade pomegranate
noisette hazelnut
noix walnut
pastèque watermelon
pêche (blanche) peach (white)
pignon pine nut
pistache pistachio
poire pear
pomme apple
raisin (sec) grape (raisin)

Planning
Your Trip

05

When to Go

Climate

Morocco has between 330 and 350 days of African sunshine a year and so, as hotels and restaurants remain open all year round, any month is a good time to visit Morocco. There are, however, seasonal variations to take into account when planning the shape of your holiday.

Morocco has been called a cold country with a hot sun. The monthly averages given here hide an often dramatic range in temperatures through each day. Even in the mid-summer months a sweater may be useful against evening coastal breezes, the cool of the mountain peaks and the desert nights. At the very least it can be moulded into a pillow for long bus journeys.

From **November to February** there is the possibility of rain, and you will find the beach resorts distinctly off-season. Winter in the mountains is cold and often damp and there is even some skiing, although it's only well provided for in Oukaïmeden in the High Atlas. At any rate, head south.

March, April and May are reliably (but not cripplingly) hot, and the countryside, with its fast-ripening harvest and busy rural souks, is at its most interesting. It is this time of year when the country is at its most lush and when the middle of the day does not force you indoors. But Morocco's autumn (**September and October**) is pleasant too, if hotter than spring, and a good time to swim in the sea.

June, July and August are the hottest and busiest tourist months, but there is little activity in evidence on the part of the locals during the heat of the day. The farmland is baked dry, and most schools, offices and industries have stopped work. The nation is on holiday, if not at the beach. These months do have most of the *moussems* (religious festivals). The High Atlas mountains, south of Marrakesh, are at their most accessible and attractive during these months.

Packing

The clothing you take will vary enormously depending on when and exactly where you go. In the winter in the mountains and desert

Average Maximum Temperatures in °C (°F)

	Jan	April	July	Oct
Marrakesh	15 (59)	20 (68)	34 (93)	25 (77)
Fez	18 (64)	26 (79)	38 (101)	28 (82)
Rabat	17 (63)	22 (72)	28 (82)	25 (77)

Average Minimum Temperatures in °C (°F)

	Jan	April	July	Oct
Marrakesh	4 (39)	8 (46)	17 (63)	11 (52)
Fez	4 (39)	11 (52)	19 (66)	14 (57)
Rabat	8 (46)	11 (52)	17 (63)	14 (57)

you will want to prepare for cold weather and possibly snow, while winter more generally in Morocco does bring some rain. While winds can add chill factor to the coast, inland the weather can spike to 40 Celsius in the summer. Pack strong sun cream if your trip is in the summer and beware the sun in the middle of the day. Sunstroke is common among tourists to Morocco. A hat and sunglasses might be your saving grace but so too are light, baggy trousers and shirts.

Morocco is no Saudi Arabia and there is a relatively liberal attitude to uncovered forearms and legs, but not to plunging cleavages, short skirts or skin-tight clothing. If you want to win respect and meet older Moroccans, and for people to give you the benefit of the doubt, it is best to stay on the conservative side if you can, covering legs and (for women) arms too, except of course at the beach or in your hotel. Be especially generous with sleeve and trouser lengths if you are visiting a mosque.

As for toiletries, you can buy them all there, but packing some water purification tablets, Nurofen and anti-diarrhoea tablets will save you making a hunt around town later. Some earplugs would be a good idea too for the cheapest urban hotels. Suntan lotion is at its most useful at the beginning of the holiday, of course. Tampons and batteries are all readily available but you are advised to bring your own contraception. A small torch in your washbag is useful for that blurry late night bathroom trip in the low-end bunkhouse. Finally, the two-pronged 220V adaptor is a small but redoubtable aid.

To ease your passage around the country, buy a stock of presents (like those that you might fill a Christmas stocking with, and especially pens) for local children who have shown you around a village, put you on the right path or guarded your car. Anything with a football motif is usually eagerly received. My mother has travelled for years with a bag filled with goodies ranging from notebooks and small sets of coloured pens to more hazardous items such as whistles and water pistols that should only be given on departure.

Festivals

National Holidays

There are secular holidays during the year when banks, government offices, schools and most shops are closed. Note also that in the summer school holidays hordes of Moroccans head to the beaches.

For a list of National Holidays, *see* box p.88.

Moroccan Calendars

The Berber calendar, a surviving form of the Julian calendar used in Rome before the Gregorian replaced it in 1582, is still used by some farmers in Morocco, especially in the south. The Islamic calendar is not suitable for agriculture since it is purely lunar, but beyond the farms Morocco runs on both the Western and Islamic calendars. Islamic holidays and festivals therefore change date, according to the Western calendar, each year, so it is best to check in advance.

The Islamic Calendar

Sequence of months	Duration (days)
Muharram	30
Safar	29
Rabi al-Awwal	30
Rabi al-Thani	29
Jumada al-Ula	30
Jumada al-Thuni	29
Rajab	30
Shaban	29
Ramadan	30
Shawwal	29
Dhu al-Qa'da	30
Dhu al-Hijja	29 (30 in leap years)

Western calendar dates of Muslim national holidays in Morocco for 2011/2012:

Mouloud (The Prophet's Birthday): 5 Mar/22 Feb

Feast of the Throne: 30 July (both)

Oued Ed-Dahab: 14 Aug (both)

Eid al-Fitr (End of Ramadan): 29 Aug/18 Aug

Eid al-Adha (Feast of the Sacrifice): 6 Nov/26 Oct

Moharran (Muslim New Year): 26 Nov/15 Nov

Important Muslim Festivals

These are based on a lunar calendar, which loses 11 days a year (or 12 in a leap year) against the Gregorian calendar.

The great event of the Islamic year is the fasting month of **Ramadan** (which will begin in August in 2011, but in July in 2012 and 2013). To be in Morocco in one of the great cities during Ramadan is a fascinating experience, but it is not a good time to travel around the country. Ramadan, the ninth month of the Islamic lunar year, is the Muslim equivalent of Lent. The fast has remained a great institution in Islam and is cherished as an act that binds the whole nation, indeed the entire Muslim community, together in a month of asceticism. For all except the sick, travellers, children and pregnant women, Ramadan involves abstaining from food, sex, drink and cigarettes during the hours of daylight. It is an ancient custom, one that was in full force when the Prophet Mohammed was a child in Mecca, when this holy month was a time when a general truce reigned over Arabia and the demands of vengeance and tribal animosity were put aside. Non-Muslims are not involved, but you will find most cafés, bars and licensed grocers firmly closed. It is insensitive to smoke, eat or drink in public during Ramadan. It can be more rewarding to join Ramadan quietly as a volunteer, sharing the exuberance at dusk when the daily fast ends with a bowl of *harira* soup, and the café-restaurants fill up with customers and music. A spirit of relief breaks out across the nation and continues deep into the night. The 26th night of Ramadan, 'holy night' (when the first verse of the Koran was delivered to the Prophet Mohammed), is particularly magical, with young children paraded in glittering costumes in an endless promenade.

The feast of **Eid al-Fitr** (or **Seghir**) celebrates the end of the month of Ramadan, when the new moon is sighted. A few months later **Aid al-Adha** (or **Kebir**) commemorates Abraham's sacrifice of a ram instead of his son, and is a great excuse for family reunions. The week before Aid al-Adha is colourful, as the streets are full of thousands of rams being led around on leashes like honoured members of the family. After the excitement of public prayers and the sacrifice on the morning of the Aid, the festival is mostly celebrated indoors. Shops, souks and some museums are closed for the week. Three weeks later is **Moharran** (or **Achoura**) the feast of the Muslim New Year, when almond cakes are baked, drums are beaten and gifts given to children and the poor. The fourth principal holiday is **Mouloud**, the Prophet's birthday, celebrated with presents for children and firecrackers on the street. In particular, there is a *moussem* (religious festival) at Zaouia-Moulay-Brahim in the High Atlas, south of Marrakesh; a candle procession at Salé; and the Aissawa *moussem* at Meknès.

Moussems and Festivals

Moussems and *ammougars* (the Berber version) were originally annual pilgrimages to the tomb of a saint; now the words are used for any festival, although most do still have religious roots. There are hundreds of local festivals throughout Morocco that celebrate a saint in either a day- or a week-long trading fair, with some feasting, dancing, religious music and *fantasia* display. In mood they are not dissimilar from an especially animated rural souk, and so for the vast majority of visitors may be of only passing interest. Even the major festival dates are impossible to predict accurately. Some depend on the harvest, the lunar cycle, the Muslim religious year, the national tourist office or the diary of the regional governor. You will have to ask the tourist office or a major local hotel for more accurate information, though even they are unlikely to know more than two months in advance.

The most rewarding festivals for a foreigner are the week-long **Folk Music Festival** staged in Marrakesh, usually in June; the week-long

Festival of Sacred Music at Fez, usually at the end of May or beginning of June; a week-long **jazz festival** in Rabat in June; and the week-long **festival of Gnaoua music** at Essaouira (accessible as a day trip from Marrakesh).

Tourist Information

The Moroccan National Tourist Board, the **ONMT**, and French-style **Syndicats d'Initiative** are found in every city and even in most small towns in Morocco. They are useful as a source of official guides, glossy handouts, hotels, the dates of local festivals, the location of rural souks and the odd local map. They are seldom informative about local history, but very keen on the regular run of tourist sites, bazaars and large hotels.

The Moroccan Tourist Board is worth visiting to stock up on the full range of handouts. There is a useful booklet of all the classified hotels, a collection of package-tour prices, a sheet with the year's maximum hotel prices and half a dozen regional leaflets. There are several branches abroad:

Australia (also for **New Zealand**): Moroccan National Tourist Office, 11 West Street North, Sydney NSW 2060, **t** (02) 9922 4999.

Canada: Moroccan National Tourist Office, 2001 Rue Universitaire, Suite 1460, Montreal QU H3A 2A6, **t** (514) 842 8111.

France: 161 Rue St Honoré, Place du Théâtre Français, Paris 75001, **t** 01 42 60 63 50

UK: Morocco Tourist Information Office, 205 Regent Street, London W1B 4HB, **t** (020) 7437 0073.

USA: Moroccan National Tourist Office, 104 West 40th St, Suite 1820, Manhattan, New York, **t** 212 221 1583

Useful Websites

The Moroccan Ministry of Tourism, *http://www.tourisme.gov.ma/index_en.htm*, is a good place to begin. Also useful is *www.visitmorocco.com. See* also p.86.

Embassies and Consulates

The Moroccan embassy and consulate websites provide the most up-to-date information on official requirements for travelling to and from Morocco.

Moroccan Embassies Abroad

Australia: 17 Terrigal Crescent, O'Malley, ACT 2606, t (262) 900755/66.

Canada: 38, Range Road Ottawa K1N 8J4 (Ontario) Canada t (613) 2367391/92; Consulate, 2192 Blvd René Lévesque, Montreal Ouest, Québec, H3H 1R6, t (514) 2888750.

Ireland: 39 Raglan Road, Ballsbridge, Dublin 4, t (1) 6609449/319.

New Zealand: (Consulate) 81 Remuera Road, Newmarket, P.O. Box 9925, Auckland, t 9520 4129. (Morocco's embassy in Australia, see above, has cross-accreditation for New Zealanders).

UK: 49, Queen's Gate Gardens, London SW7 5NE, t (020) 7225 3862; Consulate-General, Diamond House, 97–99 Praed Street, London W2 1NT, t (020) 7724 0719.

USA: 1601 21st Street, NW 20009, Washington D.C., t (202) 4627979, http://dcusa.themoroccanembassy.com/; Consulate General: 10 East 40th St, 24th floor, New York, NY10006, t (212) 2139644/7582625.

Foreign Embassies in Morocco

Australia: contact the Canadian embassy (see below) in Rabat for consular assistance.

Canada: Embassy of Canada in Morocco, 13 bis Rue Jaâfa-as-Sadik, Rabat-Agdal (or CP 709 to send mail), t 0537 687400, www.canadainternational.gc.ca/morocco-maroc.

Ireland: Irish citizens in Morocco are represented by British diplomatic staff. Irish Consulate, COPRAGRI Building, Boulevard Moulay Ismail, Route de Rabat, Aïn Sebaâ, Casablanca, t 0522 660306.

New Zealand: NZ Citizens in Morocco are represented by British diplomatic staff. Consular representation for Morocco is held at the NZ embassy in Madrid, which can be reached on t (+34) 915 230 226.

UK: British Embassy, 28 Avenue S.A.R. Sidi Mohammed, Soussi 10105 (BP 45) , Rabat, t 0537 633333. British Hon. Consulate, 55 Blvd Zerktouni, Residence Taib, Marrakesh, t 0524 420846. Consulate-Gen, Villa Les Sallurges, 36 Rue de la Loire, Polo, Casablanca, t 0522 857400, http://ukinmorocco.fco.gov.uk/en.

USA: Embassy of the United States of America, 2 Avenue de Mohamed El Fassi, Rabat, Morocco, t 0537 762265, http://rabat.usembassy.gov. Consulate-General, 8 Blvd Moulay Youssef, Casablanca 20000, http://casablanca.usconsulate.gov. For telephone enquiries, contact the embassy.

Entry Formalities

Passports and Visas

Note that the following information describing passports, visas, customs and currency is subject to change, and should be checked in advance with the relevant Moroccan embassy or consulate (see above).

A valid Australian, British, Irish, Canadian New Zealand or United States passport allows you to enter Morocco (as does any European Union passport) without a visa, as a small 90-day entrance visa is then stamped into your passport. South Africans will need a visa (which they must apply for in South Africa).

Whether arriving by air or sea you will need to have filled in a form (fiche) with personal details as you approach the immigration desk. This is perfectly straightforward, providing you avoid any flowery prose beside 'purpose of visit' and humbly write 'tourism'. If you are a journalist or spy you should pretend to have another profession while on holiday in Morocco. If you are, or could be mistaken for, a hippy and are coming off the boat into Morocco it is worth tidying yourself up. If for some reason your hair, dress and jewellery has excited the enmity of an immigration officer, then in extremis there is nothing to stop you trying a different boat and/or port on another day.

If travelling from certain parts of Asia, Africa or South America, you may need a health certificate to enter the country too.

Extending Your Stay

Visa-exempt nationals can extend their stay for another 90 days or can even (if they have proof of work in Morocco) apply for residency, but both of these processes are complicated, since you not only need three photos and your passport when you visit the police station, but also a letter from your embassy and the freedom to hang around several hours, if not several days, while Moroccan bureaucracy runs its serpentine course. Most travellers head to Gibraltar, Spain (mainly Algeciras) or to the two Spanish enclaves (Ceuta and Melilla) on the North African coast, an approach which has the best track record. Note that the Ceuta or Melilla approach will only work for EU nationals, although Australia has a special arrangement with the EU. Those wanting to head south for a while could get a new visa in Nouakchott, the capital of Mauretania, by travelling down along the wonderful coastal road on the rim of Western Sahara, but this takes careful planning.

Customs

Many people start their trip with an extra bag, a shin-bruising thing in bright yellow. But forget all the duty-free hype and stick to Moroccan products while you're there. You may bring in 200 cigarettes or 50 cigars or 400 grams of tobacco, as well as one litre of wine and a litre of spirits and 5 grams of perfume. Avoid carrying books that are pornographic or clearly critical of Morocco, its government or of Islam. Don't ask about money lest forms appear.

Cars, sporting guns and expensive electronic equipment (which generally means professional still and video camera equipment) can be imported into the country

duty-free for 90 days. The details will be entered into your passport on arrival and will be checked off as you leave. If you cannot produce evidence of their theft (police documentation) you will be presumed to have sold them and charged a punitive duty. There is no way around this; even if you have written your car off on some obscure mountain road you will eventually find yourself having to fetch the wreck and tow it on to the ferry.

Customs officers routinely check bags as you arrive and depart. They are generally courteous and correct with foreigners. When leaving, you can take 200 cigarettes or 50 cigars or 400g of tobacco plus a litre of spirits and one bottle of wine, but no dirhams (see below, Money and Banks). Residents of the USA may each take home US$400-worth of foreign goods without attracting duty, including the tobacco and alcohol allowance. Canadians can bring home C$300 worth of goods in a year, plus their tobacco and alcohol allowances.

UK Customs, t 0845 010 9000, *www.hmrc.gov.uk.*

US Customs, t (202) 354 1000, *www.customs.gov.*

Canadian Customs, *www.cbsa.gc.ca.*

Disability Organizations

In the UK

Access Travel, 6 The Hillock, Astley, Lancashire M29 7GW, **t** (01942) 888 844, *www.access-travel.co.uk.* Travel agent for disabled people: special air fares, car hire and wheelchair-accessible accommodation.

Holiday Care Service, 7th Floor, Sunley House, 4 Bedford Park, Croydon, Surrey CR0 2AP, **t** 0845 124 9971, **t** (020) 8760 0072, Minicom **t** 0845 124 9976, *www.holidaycare.org.uk.*

RADAR (Royal Association for Disability and Rehabilitation), 12 City Forum, 250 City Rd, London EC1V 8AF, **t** (020) 7250 3222, Minicom **t** (020) 7250 4119, *www.radar.org.uk.*

In the USA

Mobility International USA, PO Box 10767, Eugene, OR 97440, USA, **t/TTY** (541) 343 1284, *www.miusa.org.* Information on international educational exchange programmes and volunteer service overseas for the disabled.

SATH (Society for Accessible Travel and Hospitality), 347 5th Av, Suite 610, New York, NY 10016, **t** (212) 447 7284, *www.sath.org.* Travel and access information.

Other Useful Contacts

Access Ability, *www.access-ability.co.uk.* Information on travel agencies catering specifically to disabled people.

Access-Able Travel Source, *www.access-able.com.* Web-based database of city information, travel operators, cruise lines, hotels, equipment hire, etc. for the disabled traveller.

Australian Council for Rehabilitation of the Disabled (ACROD), PO Box 60, Curtin, ACT 2605, Australia, **t** (02) 6283 3200, **t/TTY** (02) 6282 4333, *www.acrod.org.au.* Information and contact numbers for specialist travel agencies.

Emerging Horizons, *www.emerginghorizons.com.* International on-line (or mailed) quarterly travel newsletter. Subscription-based.

Global Access, *www.globalaccessnews.com.* On-line network for disabled travellers.

Disabled Travellers

Neither the pavements of the New Town boulevards of Moroccan cities nor the narrow, packed streets of medinas are particularly suitable for visitors in wheelchairs. To set against the many stairs, few ramps and virtually complete absence of adapted toilets there is, however, the very willing and unflappable attitude to be found in Morocco. You will seldom be short of a pair of extra hands in need, though – as with any Westerner – tips or at least cigarettes should be offered around.

Only a few hotels have lifts so ground floor rooms are preferable, and catching buses and taxis is awkward in a wheelchair, though again locals will help. Hiring a car is a good approach in Morocco. Do not let the difficulties put you off. Some of the most enthusiastic accounts of North Africa I have heard have come from friends who use wheelchairs. If you are in need of encouragement, read Quentin Crewe's *In Search of the Sahara*, a book full of possibilities and adventures.

Insurance

All-eventualities **private travel insurance** covering you for medical emergencies as well as theft need not be expensive and is the best protection against any really serious health problems. Some hospitals will be reluctant to take you in at all unless you have travel insurance documents. If you have private health insurance, you may already be covered: check the fine print.

If you do forget insurance and you are afflicted by a case of Murphy's Law, major credit cards are usually accepted at hospitals. Contact **IAMAT**, (International Association for Medical Advice to Travellers, *www.iamat.org*) for a list of doctors in the region, and consider registering with them before travel if you have health problems.

In an **emergency**, dial **t 15** for **medical** help or **t 19** for the **police**.

Money and Banks

The Moroccan currency is the **dirham** (a name taken from the currency of the Byzantine empire), which divides into 100 santimat (*santim* in the singular), from the French word *centimes*. It is also the common currency of Western Sahara. The denominations of dirham notes are 200, 100, 50, 20 and 10. There are silver-coloured coins worth 5, 2 and 1 dirham, and brass ones worth 50, 20, 10 and 5 *santimat*. The currency's price is pegged to a currency basket dominated by the euro: at the time of writing (2010), it was 13 to the UK pound, 11 to the euro and 8 to the US dollar. There are no black-market rates, though tourist bazaars and carpet shops may be persuaded to accept dollars and European currencies.

You can usually **buy Moroccan money** in Málaga, Algeciras or Gibraltar, although there are restrictions against exporting dirhams from the country.

There is usually an **exchange booth** open at seaports and airports on arrival. Should you arrive at night or outside conventional hours, you may find them closed and that it is impossible to cash travellers' cheques or Eurocheques at all until the next day, let alone use a credit card, so it's best to be armed with cash as well. Local taxi drivers, again, will be only too happy to accept dollars, francs, pounds and just about any other European currency, but try not to accept wildly excessive charging, even after a long flight (*see* 'By Car and Taxi', p.78).

Keep your currency exchange slips for when you leave the country, and try to use up any dirhams you may already have exchanged before leaving. **Currency checks** are carried out at passport and customs control at departure points. You will only be allowed to change back half of any amount you are carrying in excess of about 10 dirhams, and the rest will be confiscated outright, with no compensation offered.

Cash machines (ATMs) are open 24 hours a day in all the big tourist resort cities and increasingly in the smaller towns too; use your bank service card, credit card or cash card, matching the symbols (Visa, Cirrus, Mastercard, Electron, Maestro, Interbank are all common) with those displayed on the machines. The maximum cash machine withdrawal is usually 2000dh (roughly equivalent to €180). The biggest concentration of cash machines is usually found in the *ville nouvelle*, or new town.

Standard international **travellers' cheques** in dollars or main European currencies are also easily exchanged in banks, although travellers use them less and less.

Prepaid credit cards have become increasingly popular, but shop around before purchase and carefully compare all fees and charges (a useful resource is *www.what-prepaid-card.co.uk*). Passports are required for most transactions. **Major credit cards** such as Visa and MasterCard are accepted in the smarter hotels and restaurants and a great many shops in the bazaars, though in the latter they might try to charge you a 5–6 per cent handling fee (subject to your negoti-

ating skills). You can withdraw cash on your credit cards in several of the banks too.

Moroccan **banks** display a wide range of tempting stickers on their windows but often don't match up to all their advertisements. There is usually one bank in every town that operates some form of foreign exchange desk, though you will usually save time by heading directly for either the Banque Marocaine du Commerce Extérieur (BMCE), the Banque Populaire or the Banque Crédit du Maroc (BCM), all of which accept cards, travellers' cheques, Eurocheques and, of course, cash.

Airline Carriers

UK and Ireland
Aer Lingus,(Ireland) t 0818 365 000, *www.aerlingus.com*.
Air France, (UK) t 0871 66 33 777, *www.airfrance.co.uk*.
British Airways, (UK) t 08444 930 787, *www.ba.com*.
easyJet, (UK) t 0871 244 2366, (from Ireland) t 0044 870 6000 000, *www.easyjet.com*.
Royal Air Maroc, (UK) t (0207) 439 4361, *www.royalairmaroc.com*.
Ryanair, (UK) t 08712 46 00 00, (Ireland) t 0818 30 30 30, *www.ryanair.com*.

USA and Canada
Air Canada, (Canada and USA) t 888 247 2262, *www.aircanada.ca*.
Air France, (USA) t 800 237 2747, *www.airfrance.com*, (Canada) t 800 667 2747, *www.airfrance.ca*.
British Airways, t 800 AIRWAYS, *www.ba.com*.
Delta Airlines, (USA) t 800 221 1212, *www.delta.com*.
Northwest Airlines, (USA) t 800 225 2525, t 800 328 2298 (hearing impaired), *www.nwa.com*.
Royal Air Maroc, (Canada and USA) t 800 344 67 26, *www.royalairmaroc.com*.
United Airlines, (USA) t 800 538 2929, t 800 323 0170 (TDD), *www.united.com*.

France and Spain
Aer Arabia, (France) t 08 99 19 00 23, (Spain) t 902 053 765, *www.aerarabia.com*.
Air Europa,(Spain) t 902 401 501, *www.air-europa.com*.

Air France,(France) t 08 20 32 08 20, *www.airfrance.fr*.
Iberia,(Spain) t 902 400 500, *www.iberia.com*.
Vueling,(Spain) t 807 200 200, *www.vueling.com*.

Discounts and Youth Fares

UK and Ireland
Budget Travel, 134 Lower Baggot St, Dublin 2, t (01) 631 1111, *www.budgettravel.ie*.
STA, 52 Grosvenor Gardens, Victoria, London SW1W 0AG, t 0871 468 0649, *www.statravel.co.uk*. Branches in London, and across the UK.
Trailfinders, 194 Kensington High St, London W8 7RG, t (020) 7938 3939; 4–5 Dawson St, Dublin 2, t (01) 677 7888, *www.trailfinders.co.uk*.
United Travel, 12 Clonkeen Rd, Deansgrange, Blackrock, Co. Dublin, t (01) 219 0600, *www.unitedtravel.ie*.
USIT Now, 19–21 Aston Quay, Dublin 2, t (01) 602 1906, *www.usitnow.ie*.

USA and Canada
Airhitch, 481 Eighth Ave, Suite 1771, New York, NY 10001-1820, t (212) 247 4482 or t 877 AIRHITCH, *www.airhitch.org*.
STA, t 800 781 4040, *www.statravel.com*. Branches at most universities and across the country.
TFI Tours, 1270 Broadway Suite 409, New York, NY 10001, t (212) 736 1140 or t 800 745 8000, *www.tfitours.com*.
Travel Cuts, 187 College St, Toronto, Ontario M5T 1P7, t 866 246 9762, *www.travelcuts.com*.

Getting There

By Air

Travel to Morocco has ballooned in recent years, especially since the government introduced an 'open skies' policy, thereby allowing European budget airlines into the country. The principal **airports** are at Casablanca and Marrakesh, but there are also significant airports at Rabat, Agadir and Tangier and a few international flights leave from elsewhere too, largely to France and the Benelux countries.

Prices reach their height in peak tourist season (July and August) while in the winter months prices dip with the temperature.

From the UK, direct flights serve London with Royal Air Maroc and British Airways, and for return journeys you should pay £250 off season or £350 in season (or over Christmas and Easter holidays). Ryanair, Thomson and easyJet operate direct flights from several London airports, Bristol and Manchester; a high season return flight from London Stansted to Agadir currently costs just under £100 with Ryanair if booked well in advance.

From the USA and Canada, either fly via Europe or take a direct flight from Montreal and New York (both with Royal Air Maroc). Prices start at around US$600–800 in low season, but double that in peak periods.

From further afield, fly to France or Spain and catch a ferry or plane from there.

See box, left, for airline details.

By Sea

Travelling to Morocco by boat, gently shedding the shores of Europe for those of Africa, is undeniably appealing. There are no ferries to Morocco from Britain or northern Europe, but there is a good choice of routes once you reach the shores of the western Mediterranean. Outside of the peak six weeks from late July to early September, it is usually possible to pick up tickets for a vehicle crossing at ferry ports without too much of a wait. Tickets can be purchased (or routes planned) in the UK with **Southern Ferries** (30 Victoria Street, London SW1V 2LP, **t** 0844 815 7785, www.southernferries.co.uk), which represents most of the ferry companies operating in the southern

Internet Travel Sites

www.cheapflights.co.uk
www.ebookers.com
www.expedia.com
www.flightcentre.com
www.flights.com
www.flydeals.co.uk
www.lastminute.com
www.opodo.com
www.orbitz.com
www.smartertravel.com
www.statravel.com
www.sunway.ie
www.trailfinders.com
www.traveldiscounts.com

Mediterranean. For contact information for the main ferry companies, see box overleaf, 'Ferry Companies'.

From Spain

There are numerous ferry links between Spain, Morocco, and the Spanish enclaves of Ceuta and Melilla in North Africa. The most popular routes are Algeciras–Tangier route (journey time 1hr–1hr 30 mins; prices start at around €55 return for a foot passenger; from €200 for a car plus driver), Algeciras–Ceuta (30mins–1hr, prices start at around €66 return for a foot passenger; from €250 for a car plus driver). There are longer and less frequent services between Málaga and Melilla (3hrs 45 mins, 8hrs for the overnight journey; from €108 return for a foot passenger), Almería and Nador (7hrs; from €98 return for a foot passenger), and even Barcelona to Tangier (30–33hrs; from €200 return for a foot passenger). The biggest company is **Acciona Trasmediterránea**, which also operates the **Comanav**, **EuroFerrys** and **Ferrimaroc** services. Other ferry companies include **Balearia** and **FRS** (Ferries Rápidos del Sur). FRS operate a fast service (four times a week) between Tarifa and Tangier, the shortest crossing, which takes just 35 mins.

From France

SNCM and **Comanav** operate ferry services between Sète and Tangier (36hrs; from €200 return for a foot passenger).

From Italy

GNV run ferries once a week from Genoa to Tangier with a stop in Barcelona: prices start

Ferry Companies and Routes

UK to France

Brittany Ferries, t 0871 244 0439, *www.brittany ferries.com*. Portsmouth–Caen/Cherbourg/ St-Malo, Plymouth–Roscoff, Cork–Roscoff.

Condor Ferries, t 0845 609 1024, *www. condorferries.co.uk*. Portsmouth–Cherbourg, St-Malo–Weymouth, Poole–St-Malo.

LD Lines, *www.ldline.co.uk*. Dover–Boulogne, Newhaven–Dieppe, Portsmouth–Le Havre, Rosslare–Cherbourg.

Norfolkline, t 0844 847 5042, *www.norfolkline. com*. Dover–Dunkerque.

P&O, t 08716 64 56 45, *www.poferries.com*. Dover–Calais.

SeaFrance, t 08705 711 711, *www.seafrance.com*. Dover–Calais.

Spain to Morocco

Acciona Trasmediterránea, t 902 45 46 45 (in Spain), *www.trasmediterranea.es*. Algeciras– Tangier, Algeciras–Ceuta, Málaga–Melilla, Almería–Nador, Barcelona–Tangier.

Balearia, t 902 160 180 (Spain), *www.balearia.com*. Algeciras–Tangier.

Comarit, t 956 66 84 62 (Spain), *www.comarit.es*, Algeciras–Tangier.

FRS, t 956 68 18 30 (Spain), **t** 039 94 26 12 (Tangier), *www.frs.es*. Tarifa–Tangier.

Ferrimaroc, t 902 45 46 45 (in Spain), *www.trasmediterranea.es*. Barcelona–Tangier, Almería–Nador.

France and Italy to Morocco

Comanav, t 902 45 46 45 (in Spain), **t** 0899 191293 (France), *www.trasmediterranea.es*. Sète–Tangier, Genoa–Tangier.

GNV, t +39 (0)10 209 4591, *www.gnv.it*. Genoa–Tangier.

SNCM, t 3260, *www.sncm.fr*. Sète–Tangier.

Online Ferry Tickets

www.buyferrytickets.co.uk
www.directferries.co.uk
www.ferrybooker.com
www.ferrypricesearch.co.uk
www.ukferrytickets.co.uk

at €250 return for a foot passenger, or €795 for a car plus driver. **Comanav** also run a summer-only service on the same route.

By Train

If air and water are not your preferred elements, then an overland journey to Morocco makes for a wonderful two days. (By 2015, when a new high-speed rail line is completed between France and Spain, journeys times will shrink to little over eight hours between Madrid and London.) Rail tickets can be bought from London to Algeciras, beginning by **Eurostar** to Paris, where you will need to then cross to the Gare d'Austerlitz for a sleeper train to Madrid (this service is operated by **Elipsos**, a consortium of French and Spanish railways). From there, you take a last train to Algeciras. There is a phenomenally detailed explanation at *http://www.seat61.com/Morocco.htm#How to book*. If you choose your journeys well and in advance, you can do this journey for £300 return (including a sleeper from Paris to Madrid and back) but it is likely to cost you a little more. Morocco is no longer part of the **InterRail** system, although InterRail passes may be useful on journeys through France

and Spain (for information, contact Rail Europe). Rail Europe also handles bookings for all services, including Eurostar.

Rail Europe, 1 Lower Regent St, London, **t** 08448 484 064, *www.raileurope.co.uk*.

Rail Europe (for travellers from outside Europe), *www.raileurope.com*.

Eurostar, t 08705 186 186, *www.eurostar.com*.

Rail tickets can also be booked directly through the following websites, run by the French and Spanish train companies:

Elipsos, *www.elipsos.com*.

RENFE (Spain), *www.renfe.es*.

SNCF (France), *www.sncf.fr*.

By Coach

Coach travel has little to recommend it: journey times are long (Marrakesh is about 1500 miles/2300km from London) and prices are no match for the budget airlines. There are currently no direct services from London, but you can travel via Paris with **Eurolines** (*www.eurolines.eu*) which operates direct services from the French capital to several Moroccan destinations, including Casablanca, Marrakesh, Fez and Rabat. It

Drivers' Clubs

For information on driving through Europe to Morocco, including international driving permits, insurance and motorway tolls:

AA: General enquiries, **t** 0870 600 0371, *www.theaa.com*.

RAC: General enquiries, **t** 0870 572 2722, *www.rac.co.uk*.

AAA (USA): **t** 800 222 4357, *www.aaa.com*.

costs €292 for a high-season return ticket to Marrakesh, about half that in the off-peak season, and the journey takes 2½ days.

By Car

It is possible with two drivers and very little rest to get from England to Tangier in two days, although four or five days would allow you to enjoy something other than fast driving. To effect a smooth entrance into Morocco with a car, it is best to have your paperwork well organized, with documents under one name and one address. You should have Green Card insurance for the journey through Europe (or, failing that, you can buy temporary insurance at Spanish or Moroccan ferry ports at £30 for five days per car), your Vehicle Registration Document and your Driving Licence. The pink EU driving licence is recognized in Morocco, although the more impressive International Driving Licence (available from the RAC or AA in the UK, or the AAA in the USA), with its seal, passport photograph and French translation, is preferred. (A national driving licence is not enough.) Go to *www.douane.gov.ma/mre/* to organize your documents in advance, but note that the website is French-only.

Ferry companies operating between France and the UK and Ireland are listed above left.

Getting Around

By Air

There are plenty of Royal Air Maroc (RAM) internal flights between Casablanca (handy for Rabat), Fez and Marrakesh, as well as the other principal cities of Morocco, although the timetables shift constantly. Contact the local RAM office (or head office on **t** 022 921000, *www.royalairmaroc.com*) for details but it is not generally worth flying internally

unless you're heading for Western Sahara. Note that RAM offers a 25% **student discount** on all domestic flights if tickets are bought in advance and from RAM outlets.

By Train

Travel by train whenever possible. The Moroccan state railway, the **ONCF** (*www.oncf.ma*, **t** 0890 203040), manages the difficult trick of being both colourful and efficient, although you will need to be eagle-eyed as your train slows to identify which station you are arriving at. The national train network runs on 1,893km (1,176 miles) of line on two axes, from Tangier to Marrakesh (via Rabat and Casablanca) and Casablanca to Oujda (via Rabat, Meknès and Fez).

Both of these long routes have a sleeper service, but trains are divided between *rapide* and *ordinaire*, with intercity services limited to the former. In fact, the main benefit of the *rapide* trains is their comfort and air conditioning rather than their price. Both kinds of train have first and second class but the difference between the classes is minimal.

Reservations are best made in advance. At the least, you should buy tickets in the station, as on the train there is a supplementary charge. For the cities covered in this guide, the longest single daytime train journey is from Marrakesh to Fez, which takes seven hours and costs (second-class) around 195dh (€18). In general **sleeper trains** are only worth taking if you are travelling the whole distance (or close to it) between Casablanca and Oujda or Marrakesh and Tangier.

Major trains have a bar and restaurant and the stations of major cities tend to be attractive colonial buildings in the new town (*ville nouvelle*).

Morocco is not part of the InterRail network, but the ONCF *Carte Fidélité* (149dh) earns you a 50% reduction on eight return or sixteen one-way journeys, so long as they all fall within a twelve-month span.

Train Timetables

Most railway stations have timetables in French posted on the wall, but at some you will need to ask the ticket office for a printout. In many ways it is easier to use the more comprehensive ONCF website (*www.oncf.ma*) or phone (**t** 0890 203040).

By Bus

Morocco's buses are cheap, convenient and lively, one of the best places to meet Moroccans properly, sharing food, cigarettes and travel advice. Camaraderie and magical night-time scenes make buses a more intense pleasure than the trains, though sleep may elude you. Within the major cities, there are plenty of buses and these are good for crossing town cheaply, though they can be overcrowded.

For longer distances, the carrier to choose is the **Compagnie de Transports Marocains**, or **CTM** (*www.ctm.ma*, or phone their Casablanca office on **t** *0522 458080*). Usually CTM operates out of a city's main bus station but occasionally it has its own. Reservations are best made in advance and there are first-class buses offering air-conditioning and heating, which is not always as good as it sounds. There are several other bus companies but the largest is **Supratours** (*www.supratourstravel.com*), but these leave from their own out-of-town offices. However, buses are increasingly based in a single area of town, making advanced ticket purchase that much easier.

By Car and Taxi

Driving is a good way to explore Morocco, especially around the Atlas Mountains and along the Atlantic coast. Moroccans tend to be vigorous and experimental when behind the wheel, so nervous drivers might be best to board the train instead. Petrol is relatively cheap, but refuel where possible when travelling in the Western Sahara, as the irregular gas stations often run out of petrol.

Car hire is a relatively expensive option in Morocco, although off-season you should get a 20% discount on the more unspectacular models. Alamo, Avis, Budget, Thrifty and National Car offer reasonable prices (which are often cheaper if booked online) and have offices in most cities, but you may want to organize this through a travel agent in your home country. Prices range from Fiat Unos, Renault Clios and the odd battered Renault 4 at around €350 (3,800dh) per week to Land Rovers at €1650 (42,000dh) per week.

Repairs are good in Morocco and there are plenty of spare parts available for French cars

Car Hire Companies

Auto Europe, (UK) **t** 0800 223 5555, (USA) **t** 1-800 223 5555, *www.autoeurope.com*.
Avis, (UK) **t** 0844 581 0147, (USA/Canada) **t** 800 331 1212, *www.avis.com*.
Budget, (UK) **t** 08701 56 56 56, (USA) **t** 800 527 0700, *www.budget.com*.
Europcar, (UK) **t** 08706 075 000, (USA) **t** 877 940 6900, *www.europcar.com*.
Hertz, (UK) **t** 08708 44 88 44, (USA) **t** 800 654 3131, *www.hertz.com*.
Holiday Autos, (UK) **t** 0870 400 4461, *www.holidayautos.com*.
easyCars, *www.easycars.com*.

Price Comparison Websites

The following are useful tools for comparing rental prices:
www.carrentals.co.uk
www.moroccocar.com
www.travelsupermarket.com

and for Land Rovers. You will need to bargain to get local prices.

Be aware of **safety** by allowing traffic from the right onto the roundabout first, slowing down for hairpin bends where gravel is loose (a particular danger in Morocco) and remembering that the distinction between pavement and road is not important to pedestrians, a particular danger at dusk and in the dark of night. If you do hit someone on country roads, find the police quickly lest local villagers take justice into their own hands, as has been known to happen. There is a **speed limit** of 100 km (62 miles) an hour, which drops to 40 km (or 25 miles) per hour in anything even loosely residential. Avoid city driving where possible; most hotels have their own parking.

At some point a shared *grand taxi* may be just the ticket, especially between neighbouring cities like Fez and Meknès. They are usually for six people, a little more expensive than buses and leave from around the major bus stations. You will have to negotiate a price for less-popular destinations. Be careful not to end up hiring the whole vehicle and discard your ideas about safety as you board. Avoid these vehicles by night.

There are also *petits taxis* which stay within a city's boundaries, carry up to three passengers and should use a meter if it works

(Marrakeshi taxi drivers are more likely to avoid the meter so be insistent).

Unlicensed cars are a bore because avoiding police checkpoints leads to ludicrous routes being taken. They are of course less likely to be honest with you too.

On Two Wheels (or Four Legs)

Cycling is increasingly popular for travellers to Morocco, where roads allow. Look up the **Cyclists' Touring Club** (*www.ctc.org.uk*) for thorough coverage and details on taking your own bike. You can take bikes on most trains for a small fee. **Scooters** can be fun too and are widely available for hire.

The four-legged option is also available, if **donkeys** are more your style.

Atlas Hikes

If you have the time and enjoy the mountains, a few days away from Marrakesh are one of the country's highlights. *See* p.143 for details of companies offering trips.

Travel Restrictions

There are two areas in Morocco it is a little more complicated to visit. The first is the Rif Mountains, which we advise against. Since this is where Morocco's *kif* is grown and exported in bulk to Europe, it is a dangerous area to travel through. If you have to, try to find out which villages to avoid in advance.

Western Sahara hugs the Atlantic shore southwest of Marrakesh. It is claimed by both Mauretania and Morocco, although Algeria also argues it should have its own Saharan corridor to the coast through the area too. In practice, it will be a Moroccan-Mauretanian deal that seals its fate, but the region is de facto part of Morocco currently. You no longer need any special permit for the area, but you should be careful what you photograph (not refugee camps, for example) and take plenty of water. Be sure to visit Dakhla and to take Saint-Exupéry's books with you.

Where to Stay

Morocco is as good for sleep as it is for sights. The range of options is immense and experiencing something of it is part of the joy of travel in the country. In **cheap hotels** in

Hotel Price Categories

All prices listed here and elsewhere in this book are for a double room in high season.

luxury	€€€€€	over €200
expensive	€€€€	€100–200
moderate	€€€	€50–100
inexpensive	€€	€20–50
cheap	€	under €20

the south you can sleep on a mattress on the roof for 35dh (€3). In cheaper hotels expect shared bathrooms but the rooms themselves are generally clean. **Mid-range options** are often the most practical, and rooms boast their own showers, but they are often the least interesting and many are located in the *villes nouvelles*. The occasional stay at a **top-range hotel** can offer a fabulous Moroccan night, often with a *hammam* to boot.

But tourists increasingly opt for staying in a **riad** instead, effectively a Moroccan courtyard house built around a garden. Trendiness has its cost in dirhams, however, and what began as a Marrakesh movement has spawned riad hotels across all of Morocco's larger cities. It is worth looking around a little.

Towards the bottom of the scale again, hotel **dorm rooms, youth hostels and campsites** are usually good for the purse, especially if you are in a small group. For serious hikers, the **Club Alpin Français** (*www.ffcam.fr*) offers beds in some of their *refuges* in the High Atlas. It can also be fun to stay in the house of a local family, something done on a very informal basis.

Hotel prices should include **breakfast** but sometimes do not, especially lower down the scale, so it is worth checking. You'll need your passport number when registering at a hotel and will have to pay a **government tax** of around 25 dh too (the amount depends on the rating of the hotel).

Morocco has a **hotel classification system** ranging from one star to five (with many hotels unrated) but these ratings are often limited to the *villes nouvelles*. Unclassified hotels tend to be in the historic areas of town and usually cost between €5 and €15. Cleanliness, air and light are often in short supply here, so check your room first. In some, you will at least have the fleas for company. The official Moroccan star classifications for hotels are not reproduced in this guide, as they are not necessarily a reliable indication of the relative expense or comfort level of a hotel and can be seriously confusing, especially in the middle ranges. As in many countries they are based on a fairly arbitrary list of potential facilities (whether or not a hotel has a separate reception desk, a lift and so on) more than price. It can work out that a small two-star can be a good deal more comfortable and attractive than a four-star, or that a four-star can be cheaper than a three. Instead, the classification used in the guide is simply based on prices, although this can still hide an enormous flexibility depending on room size, position, season and your bargaining ability. Always book in advance, especially during Easter, August, Christmas and (western) New Year.

Specialist Tour Operators

A variety of package tours are available both to and through Marrakesh, Fez and Rabat. Many of them will offer walking, cycling or driving tours of the Atlas mountains. Some are guided by a historian or academic.

In the UK

Bales Worldwide, Bales House, Junction Road, Dorking, Surrey RH4 3HL, **t** 0845 057 1819, *www.balesworldwide.com*. Bales offers three 'frequent departures' tours you can join (of 9, 7 and 4 days respectively) as well as even more tours for groups.

Best of Morocco, 38 Market Place, Chippenham, Wiltshire SN15 3HT, **t** (01249) 467 165, *www.morocco-travel.com*. This company specializes in arranging travel for the independent traveller and has been doing so in Morocco since 1967. Its website is exceptional too.

Cox & Kings, 6th Floor, 30 Millbank, London SW1P 4EE, **t** (0207) 873 5000, *www.coxandkings.co.uk*. Cox & Kings has excellent travel experience and networks, as well as a good selection of high-end Morocco itineraries, often at a leisurely pace.

Intrepid Travel, 76 Upper Street, London N1 0NU, **t** (020) 7354 6169, *www.intrepidtravel.com*. Offers an impressive range of reasonably priced tours to both known and less-known areas of Morocco.

Martin Randall, 10 Barley Mow Passage, Chiswick, London W4 4PH, **t** (020) 8742 3355, *www.martinrandall.com*. This company arranges an annual trip in late September, with a strong architectural and historical bias, that follows the old caravan route of the Saharan gold trade from Tangier to Sijilmassa and back to Marrakesh.

Ramblers Holidays, Lemsford Mill, Lemsford Village, Welwyn Garden City AL8 7TR, **t** (01707) 331 133, *www.ramblersholidays.co.uk*. Arranges walking holidays from Marrakesh into the foothills of the High Atlas, as well as trips to the Imperial Cities.

Sherpa Expeditions, 131a Heston Road, Hounslow, Middlesex, TW5 0RF, **t** (0208) 577 2717, *www.sherpa-walking-holidays.co.uk*. Sherpa offers week- and two-week-long hikes in the Atlas mountains.

Tribes Travel, 12 The Business Centre, Earl Soham, Woodbridge, Suffolk, IP13 7SA, **t** (01728) 685971, *www.tribes.co.uk*. Offers a range of holidays with a particular focus on culture, wildlife, trekking, and responsible tourism.

Truck Africa, **t** (01580) 761171, *www.truckafrica.com*. Safari camping tours that cross Africa from north to south, including stop-offs at Morocco's imperial cities.

In the USA

Experience It Tours, **t** 315 858 3426. This company has a range of Morocco tours and flexibility over itineraries as well as a good track record on price compared to other companies offering a similar service.

Heritage Tours, 121 West 27 Street, Suite 1201, New York, NY 10001, **t** 800 378 4555, *www.htprivatetravel.com*. Heritage offers an excellent cultural gambol through the country and its most historic spots, and offers a high level of flexibility on itineraries even though the company offers eight of its own.

Marrakesh Voyage, 865 Fox Mountain Rd, Livingston Manor, NY 12758, **t** 888 990 2999, *www.morocco-travel-agency.com*. MV has its own office in Marrakesh, offers a broad menu of travel options and has a special focus on the country's memorable music festivals.

In Morocco

Journey Beyond Travel, *www.journeybeyondtravel.com*. JBT offers a range of Morocco tours but it is their 'Bike Morocco' trip that especially marks them out.

Trans-Atlas Bike, *www.atlasmountainbiking.com*. Explores the Atlas range by mountain bike. A Dutch family has been running these tours since 2004. The company is not-for-profit, using all profits to boost employment for mountain Berbers.

Practical A–Z

06

Conversions: Imperial–Metric

Length (multiply by)
Inches to centimetres: 2.54
Centimetres to inches: 0.39
Feet to metres: 0.3
Metres to feet: 3.28
Yards to metres: 0.91
Metres to yards: 1.09
Miles to kilometres: 1.61
Kilometres to miles: 0.62

Area (multiply by)
Inches square to centimetres square: 6.45
Centimetres square to inches square: 0.15
Feet square to metres square: 0.09
Metres square to feet square: 10.76
Miles square to kilometres square: 2.59
Kilometres square to miles square: 0.39
Acres to hectares: 0.40
Hectares to acres: 2.47

Weight (multiply by)
Ounces to grams: 28.35
Grams to ounces: 0.035
Pounds to kilograms: 0.45
Kilograms to pounds: 2.2
Stones to kilograms: 6.35
Kilograms to stones: 0.16
Tons (UK) to kilograms: 1,016
Kilograms to tons (UK): 0.0009
1 UK ton (2,240lbs) = 1.12 US tonnes (2,000lbs)

°C	°F
40	104
35	95
30	86
25	77
20	68
15	59
10	50
5	41
-0	32
-5	23
-10	14
-15	5

Volume (multiply by)
Pints (UK) to litres: 0.57
Litres to pints (UK): 1.76
Quarts (UK) to litres: 1.13
Litres to quarts (UK): 0.88
Gallons (UK) to litres: 4.55
Litres to gallons (UK): 0.22
1 UK pint/quart/gallon =
    1.2 US pints/quarts/
    gallons

Temperature
Celsius to Fahrenheit:
multiply by 1.8 then
add 32

Fahrenheit to Celsius:
subtract 32 then multiply
by 0.55

Morocco Information

Time Differences
Morocco: + 1hr GMT; + 6hrs EST
Daylight saving from May to August (dates change annually: check at tourist offices).

Dialling Codes
Morocco country code: t 212

To Morocco from: UK, Ireland, New Zealand dial 00; from USA, Canada 011, from Australia 0011; then dial 212 and the number without the initial zero

From Morocco to: UK 00 44; Ireland 00 353; USA, Canada 001; Australia 00 61; New Zealand 00 64; then the number without the initial zero
Directory enquiries: 160

Emergency Numbers
Police: t 19
Ambulance: t 15
Fire: t 16

Embassy Numbers in Morocco
UK (and diplomatic assistance for visitors from Ireland, New Zealand) t 0537 633333 (Rabat); **USA t** 0537 762265 (Rabat); **Canada (and diplomatic assistance for visitors from Australia) t** 0537 687400 (Rabat).

Shoe Sizes

Europe	UK	USA
35	2½ / 3	4
36	3 / 3½	4½ / 5
37	4	5½ / 6
38	5	6½
39	5½ / 6	7 / 7½
40	6 / 6½	8 / 8½
41	7	9 / 9½
42	8	9½ / 10
43	9	10½
44	9½ / 10	11
45	10½	12
46	11	12½ / 13

Women's Clothing

Europe	UK	USA
34	6	2
36	8	4
38	10	6
40	12	8
42	14	10
44	16	12

Business Facilities

Five-star hotels in the major cities, such as the Majorelle in Marrakesh, usually have conference rooms and will rent them to both guests and non-guests. Likewise, these hotels usually have a small business office where you can send and receive faxes, make photocopies and calls and send emails. You can also access the internet in your room at the smarter hotels, if you have a laptop. Even many mid- and low-range hotels offer internet access.

Children

Children are much more of an advantage than an impediment to travelling in Morocco. Next to speaking Maghrebi Arabic or converting to Islam, they form the most enduring bridge between cultures. They cause a drastic reduction in hassle and can be relied upon to look effortlessly stoical during bargaining sessions and (unless they are absolute monsters) improve your relationship with the staff of a restaurant, café or hotel. Hotels are usually happy to provide extra mattresses or a cot in a room, usually without any extra charge.

Children's tastes should be taken into account when planning trips since they tend to be easily bored by architecture and museums but more than usually excited by snakes, minerals, working potteries, horse-drawn-carriage rides, camels, donkeys, mules and running water. The one thing you must always bear in mind, even on the most sheltered beach, is the strong undertow off the Atlantic coast.

Wide straw hats can be bought locally as necessary protection against the sun, and packets of nuts, raisins, sultanas, dates and other dried fruit can be carried around in a raffia bag for snacks. Sterilized *écremé* milk can be bought in litre cartons, but should be consumed quickly once opened. Throughout Morocco it is also possible to buy small plastic sacks of fresh milk which have their date stamped in one corner, for a couple of dirhams. However, no matter how attentive you are about mineral water and peeling fruit, it is very likely that your child will be hit by an attack of diarrhoea in the first week or two in Morocco. Try not to panic, and feed them lots of bananas.

Crime and Security

As a rule, Morocco is a safe country aside from the inevitable pickpockets and occasional wild cards. But the larger cities do have their risks, especially around the medinas at night. Conmen have been largely cleared from the major cities though expect a few to try the new face when you first arrive. In the smaller towns they are more common. Some tourists have been conned by hitch-hikers or 'breakdown' artists on inter-city highways, notably the N9 and N10, most of whom want to take you to a friend or relative's shop for some hardball bargaining.

The Moroccan police force is modelled on the French, and is divided into two: the **Gendarmerie** and the **Sûreté**. The Gendarmerie live under semi-military discipline, wear khaki serge and green berets and carry batons. They cover both cities and the countryside with a regular grid of barracks, and could be compared to a mixture of a county constabulary and a reserve regiment. The Sûreté are the grey-uniformed and armed police who patrol the roads and the cities, and to whom robberies from tourists will normally be reported to obtain a declaration for insurance purposes. They are more directly concerned with crime and law enforcement and are considered, as in France, more street-wise, sophisticated and corrupt: they are commonly referred to as 'Ali Baba and the forty...'

Grey-clad **customs officers** may be seen, particularly on the northern coast, trying to control the flow of electrical goods smuggled in from Ceuta and Melilla, and *kif* (Moroccan hashish) being smuggled out. **Prison officers** wear blue. **Firemen** wear blue with red piping and might be seen trying to sell their calendars to unwary motorists, particularly on the road south of Tangier. The **army**, by comparison, look rather underdressed in their plain lovat-green uniform.

To report a crime, contact the **police** on **t 19**, the emergency number. If you suffer a theft and want to claim the loss on insurance, you will need a stamped receipt from the local police station and will probably find it easier if you visit the station with a French or Arabic speaker. Without evidence (or a witness) you will only get a receipt for the loss of your identity documents.

Eating Out

Morocco has a very attractive national cuisine, distinctive for the quality and fresh-ness of the ingredients. Restaurants are usually open from around noon to 3pm and then again from 7pm to about 10.30 or 11pm. Less formal places are open all day. For more on local specialities and a menu-reader, *see* **Food and Drink**, p.61.

Electricity

The standard European current of 220 volts AC has now largely replaced the 110 volt AC system except in a few older buildings. You will need two-pin flat European plugs to fit Moroccan sockets, and if you have any US or Canadian 110-volt appliances you will also need a current transformer. On or off the grid, cooking, heating and lighting is largely dependent on charcoal or gas. The ubiquitous blue gas bottles fitted with a ceramic hob are subsidized by the government as one of the principal necessities of the poor.

Embassies in Morocco

Your embassy can help you by holding onto your mail, advising on emergency financial and medical problems (while being unable to actually give you money) and putting you in touch with people at home. Embassies prefer you to register with them when travelling in the country. *See* p.71.

Entertainment

Nightlife is at its Moroccan best in Marrakesh, when belly dancers, snake charmers, dance troupes and music groups take to the streets. It may sometimes be hackneyed and aimed at the outsiders, but it can make for a lively wander through town after dinner.

Morocco is reasonably relaxed about alcohol for a Muslim country, meaning that bars and clubs offer a good night out too, especially in Marrakesh. Women should keep

Restaurant Price Categories

The price categories used for restaurants throughout the book are per head for a full meal without drinks, but prices vary very widely according to what you eat, almost as much (within reason) as where you eat it.

expensive	€€€	over €30
moderate	€€	€15–30
inexpensive	€	Under €15

The cost of a bottle of local wine in most restaurants is around 100dh (€9).

to the smartest bars, as the cheaper ones tend to be seedy and the women are often prostitutes. In Fez, you might be better to pick one of the music bars or even time your stay to coincide with the wonderful World Music Festival in June, but you will need to buy tickets in advance. Rabat's drinking nightlife is passable and the capital is better for cultural offerings, from the theatre and cinema to evenings at the British Council, Alliance Française and Goethe Institut. Nearby Casablanca has something for most tastes (including many you may want to avoid) and plenty going on along the seaside, if you can stomach the prices. It also has a theatre with occasional performances in French (but most in Arabic).

If you have an ear for heavy metal, the annual Sidirock Festival has enough angry energy to make it a good spectacle, so long as the police allow it to happen.

For a quieter night out, numerous cinemas showing Moroccan and French films grace the larger cities.

Guides

Official guides of the highest (national) grade can be hired from tourist offices for 180dh (€16) for a half-day and 350dh (€31) for a full day. Local guides charge perhaps a quarter less. They are all well trained in history and anecdotes, fluent in several languages, and trustworthy.

Alternatively, if you have just arrived in a city and not yet found your way to your hotel, let alone the tourist office, you will not find it difficult to find yourself an unofficial guide. In fact, there will most probably be a profusion of them offering their services and asking where you want to go as soon as you appear on the street.

Dealing with the attention of unwanted urban guides is one of the recurring problems of travelling in Morocco, although in recent years the deployment of plain-clothes policemen has cut down the aggressive hustling of foreigners in tourist destinations such as Fez and Marrakesh. The discordant cries of hustlers just as you arrive fresh in a town or at the medina gates can be irritating. Accept this, though, as a facet of Moroccan life. There is certainly no easy way to avoid it, short of jumping in a taxi and hiding in a hotel. Use your energy not to avoid these guides, but to select the most appealing.

A little humility is also an asset. On your first visit to a large and strange town, some help in finding your hotel or a taxi will very probably actually be useful. The aggression with which many visitors cold-shoulder themselves through potential helpers and then later bemusedly consult their imported maps and guidebooks is faintly ridiculous, but a curious and revealing insight into Western attitudes. Meet the problem in a Moroccan manner, and deploy qualities of charm and enthusiasm. Enjoy the human skills required in choosing the friendliest character from a group. As in all situations of life the eyes are the true mirror of the soul, and there is no point in having a conversation with anybody while they wear dark glasses. Greet your chosen guide with a *salaam* and a handshake, praise the weather and his town and tell him how delighted you are at last to be here. If need be, check out your character judgement over a cup of tea. Tell him exactly where you want to go and what you intend to give, which, however rich you are, should never be more than 15dh per hour.

A guide's natural interest lies in directing you to the medina. For in the confusing labyrinth of medina avenues you become more dependent on him, and this is also where lurk the bazaars, where he can earn commissions (fixed at a traditional five per cent, which can win your guide a comparative fortune) and additional kudos with his neighbours. Be aware of this and, if need be, hold out a visit to a bazaar as a carrot at the end of the day. You will soon find out that the habitat of the hustling guide is almost entirely confined to bus stops and medina gates. Marrakesh and Fez have hustling reputations. But even in these cities, when you know your way around (and show an increasing lack of interest in bazaars), you will find yourself increasingly left alone.

When you feel annoyed, run over a few relevant facts. Even an industrial worker in Morocco has a minimum wage of just 10 dirhams but it is far lower for the unskilled. The chances of getting even 5 dirhams in a country of 25 per cent employment, with over half the population under 21 years old, is low, and competition is heavy. Even a European unemployment dole converts into an enviable quantity of dirhams. Under those conditions might you not try your luck at skimming off a few dirhams from often unfriendly foreigners?

Hammams

A *hammam* is a public steam bath which, before the advent of showers and private bathrooms, was one of the great urban centres of Moroccan life. Some of them are a little bit run-down from their days of glory at the turn of the 20th century, but they survive throughout this arid country as a working institution. Apart from those in tourist hotels, male nudity is taboo and the sexes are strictly divided, either by different opening hours (usually for women in the daylight hours, with men in the evening) or by a completely different set of chambers.

The *hammams* of Morocco are rarely as elaborate as the great domed, multichambered, marble-clad structures of Ottoman Turkey, though they will usually have an entrance lobby, a changing room and a double set of doors into the steam room. Here you can gently steam, wash yourself from taps, basins or black plastic buckets, or for an extra charge you can be rigorously scrubbed, massaged and expertly manipulated. In an interesting inversion of street etiquette, women often bathe with just the skimpiest pants or completely naked, and remove hair from the most intimate parts of their body, while men are very strict about wearing either a cotton wrap or swimming trunks, and wash their genitals privately facing the wall.

Several *hammams* are listed in the text, but by enquiring from your hotel you can find many others that are happy to accept foreign visitors. A minority of establishments, usually those directly attached to a mosque, do not like the presence of *Rumi*, as Christian tourists with only the slenderest relationship to Orthodox Byzantium are still called.

Health and Emergencies

You do not need **vaccinations** for Morocco but western governments and the WHO do advise being vaccinated for measles, mumps, polio, rubella and tetanus. If you're staying for very long and especially if you plan to work with animals or in healthcare, you might consider vaccinations against diphtheria, hepatitis B, rabies and TB too. There have been a very few cases of malaria in the hottest six months of the year in the country's extreme south.

Around the Sahara, there is a real chance of seeing snakes, scorpions and palm rats. Some of these have a fatal sting or bite. In this area, always wear shoes (not flip-flops) and shake your shoes out in the morning. If you get stung or bitten, do not move the affected area and seek medical aid. Even the potentially fatal bites are usually just formalities for a doctor or nurse.

You are likely to get **diarrhoea** at some point, so stick to rice, bananas and yogurt as much as possible until your stomach settles again. Packing some rehydration tablets will help, especially if you have children, although Morocco's pharmacies stock them too.

Three areas to be especially careful about as you travel are sex, food and insects or animals. Around one in a thousand Moroccans are **HIV-positive** and **Hepatitis B** is also transmitted through sex, as well as through infected blood and needles. **Hepatitis A** and **typhoid** come from contaminated food and water, so choose freshly cooked food, and some conservatism in your choice of water source might help. **Yellow fever** and **leishmaniasis** come through insects while **rabies** is a killer and very common, so avoid even licks from dogs. At the barber's, be sure they use a new blade.

If you are unwell, your hotel should be your first port of call as they can direct you to a pharmacy, dentist, doctor or hospital. Pharmacists are reliable in the big cities and your embassy can offer some advice too. For the most serious conditions, you are probably better to return home but, beyond that, Moroccan **hospitals** are perfectly passable for minor cases and **private clinics** for anything in between. A Moroccan doctor coming to your hotel should charge you anything up to around 500dh, many times what he would charge a local patient, which you can of course claim on insurance (*see* p.73).

You have probably come to Morocco for the sun as much as anything but wear a hat when you can and avoid strenuous exercise while you are still acclimatising. **Dehydration** and **heatstroke** are common among tourists and the latter requires rapid medical attention. Remember that it can get very cold at night, particularly by the sea, in the mountains and in the desert.

In an **emergency**, dial **t 15 for medical help** or **t 19 for the police.**

Internet

One of the most extensive web guides to Morocco in English is found at *www.lexicorient.com/morocco*. The country's most official websites are *www.maroc.net* and *www.visitmorocco.com*; the former is good on history, geography, culture and travel as well as links to government departments, the latter home to some stunning photos. For culture and politics, try *www.al-bab.com/maroc*, or for arts there are *www.maghreb-arts.ma* and *http://theviewfrommorocco.blogspot.com*, while for Berber culture there is *www.amazigh-voice.com*. For extensive local detail try *http://friendsofmorocco.org*, *http://riadzany.blogspot.com*, and *http://moroccanmaryam.typepad.com*. For food inspiration, check out Tara Stevens' weekly recipes at *http://cafeclock.com/*.

Kif in the Rif

In the Rif mountains in northern Morocco is grown *cannabis indica*, some of the finest common hemp in the world. The growing of *kif* has ballooned in the past twenty years despite EU attempts to curtail it and it now accounts for an enormous source of foreign currency. Nevertheless, *kif* remains illegal to grow, sell, transport or smoke. Be aware that hawkers may try to get you smoking, sell you a brick and then threaten to call the police unless you make a major payment to them. They just want your cash but you can be imprisoned for up to five years (with sentences mostly dictated by quantities carried), so it is a risk, especially in Tangier and Tetouan. Smuggling *kif* is downright foolish.

Be aware that while *kif* induces laughter, it also breeds paranoia, so environment and company is everything.

Maps

Michelin and Geocenter both do reasonable Morocco maps, while road maps are available at ONMT tourist offices. For the cities, the maps in this guidebook should suffice. Maps not showing Western Sahara as part of Morocco may be confiscated by police or border guards. The biggest bookshops in London and Dublin tend to offer decent foldout maps of Marrakesh and sometimes of Fez and Rabat too. For all maps, Stanford's Maps (*www.stanfords.co.uk*) near London's Covent Garden is hard to beat (there's also a branch in Bristol and an online shop). In New York, try The Traveller's Choice Bookstore (*www.turontravel.com*) and Complete Traveller's Bookstore (*www. travellersbookstore.com*).

The medinas of Morocco's main cities can be tough to get around and, if all else fails, the old Éditions Gauthey maps can be a great help.

Media

English newspapers have been fitful at best in recent Moroccan history, with the much-heralded *Casablanca Analyst* discontinued after just a few issues. But *www.morocconewsline.com* is a reasonable on-line magazine with broad coverage of Moroccan issues.

For Morocco's best papers, you will need French or Arabic. French papers worth reading include *L'Opinion* and *Libération*, linked to the Istiqlal and Socialist parties respectively. *L'Opinion* ventures further into contentious ground than *Libération*.

Among the leading Arabic titles is *Al Alam* (The Flag), *Al Ichtikari* (the Socialist paper), the more independent *Al Ahdath* and the government's *The Sahara* (French version: *Le Matin du Sahara*).

The Moroccan press is allowed to be critical but only within limits, and it can never criticise the monarchy or Islam. Sales and advertising could never fund the newspapers, which rely instead on an annual government allocation of around US$6 million. Self-censorship is inevitable, but in North African terms Morocco's press is fairly free. The greater problem is circulation levels, currently between one and two per cent. National literacy, which has improved considerably in the last two decades, is still below 50 per cent in Morocco.

Several European and American newspapers are available in the major cities too, including *The New York Times*, *USA Today*, *International Herald Tribune*, *Le Monde*, *The Guardian* and *Guardian Weekly* and *The Times*, as well as *Time*, *Newsweek* and *The Economist*.

But Morocco remains a good place to shed your paper habit and pick up tuning into the **World Service** direct from London on a number of different short-wave frequencies: 9.41 and 5.975mhz – 31.88 and 50.21m. **Voice of America** can be listened to at 1197 KHz or 15,205 KHz in the daytime and 1593 KHz at night. Try 97.5FM for a music radio station which covers northwest Africa.

There may be little temptation, apart from being caught in a rainstorm, to visit a **cinema** in Morocco. But if you do find yourself inside (tickets are around 12dh), you could become more fascinated by the audience than the film. The different cultural attitudes to humour, violence and romance always make fascinating study.

The best hotels provide CNN, BBC and other TV news to your bedroom.

Opening Hours

Museums, Monuments and Sites

Throughout this guide it is safe to assume that most of the museums, monuments and archaeological sites are open daily. In winter they should be open at least Monday–Friday 8.30–12pm and 2.30–5.30pm but during Ramadan (and often in summer too) that is approximately 8am–3pm. All museums are closed on Tuesdays. Official museum opening times are not always reliable, however.

As for archaeological sites, the sun sets the schedule, but opening times tend to be broad enough. Volubilis is open from 8am until dusk, for example.

Medersas follow the same schedule as museums but are often closed all of Friday. Mosques in Morocco are, with a few notable exceptions, closed to non-Muslims.

Banks, Offices and Shops

Banking hours are usually longer in resorts and big cities but the standard hours are 8.30am until 4 or 4.30pm, shortened to 9am–2.45pm in Ramadan. Post Offices (La Poste) are open in winter Monday–Friday 8–3 and in summer they take a siesta, opening from 8.15–11am and 2.15–4.30pm, although a handful are open until 11pm. Government offices are usually open from 8.30am–12pm and 2–6.30pm. Private offices tend to be open from 8.30am to 6pm, with a two-hour lunch break. Medina shops open at 8 or 9 in the morning and only close 12 hours later.

Businesses, shops and offices tend to take a longer lunch on Friday for prayer.

National Holidays

1 January: New Year's Day

11 January: Independence Manifesto – celebrates publication of Moroccan nationalist manifesto in Fez

1 May: Labour Day

30 July: Feast of the Throne, celebrated with conspicuous amounts of bunting, processions, public feasts and music

14 August: Allegiance Day

21 August: King Mohammed VI's birthday ('Young People's Day')

6 November: Day of the Green March

18 November: Independence Day

Photography

Cameras are the symbol of the modern-day tourist driven by a mania to record, to move on, before you have the time to understand. Photographs give the illusion that one has the time to study these things later at greater depth. Even if you have the time for only the slightest sketch of a building or a landscape, it will imprint the image more vividly than a thousand pictures.

As a means of preserving images of wild flowers without picking them and of wild animals without killing them, however, cameras are entirely on the side of the angels. The two invaluable tips I have been given by a professional are to photograph at dusk and never put your subject in the centre of the frame.

Excluding anything remotely military, you are free to photograph anything architectural. Do not photograph anybody, least of all a rural woman, without permission. Be very respectful in the way you photograph religious buildings close to and do not take photos during prayers. Be prepared to tip for photographing animals or people at a tariff of around 10dh. Most museums forbid flash and operate a partial restrictive policy, like that which forbids photographs of the bronzes in the Rabat Archaeological Museum. This only seems to make sense as an opportunity for tips. Common sense and *politesse* help enormously.

Postal Services

The **postal service** between Morocco and abroad does at least work and letters take around a week to reach Europe and double that to North America and Australasia. A yellow PTT sign announces a **post office** although you can usually buy **stamps** elsewhere with your newspaper and cigarettes. Try to send your letters and parcels from cities and for a speedier service you should use **Chronopost** (*www.chronopost.com*). An ordinary letter abroad will take a maximum of 5 or 6 days to European destinations, and 10 to 15 days to the USA, and cost 7dh80 (Europe), 13dh (Americas) or 14dh40 (Oceania) for up to 20 grams. A parcel costs 111 dirhams,

but don't seal them until their contents have been checked at the post office.

Poste restante is available at the main post offices of major cities. Packages can weigh up to one kilo. These deliveries are kept for 20 days before being returned.

For more on Moroccan postal services, see *www.bam.net.ma* (French only).

Shopping

Arab cities were designed with the **souk** or market at the centre of the community. Islam has none of the Christian anxiety about mixing trade and worship. The streets around a grand mosque are usually the busiest and the richest and are known as the *kissaria*. The outer walls of mosques are commonly obscured by workshops and stalls whose rent helps pay for the upkeep of the building. A new *zaouia* (religious college) or mosque was often the initial impetus that coalesced a trading community into existence. On Fridays you will notice a marked reduction in trade as the merchants shut for noon prayers.

Moroccan crafts remain active and have recovered from the exodus of more than 250,000 Moroccan Jews, who were among the most skilled craftsmen in the country. The Jews were particularly prominent in jewellery, tailoring, weaving and non-ferrous metalwork. All large towns maintain a government-run craft centre called an **Ensemble Artisanal**, where traditional trades are taught and products exhibited for sale. Tourism greatly assists the craft economy, and it has been assessed that a fifth of any visitor's expenditure is on crafts.

A visit to a typical contemporary Moroccan home reveals a subtle difference in taste from the 'typically Moroccan' souvenirs of the souks. Rich embroidered cloth (covering cushions and day beds), nylon blankets and masses of deep-carved wood are dominant. The cool tiled floors are rarely covered by carpets. Ceramics tend not to be Islamic in decoration but plain glazed earthenware or displaying a Chinese pattern for grand occasions. The radio, TV or tape recorder will be conspicuous and you notice the complete absence of any pictures (other than an obligatory photo of a Moroccan football team, the king and a calligraphic Koranic blessing). It is chiefly in the traditional embroidered kaftans worn by women, the low tables and all the impedimenta of a tea ceremony that tourist bazaar taste and the domestic economy coincide.

Moroccan Goods

The souks are all well stocked with loose-weave large brown and white **blankets** that make excellent bed covers. In the south you will come across brilliant patterns of tie-dyed cotton for the women's enveloping *haiks* and the enormous, many-coloured thick blankets of the Sahara region. Two of these can completely line a nomad tent and provide excellent protection against the bitter nights.

Only buy **carpets** for your pleasure. Moroccan carpets are not an investment, but can be a continuous delight. To my mind the so-called Royal or Rabati carpets loosely based on a prayer rug have become charmless in colour and design, unless displayed en masse over some vast hall or courtyard. Of much greater interest are the products of the countryside. Ask to see the wild discordant weavings, often on a field of purple or madder red, known variously as *Chiadma*, *Oulad Bou Sba*, *Boujad* or *Rehamna*. Of equal mass but of much greater restraint in colour range and design are the *Marmoucha* rugs, especially those with a dark grid of lozenges on a white background. Whatever your pocket, however, you must visit the great carpet bazaars in Fez, Meknès, Rabat and Marrakesh. These are often housed in magnificent interiors, and the merchants will offer you tea while they display their still wonderfully tempting wares.

The *hanbel* or *arerbal* (the Moroccan version of the familiar Turkish killim) is woven, not knotted, though a rich pattern of embroidery can sometimes confuse this distinction. On the ground they have an even shorter life than carpets, but they are more flexible and can be used as hangings and throws, and can look especially lavish for picnics or as covers for day beds or dining-room tables. They should be much cheaper than carpets, with which they share many designs as well as the traditional nomadic production areas. All the more interesting ones are produced in the Middle or High

Atlas, or at least to the traditional patterns that were developed in these tribal regions.

The Berber tribes of the Middle Atlas plateau dominate Morocco's weaving tradition. Travelling from Rabat southeast towards Midelt you will pass through or near the **main weaving tribal zones**: the Zemmour (around Khémisset), Zaér (around Rommani), Zaïane (around Khénifra, Moulay Bouâzza and Mrirt), Beni-M'tir (around El-Hajeb and Azrou) and Beni-Mguild (the old territory of which stretched between Azrou and Midelt). There is a basic similarity in texture and design throughout this large region. In their raw state at local markets, pieces are as likely to be found woven for a practical purpose and made up as saddlebags, belts, waistcoats, sacks, wall hangings, tent divisions or cushions, than as convenient lengths for your floor. A warm red, which used to be made from the madder root, provides the basic background against which the finely executed details are picked out in bright white cotton and black. Today, with the use of chemical dyes widespread, there are innumerable colour variations.

The designs, however, remain entirely geometric and generally rely on bands of plain colour alternating with richly worked bands of lozenges, diamond grids and elaborate crosses. A good weaver will brook no repetition in design and create a dazzling killim full of movement, colour and detail. A less inspired version can look static, lifeless and repetitive. The most elegant and hard-wearing killims, which rarely come up for sale, are often so heavy with sequins that the pattern is all but obscured. These are woven specifically for the weaver's wedding, and afterwards are displayed as a decorative hanging. On her death they are used as a cover for her corpse, the sequins glistening in the dusk as she is borne up to a hillside cemetery.

Another, smaller area of weaving is in the High Atlas mountains. These simple, dignified *hanbels* are known as *Glaoua*, after the Berber dynasty from Telouèt. They have a similar pattern of banded plain and decorated stripes, although they usually have no colour and are woven from plain undyed black and white wool. In the area to the south of the High Atlas and Jbel Siroua (often referred to as Aït Ouaouzguite) these plain *hanbels* are worked over with an extra layer of knotted carpet work. In addition, a full range of colours can be used to accompany the dominant saffron hue to create a rich depth of pile, geometric design and colour. You will also find some more straightforward carpets with pale-green geometric designs worked onto a saffron field, and brightly coloured tent bands loosely based on the magnificent tradition of weaving ornate coloured borders into the local white woollen cloth.

In many of the carpet bazaars you will see the so-called **message rugs** with their bright colours and vivid row of pictograms such as camels, women and goats. These are popular trading items (of a size well suited for a child's bedroom) but are not in fact an indigenous Moroccan tradition, since they originated in southern Tunisia, in the region around the desert town of Gafsa.

Morocco is rife with attractive **ceramics** too. Pottery plates or large fruit bowls, particularly the traditional geometric designs of blue on white – glazed, plain or tinted green – translate well and seldom look out of place back home. The old ceramic centres of Morocco were Fez, Meknès and Tetouan, joined by Safi in the late 18th century. Today most of the pottery on sale in Morocco is made in either Safi or Fez. Good basic earthenware pots are also made in such typical Berber areas as the Ourika Valley, Et-Tleta-de-Oued-Laou, Amizmiz and Zaouia-Moulay-Brahim, as well as on the western edge of Marrakesh. Tamegroute in the southern Drâa produces a rough, green, glazed ware identical in look (if not in quality) to the medieval wares of North Africa.

The city souks are full of the distinctive **clothing** of the Maghreb: *gandouras* (collarless cotton smocks), *burnous* (woollen cloaks with hoods), kaftans (cotton 'nightshirts' for daytime with embroidered necks) and *jellabas* (full-length woollen tunics with hoods). Though they're vital for dressing up, you need conviction to wear them well in Morocco. Back home a *gandoura* can serve as an admirable nightgown, a *burnous* is excellent as an outdoor cloak, and a *jellaba* works well as a warm housecoat. Straw hats are useful in the summer, but no one should encourage any further manufacture by buying a hateful nylon fez. There are felt ones to be found, or lambswool 'Nehru' hats.

It's still possible to find good pieces of traditional Moroccan **jewellery**, although you will have to hunt for it, and know your prices in advance. The opportunities for self-adornment are innumerable: silver crosses based on the traditional designs of the Tuareg and other Saharan tribes; green and yellow enamelled silver eggs from Tiznit; thick silver bracelets; a cascade of bangles; pairs of ornate triangular brooches linked by a chain; golden Hand of Fatima pendants; pierced coins; necklace medallions; small hanging boxes for miniature Korans or an Islamic prayer; or a thick rope of amber or cornelian beads interspaced with silver arrow heads. As well as all this there are the sumptuous necessities of a modern Moroccan marriage: golden tiaras, belts, bracelets, earrings and rings studded with emeralds and brilliants. Moroccan jewellers are an entirely courteous but comparatively restrained breed of salesmen. Even so, one sometimes returns with something that looks just too 'tribal' back home. Many an aunt and niece have become the surprised beneficiaries of Berber pieces that the buyer found impossible to wear.

Some 40 percent of Morocco's workforce are still in agriculture, many of them working with livestock, so it should come as no surprise that **leather products** are ubiquitous. The distinctive Moroccan slippers, the pointed and trodden-heeled *babouches*, are immediately useful. They are for men and come in grey, white and yellow. You can also hunt for a softer chamois-leather version in a much larger field of colours. The heavily embroidered and gilded versions are supposedly for women, but tend to have little flexibility or much use except for a dinner party. Gilt-embroidered belts can be easily absorbed into Western dress. They look better and more amusingly ostentatious the shabbier the trousers they support. Check when buying, however, that the leather isn't cardboard, that it has been stitched, not just glued, and that the buckle is strong enough. Stamped and gilded red and ochre portfolio wallets come in a range of sizes. They are generally made of fine leather and make admirable cases for letters, documents, bills you have no wish to pay, or as a detachable binding for a book. The complete desk sets found in many leather shops (a blotter, envelope stand and desk-size portfolio) are also usually of a high quality. If you have time, ask for a favourite book to be Morocco-bound.

There is a mass of decorated **brass plates** and **silver-coloured implements** in every bazaar. Candlesticks, mirrors, trays, incense burners, cake stands and ornate kettles attached to bowls (for the washing of hands before a meal) can be acquired before you even realized you had a need. The distinctive silver-coloured Moroccan teapot is the most attractive single item. The weak hinge of the lid and the failure of the insulating joints on the handle seem to be universal faults. Throughout Morocco, handkerchiefs are used for pouring and bent nails secure the lid.

For a few dirhams you can pick up superb pieces of **Sahara rose and amethyst** from the High Atlas, south of Marrakesh. The three principal fossils are the spiral swirls of the goniates, the long cones of the orthoceres, and the compressed tapeworm-like forms of the trilobites. There are plenty of stalls selling these 400-million-year-old minerals on the roadsides of the High Atlas passes, and also in Marrakesh.

Moroccan spices, principally cumin, harissa (hot pepper), paprika, ginger, saffron, cinnamon and bunches of fresh mint, coriander and parsley create the most colourful displays in the souk. The intriguing displays of the apothecary and cosmetic stalls are often found close by, selling blocks of silvery antimony, kohl (ground antimony for the eyes), henna (in leaf or powder), *ghassol* (a brown mud for washing), snib (for stopping shaving cuts), cochineal, porcupine quills, tooth-cleaning twigs, incense and dried Dadès roses.

The skilled carvers and joiners of Essaouira, which is accessible as a day trip from Marrakesh (*see* p.166), work upon odiferous thuja wood to create some of the most attractive and durable items that you can acquire in Morocco. **Inlaid chessboards, backgammon sets, polished boxes** and **carved jars** can be bought directly from the craftsmen. Watch out for the hinges, which are invariably shoddy, and hunt around for boxes that have snugly fitting lids. It is not a new trade, for the Romans were mad about thuja wood and spent fortunes on tables.

Bargaining

This is a necessary art that is fully enjoyed and understood in Morocco. For a foreign traveller, transport, hotel and restaurant prices are all fixed. It is only for the purchase of local crafts (and the odd taxi ride) that your bargaining skills will be required. A visit to a museum to remind yourself of what quality you are aspiring to, and to a state-run **Ensemble Artisanal** for the maximum price, is a good start: you will be helpless unless you have a firm and confident idea of the price you should be paying.

It is good tactics, and in the highest order of gamesmanship, to greet the shopkeeper, shake his hand and praise his colourful display of goods before he does. Look at some items other than what you are actually interested in first, and have a friend act out the negative, mean and unenthusiastic role. Accept as many cups of tea as you are offered and delay for as long as possible the mention of your first price, praising the goods but looking sad, wistful and tearful in turn at the impossible prices. Once you have named your price be obstinate, and watch out for the skilfully deployed ratchet gambit by which he gradually drops his price in exchange for a gradual rise in yours.

There are three rules:
1. Never bargain for something you don't want.
2. Don't hurry.
3. Even if you think you have just made a great financial coup, praise your opponent for his ruthless hard bargaining and great skill.

Sports and Activities

The sport of choice in Morocco (especially among the young) is **football**, played on dusty stretches of turf throughout the country. Morocco has a good national team, Lions of the Atlas, and you can watch the local teams in all major cities. Try *www.frmf.ma* (French only) for tickets but it might be easier to ask your hotel to book.

Moroccans are exceptional long-distance runners and the country hosts the infamous

Marathon des Sables in the Sahara, a 7-day, 150-mile race through the desert. If you prefer one marathon at a time, the **Marrakesh Marathon** takes place in the relative cool of January.

In the Atlas, **fishing** is particularly rich, with small trout called *farios* and some imported rainbows. There are also ocean-fishing expeditions available, notably from Mohammedia near Casablanca. Fishing permits (for coarse or fly) are available through the Administration des Eaux et Forêts, 11, Rue Moulay Abdelaziz, Rabat t 0537 762694 or its regional equivalent (ask at tourist offices).

Morocco's long Atlantic coast is a fabulous place to surf. There is good **surfing** near Agadir and Safi and excellent **windsurfing** close to Essaouira. You can even get surf lessons in some of these places, although the waves can be big and you must be especially careful of the Atlantic undertow. If you do get caught, remember not to swim against it but parallel to the beach until you escape the core of the current. **Swimming** and **water sports** more generally are popular too, and at Mohammedia and Essaouira all sorts of sports and activities have grown up around the resorts, many of them well suited to children, such as donkey rides and pedaloes.

There is plenty of **golf** to be had in Morocco in or just outside all the major cities, notably the Marrakesh Royal and the lynx course at Mohammedia. The Moroccan Royal Golf Federation in Rabat (*www.frmg.ma*) should help and can advise on eco-friendly courses too, as golf is usually not the best use of this desert country's water resources.

Morocco has cottoned onto the global love for **hiking** and provided all sorts of mountain trails, guides and rural accommodation to fuel it. Several foreign tour operators can help you with this, but the tourist offices of each city will give you brochures and other details.

Some may prefer an animal to do the work for them, in which case **riding** is your best bet. Expeditions are even available where you take tents with you, carried by mules (try La Roseraie Hotel, south of Marrakesh, p.157).

If you want no more than to say you have 'skied Africa' then Oukaïmeden in the High Atlas is close to Marrakesh and perhaps your best option.

Students

Morocco recognises the international student (ISIC) card and offers some discounts. Check www.isic.org for full details, but discounts include free breakfast when you stay at the Ibis Moussafir hotels in all the major cities covered in this guide. Museums do not generally offer student discounts in Morocco but there are many music and arts festivals where your ISIC card will get you a discount. Internal travel with Royal Air Maroc is 60% cheaper with an ISIC card.

Telephones

For assistance dial t 160.

It's best not to use your mobile In Morocco as roaming charges tend to be extortionate, especially for iPhones. But you could simply buy a local SIM card for 30dh instead.

Morocco is well-supplied with small blue Maroc Telecom shops (téléboutiques in French) where you can buy your SIM or make calls from a cubicle using coins or phone cards, which range in price quite widely, from about 20 to 160 dirhams.

There are also street phone boxes dotted around the cities, although not usually in the medina. Be aware of recent changes in area codes in Morocco, as a digit has been added to these. Do not use area codes when calling from within that code area.

Area codes within Morocco

t 0548	Agadir
t 0522	Casablanca
t 0535	Fez, Meknès
t 0234	Marrakesh
t 0537	Rabat
t 0531	Tangier

Toilets

There is no need to feel embarrassed about asking to use a lavatory for, unlike the staff in London pubs, no waiter or barman would dream of refusing a passer-by in need. Afterwards you could stop and order a drink, a simple coffee or Fanta, and leave an extra tip in grateful thanks.

Most classified hotels and large restaurants are equipped with Anglo-Saxon flush bowls, though water supplies and efficient drainage can be variable, particularly in summer. It is a wasteful system for a nation grappling with the recurring problems of drought, and has been established largely for the benefit of tourists.

Urban cafés and houses have a crouch hole and no paper, but a tap for washing your left hand and an old tin for sluicing. Outside the largest cities, public lavatories are unknown. Hedgerows, dung heaps, beaches and ruins are freely used by the locals.

Women

Moroccans traditionally have an uncomplicated attitude to sex – chauvinist to women and liberal to men – but a great respect for outward modesty. Homosexuality is treated as essentially a matter of taste but is to be kept out of public view. The Koran, unlike Judaism and Roman Catholicism, celebrates the pleasure of sex and encourages it.

Aids awareness is limited but growing. Prostitution is prevalent in Morocco (where is it not?) and many Moroccans still view Aids as a western disease, but known infection rates remain low in the country at less than 25,000, according to the Health Ministry.

Life is much improved for women in Morocco since a raft of reforms were introduced to family law in 2004. As a result, women are now allowed to file for divorce and men are less free to swiftly cancel the marriage almost whenever they wished. But Morocco remains a man's world nevertheless and attitudes to women are complicated. If you are a woman travelling alone, you would be wise to cover arms and legs much of the time and avoid staying out late in the evenings on your own.

In general, Moroccan men conceive of mature women in three guises: the mother whom they adore, the wife in whose modest conduct rests all the honour of her husband, and all other women, who are potential objects of their desire. This is particularly true of women who show themselves in the public domain of streets and cafés, let alone in bars and restaurants. Western women (especially in view of their power to bestow a foreign passport on the father of their children) are all near-automatically placed in the third category to a greater or lesser degree.

Morocco consequently tends to divide women travellers between those who couldn't cope and those who loved it. Dig a little deeper and you will often find that the former went alone or with another woman, and had never been to a Muslim country before. Of course there are single women who have holidayed happily in Morocco, but they tend to have a proven track record as independent travellers. If in doubt, err on the cautious side. There's no point in having a miserable trip, and no stigma attached to not feeling comfortable in a country where the men tend to see white women as possible lays and have little respect for them. If you do travel with a man, the most irritating thing will be the way in which any decision will be instantly referred to him by Moroccans. The easiest way to cope if you're alone is to play one of the stereotyped but recognizably 'less available' roles: the wife, the mother, the intellectual or the sportsperson.

There are no easy ways to deal with a hand where you don't want it, but being soberly dressed will make you less of a target. Be open and straightforward, and don't be embarrassed to yell loudly at the man, in any language. He'll understand, and suffer the indignity of a public reproval. A sharp slap, satisfying as it might be, only seems to make things worse. In some of the larger towns it is not advisable for single females, or even female couples, to stay in the cheapest medina hotels.

For a sense of sorority go to the local women's *hammam*. Laughter and curious communication, if not outright friendship, will result. By way of reading matter, any of the studies of women and sexual politics by Fatima Mernissi make compelling – if depressing – reading (*see* Further Reading p.304). It is much, much more difficult for Moroccan women than one can possibly imagine. As Fatima Mernissi has observed, *'The conception of the woman as a lust-driven animal that must be kept under lock and key is one of the sickest and most disgusting aspects of Arab culture.'* So is the sad record of male divorce and the neglect of their responsibilities as a father, though this has much more to do with poverty and lack of opportunity than any cultural determinant.

Marrakesh

Marrakesh the Red is the heart that beats an African identity into the complex soul of Morocco. The city walls, overlooked by the Koutoubia minaret, are framed by the towering blue wall of the High Atlas mountains. From outside, the city promises much, but at first it may seem to contain nothing more than a vast transitory souk. The Jemaa el Fna, the celebrated square at the centre of the medina, is full of visiting farmers, as well as snake charmers, storytellers and fortune-readers.

Marrakesh is strikingly African compared with the Atlantic character of Casablanca, and the intensely Arab attitude of Fez; yet it is not some desert border town but a city with a long and proud record as an imperial capital.

07

Don't miss

1 Market streets
Medina souks p.108

2 Cloistered beauty
Ben Youssef Medersa p.113

3 Unearthly sepulchres
Saadian Tombs p.122

4 The Vizier's garden mansion
El Bahia Palace p.128

5 Technicolour traditions
Tanneries p.133

See map overleaf

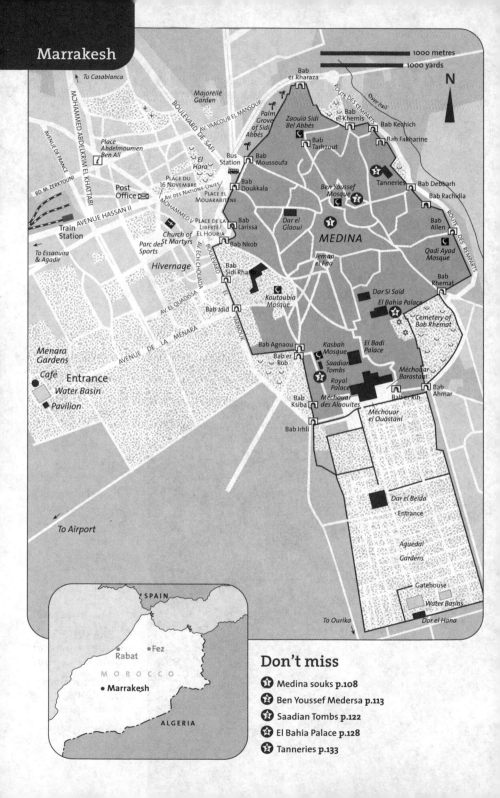

The name Marrakesh, corrupted by European travellers, has provided us with the word Morocco. The derivation of the word Marrakesh is more problematical. It means to 'cross and hide', a reference to its first role as a fortress beyond the mountains.

The Phoenicians, Romans, Arabs and Idrissids ruled over a mere portion of Morocco, a patchwork of hills and the northern Atlantic coast. The Empire of Morocco was first created not by any of these distinguished, alien powers, but by a Berber tribe from the depths of the western Sahara. They were the first to forge a Moroccan identity by linking a vast continental hinterland to the civilized lands of the northwest. Marrakesh was the Berber capital, a city where they embraced Islam and an urban culture on their own terms. Here they brought together, like heraldic symbols of the future state, palm trees from the desert and craftsmen from Andalucía. The composite identity they created remains to this day.

The city's guaranteed dry heat, the heady atmosphere of its souks, its celebrated monuments and the nearby mountain valleys of the High Atlas have a universal appeal. It is a fascinating city, the central objective of most visitors to Morocco, but be aware that you will not be alone: Marrakesh is, alongside Agadir, Morocco's chief tourist destination. In recent years it has turned some five hundred riads into small hotels; Hollywood stars and European bankers alike have acquired holiday houses in the city; and Ryanair and easyJet have brought it into the European budget airspace. Marrakesh remains a Muslim city on the edge of the Atlas Mountains and Sahara desert, but its orientation may be shifting.

Rural Moroccans have moved here in increasing numbers too. The farming fields that surrounded the airport just a decade ago are now home to large housing developments and the city's population is now around 1.65 million. There are still beggars and madmen aplenty on the streets of Marrakesh but unemployment, the bugbear of estranged neighbour Algeria, has been in decline in Morocco (except in the wake of the global financial crisis) and the Red City must take some of the credit.

Yet Marrakesh is also undeniably demanding. As always in Morocco, take things slowly and do not try to rush your way through its precious store of monuments or its labyrinthine markets. Marrakesh has stood for a thousand years, has endured generations of star-struck travellers, and its thick-lidded eyes will not be stirred by much.

History

Orientation around the city is best managed by remembering the contours of the medina, shaped a little like a lollipop with the Royal Palace and Aguedal Gardens to the south forming the stick. Within the medina itself you cannot usually see the Koutoubia minaret for the narrowness of the alleyways but the Jemaa el Fna forms the vortex of everything and you are best to ask a shopkeeper for directions, since he is less likely to insist on guiding you there in return for money.

Foundation and Empire (1062–1147)

Archaeologists have found that the site of Marrakesh has been almost continually occupied since Neolithic times, but the modern city has its origins in an Almoravid garrison town of the 11th century. In 1062, Abu Bekr, an early commander of the Almoravids, threw up a wall of thorn bushes to protect his camp and built a fortress amid his tented army, the Ksar el Hajar, 'the tower of stone'. Nine years later he appointed his young cousin, Youssef ben Tachfine, to command this new post. The meteoric conquest of Morocco and Spain by Youssef ben Tachfine from this base marks the true foundation of both the city and the Almoravid Empire. Marrakesh's position on the border of three agricultural regions meant that it soon eclipsed the older towns of Aghmat and Nfis to become the main market for the farmers of the Tensift valley, the nomadic pastoralists of the plains and the Masmuda Atlas tribes. It still has that feel to this day. It was Youssef ben Tachfine's son and successor, Ali ben Youssef, who built the great circuit of walls, two large mosques, palaces and fountains, which were all superbly decorated by Andalucian carvers. The Almoravids brought the technology of desert survival and used it to improve the city's seasonal water supply. Long *khettera* (pipes) were built to carry water underground from the High Atlas mountains to the houses and gardens of Marrakesh. But the Almoravids were undone by trouble in their border regions, including their campaigns to defend Muslim Andalucía, and by their eager acceptance of the imams' political counsel.

The Capital City of the Almohad Empire (1147–1269)

After decades of warfare between the Almoravid Sultans and the Almohads, whose headquarters were tucked up in the High Atlas mountains, the walled city of Marrakesh finally fell in 1147. The new ruler had studied in the Levant, probably in Cairo or Damascus, and preached a stricter social code than the city had known, including the veiling of women. Sufism and scholarship combined to make the city a centre of Muslim learning. The Almohads deliberately demolished any evidence of the previous dynasty and remade the city in their own image. It did, however, remain the capital city of a great empire, and the monumental buildings of this period – the Koutoubia Mosque, the El Mansour Mosque, the Bab Agnaou – still dominate the city. Almohad princes ruled on in Marrakesh decades after the rest of their empire had fallen into the hands of rival dynasties. Like the Almoravids before them, they were fated to die defending the walls of the city, which were finally breached by the Merenids in 1269.

A Decaying City (1269–1524)

Under the Merenid sultans (1248–1465) Morocco was ruled from Fez, Marrakesh stagnated into a provincial town and the gold routes moved further east. Tribal forms of government also detracted from the city's success, since they lacked the bureaucratic weight of manpower. By the early years of the 16th century even this period's limited prosperity had ended. Portuguese cavalry raided the region, reaching as far as the walls of the city, Ottoman Turks were poised to advance from the east, and the authority of the central government, threatened by dozens of rival dynasties, had shrunk to the area around Fez. In 1524 the dilapidated city welcomed the rule of Mohammed ech Cheikh, forceful founder of the Saadian dynasty, whose power was based on the tribes of the south. Using Marrakesh as his base, Mohammed ech Cheikh succeeded in subduing the rest of the country. He was murdered in a High Atlas valley by an Ottoman assassination squad. The governor of Marrakesh promptly ordered the murder of six of his sons, to clear the succession for Abdullah el Ghalib.

The Golden Capital of the Saadians (1524–1668)

The reigns of Abdullah el Ghalib and his half-brother Ahmed el Mansour, 'the victorious' (also known as El Dehbi, 'the golden'), witnessed a magnificent revival in the prosperity of Marrakesh. Abdullah founded the Mellah, rebuilt the kasbah and the Ben Youssef Mosque and Medersa, and built a hospital and the new Mouassine Mosque. Ahmed built the incomparable El Badi Palace and the Saadian Tombs, and sprinkled the city with fountains, fondouqs, libraries and *hammams*. The prosperity of Marrakesh in these centuries was partly based on a thriving trade in sugar, saltpetre, cotton and silk. The city became the collection and transit point for the produce of the Sahara and sub-Sahara – slaves, gold, ivory, gum arabic and ostrich feathers – which was then exported through the Atlantic ports.

Alaouite Marrakesh, the Twin Capital (1668–1912)

The vicious civil wars of the late 17th and early 18th centuries, in which Marrakesh was repeatedly besieged and plundered, were a disaster from which it never entirely recovered. Sultan Moulay Ismaïl (1672–1727) restored the religious shrines of the city but decided to rule from a new capital in Meknès. Later Alaouite sultans attempted to check the city's continued decline by

Getting to and away from Marrakesh

By Air

The Menara **international airport** in Marrakesh (t 0524 447865, *open 8am–6pm*) is 5km southwest of town and has two terminals: a third is slated to open in 2012. There is, theoretically, a bus (no.11) to the city every half-hour. There are *grand* and *petit taxi* ranks at the airport: drivers can be quite extravagant in their demands, though 50dh is usually considered an acceptable tourist rate. As well as international flights there is a regular schedule of internal RAM services to Casablanca (not far from Rabat) and Agadir. Further information and prices are available from the RAM office (*see* below) or from Atlas Blue. Return tickets should be reconfirmed here a day or two before departure. For international flights, *see* Planning p.75.

Airline Offices

These tend to be in the *ville nouvelle* (Guéliz) or at the airport itself.

Air France: No Marrakesh office. Contact them in Casablanca or Rabat. 15 Ave des FAR, Casablanca, t 0890 201 818, *www.airfrance.fr; open Mon–Fri 8.30am–12pm and 2pm–6.30pm, Sat 9am–12pm*. 281 Ave Mohammed V, Rabat; *open Mon–Fri 8.30am–12pm and 2pm–6.30pm, Sat 9am–12pm*.

Atlas Blue: Menara (Marrakesh) Airport, t 082 009090, *www.royalairmaroc.com*.

British Airways: 47 Rue Allal Ben Abdullah, Centre Allal Ben Abdullah (7th floor), Casablanca, t 0522 433300, *www.ba.com; open 8.30am–12pm and 2.30pm–6pm, Sat 9am–12pm*. Also at Menara (Marrakesh) airport, t 0524 448951.

Royal Air Maroc: 7 Ave Mohammed V, Marrakesh, t 089 000 0800 , *www.royalairmaroc.com*.

easyJet (*www.easyjet.com*) and **Ryanair** (*www.ryanair.com*) do not have offices in Morocco.

By Train

Marrakesh's monumental **railway station** (t 0524 446569), reopened in 2009, is in the *ville nouvelle* opposite the Royal Theatre. It sits on Ave de France just off the crossroads with Ave Hassan II. Nine trains a day travel north to Casablanca (4hrs) and some five a day to Fez (via Rabat and Meknès). These last trains tend to leave on the odd hours from about 11am. There is also a sleeper train to Tangier which should be booked well in advance. The regularity of services between Morocco's main cities has increased at an impressive clip in recent years so check timetables.

Train is the best means of travel between the large cities and is inexpensive. It is generally best to book first class, since the difference in price is minimal, it ensures you a seat and, as one fellow traveller explained, there is a high chance the air conditioning might work too.

Arriving in Marrakesh, you are likely to be met by touts as you leave the station. Take a *petit taxi* (licensed for up to three people) and get rid of your luggage at a hotel. Thankfully, a sea change in manners has occurred since some of the taxis have started using their meters. If the meter is not working, allow 15dh for the drive to your hotel. Alternatively, catch a no.3 or a no.8 local bus from the station to the Jemaa el Fna.

Buying tickets at the station is very straightforward as staff speak some English and all tickets are bought at the same counters. If you have time to kill, there are a few fast-food restaurants and, if you cross the main road and turn left along the next street up (i.e. not Ave de France but Ave Muhammed), there's a very well-stocked camera shop on the left just after you turn.

By Long-Distance Bus

Most buses depart from the modern depot just outside the Bab Doukkala on Place el Mouarabitène, around 10–12dh by taxi from the Jemaa el Fna. It is usually worth buying tickets a day in advance and you should note that some services leave as early as four in the morning. Take your time to sort out the various alternatives on sale from the kiosk windows, and you can mull over the final details of your travel plans in the station's garden-café. Otherwise, facilities are generally unpleasant but at least there is a working left-luggage office. Casablanca, Rabat, Fez and Meknès are favourite destinations from here (and you take a more direct, but still a little slower, route than the train for Fez and Meknès).

There are currently around eight buses a day to Rabat (5–6hrs), almost hourly departures for Casablanca (4hrs) and three a day to Fez (11hrs).

CTM, t 0524 438202, is the best company to use and, although their services leave from the same station and they do have a ticket window there (number ten), it might be easier to buy from their office at 12 Blvd Mohammed Zerkhouni in the *ville nouvelle* (note that their international bus services to Paris and Madrid depart from outside the office). Bus is an especially good way to reach Essaouira, taking around three hours, but it's a popular line and you should buy tickets well in advance.

Supratours, t 0524 435525, is good for buses to the coast, and is based near the train station on Ave Hassan II.

By *Grand Taxi*

These leave from on the northern side of the main bus station, beside the train station and off the Jemaa el Fna. They offer two challenges. The first is to negotiate a reasonable price. The second, if you are a group, is to ensure exclusive use of the vehicle, since drivers will want to pick up other paying travellers which usually means taking detours to get them to their destination. You are best to organize a *grand taxi* through your hotel or riad if possible. Failing that, be prepared to put in a good performance to get your desired price. Expect to pay around 130dh for a seat to Essaouira and very slightly less to Agadir. If you are taking a *grand taxi* to nearby areas (such as the Ourika Valley for 20dh), catch it by the Royal Palace. A taxi for the day to Ourika or up the Tizi-n-Test should come to 300–330dh.

By Car

You will not need a car in the city until it is time to leave. The smaller car hire companies offer cheaper deals, but this is often reflected in the condition of their cars and their legal contracts. One misadventure that ended up with a protracted two-day negotiation at a police station has given me a bias towards the more reputable mainstream operators:

Avis: 9 Ave Mohammed V, **t** 0524 432525; airport office **t** 0524 433169.
Europcar: 63 Blvd Zerkhtouni, **t** 0524 431228.
Hertz: airport, **t** 052 447239; 154 Ave Mohammed V, **t** 0524 439984.
Always: Complex Kawkab Centre, Guéliz, **t** 0524 446797. With an English-speaking team, and delivers the car to your hotel.
Concorde Cars: t 0524 431116.

You can **park** anywhere off the Ave Mohammed V in the New Town – providing the pavement is not decorated with a red-and-white no-parking stripe – in any big hotel, or at the Jemaa el Fna in front of the Hôtel de Foucauld. There is also a car park in an old covered bus depot immediately beside the CTM Hotel. Another useful place is the car park behind the Koutoubia Mosque, approached off Ave Mohammed V. In the old town, you can usually park next to the main gates into the medina, sometimes in a car park (around 30dh) or else under the watchful eye of a blue-uniformed attendant, who you should pay 10dh to on returning to your vehicle.

Mopeds can be rented from Marrakesh Motos at 31 Ave Muhammed Abdelkrim el-Khattabi, **t** 0524 448359, which stays open until 10pm, and from Aboul Abdallah, 14 Blvd El-Khattabi, **t** 0524 432238.

Bicycles can be rented in several places around the medina including Hotel Ali, **t** 0524 444979. For sturdy mountain bikes to head outside town and perhaps into the hills, Marrakesh Motos and Aboul Abdallah (*see* above) are better options.

alternating government between Fez and Marrakesh, and many of the city's finest buildings date from the 18th and 19th centuries. The comparative order and prosperity of Moulay Hassan's reign (1873–94) is revealed in the large number of opulent merchants' houses and the palaces of the Bahia and Dar Si Saïd, built by viziers during the minority of his son, Abdul Aziz.

But the city remained pitifully backward. At the turn of the 20th century, as rebels traded guns and slaves and gold across the Sahara to Marrakesh, there were still no wind or steam mills in the city, and trade depended on pack animals being safely escorted past the Rehamna tribe to Essaouira. While Morocco's trade with Britain and Spain ballooned, Marrakesh stayed in the background.

The 20th Century and Beyond

Growing European influence was bitterly resented, culminating in the lynching of a French resident, a Dr Mauchamp, after he attached an aerial to his roof in 1907. Personal resentment against Dr Mauchamp was intense, from both native healers and city traders who were infuriated that with his aerial the doctor could discover prices in Essaouira days before they could. The city mob, for their part, was convinced the aerial was a sorcerer's device, for it was well known on the streets, and with some truth, that Mauchamp had great knowledge of the occult. This lynching proved to be one of several incidents that provided the excuse for the French landings in Casablanca in the same year. Five years later the French army occupied the city, having destroyed the tribal army of El Hiba, the Blue Sultan, at Sidi-Bou-Othmane. Marrakesh became an important centre of French influence in the south, though the city's old predominance was deliberately shattered with the location of the new commercial centre at Casablanca. In Marrakesh the French built a new town, 'Guéliz', to the west of the old city, its ordered avenues and quiet leafy suburbs overlooked by their enormous army barracks. Within a generation they had adorned the region with roads, hotels, pylons, railways, schools, irrigation works and hospitals. Apart from the roads, these technical advances were for the benefit of colonial farmers and the caidal allies of the French. Their chief ally was Si Thami el Glaoui, the fabulously wealthy Pasha of Marrakesh, who ruled a medina in which an estimated 20,000 registered prostitutes lived.

Independence in 1956 brought a swift and bloody end to the pasha's corrupt regime. Greater Marrakesh today houses a rapidly expanding population that may not be far off two million. It is the most important administrative and industrial centre of the south, and earns valuable foreign currency as a tourist destination. The spread of car and scooter ownership, while an encouraging indicator of the distribution of wealth, has had a damaging effect on the air. It is very doubtful that today you could follow Churchill's example and visit the city as a cure for bronchitis. Marrakesh is a more international city than it has ever been and no stranger to the bulging wallets of Europeans or even the bottomless bank accounts of visitors from the Gulf. But it is still a natural marketplace, with a cultural life that recalls both the splendour of its periods as an imperial capital and the traditions of its rural Berber hinterland.

Highlights of Marrakesh

For those with limited time in Marrakesh, an effort should be made to visit the magnificent cloistered Ben Youssef Medersa and the evocative Saadian Tombs. A walk through the souks with dinner in the Jemaa el Fna is the best way to experience the city's vigorous street life and playful, artistic bargaining culture.

To retreat into the Marrakesh's best natural scenes, the Bahia Palace and Aguedal Gardens are exceptional. As for ruins, the monumental El Badi Palace is without rival.

Orientation

Central Medina and Jemaa el Fna

The Jemaa el Fna is the variety show at the centre of Marrakesh and always a useful landmark by which to navigate, as everyone knows where it is. To its west, the Koutoubia minaret is visible from many parts of the city and, if you are really lost and need to find something familiar, a roof terrace may be your salvation. North, south and east of the main square lie the city's principal souks, which are perhaps the most disorienting areas in Marrakesh.

Southern Medina

The southern parts of the medina are some of the most attractive and the Place des Ferblantiers usefully marks the middle of its northern side. The Mellah became the home of the city's Jews in the 16th century and next to it is the old Jewish cemetery. But to the north lies the the Bahia Palace and its glorious plants while a few minutes walk directly west bring you to the idyllic Saadian tombs and the expansive ruins of the Badi Palace. The southern extreme is filled by the idyllic Aguedal Gardens.

Northern Medina

Immediately north of the souks that flank the upper side of Jemaa el Fna is the most elegant building in Morocco, the Ben Youssef Medersa. Further north again, wasted spaces, cracked concrete and graffiti become more of a feature, but the mosques of Sidi ben Slimane and Sidi Bel Abbès are both up here.

Ville Nouvelle: Guéliz and Hivernage

The *ville nouvelle* was the French answer to mixing colonialism with respect for the local way of life and it emanates from the Place du 16 Novembre. The new railway station and royal theatre are a little to the west. The main part of this area is Guéliz, imprecisely named after the Roman Catholic cathedral.

The Medina

The Koutoubia Mosque

The minaret of the Koutoubia Mosque appears at its most elegant from a great distance. Approaching Marrakesh from the High Atlas, the tower rises magnificently above the barely perceptible city, and you can begin to understand the veneration in which it is held locally. The interior of the mosque (and minaret) are, of course, closed to non-Muslims. The dusty wasteland that once surrounded it has been converted into a sparse, somewhat tired garden, while the surrounding ruins – of the earlier mosque and elements from the Almoravid palace – have been exposed, stabilized and enclosed within a piazza. An elegant new paved street now allows the visitor to walk right up to the mosque and pass below the towering minaret.

This wasteland was once the centre of the city. The Almoravid Sultan Ali ben Youssef rebuilt his father's mosque and added a new palace to the south, on the site of the present Koutoubia, but both buildings were razed to the ground when the Almohads captured Marrakesh in 1147. Abdel Moumen, the Almohad sultan, immediately started on the construction of a new mosque, but the work was pushed forward too quickly. It was found wanting (among other faults it was incorrectly aligned to Mecca) and was dismantled soon after its completion. The excavations have clearly revealed this first mosque immediately to the north of the present one. Undeterred by this failure, Abdel Moumen ordered a fresh start. This, the Koutoubia, followed the same plan, though it was slightly wider and with an interior dominated by a forest of horseshoe arches resting on solid square pillars decorated by pairs of pilasters. Five domes rise along the high, wide central aisle to focus attention on the *mihrab* prayer niche. At the opposite end, the open-air *sahn* courtyard, the place for ritual ablutions, also served as the customary place for lectures on the Koran and Islamic law before the construction of *medersas* in the 13th century.

Owing to the vagaries of the site, the minaret was positioned in the northeastern corner of the mosque. It was only completed in the reign of Abdel Moumen's grandson Sultan Yaacoub el Mansour, one of the world's greatest architectural patrons, who was also responsible for the Giralda Tower in Seville and the Hassan Tower in Rabat. From its 12m by 12m base the minaret rises to almost 70m. It was built from an internal ramp that climbs between its double walls. This connects six rooms that increase in delicate ornamentation as they ascend. Each side of the minaret has a different decorative scheme, and the boldly carved lancet windows are a study in Almohad design. The decoration grows more intricate as you cast your eyes from ground to apex, beginning with basic keystone arches, then adding scalloping to them before culminating in the rich interlinked arches of the top storey, above which is a last surviving band of faïence decoration. This work would originally have been obscured by pinkish plaster and decoration, as the restored minaret of the Almohad Kasbah Mosque shows. Fortunately, restoration work on the Koutoubia has revealed the original stonework.

Above the faïence band a decorative battlement frames the domed minaret, which was built in a strict one-to-five proportion to the tower, the golden rule for all Maghrebi minarets. On the summit are the wooden gallows common to minarets across Morocco, and which always point towards Mecca. On them flies a blue or green prayer flag on Friday, next to three golden balls surmounted by a tear. These are thought to be the gift of Yaacoub el Mansour's wife, who melted down all her jewellery in penance for having eaten three grapes during Ramadan.

The new mosque was once enclosed by streets where hundreds of copyists, scribes, binders and booksellers kept stalls. It is from this surrounding souk of books, the *kutubiyyin*, that it takes its name. For its inauguration in 1158 Abdel Moumen had a

Getting around Marrakesh

Petits Taxis

Petits taxis are found along the length of Ave Mohammed V, by the covered market in the New Town, by the bus station, train station and by the Jemaa el Fna. Bargaining a decent price used to be an exhausting part of Marrakesh life, but the use of meters is now widespread. Take advantage of these little cabs whenever possible. Your driver may mock-refuse to use the meter; a good-humoured, gesticulating insistence should help.

By Carriage

For a horse-drawn carriage that seats five, 100dh an hour is a generous price, but it may be easier to settle one overall price for a tour of the ramparts and gardens, which will cost perhaps 140dh and take an hour-and-a-half. In the last few years the carriages have been equipped with a municipally approved list of maximum prices, which is an aid but not a conclusive element in the bargaining process. To go anywhere in the medina should cost 15dh, thanks to state-fixed prices.

On one trip, when my birthday coincided with the feast of Achoura, this rather hackneyed tourist excursion proved to be one of the most enchanting journeys of my life. We set off before dusk with both of the kerosene side lamps lit, and drove for hours, passing mosques with their silent queues of seated paupers waiting for the traditional festival charity, and through unknown back streets thronged with young children beating their festival drums, demanding presents and dancing around bonfires that scattered wild shadows on the glowing red walls. When it came to paying, the driver had lowered his price (perhaps because the back wheel came off twice), but we then doubled it as our two-year-old daughter, who had sat mesmerized with delight on the driving bench, had clearly fallen in love with both the ancient driver and his horse.

By Bus

Local buses depart from Rue Moulay Ismaïl, beside the triangular garden at the southern end of the Jemaa el Fna. Useful routes include:

No.1 goes right along Ave Mohammed V to below the Guéliz hill
No.2 passes the Bab Doukkala bus station
Nos.3 and 14 head along Ave Mohammed V and Ave Hassan II to the train station
No.4 goes along Ave Mohammed V and then on to the El-Jadida road
No.5 goes on to the Béni-Mellal road (useful for Souk el Khemis)
No.6 passes the Quartier Industriel (and the youth hostel)
No.7 goes to Ave Hassan II and farther northwest
No.8 runs along Ave Mohammed V and Ave Hassan II
No.10 goes to Bab Doukkala and the Safi road
No.11 runs to the airport via the Menara Gardens.

spectacular trophy to display, for he had just acquired from conquered Córdoba one of the four original copies of the third Caliph Uthman's official compilation of the Koran. From these all later texts descend.

The imposing walled building just to the southeast of the Koutoubia is the French consulate. South of this stands the Place Youssef ben Tachfine, overlooked by a modest tomb. This is the traditional tomb of the great warrior and founder of Marrakesh. His grave was despoiled by the Almohads but reconsecrated by the Merenids in the 14th century. The tomb is left open to the sky, the only dome that the spirit of this desert warrior will accept.

The Jemaa el Fna

Three hundred metres east of the Koutoubia Mosque lies the great central square of the medina, the Jemaa el Fna, popularly translated as 'the place of the dead', a suitably chilling phrase which adds a whiff of exoticism and savage justice to an otherwise undeniably lively place. A less entertaining but probably correct translation is 'the mosque that came to nothing' – a sly reference to the Saadian Sultan Ahmed el Mansour's abortive attempt to build a mosque here.

The square has always been at the centre of medina life, and started as the formal *méchouar* (an open space generally next to a palace in which to make pledges of allegiance) in front of the Almoravid kasbah. When the Almohads moved the kasbah to the south of the city, official processions were increasingly staged there, but in essence the Jemaa el Fna has always been as it is now, a popular forum for entertainment, celebration, riots, gossip and business.

At dawn it is an empty wedge of tarmac, surrounded by parked cars, shuttered cafés and bazaars, an area of no architectural interest. As the morning progresses a perimeter is formed by lines of barrows selling nuts and freshly squeezed orange juice, and the edges of the square erupt in a sea of shops. The centre is filled by a random and changing assortment of snake charmers, storytellers, acrobats, dentists, water-sellers, scribes, bands of musicians, monkeys, clowns and dancing boys, who during the day direct most of their skills to camera-carrying tourists.

But at dusk the Jemaa el Fna comes into its own, and returns to its true audience of visiting Berber farmers from the plains, desert and mountains. Lines of kitchens set up their groaning tables, braziers and benches beneath hissing gas lamps. Here you can dine on an assortment of salads, vats of brewing goat's-head soup, fresh grilled or fried vegetables, chicken, fish and mutton. You can move from table to table trying different platefuls and break off to wander among the musicians and the storytellers. Sharp young street kids hiss 'Hashish!', veiled women offer trinkets, or sit beckoning by their stock of woven baskets and woolly hats. Blind beggars cry 'Allah!' as they extend a bowl or fix you with one accusing, rheumy eye. Innocent-looking children with beguiling almond eyes solicit, or try rather clumsily to pick your pockets. From worn tarot cards, the waddle of sacred doves, ink dots, cast bones or your palm, incidents from a possible future will be divined by hunched figures perched on low stools, surrounded by the instruments of their trade. As the evening progresses, the crowds

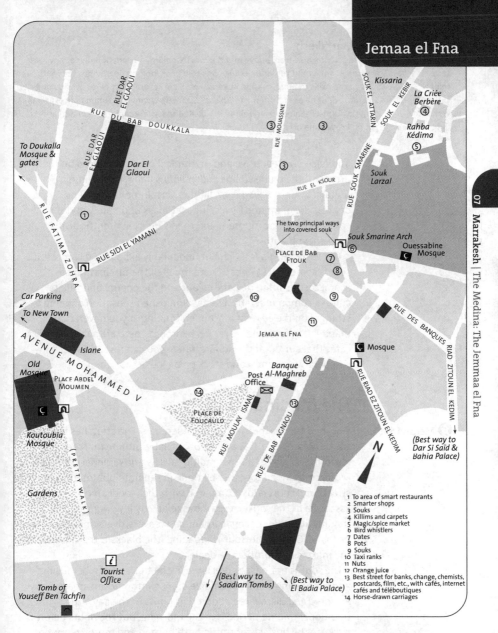

Map labels:

Kissaria
SOUK EL KEBIR
La Criée Berbère (4)
SOUK EL ATTARIN
Rahba Kédima (5)
RUE SOUK SMARINE
RUE DU BAB DOUKKALA
RUE DAR EL GLAOUI
RUE DAR EL GLAOUI
RUE MOUASSINE
Souk Larzal
RUE EL KSOUR
Dar El Glaoui
To Doukkala Mosque & gates
RUE FATIMA ZOHRA
RUE SIDI EL YAMANI
(1)
The two principal ways into covered souk
Souk Smarine Arch (6)
PLACE DE BAB FTOUK (7)
Ouessabine Mosque
(8)
(9)
(10)
(11)
RUE DES BANQUES
JEMAA EL FNA
Car Parking
To New Town
AVENUE MOHAMMED V
Islane
Old Mosque
PLACE ABDEL MOUMEN
Mosque
RIAD ZITOUN EL KEDIM
Banque Al-Maghreb
Post Office (12)
(14)
PLACE DE FOUCAULD
(13)
Koutoubia Mosque
RUE MOULAY ISMAÏL
RUE DE BAB AGNAOU
RUE RIAD EZ ZITOUN EL KEDIM
(PRETTY WALK)
(Best way to Dar Si Saïd & Bahia Palace)
Gardens
N
Tourist Office
(Best way to Saadian Tombs)
(Best way to El Badia Palace)
Tomb of Youseff Ben Tachfin

1 To area of smart restaurants
2 Smarter shops
3 Souks
4 Killims and carpets
5 Magic/spice market
6 Bird whistlers
7 Dates
8 Pots
9 Souks
10 Taxi ranks
11 Nuts
12 Orange juice
13 Best street for banks, change, chemists, postcards, film, etc., with cafés, internet cafés and téléboutiques
14 Horse-drawn carriages

thin, the kitchens close and small knots of musicians are left, surrounded by a crouching audience furtively smoking pipes. This is the right time to seek out powerful music influenced by the many spiritual brotherhoods – the Aïssoua, Derkaoua, Hamadasha and Gnaoua – freed from the irrelevancies of a purely tourist

Looking Down on Marrakesh

Marrakesh is a fantastic city to view from above and it is worth looking up occasionally for any roof terraces where you could sit for a mint tea, orange juice or a cold beer, looking down onto the roofs, minarets and even up to the Atlas mountain range beyond. There are several lofty cafés overlooking the Jemaa el Fna and most riads have a roof terrace. One or two medina café-restaurants are especially well placed, including the Café des Épices (overlooking Rahba Kédima, *www.cafedesepices.net*) and Café de France (right on the Jemma el Fna).

audience. The repetitive and rhythmical music produced on their drums, flutes, crude violins and *guenbris* (long, few-stringed guitars) is far removed from light entertainment. Shuffling dancers are animated by a spirit that plays upon piety and continence at one moment and then sends lewd, erotic displays in the next breath.

The Jemaa el Fna is a rich but undeniably exhausting carnival. It seems somehow to encapsulate much of the fascination of Morocco: the difference, the colour and the energy of its alien culture, compounded by a rarely diminished sensation of being a stranger on the edge of any understanding. If you haven't managed to find a nearby hotel bedroom, there are a number of cafés that surround the square where you can rest and watch in comparative serenity, and stock up on loose change.

The Medina Souks

⭐ Medina Souks

Beyond the northern edge of the Jemaa el Fna stretches the great souk of Marrakesh. It is a triumphant, labyrinthine marketplace, a glittering display of all the traditional arts and regional crafts of Morocco, grouped together by trade in separate but interlinked streets and courtyards. Compared with the woodcarvers' areas in Essaouira or the souks of Fez it has relatively few workshops, though there are turners, carpenters, weavers, dyers and tailors to be found. Only in the Souk Haddadine (the blacksmiths' quarter) do the makers outnumber the dealers.

The souk is not best appreciated at the tail-end of a bemusing and exhausting tour. It should be dipped into: chosen areas gently explored and discovered at different hours of the day. The traditional trading period is in the morning, but the hours before dusk are the busiest for traffic, both human and motorized, when the souk becomes so packed that the crowds of people seem to sway and move in unison.

For your first visit employ a guide to show you the main streets and features. Then, armed with a little knowledge of the street pattern, you can afford to explore – the earlier in the morning the better.

Rue Souk Smarine

Along the northern edge of the Jemaa el Fna a range of bazaars and the Ouessabine Mosque hide the main, arched entrance to the principal street, the Rue Souk Smarine. Here, before entering the souk proper, you can find a pottery and a spice market. The whole area is often obscured by shifting displays of clothing laid out on canvas. These pavement vendors are constantly on the look-out for police; they operate against an echoing soundtrack of bird whistles and hustling calls.

Rue Souk Smarine is, however, easy enough to identify and not only thanks to a small sign some fifteen feet up. It is broad, well paved and shaded from the sun by a high trellis cover. Commercially, it is dominated by the cloth merchants, whose shelves groan under the weight of hundreds of bolts of bright silks and embroidered cloth for kaftans, but it is also full of clothes, leather goods, jewellery and carpets.

Interspersed amongst the cloth merchants are tailors, who have been joined by a number of upmarket bazaars with halls stacked full of carpets half-hidden behind gleaming gates of brass, and who accept all manner of credit cards.

Rahba Kédima (Magic Market)

About 150m along Rue Souk Smarine two right turns lead into a distinctive open space, the triangular-shaped piazza known as Rahba Kédima, which used to be the old corn market. Until the 19th century it was forbidden to export grain, as it was considered immoral to profit by feeding Christians to the discomfort of poor Muslims. There are a few vegetable stalls at the far end of the square, but the spice and magic stalls at the Jemaa end are diminishing. Still, this remains a good spot to pick up an inexpensive wide-rimmed straw hat, spice jars and perhaps even a Moroccan teapot. An atmospheric courtyard brimming with metalware sits just off the square.

The spice and magic stalls here are hung with strange curtains of dried eagles, mountain foxes, hedgehogs, snakes, porcupines, lizards and unnamed grim relics in pots. These ingredients are used in the concoction of love potions, stimulants and aphrodisiacs – a female magic which helps to balance the many male-dominated features of Moroccan life.

The trinity of Maghrebi cosmetics are very prominently displayed: silvery blocks of antimony which are ground into kohl – a powder which both outlines the eyelids and stimulates an attractive watery sheen that protects eyes from soot and dust; henna in all its variety – green leaves, powder or ready-made pastes for dyeing hair and the intricate decorative tattooing of hands, face and feet;

and pottery saucers of cochineal, which is used as a rouge. Also look out for sacks of dried Dadès roses, a deliciously fragrant and cheap potpourri.

In the centre, veiled ladies sell knitted woollen hats and reed woven shopping baskets and raffia trays. The northern face of the piazza is usually hung with killims and carpets – a bright blaze of madder red and saffron yellow which almost obscures the two entrances to La Criée Berbère, the dark textile marketplace.

Before entering this haven of carpet dealers you might discover two other small places to the south of the Rahba Kédima. **Souk Btana** used to be dedicated to the auction of sheep and goat skins, cured and uncured, but has now been tidied up. The pungent goods have been replaced by dozens of stall-holders and you might buy your kaftan here. **Souk Larzal**, a small rectangular square with a small covered arcade in its centre, has kept more of its medieval atmosphere. Wool is still auctioned off to spinners and dyers, but in the evening the square is transformed into a second-hand clothes market with some fine embroidered kaftans and gilt work to be discovered amongst the tat for the patient and determined customer.

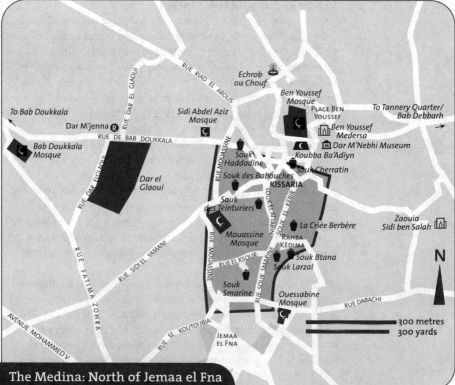

The Medina: North of Jemaa el Fna

You may want to eat lunch on the first floor or roof terrace of the Café des Épices here, watching the stalls and interactions below.

La Criée Berbère

Off the northern side of the Rahba Kédima two entranceways lead into the narrow Criée Berbère, a tight, enclosed space lined with displays of killims, killim cushions, killim waistcoats, carpets and woollen *burnouses*. Here you can find relief from Marrakesh's African sun. Most trading in the Criée Berbère is done from the shops, but auctions of goods are often held in the morning and evening. Moroccan auctions are distinctive affairs: the auctioneer walks around with odd composite bundles of stock, shouting the current price in the hope of attracting a larger one. Buyers and sellers sit to one side eyeing each other. Nothing seems to get sold very quickly.

This auction square was used before 1912 for the sale of slaves, at dusk on Wednesdays, Thursdays and Fridays. These auctions were only for the disposal of stock at the lower end of the domestic market, as influential clients would expect private and advance viewing. Galla women were considered the most attractive, but girls of the Hausa country fetched the best prices as they were considered more cheerful and neater. In the 1840s about 4,000 slaves were sold in Morocco each year, but by 1870 there was such a glut that prices dropped below $3. Even before then the common rate was two slaves for a camel, 10 for a horse, and 40 for a civet cat.

A left turn from here leads you past an artful selection of bazaars to the main street, or you can retrace your steps to Rue Souk Smarine.

The Kissaria: Souk el Kebir and Souk el Attarin

Just past the Rahba Kédima turning, Rue Souk Smarine splits into the Souk el Kebir (on the right) and the Souk el Attarin (to the left).

The Souk el Kebir passes a jewellers' alley on the right, before the alleys of the Kissaria open up on your left. The Kissaria is traditionally the heart of a souk, and in Marrakesh specializes in clothes, with stalls selling modern Western clothes, traditional cotton *gandoras*, woven blankets and arrays of Western-influenced open-necked kaftans for women.

Farther along Souk el Kebir are the aromatic stalls and small courtyards of the carpenters and wood-turners who make wooden screens and book holders. On the right-hand side, after an arch labelled Souk des Sacochiers, a skilled craftsman makes elaborate embroidered saddles and all the trappings of an Arab cavalier. Almost opposite, at 127 Souk Chkaria, craftsmen will Morocco-bind a favourite book for you, although covers for video cassettes are more in demand. If you bear left at the far end of the souk, you will find yourself in **Souk Cherratin**, a collection of alleys with a few leather, wood and metal craft stalls.

The Souk el Attarin takes you on much the same journey as the Souk el Kebir, though the alleys of the Kissaria will appear on the right. There are, however, three of Marrakesh's most celebrated sites to be discovered just on or off this alley.

The first, and easiest to find, is the **Souk des Babouches**, the section of Souk el Attarin devoted to the sale of slippers. This quarter, with its dazzling display of bank after bank of gilt-embroidered slippers, arrayed in every colour alongside those in fake animal skin, suede, polished leather, burnished leather or velvet, is like swimming in a jewellery box.

Continue farther along to the narrow turning into the **Souk Haddadine** (blacksmiths' quarter). During working hours the cacophony of hammer blows is enough to guide you there with your eyes closed. It is a triumphantly messy zone, full of rusting sections of iron plates and cut rods. The ice-blue glow of acetylene torches illuminates the tiny workshops packed full of industrious smiths dressed in grime and denim. They can make anything here, but at the moment the souk is producing vast quantities of lanterns, fire tongs, weather vanes, tables and yet more lanterns to be exported to Europe.

The third great site in this area is the **Souk des Teinturiers** (dyers' quarter) – reached by either of two alleys to the left of Souk el Attarin. On a good day the whole alley can be hung with vast swatches of wool drying in the sun. The combination of bright primary colours is irresistibly photogenic. As a passing tourist you might snap away free of charge, although film crews will be charged for the pleasure. There are some good shops in this section: old junk shops as well as a young man making genuine felt hats and fezzes. If you continue, passing under an arch, you will emerge out by the **Mouassine fountain** on your left – a triple-bayed recess with one or two working water taps. The great bulk of the **Mouassine Mosque** is hidden behind houses.

A left turn past the Mouassine Mosque takes you down the wider and uncomplicated Rue Mouassine, lined with some of the better-stocked tourist bazaars, which brings you out into the Place de Bab Ftouk and the Jemaa el Fna.

Ben Youssef Medersa, Koubba Ba'Adiyn and Dar M'Nebhi

There are three monuments open to non-Muslims in the medina: the Saadian Ben Youssef Medersa, the Almoravid Koubba Ba'Adiyn and the private museum housed in the magnificent 19th-century Dar M'Nebhi palace. The Ben Youssef Medersa and the Koubba are two of the finest buildings in Marrakesh, some would say in all Morocco, and no visit, however short, should exclude these architectural treasures. They are relatively easy to find as they are both associated with the Ben Youssef Mosque, just to the north of the covered souk. Both are proof of the rich Moorish heritage in southern Spain, which spawned Morocco's 'Andalucian' architecture.

From the Jemaa el Fna, head up the main souk artery, the Rue Souk Smarine/Souk el Kebir for 450m, turn left at the far Y-junction and then right under an arch and left again along a broader street to reach an open square, the Place Ben Youssef. At least one football game is usually underway here, set against the colourful backdrop of the mosque walls, draped with long, spinning strands of tailors' silk. The entrance to the Koubba is behind the wall on your left, the museum is on the right, and the *medersa* down the alley to the right of the mosque.

The Ben Youssef Mosque

Above the square rises the green-tiled roof and minaret of the Ben Youssef Mosque. A mosque was first built here by the Almoravid Sultan Ali ben Youssef, in the 12th century, as the central mosque of the medina. It was then twice as large as the present building. The Saadian Sultan Abdullah el Ghalib attempted to make Ben Youssef the most popular and esteemed mosque in Marrakesh. By this time it was in ruins, so he had to rebuild it entirely, along with the neighbouring *medersa*, and to cap his work he presented it with a large library.

The mosque, however, did not survive the well-intentioned improvements of his successors. What you now see dates entirely from the early 19th century, when an ancient and beautifully carved Almoravid fountain was also destroyed. The best view of the minaret (for non-Muslims) is from the neighbouring Koubba Ba'Adiyn (*see* below).

The Ben Youssef Medersa

The *medersa* was founded by the philanthropic Merenid Sultan Abou Hassan in the 14th century as part of an educational programme that established Koranic colleges in Fez, Taza, Salé, Meknès and Marrakesh. In 1564 it was restored by order of Saadian Sultan Abdullah el Ghalib, who created the largest *medersa* in Morocco, a feat which was completed in under a year. It was part of his ambition to make the Ben Youssef Mosque an intellectual centre to rival Fez. Dedicatory inscriptions to the sultan can be seen on the lintel of the entrance gate and along the prayer-hall.

⚄ Ben Youssef Medersa

open 9–6; adm, also included as part of a three-monument pass that includes the Koubba and nearby Dar M'Nhebi museum, see overleaf. Note that the ticket must be used in order, beginning at the museum

You may have to knock at the inconspicuous door to the right of the covered arch to enter. A long twisting passage then leads to the entrance hall, a secretive Marrakeshi feature not found in any Merenid *medersa* (they have proud portals and direct entrances). From the hall, stairs lead up to over a hundred plain wooden rooms where students lived, each sharing small courtyard skylights. This is another distinctive feature, for earlier *medersas* used windows overlooking the central courtyard to provide a central decorative theme.

The open **courtyard**, a great interior space of peace and silence, centres on a marble basin and is flanked by two galleries of solid pillars. Directly opposite is the entrance to the prayer-hall. The richness of decorative detail never disturbs the graceful simplicity of the plan: an initial height of *zellij* mosaic is broken by two bands of tile and plaster carved with Koranic inscriptions, which lead up into the ornate plaster and cedar carving. The carved pediments that support the wooden beams are exceptionally elegant and the geometrically-proportioned arabesques of Koranic scripts emphasise both the Word of God and the practice of the mathematical sciences. The courtyard has a distinctive grandeur touched with an element of severity not found in more intimate Merenid *medersas*.

The **prayer-hall** is divided into three aisles by four marble columns, and a further four enhance the arched *mihrab*, which carries the two traditional inscriptions of the Muslim declaration of faith. Go upstairs to see the students' rooms arranged around internal lightwells, their sparse dignity enlivened by the elaborate details of the carved wood balconies and turned window frames. The students (known as *tolba*, or reciters) were allowed to lodge here for six years whilst they memorized the Koran and studied the commentaries and laws. In the summer they wandered through the country, begging, listening to *marabouts*, and reciting their verses throughout the night at rural festivals.

The Ben Youssef Medersa is a building turned in on itself, something you expect to see in the veiled beauty of Fez rather than in the public spectacle that is Marrakesh. But that inwardness is proof of the building's very Muslim ambitions to become an intellectual generator renowned across Islamic lands.

On the north side of the Ben Youssef *medersa* you will find the **Fondation Culturelle Dar Bellarj**, an arts centre which hosts exhibitions, film screenings and master classes in various traditional crafts. Set around an idyllic central courtyard, the centre usually has exhibitions running and makes an excellent place to stop for a *whisky marocain* (mint tea). There's a small entrance fee for visiting exhibitions and the centre usually closes for lunch.

Fondation Culturelle Dar Bellarj
9 Rue Toualate Zaouiate Lahdar, t 0524 444555; adm for some temporary exhibitions

The Koubba Ba'Adiyn
(Kobbat el Mourabitine, Kobba el Baroudiyine)

When this building was rediscovered in its sunken position in 1948, French art historian Gaston Deverdun exclaimed that '*the art of Islam has never exceeded the splendour of this extraordinary dome*'. The Koubba is all that remains to hint at the glory of 12th-century Almoravid Marrakesh. It is a small pavilion covering a shallow ritual washing pool in the outer courtyard of the mosque, and is still surrounded by brick cisterns and latrines that once enclosed it. The Koubba introduces many of the shapes that become so familiar in later Islamic architecture.

The plan itself is simple enough: a rectangular two-storey domed structure pierced by arches. At ground level a pair of scalloped arches face each other; there are twin horseshoe arches on the longer sides. These silhouettes are repeated like chess pieces in the rows of three and five inset window arches on the upper storey, where scallop and horseshoe have been joined by an impaled turban motif. An ornate battlement frames the dome, which is decorated with a band of interlocking arches and surmounted by a series of diminishing seven-pointed stars.

Standing inside you look up into a dome of astonishingly bold, confident, solid yet supremely elegant and disciplined carving. The remains of a Kufic frieze announcing its creator, Ali ben Youssef, can just be made out. Above this rests an octagonal arched dome, its interlaced scallop arches infilled with rich foliate carving upon which hang shell-shaped palmettes. The corner squinches are framed by *muqurnas*, elegant spanning arches that in later centuries degenerated to appear like dripping stalactites. The *muqurnas* ring a seven-pointed star that frames an eight-podded dome, which in turn echoes the triumphant, deep carving of the central cupola.

Both the exterior and interior carvings play with the strong African sun to create pools of dark shadow and contrasting patches of light. The light shows up well the confident architectural origins of the Spanish Moorish style. The gradual debasement of this style into a mere veneer of decoration can be seen progressively at the *medersa*, the Saadian Tombs, the Dar M'Nebhi, and finally in the modern hotels of Marrakesh.

The Dar M'Nebhi (Musée Privé de Marrakesh)

This opulent turn-of-the-20th-century palace has been converted into a museum owned by a charitable foundation, supported by an American-style Association of Friends. To one side of the entrance courtyard there is a well-stocked bookshop full of posters, art books and cards, and there is also a **café**. The museum's exhibits are mainly items on loan from state museums or rarely seen pieces

The Fortunes of the Menebhi

The M'Nebhi (Menebha) family no longer possess either of the great palaces in Fez and Marrakesh that bear their name. They are descended from a clan of the Arab nomad tribes that held a privileged military position and were settled by the Alaouite sultans on the good grazing ground between Marrakesh and Essaouira. The family rose to a great position at the turn of the 20th century, when one of the most promising young cavalry officers in Sultan Moulay Hassan's army, El Mehdi bel Arbi El Menebhi, rose to become Minister for War to the boy sultan Abdul Aziz. As was customary, this Menebhi made a great fortune from his position and elevated his less talented nephews and sons to various official positions.

After Moulay Hafid replaced his brother on the throne, Menebhi arranged for his transfer to Tangier, where he served as the *mendoub*, the sultan's representative. His charm, erudition, bubbly wit and hospitality endeared him to the foreign community and especially to the British, who showered him with honours, including a knighthood. He attended the coronations of three kings at Westminster Abbey. Even as an old man, seated on a comely mule, he was delighted to escort his guests out to picnics and pig-sticking parties in the woods around Tangier. On one such expedition, when things were on the point of getting ugly, the old minister plucked a lance from a neighbour and deftly transfixed a maddened boar so that nine inches of spear protruded on the farther side. The startled onlookers were left wondering what he had been like in his prime.

drawn from Moroccan private collections. The cool, echoing central courtyard is a pleasant place to sit and is dominated by a remarkable hedgehog chandelier.

The heart of the museum is the enormous internal courtyard, in which three marble fountains play beneath the subdued light that filters through the modern steel-and-stretched-canvas roof. Exhibits on show in the neighbouring galleries include two vast plates, one imported from Andalucía, the other from the Saharan oasis of Tafilalt; a circumcision kaftan; an 18th-century painted dowry coffer from the Rif; a sumptuous red velvet- and gold-embroidered Jewish wedding dress; and Lucine Vola's collection of textiles. The latter includes two fine Glaoua *hanbels*, but is richest in Beni Yacoub and Aït Ouaouzguite work. These two tribal regions on the southern slopes of the High Atlas have specialized in producing restrained bands of brightly coloured embroidery on cream or white woollen *haiks*, though the work currently on sale in the south has long since fallen from these high standards.

A secondary courtyard host exhibitions, often of modern Moroccan art. You may still be able to see some of Hassan el Glaoui's work, including his view of a royal procession centred on the mounted figure of the sultan with his crimson parasol.

The museum has a wonderful collection of photos offering a tantalizing glimpse of Morocco past. The 1935 *Danse de l'Alhouach* is a striking scene as is the enchanting image of tents pitched on the Jemaa el Fna in 1920.

The Andalucian-inspired jewellery, Moroccan *broderie* and ceramics from Fez begin to give you a sense of the cultural breadth and artistry running through Morocco's history.

The palace's toilets are also a wonderful feature, once (but no longer) adorned with some of the oldest *zellij* tiling in existence. Even now they may even inspire you to enliven your own bleach-white facilities back in London, New York or Sydney.

A Walk Past the Lesser Monuments in the Northern Medina

North of the *medersa* stretches the great bulk of the medina, without souks, bazaars, guides or many tourists. Modern houses have for the most part replaced the *pisé* buildings, but the streets retain their labyrinthine design and you can wander freely through this living maze, catching glimpses of old *fondouqs*, mosques, *hammams* and bakeries. The route outlined here takes you past the notable sights of the area, and will give you a feel for this less-explored section of the medina. Unless you are a Muslim, however, you can only look at the monuments in this area of the medina from the outside. It is a long walk: if you are short on time or energy, leave it for another visit.

Turn right from the Ben Youssef Medersa, and then left down a covered passage. As you re-emerge into daylight you face a crossroads where Rue Baroudienne joins Rue Amesfah. Both these streets are lined with a number of elegant 16th- and 17th-century *fondouqs*, which are still very much in use as craftsmen's and tradesmen's courtyards. They are well worth a discreet look inside.

Turn right up Rue Assouel, passing several more *fondouqs*, the most elegant of which is beside the monumental decorated fountain on the left, the **Echrob ou Chouf**, which translates as 'drink and admire'. A left turn by the fountain, up Rue Diar Saboun, takes you into Rue de Bab Tarhzout, which is often half-filled by a souk of second-hand clothes.

In medieval times the **Bab Tarhzout** marked the northern edge of the city, but in the 18th century Sultan Sidi Mohammed extended the walls to include the *zaouia* suburb of Sidi Bel Abbès, one of the seven saints of Marrakesh, within the city.

Zaouia of Sidi Bel Abbès

The direct approach to the shrine is through an arch lined with an expensive and elaborate arcade of jewellers. The *zaouia*, mosque and tombs are forbidden to non-Muslims, but by going to the left or the right of the main entrance you can get impressive views into the extensive complex and of the great pyramidal shrine. The imam here is especially friendly and the mosque forms part of an integrated local community. Local blind men gather under the arches opposite the mosque's entrance to chatter and listen to the radio. (Avoid the temptation to take a photo of them if you can as it is not appreciated by those locals blessed with sight, not least the imam.)

The *zaouia* rose beside the grave of the Sidi in the cemetery of Sidi Marwan, which at that time was just to the north of the city walls. The existing buildings are the work of the 18th-century Alaouite Sultan Sidi Mohammed, who, apart from extending the city walls and rebuilding the entire shrine complex, added a further gift of a *medersa* courtyard with two flights of horseshoe arches.

The *Zaouia* of Sidi ben Slimane al Jazuli

Turning back through Bab Tarhzout, a right turn takes you past the covered Souk el Mjadlia and out below the *zaouia* of Sidi ben Slimane al Jazuli, another of the seven patron saints of Marrakesh. Its distinctive green pyramid roof and neighbouring mosque can be seen from alleys to the north and south of the *zaouia*, but the street beside it is closed to non-Muslims.

Sidi ben Slimane al Jazuli was one of the great Sufi mystics of Morocco, and his followers went on to found important religious institutions throughout the country. Al Jazuli's book, *The Manifest Proofs of Piety*, remains a seminal mystical text. As well as being famed as a spiritual teacher, he was a leading figure in the struggle against Portugal and his embalmed body would became a powerful totem in the *jihad*. Buried at Afugal in Haha province for a few decades, his body was brought to Marrakesh by the Saadians in 1523. Six Saadian princes were murdered shortly afterwards in a palace coup. They were buried together beneath a single *koubba* beside Al Jazuli's shrine, giving a further bizarre resonance to the legend of the seven.

Walk down to a dusty crossroads square below the *zaouia*. Ahead and to your right you will see the minaret of the **Sidi Bou Ameur Mosque**. Turn left below the minaret to walk down Rue Dar el Glaoui.

The Dar el Glaoui

At the junction between Rue Dar el Glaoui and Rue de Bab Doukkala is the massive bulk of the **Dar el Glaoui**, the palace of Si Thami el Glaoui, Pasha of Marrakesh, which was built in the early years of the 20th century. Impressive in scale if not in detail, it is now in use as a Trade Union headquarters. In recent years there have been rumours of visitors being allowed to see the gardens but there is little evidence of the possibility. Call the tourist office for the latest developments on this.

Dar el Glaoui was a place of legendary hospitality which, from the 1920s to 50s, entertained an international social élite including Roosevelt, Churchill and Patton. Beautiful Berber girls or boys,

Es-Sebti, the Seven Saints of Marrakesh

Combinations of seven saints or seven sleepers reach back beyond Islam and Christianity to an older universal myth. In Morocco, Ceuta, Jbel Hadid, Fez and Marrakesh all share in this common tradition. In the 18th century, Sultan Moulay Ismaïl removed various unorthodox Berber aspects of the annual celebration of Marrakesh's es-Sebti, and at the same time rebuilt the sanctuaries of the historical, orthodox saints. A new week-long *moussem* was established, which began at the shrine of Sidi Lyad, moved on to Sidi Youssef ben Ali, Sidi Abd el Aziz, Sidi el-Ghawzani, Sidi es Suhayi and Sidi ben Slimane al Jazuli before culminating at the major shrine of the city, that of Sidi Bel Abbès.

Sidi Bel Abbès (1130–1205) was born in Ceuta but moved south to establish a hermitage outside Marrakesh. His learning, moral sermons, miracles and ascetic lifestyle gained him a widespread popular following. The Almohad Sultan Yaacoub el Mansour invited him into the city and presented him with buildings and funds to carry on his good works. Centred on his shrine, these continue today: city merchants support the *zaouia* in running a number of schools and hostels, and in feeding the blind each evening. A number of potent legends still circulate in the city – that Christians venerate Sidi Bel Abbès as St Augustine, for instance, and that he haunts the minaret of the Koutoubia Mosque each night until he is certain that all the blind have been fed.

opium or marijuana, Lafitte or Latour were offered to guests with the freedom and nonchalance with which other Moroccan houses offer mint tea. Compliant European females could rely on a parting gift of emeralds, and society figures fought for the chance to have been the pasha's friend for a night. However, behind the pampering of sophisticated guests lay French 'loans', illicit taxes, bribery, blackmail and protection rackets, and it was common knowledge that the thousands of Marrakesh prostitutes had the pasha as their ultimate pimp.

Only hours after the pasha's death in 1956 a crowd broke into the Dar el Glaoui. Such was their hatred for the pasha, who had allied himself very closely with the French colonists, that they preferred to destroy rather than loot the palace and even the cars were smashed and set on fire. The mob then had their vengeance on the traitorous henchmen and officials of the pasha, who were hunted through the streets of the medina. They were treated like the cars: beaten, stripped and then burnt alive on the rubbish dump outside the Bab Doukkala. It is said that King Mohammed V would not eat for seven days when he heard of this brutality, even though the men killed had been his bitterest enemies.

From the Dar el Glaoui you can walk due west along Rue de Bab Doukkala, which runs towards the gate of that name, to look at the **Bab Doukkala Mosque**, on your left. This was built in 1558 by Lalla Messaouda, daughter of a *caid* of Ouarzazate, wife of a sultan and a redoubtable mother. While in exile in Istanbul she educated her two sons, later to be the great Saadian sultans Abdel Malik and Ahmed el Mansour. All that can be seen by non-Muslims is the slender elegant minaret to the northeast of the mosque and the elegant **Sidi el Hassan Fountain**, named after one of the founding professors of the *medersa* that used to be attached to the mosque.

Walk back to the Dar el Glaoui and go east for 300m until you reach the prominent crossroads with Rue Mouassine. Just up the street to the left is the **mosque and shrine of Sidi Abdel Aziz**, another Sufi follower of the teachings of Al Jazuli, who died in Marrakesh in 1508 and has entered the pantheon of the seven saints (*see* box, p.119).

While on this crossroads, look out for the gates to half a dozen *fondouqs*, some of which may be open. Try Nos.192 or 149 Rue Mouassine, which will reveal courtyards surrounded by galleries supported by high simple pillars and graceful cedar beams.

The Mouassine Mosque

South from the crossroads, 150m down Rue Mouassine, is the Mouassine Mosque, a monumental building established by the Saadian Sultan Abdullah el Ghalib in 1560, complete with baths, *medersa* and exterior fountain. The mosque has an equivocal local reputation. It is named after a prestigious local *shorfa* family but, during the building of the foundations, a 14th-century Jewish plague cemetery was unearthed. This is considered to have reduced the sanctity of the site, and rumours of a curse released in disturbing the grave of a cabbalistic rabbi began to circulate. The mosque is largely hidden from non-Muslims by the surrounding buildings, and there is little indication of the reported magnificence inside. The large triple-bayed **Mouassine Fountain**, with its ornate portico, is in a small square found just to the left of the mosque.

A good walk east of the Ben Youssef mosque, but still in the medina, is the **Fondouq Moulay Hfid**, where you can see traditional Moroccan weaving first-hand. The *fondouk* is located at the northern end of Rue Bab Ahmad, just before it becomes Rue de Bab el Khemis and a stone's throw from the Riad Djebel. It is based in an 18th century travellers' inn, and visitors can watch weavers operating traditional looms and perhaps buy the fabrics – which include carpets, blankets, slippers, *jellebas* and *gandoras* – too.

**Fondouq
Moulay Hfid**
*www.foundoukmoulay
hfid.com*
t 0613 879452

Imperial Marrakesh

The Marrakesh of the sultans has grown up since the 12th century in what is now the southern area of the medina. Here, the Almohads first established their kasbah, palaces, barracks and a royal mosque. Successor dynasties continued to develop the southern district into an Imperial City, but in a typically Moroccan way paid scant regard to the achievements of their predecessors. The Royal Palace – not open to the public – therefore stands on ground that has seen a dazzling succession of pavilions, courts and gardens.

The glories of imperial Marrakesh include the massive and very impressive ruins of the 16th-century Saadian El Badi Palace, which contrast perfectly in their state of decay with the Saadian Tombs, which have survived completely intact from the same period. Apart from exploring two 19th-century viziers' palaces, the Bahia and the Dar Si Saïd, you can also lose yourself in the dark alleys of Marrakesh's ancient Jewish quarter, the Mellah.

The best way to approach this quarter is on foot, walking south from the Jemaa el Fna. Start by heading down the café-lined and pedestrianized **Rue de Bab Agnaou** to a roundabout dominated by the Tazi Hotel. To your right is the **Place Youssef ben Tachfine**. Cross straight over, passing a fort and keeping the medieval kasbah wall to your left, and stop in front of two imposing gates 500 metres south. The intermittent wall on your left is not an old city wall but marks out the inner city, the kasbah quarter of sultans, the Imperial City.

Bab Agnaou and Bab er Rob

The official entrance into the city lay through the Bab er Rob; the Bab Agnaou guarded the entrance into the kasbah quarter, the city within the city. *Agnaou* is a Berber word that translates as 'the mute ram without horns'. A less idiosyncratic but more logical translation names it 'the Guinea gate' – the southern gate leading to black Africa, the homeland of the sultans' guards. It was built on Sultan Yaacoub el Mansour's orders in 1185, and has added prestige as one of the few stone structures in this city of pink *pisé*. It is carved from local 'blue' Guéliz stone, which is still being quarried to the north of Marrakesh. The semi-circular frieze has been delicately cut but is surprisingly assertive and strong.

The Kasbah Mosque

Passing through Bab Agnaou you approach the Kasbah Mosque, finished in 1190 by Sultan Yaacoub el Mansour. The long white exterior wall is capped with decorative battlements and for once left free of encrusted buildings to give an indication of its impressive extent.

The Merenids added a famous *medersa* to the Almohad mosque, but this was destroyed in a gunpowder explosion in 1569. The Saadian Sultan Abdullah el Ghalib restored the damaged mosque, which has been touched up every 200 years since, by Sidi Mohammed in the 18th century and more recently by Hassan II. These pious restorations have kept it from looking its age. The minaret, however, retains its original decorations: the simple *revêtement* of celadon green tiles, the first stirrings of Morocco's love affair with *zellij* (geometrical mosaics of cut tile). For a Muslim the principal approach is through the great domed northern gate which looks across the extensive open *sahn* court to the domed *mihrab* flanked by four Omayyad columns of jasper. Beside the *mihrab* a door leads to the enclosed garden courtyard of the 16th-century royal necropolis – the Saadian Tombs.

The Saadian Tombs

⭐ Saadian Tombs
open daily 9am–4.45pm; adm, visits often in the company of a guide, tips accepted.

The tombs are one of the most visited sites in Morocco, so in order to recapture some sense of serenity and isolation try to go either early in the morning or in late afternoon. A tight, thin passage to the south of the mosque was cut through the protective Saadian walls in 1917 for the use of non-Muslims. (Before this the only entrance was through a postern gate beside the *mihrab*.) Coming through it, you enter an ancient rectangular enclosed garden, planted with trees, cascading shrubs and rosemary hedges and bordered by the impressive *pisé* wall so typical of Marrakesh. This is the cemetery of the *shorfa*, the descendants of the Prophet, which had been in use for centuries before any Saadians arrived in Marrakesh. The identity of most of the open-air mosaic graves is lost, but the Merenid sultan Abou Hassan was buried here before his corpse was moved on into the greater state of Rabat's Chellah in 1351. The first Saadian sultan, Mohammed ech Cheikh, was buried here in 1557, in a tomb covered by a simple *koubba*. The existing *koubbas* were all built by Mohammed ech Cheikh's third ruling son, Ahmed el Mansour, in two stages. First he built a pavilion around his father's simple tomb, where he also buried his mother, Lalla Messaouda, in 1591. Later he built the hall of twelve columns to be his own mausoleum, and attached to it a prayer-hall. The extraordinary interiors of both *koubbas* can be examined from their thresholds.

The **prayer-hall** is the first hall on your left as you enter; it extends south of Ahmed el Mansour's tomb. Four clean pillars support elegant high horseshoe arches which, with the skylight, divide the roof space into eight rectangles. The decorated *mihrab* niche can be seen to your left. Although it has the most pleasing dark, simple sepulchral quality of them all, this was never intended as a tomb. It contains, however, a plethora of them, mostly the resting places of Alaouite princes from the 18th century. There is a sad little nest just to the left of the *mihrab* where half a dozen plague victims, the children of Sultan Sidi Mohammed, were buried between 1756 and 1777. The large tomb to the right, surrounded by a wooden

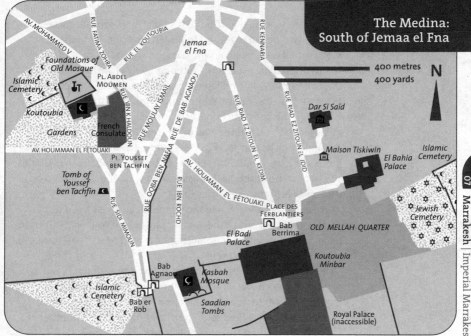

balustrade, is one of the many resting places of the Black Sultan, the Merenid Abou Hassan.

The **Hall of Twelve Columns** is the central mausoleum of Ahmed el Mansour. The three central tombs are surrounded by a colonnade of twelve decorated marble pillars, and the intensely carved upper plasterwork appears like gilded lace. The dome is even more fantastically rich, and prolonged inspection induces an almost physical sense of nausea. Decoration has overwhelmed form to produce a heady mystery, a pointillist scattering of reflected gilded light and depth that verges on a spiritual unworldliness. It is with relief that you concentrate on the layer of white script interwoven with black flowers, the lower area of *zellij* mosaic and the clean sober tombs at ground level. Appropriately, the tomb is a journey upwards for the eyes, from the mosaic border along the lower wall, through the plain stone and foliate carving above it, to the greens, pinks and vermilions of the upper walls and finally to the deeper red of the ceiling dome, where the illumination seems to be entirely soaked up. A grille covers a small upper window, allowing a narrow beam of filtered light to descend on the scene. The result is ethereal, weightless and otherworldly. Tamerlane's spectacular resting place in Samarkand may be a triumph in silver and gold, but this founder's tomb is altogether more uplifitng. The central sarcophagus is of course that of Ahmed el Mansour, who died in 1603. To his right is his son and successor Zaidan, who died in 1628, and to his left that of his grandson Mohammed ech Cheikh II, who died in 1655. There are 33 other tombs of Saadian princelings, although only 15 are identifiable by their inscriptions. Immediately behind the tomb of Ahmed el Mansour is an inscription commemorating his father.

Through this magnificence, a small darkened room can be glimpsed to the right: the **Hall of Three Niches**. An inscription in the middle niche commemorates Ahmed el Mansour's elder half-brother, the great building sultan of Marrakesh, Abdullah el Ghalib. The large tomb at the back is associated with Abou Hassan, who died an exile in the High Atlas in 1351.

Crossing over unidentified *shorfa* tombs, you pass the old entrance that led out of the Kasbah Mosque on your left. This used to be covered by another dome, but now the three sheiks' tombs are left open to the elements.

The **Second Koubba** is overlooked by two ornate loggias and a prayer-hall which was Ahmed el Mansour's first creation. The loggias' slim white marble pillars bear a lintel of carved cedar that supports the green-tiled roof. The prayer-hall, where a number of Saadian and a few 18th-century Alaouite princes are buried, is refreshingly clear of decoration other than the tranquil patterns of *zellij* mosaic, although the side-arch has impressive niche carving and a well-proportioned balancing of wood and stone. The burial chamber is decorated with stalactites and contains four tombs. Ahmed el Mansour's mother, Lalla Messaouda, is buried in a niche next to the wall on the right, beneath a commemorative inscription. The tomb to her left is that of the Sultan Abdullah el Ghalib, to his left that of Sultan Mohammed ech Cheikh, who died in 1557. The final tomb is that of the mad Alaouite Sultan Moulay el Yazid, who reigned for three years before his death in 1792.

From the Saadian Tombs to El Badi Palace

To find El Badi Palace from the Saadian Tombs, return to Bab Agnaou, turn right and retrace your route back up Rue Oqba ben Nafaa for about 150m and then turn right again on to Ave Houmman el Fétouaki. After about 600m you will arrive in the dusty square known as the **Souk du Mellah**, where oranges, fruits and olives are often sold. From the Souk du Mellah pass through one of two gates to the right into the Place des Ferblantiers, a large rectangular *fondouq* where metalworkers can be seen at work. Among other unusual processes, strips of unused Safi canning metal are cut to make intricate brass lanterns. Passing through the southern gate, the Bab Berrima, you enter a double-walled space familiar to anyone who has tramped the Imperial City of Meknès.

The outer wall divides the imperial kasbah district from the civil medina; the massive wall further south, decorated by storks' nests, encloses El Badi Palace.

El Badi, the Incomparable

El Badi Palace
open daily except hols
9–4.45p; adm

The palace was started in 1578, five months after the Battle of the Three Kings put enormous wealth from Portuguese ransoms and captured booty into the hands of Ahmed el Mansour, 'the victorious', who was further boosted by efficient management of the Sous sugar trade and the capture of Timbuktu in 1598, so that el Mansour also became known by the honorific *el Dehbi*, 'the golden'. He employed the finest craftsmen in the world, and Montaigne, on his travels in Italy, saw sculptors carving marble pillars of extreme height and delicacy for the palace. It was he who recorded that the Moroccan sultan exchanged sugar, pound for pound, for these marbles. But materials came from elsewhere too, notably gold from Sudan, most of which was then stripped to provide for the royal palace at Meknès.

Entering the Badi palace, now in ruins, through a series of crumbling walls, you find yourself in a massive empty rectangular courtyard, crossed by a rigid grid of paths which lead to a central pool – 90m long with an island – and flank four sunken gardens. The paths were actually raised to allow room for a great vaulted underground water system. The four sunken gardens would have been planted with sweet-smelling flowers: roses, violets, jasmine, acacia and hollyhocks. Happily, the orange trees have returned and are increasingly flanked by flowers too. A Moorish garden drew its chief glory from the arrangements of trees and running water, and flowers were almost entirely prized for their scent. This quadripartite garden design is a widespread Muslim phenomenon which derives from Persia and traces its inspiration to the four Biblical rivers that marked off the edges of Garden of Eden.

In the centre of each of the four massive walls pavilions were built, flanked by smaller pools and fountains. The largest of these was known as Koubba el Hamsiniya, the pavilion of fifty pillars. Opposite it stood the Crystal Pavilion, to the north was the Green Hall and to the south 'the Hayzouran', named after the sultan's favourite wife.

In his book *Black Sultan*, Wilfrid Blunt describes:

> ...walls and ceilings encrusted with gold from Timbuktu...gaily decorated boats to entertain the King and his guests in the cooler hours of the evening... Its vast halls were filled with fountains, and in looking-glass ceilings far overhead the fish appeared to swim,

*reflected from the cool waters of marble basins. There was a
domed hall where golden stars set on a blue ground gave the
appearance of the heavens themselves. Long fish ponds between
the alleys ended in grottoes and arbours.*

In the northeastern corner a staircase gives access to a viewing
platform (which used to be closed and occupied by a military
guard whenever the Royal Palace was in occupation). The prospect
of the palace is superb, as are the views south to the Jbilet hills
across the medina. In the northwestern corner of the palace
courtyard a staircase leads down into the so-called apartments of
the ambassadors. Excavations have exposed the courtyards of a
terrace of three 'houses', each of which was centred on a little
fountain courtyard.

In the southeastern corner of the courtyard, a gate leads to a
smaller series of yards and cellars. In the shadow of the present
Royal Palace, this is an intriguing area where you can see the
slave pens, old potteries, baking ovens and the remains of the
hammam. These ruins only constitute the ceremonial court of the
palace: el Mansour's private apartments for himself, four wives,
dozens of concubines, children and ministers extended to the
south and west.

El Badi, an almost impious borrowing of one of the 99 names of
God, was finished in 1603 only a few months before the death of its
creator. Descriptions of the celebratory feasts and inaugural gifts
are of almost unsurpassable splendour. During a lull in one of the
festivals, the ageing sultan asked his fool for a compliment on the
palace, to which was returned the famous reply that 'it would
make a fine ruin'. Indeed, before the century was out, in 1696,
Moulay Ismaïl had spent twelve years stripping the palace bare in
order to embellish Meknès.

The Koutoubia Minbar

Koutoubia Minbar
*open as part of El Badi
complex; small extra
adm payable at
entrance*

A room in the southeastern corner of the courtyard has been set
aside to display the *minbar* of the Koutoubia. This pulpit is one of
the world's great treasures to have survived from the early Middle
Ages. Commissioned by the third Almoravid sultan, Ali Ibn Yusuf
Ibn Tashfine, in 1137 from the craftsmen of Córdoba, it took eight
years to make the one thousand panels which were then
assembled in Marrakesh. It stood to the right of the *mihrab* in a
special hidden recess from out of which it rolled, almost
miraculously, so that the imam, staff in hand, could ascend halfway
up and deliver the noonday Friday sermon. Revered even by the
Almohads (who destroyed everything connected with the previous
dynasty), it remained in use until 1962. A beautiful book and
multilingual storyboards explain every detail.

The Mellah

From the Bab Berrima, Rue Berrima runs east of the El Badi outer walls past intriguing dark entrances into the heart of the Mellah. You will emerge, after 600m, in a *méchouar* outside the present Royal Palace, where the walls and guards are distinctly off-putting.

In 1558, some hundred years after it occurred in most of Morocco's other cities, the Jews of Marrakesh were moved into a Mellah on the orders of the Saadian Sultan Abdullah el Ghalib. The sultan created a secure quarter for them beside the royal palace, protected by walls and entered through only two gates. They were a talented community of traders, metalsmiths, bankers and linguists, a useful and valuable asset for the sultans, who have seldom shared the anti-Jewish feelings of their subjects. The community was governed by an *ulema*, a council of rabbis, ruled by a separate *caid*, and maintained its own cemetery, gardens, souks and fountains.

For some time the Jews prospered as middlemen between Moroccan Muslims and Christian merchants, but were recurrently accused by the populace of spying whenever there was a war. This antagonism grew with the strength of Portugal in the 15th and 16th centuries. Whereas learned rabbis had once been invited to lecture in mosques, it became accepted practice that if a Jew strayed into a mosque he was given the choice of immediate conversion or being burnt alive. Jews had to remove their hats and shoes when walking past a mosque, and in a royal city were forbidden to wear any shoes at all outside their own quarter.

But within the Mellah walls the community grew into one of the most populous and overcrowded in Morocco. Before 1936 there were 16,000 Jews living here, but with the foundation of Israel in 1948 and the Suez Crisis in 1956 the community disintegrated, either moving to more tolerant Casablanca or emigrating.

Only a handful of Jews are left here, but the distinctive tall, cramped houses lining low but regular narrow streets remain. Within the quarter, mostly to the north, the traditional Jewish specialist trades of jewellery, textiles and tailoring remain. At the centre of the quarter is the small **Place Souweka**, with its fountain. If you are interested in visiting the **old synagogues** which have now been converted into houses and shops, you should find a young guide here or ask advice from the Jewish-American hostel in the Mellah. **Fessaine Synagogue** (or Asim), built in 1840, remains in use as a small 20ft by 20ft house of prayer. On the eastern edge of the Mellah is an extensive Jewish cemetery separated from the larger Muslim one by the city's outer wall. Until a few years ago it was a wilderness of overgrown shrubs, but now it is kept secure and the tombs are frequently repainted. You can simply wander in past the beggars at the gate.

El Bahia Palace

⚜ El Bahia Palace
open daily 9–4.30, but sometimes closed for receptions and conferences; adm

From the Place des Ferblantiers, which stands just before El Badi Palace, follow the road north and then east to the long garden entrance of the palace ahead. If you manage to get into the palace, you will find it a perfect contrast to the vast sunbaked simplicity of El Badi, especially as you amble down the driveway, flanked by flowers and fruit trees. El Bahia, 'the brilliant', contains a series of paved courtyards, dark interior reception halls and Andalucian gardens, built by two generations of 19th-century grand viziers.

Si Mousa was vizier to Sultan Sidi Mohammed ben Abderrahmane (1859–73), and his son, Ba Ahmed, served Sultan Moulay Hassan and became the powerful regent of the child-sultan Abdul Aziz. Their choice of architecture was highly traditional and, as father and son gradually amassed over eight hectares of the city, they created a maze of passages, connecting doors, courtyards, gardens and pavilions. However, fortunes created by a sultan's officials always return to their master eventually. Ba Ahmed was exceptional in having been able to enjoy his father's inheritance and his own wealth until the hour of his death, for a provincial *caid* or pasha in Morocco could expect to be squeezed of his ill-gotten gains any time after just a decade in office. Not until Ba Ahmed lay dying did the sultan's guards quietly replace the viziers at the doors of the Bahia Palace. Before the corpse had grown cold, they had stripped the palace of all portable possessions, and a few days later nothing remained but the great empty building as it is seen today.

The Oriental complexity of plan, the locked side doors, beckoning passages and the ghosts of French and Moroccan courtiers (it was lived in by the resident-generals after 1912 and is still used on occasions by the Royal Family) give it an undeniable charm. The guided tour will take you through a dazzling series of reception halls with their great panelled Moorish ceilings of carved, painted and gilded wood. It is, though, the low empty range of the extensive concubines' courtyard, the garden courtyard and the courtyard of the four official wives that provide some of the most powerful, enduring and melancholic images of this palace. It is impossible not to feel sympathy for the imprisoned women who once inhabited this gilded cage, even though they themselves no doubt felt protected, pampered and privileged.

The Dar Si Saïd (Musée des Marocains)

Dar Si Saïd
Riad ez Zitoun el Jdid,
t 0524 442464; open
Wed–Mon 9–4.45; adm

Walking up Rue Riad ez Zitoun el Jdid towards the Jemaa el Fna, turn right opposite the neighbourhood mosque to find this secluded museum. Si Saïd was the idiot brother of Ba Ahmed, though they shared the same slave mother and powerful vizier father. He held a number of court posts as extra sinecures for his brother, whose palace communicated with the Dar Si Saïd by an underground tunnel. The Dar Si Saïd is more modest and attractive in plan than the Bahia, and greater attention has been paid to the detailed decorative work. Worthy of attention in its own right as a town palace, it also houses an important collection of the decorative desert arts of southern Morocco.

The entrance passage of the **Museum of Moroccan Arts and Crafts**, lined with doors rescued from the decaying kasbahs of southern Morocco, leads to a magnificent marble fountain bowl carved some fifty years before the founding of Marrakesh for Abdelmalik ben Abi, grand vizier to the Omayyad Caliph of Córdoba, Hisham II. It was carried away from Spain by the Almoravid Sultan Ali ben Youssef to embellish the Marrakesh mosque that bears his name. The figurative carving (on the sides a central imperial eagle is seemingly supported by two mountain goats, with a pair of apes on the outspread wings) would not have survived the fundamentalist cleansing of the Almohad period since figurative art is outlawed in the Koran, and it was fortunate to have lain buried in ruins until discovered by excavations in 1926. The entrance passage opens into the delightful courtyard, with green and white pavement, fountain and central pavilion almost lost among bird-filled trees, like some overgrown colonial-era conservatory.

In the long room to the left is an uplifting display of the many **Berber jewellery** traditions of southern Morocco: the gorgeous fibules and green and yellow enamel eggs of Tiznit, the red stones set in dark silver from the western High Atlas, the elaborate filigree from Jbel Siroua, the black-on-silver *repoussé* designs from the Tafilalt Oasis, and thick bracelets from Jbel Bani. On the other side of the courtyard there is male jewellery, as worked into ornamental daggers, powder horns and long-barrelled flintlocks. The two smaller rooms are dedicated to **ceramics**: one housing the traditional yellow, green and blue decorated wares produced in the great centres (Safi, Marrakesh and Fez), and also the traditional green slipware of Tamegroute, while the other is filled with different examples of the local red wares produced in the countryside and the mountains.

The **collection of carpets** includes many of the best examples you will find in southern Morocco and are on display downstairs, next to a corridor of beautifully emblazoned leather wallets. Stylistically the carpets are divided between Berber and Arab. Those produced by the Arab tribes of the plain are sometimes collectively known as Tensift, or individually identified as Rehamna, Oulad Bou Sbaa, Chiadma, Ahmar or Boujad. Typically they are very long and narrow (to fit the dimensions of a tent, or the interior of a kasbah), and dominated by fields of madder red and purple with an almost abstract use of geometric designs floating in and out of scale with each other. By way of a contrast those carpets and *hanbels* (similar to killims) produced by Berber tribes such as the Glaoui of the High Atlas and the Aït-Ouaouizarht of the Jbel Siroua region are set against a predominately black and white background with details worked in gold, yellow, red and blue. They are both more ordered and more colourful, though once again they use an entirely geometric repertoire of patterns. The figurative shapes – those brightly coloured strip pictograms so beloved of the bazaars – are not indigenous to Morocco, even though their influence was already apparent in the 19th century. They come instead from southern Tunisia, and in particular the Gafsa region.

The magnificent **apartment** upstairs is worthy of a visit in its own right but also has a small selection of velvet and cotton embroidered robes, as well as traditional dagger sheath belts and shoes. Perhaps the most intriguing exhibit is the four carriages of a hundred-year-old, three-metre-high wooden Ferris wheel for toddlers (pictured in an early photograph).

The collection concludes with some ornate and sometimes beautiful pieces of local **carved cedar** – heavy dark doors, the delightful doors within painted Moorish gates, turned window frames and screens, among them some 16th-century Saadian work recovered from El Badi.

Maison Tiskiwin (Bert Flint Museum)

Maison Tiskiwin
8 Rue de la Bahia,
t 0524 389192; open
10–12.30 and 3–8; adm

The entrance to this private museum is reasonably easy to miss – overshadowed by the group of three neighbouring bazaars. It houses another collection of Moroccan decorative art, put together by the Dutch anthropologist Bert Flint during several decades of field work in Morocco. The house, ranged around a traditional Moorish courtyard, is itself reason enough for a visit, and the exhibits offer an overview of the traditional material culture of Morocco.

In 2000, Bert Flint moved his Agadir exhibits here too, so the collection is now considerable. One particular highlight of the collection is the **Zemmour room**, with its dense collection of Middle Atlas weaving on floor and walls, forming a bit of textile heaven for the urban visitor dreaming of a free, nomadic existence.

The vivid patterns on the leatherwork he has collected from around the various Sahara regions are enough to fill a sketchbook with dozens of derivative designs. The exit from the museum rooms goes through the kitchen courtyard with its orange tree, and you are meant to pass quickly through the private rooms, which are, however, equally intriguing. You might have to pinch yourself to prevent the feeling of having strayed into a design-magazine article as you take in the faultless blending of traditional High Atlas weaving and bold modern carpets.

A Tour of the Ramparts

The *pisé* walls of Marrakesh respond with a dazzling range of colours to different degrees of light. They glow with changing hues of pink, ochre, gold and brown against the startling backdrop of High Atlas peaks and clear blue sky. Stretches of the walls wind through a wilderness of dusty graves; elsewhere they are overhung by rustling palms or interrupted by frantic streams of traffic. Elsewhere again they are found decorated with drying skins, sheltering a souk or a passing flock, or enclosing the processional court of the palace of a king. The walls are a shifting pattern of colour and life, at once both monotonously extensive and the city's richest aesthetic treat.

Alarmed by the growing Almohad threat from Tin-Mal, the Almoravid Sultan Ali ben Youssef decided to protect Marrakesh with walls in 1126. He asked his generals for tactical advice and consulted his astrologers for an auspicious date to start work on them. Within a year, a 10km circuit of 9m-high walls, defended by 200 towers and pierced by 20 gates, had been built. This has been constantly repaired and occasionally expanded but still substantially follows the 12th-century plan.

A 16km walk around the city walls of Marrakesh would be arduous at any time of the year. Ideally you should travel by **horse-drawn cab**. The trip can be broken at Bab el Khemis for the souk, and Bab Debbarh, for a look at the tanneries, but the rest of the gates are likely to be of only passing interest. A circuit of the walls would ideally end with a leisurely afternoon picnic in the Menara or Aguedal Gardens.

Leave from the Jemaa el Fna, where horse-drawn cabs, taxis and bicycles are easy to find, and take the Ave Mohammed V, passing the town hall on your right and the orange-tree-shaded park of Moulay Hassan opposite. Crossing through the line of the city walls at the Bab Nkob breach, follow the walls round to the right, passing the double crenellated towers of the Bab Larissa in the corner to approach the Bab Doukkala.

Bab Doukkala

The massive but unequal towers of this Almoravid gate are now isolated to the left of the modern entrance to the medina. If the doors are open, go in to examine its dark, twisting defensive passages. The gates guarded the road to Doukkala, the fertile coastal region between El-Jadida and Safi inhabited by Arabic-speaking Berber tribes who were considered to be among the more loyal and dependable subjects of the sultan. Just within the gate, to the right, are the impressive modern green-tiled law courts.

The area outside the gates, despite being used by a busy and modern bus station and passing fairs, retains a melancholy air. To the south of the bus station is the cemetery and *koubba* of **Sidi Bennour**, which belonged to the El Hara, the old leper colony.

Pass two small gates, Bab Boutouil and Bab Moussoufa, to reach the palm grove of Sidi Bel Abbès. Inside the walls here is the *zaouia* of Sidi Bel Abbès; despite the fact that he was the venerated patron saint of Marrakesh, his *zaouia* was in a suburb outside the city until the walls were extended in the 18th century.

Souk and Bab el Khemis

The northern end of the medina has spilled beyond the walls around the Souk el Khemis, the Thursday market. Fruit and vegetables are sold throughout the week here, though livestock trading is still concentrated on Thursdays.

From the souk enclosure, a road passes between the cemetery of Sidi Ahmed Ez Zaouia and a lunar landscape of baked mud and refuse to approach the old Almoravid Fez gate which when rebuilt became known as Bab el Khemis. Just before the gate, on the left is the *koubba* of **Sidi el Barbouchi**, the saint of the slippers, and straight through the gate within the walls is the *zaouia* of the **Derkaoua Sufi brotherhood**. The road to the left leads to a series of yards where scrap, broken machinery and bruised food are traded by the most impoverished on the grounds of the old Christian cemetery. It is a powerful, disturbing place, threatening only through its misery. It was at the centre of an insurrection in January 1904. A revolutionary mob led by the cobblers' guild marched under black flags to the cemetery and there exhumed the graves of Christian missionaries. The skulls were impaled to serve as standards that led the mob in its assault on the money-lenders in the Mellah, the merchants in the souk and the kasbah of the pasha.

Return outside the city walls, then follow the road south beside a magnificent stretch of wall and an extensive **cemetery** through which snakes the dry bank of the river Issil. The cemetery is often flecked with the bright colours of drying skins as you approach Bab Debbarh, the tanners' gate.

Bab Debbarh

The entrance to the **tanners' quarter** is beneath the ancient Almoravid towers of Bab Debbarh, through a twisting three-chambered passage. By one of the gate-towers there is a door to the precarious roof, which, if open, provides the best view over the tanneries. If the gate is closed there will be no difficulty in finding a young guide to give a quick tour of the tannery vats. They are at their busiest and least pungent in the morning.

☆ Tanneries

Continue south, past Bab Rachidia, to reach **Bab Ailen**, a strong portal named after a Berber tribe that inhabited land to the east. In 1130 an Almohad army descended from the High Atlas to besiege the city. They concentrated their assault on this gate, but were driven off by Almoravid cavalry who sallied out from the neighbouring gates. Just within the gate is the minaret and extensive shrine of the **Qadi Ayad Mosque**. This was built by Sultan Moulay Rachid in the 17th century to hold the tomb of Moulay Ali ech Cherif, the holy ancestor of the Alaouite dynasty. Two later sultans, Moulay Sliman (1792–1822) and Mohammed IV (1859–73), chose to be buried here beside him.

The Southern Ramparts

The angle in the southeastern corner of the walls is filled by the enormous **cemetery of Bab Rhemat**. To the east stretches a modern suburb, and a green-tiled *koubba* peeks over the houses to your right. This shrine covers the grave of a 12th-century saint, Sidi Youssef ben Ali, who is remembered for his great piety – he continued to praise and thank God even for the gift of leprosy that killed him. The twin towers of the **Bab Rhemat/Aghmat** were betrayed by a Christian regiment in the service of the Almoravid sultans, who opened the gate to the Almohads in 1147. If you pass under the gate here and continue a kilometre into the medina along Rue Ba Ahmed you can see the exterior of the *zaouia* **of Sidi ben Salah**, its carved minaret inset with green tiles rising above a jumble of roofs, arches, passages and gates. This complex was built in the 14th century by the Merenid Sultan Abou Said Othman.

Continuing outside the city walls, pass beside the cemetery wall to reach the **Bab Ahmar**, which was rebuilt by Sultan Sidi

Mohammed in the 18th century. The gate was reserved for the use of the sultan on the feast of Mouloud. The area inside the gates used to house the barracks of the Bouakher regiment of black soldiers, who had a religious cult based around a Jujube tree that grew from the gate. To the south, 3km of walls enclose the Aguedal, the private gardens of the sultan.

Pass through the Bab Ahmar to enter a number of processional squares or *méchouars* to the south of the royal palace. From **Méchouar Barastani** pass through 'the gate of the winds', the Bab er Rih, to go into the smaller **Méchouar el Ouastani**. In the southwestern corner a double wall allows private communication between the palace and the Aguedal. The Bab El Arhdar, just before this on the left, may be left open for the use of the public. Beyond is the great **Méchouar des Alaouites**. The **pavilion of Essaouira** in the middle of the southern wall and an artillery magazine in the corner were both built by Sidi Mohammed in the 18th century. The pavilion was used for diplomatic receptions, parades and for reviewing *Fantasia* displays. Pass out through the city walls at **Bab Irhli** and turn left.

The *koubba* **of Sidi Amara** is just south of here, on the right, and 800m farther on is the **Sqallet el Mrabit**. This elegant ramped fortress was built by Sidi Mohammed in the 18th century to house a mobile squadron from the 600-strong regiment of cavalry he kept permanently posted to defend against the Rehamna tribe. Beyond it you can see the white *mihrab* of the *msalla*, an open-air mosque used during religious festivals.

Just north of Bab Irhli, the **Bab Ksiba** leads to the Derb Chtouka district, once the site of an Almohad fortress. In the 19th century this was still a government kasbah, occupied by the Mokhazines who guarded the sultan's prison.

From Bab er Rob to Bab Sidi Rharib

After extending the city to the south in the 12th century, the Almohads were left with a potentially vulnerable angle in the southwestern wall, which they protected by building the Bab er Rob. *Grands taxis* collect up passengers and local buses stop here. There is a souk for cheap pottery and fruit extending around the gate, which is named after raisin juice, perhaps a memory of an old dried-fruit market or a morbid reference to the executed heads that in former times were displayed from the battlements. Just inside the Bab er Rob is the most elegant gate in Marrakesh, the **Bab Agnaou**. This carved stone arch once led from the medina to the Imperial City.

To the west of the Bab er Rob the walls are hidden by the **cemetery of Sidi es Soheili**, another of the seven saints of Marrakesh, whose *koubba* is beside the cemetery gate, Bab ech Charia. After a detour around the outside of the cemetery you will eventually reach the long wall that contains the garden of the Mamounia Hotel, the entrance of which is just inside the next gate, the **Bab Jdid**. North of this gate is the **Bab Makhzen**, which used to form a direct entrance to the 12th-century Almoravid kasbah and today is still reserved for the use of the king. This is no inconvenience, as the **Bab Sidi Rharib**, just 200m north, will lead you just as directly back to Ave Mohammed V, with the main streets of the New Town to the left and the Jemaa el Fna and the medina to the right.

The Gardens of Marrakesh

The gardens of Marrakesh are often packed with locals and visitors alike, but do not let this discourage you: there is no better way of sheltering from the afternoon heat than by picnicking in the Aguedal or the Menara gardens. The main market on Avenue Mohammed V in the New Town sells everything you need: wicker baskets, wine, cheese, fresh bread, pâté and a bewildering selection of olives, nuts and fresh fruit.

The Aguedal Gardens

Aguedal Gardens
open erratically, but usually Fridays and Sundays; often closed if the Royal Palace is occupied

Pass down the dirt track through the orchards to the 200m-square main tank, the Sahraj el Hana, or 'pool of health', next to the pavilion of **Dar el Hana**. You can still enjoy its tranquil rooftop view south to the Atlas peaks, or join the knots of Moroccan families picnicking under the shade of the surrounding trees. On the far side the ruins of a gunpowder factory have been turned into a waterfront palace. From the roof of the Dar el Hana you might have witnessed the death in 1873 of the Sultan Mohammed IV, who drowned while boating with his son on the tank. A forlorn, almost wistful, acceptance of fate is beautifully expressed in the official epitaph: '*He departed this life, in a water tank, in the expectation of something better to come.*'

He was not the only sultan to die in the Aguedal Gardens. On 9 April 1672, after the feast of Aid el Kebir, Sultan Moulay Rachid took out a spirited horse to gallop away his *ennui* through the orange groves of the Aguedal. In the morning, the court poets sang:

The tree's branch did not break the skull of our imam out of cruelty; nor from ingratitude, unmindful of the duties of friendship.

It was out of jealousy of his slender figure, for envy is to be found even among trees.'

These gardens were established in the 12th century by the Almohad Sultan Abdel Moumen. Two enormous tanks were built and filled by pipes that tapped the Ourika stream. By the 18th century, however, the walls had decayed, the water had been diverted and tribesmen grazed the orchards. The present garden is the creation of Sultan Abder Rahman (1822–59), who reclaimed the water rights and rebuilt the walls, although his successors still had to keep a constant guard against tribesmen, especially the nomadic Rehamna, who enjoyed nothing more than raiding the sultan's garden.

In the 19th century a succession of pavilions was built in the gardens, most notably the **Dar el Beida** provided for the *harem* of Moulay Hassan. However, the garden's primary purpose was always to be an efficient and very profitable private agricultural estate. Two visitors from Kew who saw it in 1840 estimated that its 40 acres gave the sultan produce worth at least £20,000 each year. The gardens cover forty acres and make an excellent escape for an afternoon.

The Menara Gardens

Menara Gardens
open daily 8:30–5; free, adm to Royal Pavilion

The Menara Gardens are 2km west of Bab Jdid. The Menara is an agricultural estate of irrigated olive orchards and gardens that have been planted around a massive water tank. Like the one in the Aguedal Gardens, the tank was built by the Almohads in the 12th century, but what you now see was established in the 19th century by the Alaouites. Mohammed IV replaced the outer walls, refurbished the tank and built the green-tiled pavilion in 1869 to replace a ruined Saadian one. There is a a wonderful, tranquil view over the great expanse of water from its open, balconied first floor, where the royal party would picnic whilst musicians played out of sight on the ground floor. Walk around the tank to catch the celebrated view of the pavilion set against the High Atlas mountains and reflected in the waters. Stop for a sandwich at the café or just to buy bread to feed the enormous carp, which will churn up a small frenzy of turbulent water with their gaping wide mouths as they descend on leftovers.

Marjorelle Garden
*www.jardinmajorelle.
com, t 0524 301852;
open Oct–April daily
8–5.30 and May–Sept
8–6; Ramadan
9–5; adm*

The Majorelle Garden

The Majorelle is a privately owned botanical garden off a side street in the New Town, north-west of the medina opposite the wholesale market on Avenue Yaacoub el Mansour. It was created by two generations of French artists, Jacques and Louis Majorelle, and was then owned by the couturier Yves Saint-Laurent (who was born in Algeria). It is an immaculately manicured walled garden full of pavilions, paths and rills painted a bright Mediterranean blue. The admirably lush botanical collection is especially strong in cacti. The Majorelles' old studio has been turned into a small **museum** (*closed indefinitely; check with the garden administration for the latest updates*), which displays the present owner's idiosyncratic collection of Maghrebi decorative art: carpets, ceramics, textiles, woodwork and jewellery, as well as a gallery filled with some of the Majorelles' original canvases. After he passed away in 2008, Yves St Laurent's ashes were scattered across the garden.

The Mamounia Garden

Mamounia Garden
Ave Bab Jdid,
t 0524 388600,
www.mamounia.com

This lush formal garden with its central pavilion was established in the 18th century by Pasha Mamoun, governor of Fez, and was later bequeathed to the sultan. It then served as the crown prince's residence, and was occasionally lent to visiting diplomats, until the era of French rule when it was turned into a luxury hotel (*see* p.145). The hotel's charm was drastically reduced by its 1986 renovation, and somewhere in its marble halls there should be installed a constant video of the old interior as preserved in Hitchcock's 1956 film *The Man Who Knew Too Much*. The 300m sweeping wall of bougainvillea and the quiet, undisturbed half-dozen regular plots of olive and palm trees are now part of the phenomenally sumptuous Mamounia Hotel. Buy a cup of coffee on the terrace and then take a wander.

The Palm Grove (La Palmeraie)

Follow the Fez road east for a kilometre past the Bab el Khemis, then take a signposted left turn for an 8km drive through the palm grove to the north of the city. The Almoravids are credited with planting this grove, but palms in Marrakesh are useful only for wood, shade and desert imagery, for they are too far north ever to bear fruit. Olives or oranges would be a more useful crop, and the palm grove has a deserved aura of neglect. The *pisé* walls, fragments of irrigation systems and barren palms might be entertaining if it weren't being turned into a smart suburb of villas, time-share holiday homes and hotels.

New Town (Guéliz)

The New Town (*ville nouvelle*), the French-built city of neat avenues and apartment blocks to the west of the old walled city, is known as **Guéliz**. The name derives from a local corruption of '*église*', for the **Catholic Church of St Martyrs** was the most remarkable building throughout the 1920s and 30s. Arguably this is still true today, with its cool, spacious interior lit by a clerestory of yellow and red glass to flood the basilica with warm light. It is dedicated to the five early Franciscans who travelled from Italy to Muslim Seville and then on to their martyrdom in 1219. Fortunately the priest and the imam of the mosque (both on Rue Imam Ali) now maintain an excellent relationship.

The **Hivernage**, a garden suburb of hotels and villas, stands immediately west of Bab Jdid and Bab Makhzen. The mature gardens of the interlinked Hotel es Saadi and the Casino make for a pleasant, tranquil stroll, particularly when combined with a drink beside the hotel pool or the piano bar.

There are also some recent buildings in the New Town that toy with the New Carthage style, a fusion of traditional Moorish and Saharan styles spiked with the odd detail from Egypt and Tunisia, that might be of interest. In particular, look for the recent work of the Tunisian-born French architect Charles Bocarra, responsible for the design of the much talked-about Tichka Hôtel (now the Tichka Salam) and the opulent Les Deux Tours villa in the Palm Grove (see 'The Gardens of Marrakesh' earlier), as well as the great mass of the **Marrakesh Opera**, which now dominates the junction of Avenue de France and Avenue Hassan II, near the railway station.

The **art galleries** around Rue de la Yougoslavie are certainly worthy of a browse and you may want to stop for lunch or dinner around Hivernage.

ⓘ **Marrakesh >**
Tourist Board, Place
*Abdel Moumen Ben
Alion (on the Ave
Mohammed V in the
ville nouvelle),
t 0524 436131; open
Mon–Fri 8.30–4.30*

*Tourist Information
Office*, or Syndicat
*d'Initiative, 176 Blvd
Mohammed V,* **t** 0524
432097/434797

Information and Services in Marrakesh

Tourist Information

Like all major Moroccan cities, Marrakesh has two tourist offices.

The **Tourist Board** has a few leaflets and maps as well as offering guides.

The **Tourist Information Office**, or *Syndicat d'Initiative* is less helpful: 'initiative' is not a feature of Moroccan tourist offices, despite the name.

Tourist Police

The tourist police are one of the reasons Marrakesh has been able to become such a favourite tourist destination, since they put a stop to the more unreasonable hawking techniques used on tourists. You will see them in their blue uniforms ready to assist should you need it, whether you just need directions or someone will not leave you alone.

The city's central **tourist police office** (**t** 0524 384601) is located just south of the Koutoubia Mosque.

Communications

Telephones

In 2009 Maroc Telecom added an extra digit to all urban area codes in the country, meaning that Marrakesh's **area code** is now **t** 0524 (formerly **t** 044, and then **t** 024). As some business cards and hotel brochures have not yet caught up, you may need to add the 5 after the initial zero. The number of Maroc Telecom's head office in Marrakesh is **t** 0524 436512. Always begin with a zero if making a call within Morocco.

Telephone booths are dotted around the streets (and most take coins), often outside petrol stations or by major crossroads if they are in the *ville nouvelle* or in small Maroc Telecom shops in the medina. For the latter, look out for the blue signs with orange lettering. But for long-distance calls you are usually better asking at a hotel where, though perhaps double the price, at least the line is clear and you should be able to escape any background noise.

Email and Fax

Internet cafés are dotted around the city although they are more common in the new town (*ville nouvelle*). They tend to pop up and disappear with alarming speed. Most hotels and riads have wifi these days, as well as a computer terminal you can use; if not, they can point you to somewhere nearby.

Occasionally you may see 'FAX' written in the window of a very small and rudimentary shop but for the most part you are best to find a hotel.

Post and Telegrams

The Central Post Office is in the *ville nouvelle* (Place du 16 Novembre on Ave Mohammed V, in Guéliz, **t** 0524 431963; *open Mon–Fri 8am–4.15pm, Sat 8am–11.45am*). The main post office in the medina is on the Jemaa al Fna but there are also branch post offices dotted through the city – you can find a fully comprehensive list at *www.bam.net.ma.* (Click on the small yellow '*bureaux de poste*' icon at the top and select the city.)

For fuller details on **telegrams, letters and parcels** in Morocco, *see* Practical A-Z, p.88.

Courier Services

DHL, 113 Ave Abdelkarim El-Khattabi, **t** 0524 437647; *open Mon–Fri 8.30–4.30, Sat and hols 8.30–12.30.*

FedEx, (same address as DHL, above), **t** 0524 448257; *open Mon–Fri 8–6, Sat 8–12.15.*

TNT: 240 Z.I. Sidi Ghanem, **t** 0522 276728 (general Morocco number), *accueil@tnt-maroc.com*

Chronopost, 3 Immeuble le Verdroyant, Ave Hassan II, **t** 0522 422020, www.chronopost.com. This French service is both cheaper and slower than its more globally recognised cousins.

Emergencies

Police: t 19

Fire Service: t 16

Ambulance: t 15

Private ambulance: 10, Rue Fatima Zohra, t 0524 443724

Telephone Enquiries: t 160

Hospitals and Medical Care

Travel insurance is a necessary expense for travelling in Morocco, since it saves you a lot of cost and even trouble. For more on Insurance, *see* Planning Your Trip, p.73.

Marrakesh is very well-equipped with medical services. A Moroccan doctor will come to your hotel, and may charge up to 500dh, which can be claimed back on insurance. The UK embassy recommends **Dr G. Michaelis Agoumi**, who speaks fluent English, especially useful when trying to describe symptoms and understand diagnoses. His office is in the *ville nouvelle* at 7, Rue Ibn Sina, Quartier de l'Hopital Civil, Guéliz, **t** 0524 448343. If you require hospital treatment, the following are recommended:

Polyclinique du Sud, 2 Rue Yougoslavie, Guéliz, **t** 0524 447999. This is a reliable private clinic which is recommended by travellers and embassies.

Polyclinique de la Koutoubia, Rue de Paris, **t** 0524 438585. This is convenient if you are closer to Hivernage.

Hôpital Ibn Tofail, Centre Hospitalier Universitaire Mohammed VI, Rue Mohammed El Beqal, **t** 0524 439395. A reliable public hospital.

Hôpital Avenzoar (Ibn Zuhr/Zohr), Quartier Sidi Mimoun (beside the Mamounia Hotel), **t** 0524 384145. Another good public hospital.

If you do need a doctor or **dentist**, it is worth asking at your hotel for a recommendation. You are spoilt for choice when it comes to preserving your ivories but you would be best to avoid the many amateur enthusiasts whose handmade 'dentist here' signs are a feature of Morocco's medinas.

Marrakesh is endowed with plenty of well-stocked **pharmacies** across the city. There is one on the Jemaa el Fna and there are many along Ave Mohammed V. Most shut for lunch but are open from 8.30am and only close at dusk. **All-night pharmacies** exist on the Jemaa el Fna beside the police headquarters and on Rue Khalid ben Oualid in the *ville nouvelle*. If in doubt, ask at your hotel. Pharmacies are often much more willing to sell you medications that in western countries would require a prescription (notably antibiotics), which can be useful if you are in urgent need. Pharmacies are also useful if you need to purchase cosmetics and toiletries.

Maps

Tourist offices often have the most recent maps and will give you a copy for free but they tend to deteriorate quickly. A reasonable map of Marrakesh is printed by International Travel Maps and is called '*Marrakesh and Northern Morocco*'. Insight do a laminate, flexible city map that's very handy. You will not find a map with all medina alley names marked.

(★) **La Porte d'Or >>**

Money

There are a few **banks** on the south side of the Jemaa el Fna and a BMCE around the corner on Rue Moulay Ismail near a WAFA bureau de change. But there are considerably more banks in the *ville nouvelle*, many of them on Ave Mohammed V (Crédit du Maroc, CIH, Attijariwafa, etc). These days banks tend not to take a lunch break.

It is generally best to rely on **cashpoints** (ATMs) in Marrakesh although on Sundays those in the medina sometimes run out, at which point you should head to Guéliz.

Shopping in Marrakesh

Although Marrakesh souk has an extensive a range of Moroccan crafts as anywhere in the country, the bazaar merchants are also used to extracting some pretty fabulous sums from rich and careless visitors who have come straight off the plane into this Aladdin's Cave. You may find that you will have to spend even more time and energy than normal bargaining things down to a decent price. Check out the prices and quality of the crafts on offer at the **Ensemble Artisanale**, Ave Mohammed V, **t** 0524 443503, in the *ville nouvelle* first if you lack confidence over haggling.

It is worth finding a map and then you might begin in Rue Souk Smarine. This last street runs north from the Jemaa el Fna for 250 metres before forking into Souk el Attarin (to the northwest) and Souk El Kebir (to the northeast). El Kebir leads up towards the Ben Youssef Mosque and Medersa. Otherwise, however, products tend to cluster around particular neighbourhoods along the alleyways that flank these three arterial streets.

Shopping is a good way to spend the hot, middle hours of the day if you have the energy, since the souks are largely in the shade, although in high summer the midday temperatures are simply too much for many tourists, even in the souks.

Antiques

La Porte d'Or, 115 Rue Souk Smarine. This is the best place to start your search for Moroccan antiques, before fanning out into neighbouring shops. Always get a receipt for major items in order to avoid export tax.

Apothecary

Around the **Rahba Kédima**, there are still a few stalls which sell the strange herbal remedies, love potions, aphrodisiacs and animal skins favoured by medieval doctors and mystics alike.

Books and Prints

There are a few bookshops that stock foreign titles, with French being the most common but English very much on the increase. Paperbacks are often available at the kiosks found in or near the smarter hotels.

Café du Livre, 44 Rue Tarik ben Ziad, **t** 0524 432149. A good place for lunch and a sleepy afternoon read, this has café tables and sofas and more than 2,000 titles in English, as well as hundreds in other European languages. It hosts the odd book launch and poetry reading too. *Open Mon–Sat 9.30am–9pm.*

ACR Librairie, 55 Blvd Zerktouni, Guéliz, **t** 0524 446792. Sumptuously illustrated coffee table books, plus a small range of guidebooks in English.

Librairie Dar El-Bacha, **t** 0524 391973, *www.darelbacha.com.* Another largely French bookshop, with regular book signings.

Marrabook Café, 53 Derb Gebbada (off Ave des Princes), no tel, *www.marrabook.e-monsite.com.* Close to the Jemaa el Fna, this stocks plenty of English and French paperbacks (and also offers a book exchange service). It also serves reasonably priced Moroccan and French dishes, which you can eat out on the terrace. *Open daily 9am–9pm.*

Several of the museums and palaces have decent bookstores which are worth a glance; they are particularly good for lavishly illustrated photography books.

Carpets, Blankets and Weaving

Marrakesh is a good but not brilliant place to buy your Berber carpets. **Souk Smarine** has plenty of carpets while **Dar Nejjarine Carpets** has perhaps the best service of any single outlet. **La Criée Berbère**, on the north side of Rahba Kédima (a square less than 200 metres north of the Jemaa el Fna) is the best spot to see them all hung out on display. (It was once the slave market.) Be prepared for outrageous price quotes (even as much as €1,000) but, with time and patience, you can get a reasonable deal, although it is cheaper to buy outside the city.

If in doubt, the tougher and more unusual Berber rugs tend to be less obviously conceptually unified, a maze-like collage of patterns (with occasional spaces flecked with the odd macabre sign) whereas the Arab rugs emphasize grandeur and luxury in both style and substance, if not always imaginatively.

Ceramics

These are an exceptional Moroccan craft and worth more than a few dirhams, if you can get them home in one piece. *Tagine* pots (with their round bases and conical lids), soup tureens and spice jars are all good investments in Marrakesh's markets. Some of the more decorative items, many of them made in nearby Safi, are for sale in the Mouassine area, while everyday ware is available throughout the souks. You will get mildly better prices in Safi or Fez but, if you see something you like, it is usually worth the few dirhams' difference to have it in your hand.

Copper, Brass and Ironwork

Opposite the southern end of the Mouassine Mosque, and huddled around its 16th-century fountain, are the coppersmiths, hammering out their vessels. Here you can buy cooking pots, intricately-latticed lamps and an assortment of goods.

The Mellah (Jewish quarter) still has plenty of excellent metalwork available. Brass is ubiquitous as ever but ironwork has increased in popularity in recent years. **Souk des Tamis** has forged iron goods and lies just east of the Mosque Al-Mansour.

For lanterns, try **Souk Haddadine** (the blacksmiths' souk), close to Rue Bab Doukkala, although it is also excellent for ironwork generally. Also very good for copper lanterns is the shop at 28 Souk des Teinturiers.

Fabrics

The **Dyers' Souk** is largely enjoyed for the spectacle of colour but you can buy freshly-dyed fabrics here too.

The covered *kissarias* are a good place to root around for fabrics and

(★) Kif-Kif >

clothes (including kaftans, *jellabas* and other cloakish garments) but you could also leave haggling behind at Kif-Kif at 8, Rue Laksour (*www.kifkifbystef.com*), a small outfit offering all sorts of surprising and inventive bags, clothes and jewellery for all ages and made by local artisans. (A percentage of their profits goes towards a local charity for disabled children.)

The **Souk Marine** on the east side of Souk Smarine and close to Jemaa el Fna is the textiles souk and **Souk Larzal** (for wool) is just north of it.

Jewellery

A little north of La Criée Berbère is the **Souk des Bijoutiers** (or Bijoux) or Jewellers' Souk. This is an excellent place to find the solid shapes of Berber jewellery, with precious and semi-precious stones crowded alongside beads, stones and wooden teeth. The finer jewellery generally left the city with the Jews but survives in Fez. The **Boutique Bel Hadj** at 22 Fondouk Ourzazi (second floor) in Place Bab Ftueh is also well worth a visit for its fabulous workmanship.

Leatherwork

The **Souk Cherratin**, a stone's throw south of the Ben Youssef Mosque, is the best place to buy leather goods.

A visit to the **tanneries** (*see* p.133) is a wonderful experience, even though you can only peer down on them from a little distance. Set out in gulleys the tanneries look like a painter's palette and the colours are at least as rich. Jackets and belts are a good investment here.

Slippers

On the northwest side of the Kissaria is the **Souk des Babouches** (Slipper Souk). Slippers tend to conjure in western minds the crested velvet retirement wear of the well-to-do, but Moroccan slippers (*babouches*) are leather, pointed and in a range of flamboyant colours. They make excellent presents and a good haggle might win you a plain pair for 50dh.

Spices and Scents

The famous **Souk El Attarin** (Spices/Perfumes market) is the traditional centre for cumin, cinnamon, paprika or mint as well as scented waters, but also an increasingly overwhelming array of unlovely trinkets. You can buy spices throughout the markets. One good spot is in the long, thin end of the little square of Place Rahba Kédima (also home to the Café des Épices), just off the Jemaa el Fna.

Woodwork

Just north of the Dyers' Souk you can find carpenters at work in the **Souk Chouari**. Woodworking is engrained in Moroccan culture and here you can buy doors, shutters, candlesticks and the like. **La Porte d'Or**, 115 Souk Smarine, is a good place to hunt these down. You may find a jewellery box or chest here but if you are travelling to Fez or Meknès it might be worth waiting.

Sports and Activities

Marrakesh is well equipped for the athletic traveller – although the heat might ensure that even the most determined fitness fanatic may opt for another *hammam* and massage instead.

Cycling and Running

Many hotels hire out bicycles, especially in the medina, but cycling on main roads is not wise in Marrakesh. If you need a mountain bike for heading out of town, contact **Marrakesh Motos**, 31 Ave Muhammed Abdelkrim el-Khattabi, t 0524 448359, or **Aboul Abdallah**, 14 Blvd El-Khattabi, t 0524 432238.

The most rigorous runners might consider the annual **Marathon des Sables**, a 240-kilometre run across the Sahara (usually held in April). Moroccans are exceptional runners and there is an annual **Marrakesh marathon**, too (in January). If running alone, an early medina run could be quite fun as the shops are opening. Following the ramparts would suit a true long-distance runner and one or two of the parks would work well if you arrived early enough, particularly the Aguedal Gardens (*see* p.135).

⭐ **Les Bains de Marrakesh >>**

Desert and Mountains

Besides the multi-marathon above, there are also **trips by jeep** that can be made into the Sahara. **Quad-biking** is very popular too and can be done at La Palmeraie (*see* p.137) or through a number of agencies in Marrakesh. Try **Trek Morocco** if you want an organized trip (*www.trekmorocco.com*) or just hire one from **Marrakesh Motos** at 31, Ave Abdelkarım El Khattabi in the *ville nouvelle*, **t** 0524 448359.

The Atlas Mountains offer a wealth of **trekking** possibilities. From Marrakesh, you are best to head for the Ourika Valley (*see* p.158) by bus or taxi (45 minutes) and spend a night or two at the charming **Ourika Garden hotel** (*see* Where to Stay in the Ourika Valley, p.161). They can organize treks or cultural trips for you too.

For outdoor and extreme sports generally close to Marrakesh, try **Dunes Desert**, **t** 0661 246948, *www.dunesdesert.com*.

Golf and Health Clubs

The 1920s' **Royal Golf Club**, six kilometres down the road to Ouarzazate, is exceptional and was a favourite of Winston Churchill, **t** 0524 444341. The Atlas mountains provide the backdrop.

With its seven lakes, the **Palmeraie golf club** is a beautiful course built for some serious golf. It is located in the Jardins de La Palmeraie, Circuit de la Palmeraie, **t** 0524 301010.

Amelkis has excellent Atlas views and hosts the Moroccan Open. A tough course, it is on the same road as the Royal, **t** 0524 449284.

For **health clubs**, the hotels are generally best, although there are some cheap gyms in the *ville nouvelle*. **La Pause** (*www.lapause-marrakech.com*) is a little under an hour's drive from Marrakesh and offers a more sustainable form of 'cross-country' golf than you are likely to find elsewhere. (It also offers B&B accommodation, horse-riding, dining under the stars, olive oil tastings, and a host of other activities.)

Hammam

Les Bains de Marrakesh, 2 Derb Sedra, Bab Agnaou, **t** 0524 381428, *www.lesbainsdemarrakech.com*. This riad-*hammam* on the edge of the medina (just inside the ramparts and close to the El Mansour mosque) makes an excellent stop after the rigours of a day's sightseeing. A 45-minute *hammam* costs 150dh, and a 2hr massage-and-*hammam* treatment costs 500dh. They also have a pool. (Note to women: you will be asked to remove bikini tops. Be sure to wear bikini bottoms instead of shorts if you want to keep them on.)

For more on *hammam* etiquette, *see* Practical A–Z, p.86.

Riding

Marrakesh's **Royal Polo Club** on the Asni Road out of the city offers riding and other equestrian sports, **t** 0524 448529, but you could also try **Club Atlas**, **t** 0524 431301. Closer to home, you might pick up a **horse and cart** on the edge of the Jemaa el Fna (towards the Koutoubia minaret) and go for a tour of the ramparts, especially as dusk approaches.

Spectator Sports

Kawbab Marrakesh, the country's first official football club, has a large stadium (45,000). Tickets are best organised through your hotel or via the French-language website at *www.kawkabi.com*. Elsewhere in Marrakesh football games are often wonderfully spontaneous.

Swimming

Many of the hotels have swimming pools and the smarter riads tend to have plunge pools.

There is a popular and inexpensive **municipal pool** in Moulay Abdessalam Garden that you enter opposite the Ensemble Artisanale in the *ville nouvelle*, which attracts an energetic, teenage gathering.

The **Cascades d'Ouzoud** (about 165km from the city) make for a good swim among waterfalls. Take a bus to Azilal from where you can catch a *grand taxi* to the waterfalls for 25dh. There are several hotels and restaurants in the area. If you're coming for the day, it's best to leave Marrakesh by 9.30am.

For a swim at the Mamounia Hotel (see Where to Stay, below), you might want to combine it with a pre-dinner drink at the Churchill bar. They can be snooty about non-guests, so be sure to dress smartly and don't let the moody doormen put you off.

Where to Stay in Marrakesh

If you have not already made a reservation, the information desk at Marrakesh's Menara airport will be able to help; they can book a hotel and a taxi to get you there (without overcharging you for the journey).

All hotels in the luxury category (see Planning Your Trip, p.79 for price categories) will have air conditioning and a TV with satellite stations, and the moderate-priced hotels probably will do too. Most will have *hammams* but you will usually need to pay extra for a massage.

New hotels are constantly appearing in the city and prices continue to track upwards. One new hotel outside Marrakesh reportedly charges €30,000 a night and serves visitors from the Gulf states, while, for your ordinary rich, the Mamounia and Palmeraie still have their long-established cachet.

While in Fez there are still old hotels decked out in 70s or 80s furniture and fabrics, you are less likely to find this in Marrakesh and certainly not in the centre. The city's popularity with filmstars and bankers alike has created a luxury market while interior designers flock to the souks for its fabrics, woodwork and metalwork. There is no need to stay in a dowdy hotel in Marrakesh.

Mid-range travellers increasingly stay in **riads**, the old courtyard houses that can usually only offer around ten or twelve rooms at most. These are an excellent option and many are hidden down narrow alleyways, unannounced behind a heavy wooden door except for a small brass sign. Inside, they are cool, restful places, often with a plunge pool at the centre. If you value

high levels of privacy or are an exceptionally light sleeper, a riad may not be for you.

If you have young children, riads are usually less restful because of the many hazards: pool, stairs, balconies and more. But many riads are quite safe, especially if you can get a ground floor room. (Try the following websites for more riad options in Marrakesh: www.riadreviews.com and www.31best-riad-marrakesh.com).

At the lowest end of the spectrum, riads are scarce since their dimensions mean they cannot operate as economies of scale. Off-season you can often haggle down prices and in the balmy Marrakesh summer you can usually sleep on a riad's roof for very little indeed, which is a memorable way to spend your waking hours.

Aside of price, your other important choice is whether to stay in the medina or the new town, the latter being more convenient for train connections but less interesting and picturesque. Within the medina, either aim for accommodation within a stone's throw of the Jemaa el Fna (and certainly not far north of it) or go south towards the kasbah, where some of the best monuments and sights are, such as the Bahia Palace, El Badi Palace and Mellah. Outside the city, the Palmeraie area has luxury hotels aplenty, as well as scores of more energetic activities available.

All the luxury and expensive hotels and many of their moderate underlings will pick you up from the airport, which saves hassle and money. Others will do so for a fee, which is worth paying, as Marrakshis drive a hard bargain.

Luxury

Hotel Amanjena, Route de Ouarzazate (12km outside the city), t 0524 399000, www.amanjena.com. Amanjena has some fabulous buildings and gardens, wonderful service and some excellent views. You will be well-fed and pampered although the hotel occasionally feels like a luxury theme park.

Les Jardins de la Koutoubia, 26 Rue de la Koutoubia, near Place de Foucauld, t 0524 388800, www.lesjardinsde

★ Riad
Farnatchi ›››

★ Riad Kniza ›››

lakoutoubia.com. This 72-room hotel has a piano bar, several pools, underground parking and a patchwork quilt of patios, terraces and lawns. Parts of it are very attractive and the food is very good.

Jnane Tamsna, Douar Abiad, La Palmeraie, t 0524 328484, *www. jnanetamsna.com*. This exceptional hotel is in the Palmeraie outside the city and one of several in the area. With all the usual facilities, it also has beautiful gardens and an excellent track record with return guests. You can stay in a villa, house or room in the main hotel, a decision which will dictate where on the sliding scale of prices you find youself (€250–€430). Expect a blissful environment and wonderful food if not necessarily luxury-level service.

La Mamounia, Ave Bab Jdid, t 0524 388600, *www.mamounia.com*. Winston Churchill's favourite hotel was renovated between 2006 and 2009 but retains most of its fabulous art deco grandeur, even if some of its old-world understatement is lost and the décor can be a tad fussy. Its elegant gardens and procession of superb interiors distinguish it from all of Marrakesh's other offerings. The hotel is enormous but successfully scatters its guests among the various bars, restaurants and terraces. Scantily clad blondes may dominate the poolside but you will need a tie for dinner. Although the food is perfectly good, it is probably the hotel's least notable feature and you should splash out somewhere else. Mamounia's oft-reported organizational problems seem to be in retreat.

Riad El Fenn, Derb Moulay Abdullah Ben Hezzian, Bab El Ksour, t 0524 441220, *www.riadelfenn.com*. Begun as a single riad hotel by Richard Branson's sister, El Fenn now stretches across several, with three pools, a *hammam* and plush rooms with large, marbled bathrooms. Afternoon tea and cakes are served as standard in the central, leafy courtyard by the amenable staff, and an excellent breakfast roof terrace looks onto the nearby Koutoubia minaret, emblem of the city. Rooms begin at around €250

per night, although they regularly offer great packages on the website.

Riad Farnatchi, Derb el Farnatchi, Rue Souk el Fassis, Qua'at Ben Ahid, *www.riadfarnatchi.com*. Farnatchi is in the centre of the medina but is restful and elegant with excellent service. The rooms are attractive, comfortable and quiet while it has all the facilities you could hope for. If you want luxury and every service imaginable (such as personal shoppers) without glitz or excessive remove from the city's heart, this is your best bet. Rooms are around €350 to €450.

Riad Kniza, 34 Derb l'Hotel, Bab Doukkala, t 0524 376942, *www. riadkniza.com*. A beautiful riad with just eleven luxurious rooms and suites set around a trio of courtyards, all lavishly furnished with exquisite Moroccan crafts and antiques. There is also an exceptional restaurant (*see* Where to Eat, below). Also renowned for its tours, which, while pricy, are imaginative and well-organized.

Expensive

Dar Attajmil, 23 Rue Laksour, t 0524 426966, *www.darattajmil.com*. An attractive, leafy medina riad with elegant rooms and some wonderful rugs. It is handily located a little northwest of the Jemaa el Fna.

Ksar Anika, Route Makbara des Juifs (next to the Mellah), t 0524 391739, *www.ksaranika.com*. Free to the under-3s and wonderfully located beside the Badia Palace and therefore good for exploring the Kasbah area, Anika has a wonderful *pisé* roof terrace with excellent views and is otherwise restrained and quiet with plenty of attractive rooms. You can idle away time in the mini cinema or slip into the diminutive plunge pool for a dip but it is the gentle friendliness and helpfulness of its Moroccan owner and staff that especially sets you at ease. Room prices start around €190.

La Maison Arabe, 1 Derb Assehbé, Bab Doukkala, t 0524 387010, *www.lamaisonarabe.com*. La Maison Arabe has been hidden away in the medina since its founding in 1946 and remains one of the best places in Marrakesh to lay your head. The service, food and facilities are all good but the décor is probably what you will take away with you: comfortable, elegant and unfailingly Moroccan. The pool patio is especially enticing. Rooms begin at around €140 in the off season.

Maison Mnabha, 32/3 Derb Mnabha, **t** 0524 381325, *www.maisonmnabha. com*. This Aladdin's Den of antiques, rugs and beautifully carved wooden doors is ideal for the shopping traveller interested in buying antiques (by drawing on the considerable knowledge of Peter Lawrence, one of its owners). With excellent food, this is a good choice if you want to stay in the Kasbah area, and enjoy a room decorated with items only a truly discerning collector could have gathered.

Palais Donab, 53 Dar El Basha, Bab Doukkala, Medina, **t** 0524 441897, *http://dardonab.com/*. Centred on a lush, flower-filled and sunny courtyard with a good-sized pool, Donab's rooms are redolent of the kitsch glamour of Egyptian TV soaps, all white and gold. In a good location for the southern sites (close to the Kasbah), the hotel has an exceptional roof terrace with excellent views, which is good for breakfast or a chilled beer at sunset. Generally at the top of this price category, but some rooms drop as low as €130 in the off-peak season.

Riad Dar One, 19 Derb Jamar El Kabir, Hay Salam, **t** 0661 306328, *www.riad-dar-one.com*. This medina riad is elegant, minimalist and well cared for. Dar One is closest to the Bahia Palace and has an enthusiastic staff. Breakfast is included in the price, and dinner can be arranged if you book in advance. At the bottom end of this price category.

Riad Tizwa, Derb Gueraba, 26 Dar El Bacha, **t** 0668 190872 (UK: **t** 07973 238444), *www.holidaymarrakesh.com*. At the lowest end of this price bracket, Tizwa was the first riad in Marrakesh to receive the international Clef Verte for its environmentally sensitive management. Founded by two very amenable and friendly Scottish brothers who spend several months a year there, Tizwa is very attractive, understated and reasonably priced, and employs Moroccan fabrics and designs. With rooms beginning at €95 a night and charming bilingual staff, it makes a wonderful base. They have a beautiful riad in Fez too (*see* Where to Stay in Fez, p.214) which can make organising two-city accommodation (and airport taxis) that much easier.

Moderate

Riad Akka, 65 Derb Lahbib Magni, Riad Zitoun Jdid, **t** 0524 375767, *www.riad-akka.com*. Contemporary art and traditional Moroccan furnishings are stylishly combined at this boutique-style riad, with just five ultra-chic bedrooms set around a central patio. There's a small pool and *hammam*, and they offer delicious local cuisine (dinner must be reserved in advance), and a roof terrace with views over La Bahia palace. They can arrange tours throughout the region as well as guided visits in Marrakesh. Rooms start at €80–€100.

Riad Croix Berbère, 8 Derb Fhal Zefriti Laksour, **t** 0524 375503, *www. riadcroixberbere.com*. When the author stayed there the Croix Berbère was being run by Berbers, and is fitted out with Berber designs and fabrics. Cosy and colourful, it has an attractive roof terrace and a small, ice-cold plunge pool. A useful and inexpensive central *pied-à-terre* but space is short so this is not a place to while away the hours, unless you head for the terrace or pay for a larger room (€70–80 for the larger double rooms).

Riad Eden, 25 Derb Jdid, Riad Zitoune Lakdim, **t** 0672 046910, *www.riadeden.com*. Eden is a colourful, welcoming city base – cosy and sociable. The bedrooms are all different and often imaginatively decorated. Doubles start at €50.

Riad El Borj, 63 Derb Moulay Abdelkader, Derb Dabachi, **t** 0524 391223, *www.riadelborj.com*. A simple but pleasant riad which centres on an old tower (*borj* in Arabic). Berber rugs hang from the walls and the overall effect is of gleaming whitewashed walls, a profusion of plants and dappled light. The Café de France is next door.

★ Riad Akka >>

★ Riad Tizwa >

Riad Laksour >

Riad Laksour, 9 Derb El Boukili, **t** 0524 426865, *riadlaksour@hotmail.fr*. This charming and traditional riad has just five rooms and suites, set around a patio filled with luxuriant plants and trees. It's well located just off the Jemaa el Fna, and the delightful French owners are happy to arrange airport transfers and offer advice. There's a small plunge pool and fabulous views from the roof terrace.

Tlaatawa-Sitleen, 63 Derb El Ferrane, Riad Laarouss, **t** 0635 99223, *www.tlaatawa-sitteen.com*. This pleasant and quiet little riad is more modest than many, a good hide-away from the brash colours and luxury of much of tourist Marrakesh. It has an sweet courtyard and terrace and a friendly, helpful owner.

Inexpensive

Dar Tayib, 19 Derb Lalla Azzouna, Kaat Bennahid, **t** 0524 383010, *www.riad-dartayib.com*. An attractive riad just west of the tanneries, Tayib is clean, simple and reasonable with a pleasant, comfortable terrace and plenty of plants.

Hotel Central Palace, 59 Sidi Abou Lwakat, **t** 0524 440235, *http://lecentralpalace.com*. Located close to the Jemaa el Fna as well as the train and bus stations, Central Palace is an attractive, capacious building with a fantastic roof terrace, a well-conceived courtyard and a grandeur beyond its price. As if to redress the balance, the staff can be haughty and unhelpful. (For this reason, your day-trips or guides are best booked elsewhere.)

La Gallia, 30 Rue de la Recette, **t** 0524 445913, *www.ilove-marrakesh.com/hotelgallia*. A colourful and often surprising hotel, what La Gallia lacks in unifying vision it makes up for with variety and strong colours. A fun place to stay which has been around for years, so you will need to book well in advance.

Jnane Mogador, 116 rue Zitoune Kedim, Derb Sidi Bouloukat, **t** 0524 426323, *www.jnanemogador.com*. With an attractive courtyard and roof terrace, Mogador is popular with old Morocco hands. Beds and rooms are

Hotel Essaouira >>

variable in comfort and quality but this is a good place to pick up tips about the city. There have been reports that they can be a little less than service-oriented when you try to book in advance (which you will need to do in high season).

Cheap

These are often perfectly attractive, frequently clean (though beware bedbugs) and sometimes well-managed options but, since many of them are clustered very close to the Jemaa el Fna, the trade-off tends to be in noise, either from the Jemaa and its buoyant side streets or, much louder and more sleep-destroying, from the muezzin's much-amplified, pre-dawn call-to-prayer from the Koutoubia Mosque. If you are a light sleeper, check which way your room faces in advance and pack ear plugs. Here are a couple of the more established ones, but there are many more on and just off the square.

Hotel Ali, Rue Moulay Ismail, **t** 0524 444979. A simple, slightly grimy but ever-popular option, a room at the Ali may have broken lights or dirty carpets but the location remains fantastic and it's a good option for the unfussy traveller with a light wallet. Wonderful roof terrace. The food, unfortunately, is poor.

Hotel Essaouira, 3 Sidi Bouloukate, **t** 0524 443805, *essaouira@jnanemogador.com*. A great terrace and a hotel with a glamorous hippie past, the Essaouira is a backpacker's haven and rightly so. A good social hub – but noise and the constant press of people are the potential downsides.

Camping

There is a campsite called **Camping Ferdaous**, which lies 13km out of town on the Casablanca road, and is a good, well-kept site.

If you yearn to be under a grander kind of canvas, **Les Jardins d'Issil** (*www.jardinsissil.com*), about 13km from the city centre on the Route de l'Ourika, is attractive and has capacious, luxurious tents but takes advantage of its isolation by overcharging you for everything else.

Eating Out in Marrakesh

In this city you can dine lavishly in magnificent surroundings, and eat cheap fresh local food in one of the world's great public spaces. However, food should be one of the highlights of a visit to Marrakesh, so it is worth planning to visit a good restaurant or two. It is worth remembering that Marrakesh's sensitivity to fashion and trends mean some restaurants may look sensational but serve indifferent food. Medina restaurants generally lack a licence to serve alcohol, though there is some variation on this.

Expensive

L'Abyssin, Palais Rhoul (on the Fez road, a kilometre outside Bab El Khémis, the city's northern gate), **t** 0524 328584, *www.restaurant-labyssin.com*. White, minimalist and trendy, L'Abyssin makes a stunning setting for a memorable dinner. The menu is largely French with a few Moroccan dishes.

Aman, in the Hotel Amanjena, Route de Ouarzazate (12km outside the city), **t** 0524 399000, *www.amanjena.com*. Aman has an excellent chef who does largely Moroccan food but a few Mediterranean dishes too. The hotel enjoys a fabulous setting a few miles out of town – it would be worth arriving before dusk for a stroll and drink before dinner.

Dar Marjana, 15 Derb Sidi Tair, Bab Doukkala, **t** 0524 385110, *www.darmarjanamarrakesh.com*. A wonderful riad for a Moroccan dinner. The setting is idyllic and the food's value lies not in its originality but in the quality of the familiar Moroccan dishes. Marjana's set menu is around €55 and offers a great night, complete with belly dancers, even if the service is variable.

Dar Moha, 81 Rue Dar El Bacha, **t** 0524 386400, *www.darmoha.ma*. In a former palace, this has a fabulous setting, especially if you can sit beside the mosaic-floored pool. The wine list is strong and the chef has profited from more than a decade in Switzerland. His takes on traditional Moroccan dishes are often excellent.

Birds overhead can be a problem if they target your table but this is otherwise best for a romantic dinner. Ask for an umbrella. The set menu is around €50, and desserts a feature.

Dar Yacout, 79 Sidi Ahmed Soussi, **t** 0524 310104/382929, *contact@yacout.com*. This Marrakesh institution is a sensation. You always start with a drink on the roof terrace before a generously-proportioned meal that is good enough to draw even Morocco's king. Service is exemplary and the fabulous refurbishment was done by the late architect Bill Willis. Expect to pay €75 a head and try the lemon almond chicken *tagine*. Book in advance.

Dar Zellij, Kaasour Sidi Ben Slimane, **t** 0524 382627, *www.darzellij.com*. This atmospheric 17th-century riad offers several Moroccan menus, starting at around €55. The setting is phenomenal and makes a visit worthwhile, especially in the evening, even if the food is overpriced.

Le Foundouk, 55 Souk Hal Fassi, **t** 0524 378190, *www.foundouk.com*. Beautifully presented Moroccan food. Many *tagine* options here and some sweet French desserts.

Riad Kniza, 34 Derb l'Hotel, Bab Doukkala, **t** 0524 376942, *www.riadkniza.com/marrakesh-restaurant*. A Marrakesh favourite, the restaurant at Riad Kniza is exceptionally good from every angle. This is a good place for vegetarians too. Food choices must be made 24 hours in advance.

La Trattoria de Giancarlo, 179 El Beqal, Guéliz, **t** 0524 432641, *www.latrattoriamarrakesh.com*. This idyllic Hispano-Moresque building makes for a picturesque meal but the Italian food is as good as anywhere in the city. Although in the *ville nouvelle*, you wouldn't know it once you have stepped inside.

Moderate

Le Bis-Jardin des Arts, 6–7 Rue Sakia El Hamra, Semlalia, **t** 0524 446634, *www.lebis-jardindesarts.com*. The food is usually excellent here and the ice-palace décor makes it one of the city's more appealing mealtime stops. Mostly French dishes. The terrace is exceptional.

 Dar Yacout >>

 Riad Kniza >>

 Le Bis-Jardin des Arts >>

Grand Café de la Poste, Blvd El Mansour Eddahbi (junction with Ave Imam Malik), **t** 0524 433038, *www.grandcafedelaposte.com*. This old bastion of French colonialism and cooking remains excellent. Although there's the odd Moroccan dish, come here for the French cooking and the graceful, rustic interior.

Grand Hôtel Tazi, Rue de Bab Agnaou, **t** 0524 442787. Slightly further down the culinary pecking order, but the terraced bar tends to stay open longer. The latter is popular with impecunious beer-drinkers, whether foreign students or locals when they finish work.

Hôtel de Foucauld, Ave El Mouahidine, **t** 0524 445499, *http://hotel-foucauld-marrakesh.com*. This offers a filling five-course set meal at a reasonable price, as well as a mixed Moroccan-French and Italian menu (and has a drinks licence). The cooking is sound if uninspired, but you get to eat and drink in an atmospheric high-ceilinged Moorish dining room with a fine old whirring fan.

Kanyama, 22 Rue Moulay Ali, **t** 0524 421494. A convivial French restaurant with a warm welcome and exceptional steak.

Ksar Es Saoussan, Rue des Ksour 3, Derb El Messoudyenne, **t** 0524 440632, *www.essaoussane.com*. The décor is strangely convoluted but the set menus offer good Moroccan fare, and it has a licence to serve drinks.

Pizzeria Venetia, 279 Ave Mohammed V, **t** 0524 440081. This is the roof-top restaurant of the Islane Hotel. It looks directly out at the Koutoubia Mosque and has a number of classic Moroccan dishes on its menu as well as pizzas and the familiar Italian standards.

★ **Restaurant El Fassia >**

Restaurant El Fassia, 232 Ave Mohammed V, **t** 0524 434060. This is an exceptional place, run by a staff of women who have achieved the rare balance of a committed approach to Moroccan cooking without degenerating into an orientalist feast. Here you can order single dishes, not whole meals, from a well-thought-out menu in a modern Islamic-style interior. The main courses are the culinary highlight.

Restaurant Le Jacaranda, 32 Blvd Mohammed Zerktouni, **t** 0524 447215, *http://jacaranda.chez.com*. At the northern end of the New Town opposite the strategic tables of the Brasserie des Négociants on the busy Place Abdel Moumen ben Ali, has a fire in winter, air conditioning in summer and a French menu that takes full advantage of the fish and shellfish available from the coast. It's been here for sixty years.

La Sultana, 403 Rue de la Kasbah, **t** 0524 388008, *www.lasultanamarrakesh.com*. Service may not be exemplary but the food and setting are both appealing, whether for lunch or dinner. Set menus start at €11.

Terrasse des Épices, 15 Souk Cherifia, Sidi Abdelaziz, **t** 0524 375904, *www.terrassedesepices.com*. Simple and tasty food at this terrace restaurant. It is especially idyllic when Chinese lanterns are lit at night. No drinks licence.

Villa Flore, 4 Derb Azzouz (Mouassine district), **t** 0524 391700, or book via website messaging at their site: *www.villa-flore.com*. Funky, attractive riad restaurant where art deco provides the backdrop for tender Moroccan dishes.

Inexpensive

Many of the best cheap options are scattered around the Jemaa el Fna. If you buy here, be sure the food is fresh but street *tagine* can be very good and the main square is a pretty picture by night.

There are also several café-restaurants with terraces which overlook the Jemaa el Fna, including the **Café de France**, **Restaurant Argana** and others. The **Café Glacier** sits next to the CTM. Rue Bani Marine and Rue de Bab Agnaou, which emanate south from the square, also have a few cafés and the well-positioned **Café des Épices** (with its roof terrace) sits on the Place Rahba Kédima. **Chez Chegrouni** just off the northeast corner has a terrace and offers a healthy lunch and the rooftop **Café-Restaurant El Badi** (by the palace of the same name) in the southern medina is a good place for lunch. It sits just west of Place des Ferblantiers.

A few other options include:

Café Agdal, 86 Ave Mohammed V. A good place to buy a snack or small lunch in the new town

Café Arabe, 184 Rue Mouassine, t 0524 429728, *www.cafearabe.com*. Delightful Italian-Moroccan café with well-presented food and a range of drinks.

⭐ Earth Café >

Earth Café, 2 Derb Zawak, Riad Zitoun Kedim, t 0660 544992, *www.earthcafe marrakech.com*. Vegetarian and vegan café in a colourful riad. One of the better places for lunch in the city. Non-carnivores swear by it.

Le Petit Poucet, 56 Ave Mohammed V, t 0524 431188. On the corner of Rue Mohammed el Bequal is another survivor from the colonial era.

Entertainment and Nightlife in Marrakesh

Marrakesh is never short of a party and there are bars and clubs across the city open until all hours.

Cinema and Theatre

Cinema Eden in the medina is an attractive spot although the best cinemas are generally in the *ville nouvelle*, notably the **Ciné Colisée**, Blvd Mohammed Zerktouni, t 0524 448893. Check the website *www. savecinemasinmarocco.com* for details of latest showings across town and of any film festivals. Check *www.festival-marrakesh.com* for details of the annual international film festival in December.

The majestic and cavernous **Theatre Royal**, t 0524 431516, sits opposite the railway station and has both a theatre (1,200 seats) and an opera house (800 seats). The annual summer **Marrakesh Festival of the Arts** (*www.marrakesh festival.com*) usually has events here.

Bars

Le Churchill at the Mamounia remains the doyen of the city's bars, but most of the smart hotels have good bars now. There is an attractive piano bar at **Les Jardins de la Koutoubia** (*see* p.144). For an old-school, leather-armchairs bar try the **Maison Arabe** by Bab Doukkala, but if you want to sing you should head to

CantoBar (38–39 Blvd Moulay El Hassan, Hivernage, t 0524 433350), an upmarket karaoke bar.

Trendier bars include **Kosybar** beside Place des Ferblantiers and especially **Comptoir Darna**, (*www.comptoirdarna.com*) where the first floor bar is exceptionally stylish.

Nightclubs

These range from clubs where all the women are working (and foreign women are sometimes not even allowed in) to more expensive bars where foreign women get in free. Between those extremes lie all sorts of possibilities, from belly dancing to hip-hop to karaoke, at an enormous range of prices. Entry could be anything from 50 to 200 dirhams. Most of the luxury hotels listed above offer some kind of club of their own which you may like to try.

Both **Paradise** (Pullman Mansour Eddahbi Hotel) and the **Cotton Club** (Hotel Tropicana, Lotissement Semlalia, t 0524 433913) are trendy discos that rarely overfill.

Equally trendy but more of an adventure is **New Feeling** (in the Hotel Golf, Jardins de la Palmeraie). The taxi ride is worth the glamorous club at the other end.

Straight and gay alike dance beneath mirrors to house and hip-hop at the glitzy **Le Diamant Noir**, Le Marrakesh Hotel, Place de la Liberté, t 0524 434351.

Often billed the biggest club in Africa, you will have to arrive early on weekends to get into **Pacha**, Complexe Pacha Marrakesh, Blvd Mohammed VI, t 0524 388405, *www.pachamarrakesh. com*, but on weeknights there'll be plenty of dance room to spare.

In the grounds of the Hotel Es Saadi and worth a visit is the popular **Teatro**, Hotel Es Saadi, Rue Qadissia.

Live Music

If you prefer to avoid the city's nightclubs, then you could either head to the Jemaa el Fna to hear some of the visiting bands. Or you could try **African Chic** at 6, Rue Oum Errabia in Guéliz (t 0524 431424, *www.african-chic.com*) where bands are scheduled.

Day Trips from Marrakesh

The highest and most dramatic range of mountains in North Africa, the High Atlas, rises immediately south of Marrakesh. This jagged horizon of ethereal blue peaks is a lodestone that draws visitors out from the city. The two great sights of the region, the **kasbah of Telouèt** and the **mosque of Tin-Mal**, however, make lengthy day trips from Marrakesh. The High Atlas can be crossed by only three mountain passes, of which only one, the Tizi-n-Babaou that links Marrakesh to Agadir, is open all year round. The Tizi-n-Test, that connects Marrakesh to Taroudannt, and the Tizi-n-Tichka to Ouarzazate are cut off by falls of snow and rocks for several weeks every year. As well as these crossings, three other tarmac roads intrude into the mountainous region, allowing easy access to the **Ourika Valley**, Jbel Oukaïmeden and the village of Amizmiz. For a day trip into the mountains, the Ourika Valley, with its selection of restaurants, is the obvious choice. The Ourika river sparkles and gurgles over rounded boulders and through the dappled shade of poplars, and even in the midsummer heat of Morocco the valley can appear like some image from an English pastoral poem. And yet, amid this tranquillity it can reveal a darker nature. One night a few Augusts ago it was suddenly transformed into a raging torrent for a few murderous hours, when a thunderstorm up among the distant peaks of the High Atlas announced the unleashing of a violent rainstorm that took the whole region by surprise. Roads, houses, bridges were swept aside in the confused hours of the night, and when by morning the water had receded it left a residue of drowned animals and humans – rarely from the indigenous Berber communities, who had kept to the hillside dry-stone houses of their ancestors – mixed among uprooted trees and river-flung boulders. This is a land that has always demanded great hardiness from its inhabitants.

Long before Marrakesh was founded, the Berber tribes of the High Atlas region practised a seasonal migration. In the winter they brought their flocks down to the plains, planted crops during the brief spring, and then through the summer slowly worked their way back up to the cooler Alpine grazing of the highland peaks. The foundation of a strong central authority at Marrakesh in the 11th century disturbed this pattern. The Almoravids, with their desert technology, improved the irrigation of the plain and established efficient gardens and a sedentary population on the most fertile tracts. Arab tribes who came to the region in the service of the sultans were rewarded with tracts of Berber tribal land below the foothills of the Atlas. By the 19th century most of the Berber tribes had been expelled from the plains by the fierce cavalry of these nomadic Arab tribes. The Berbers either stayed to

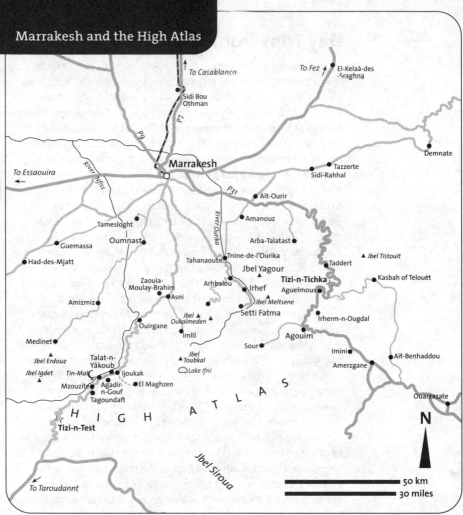

work as sharecroppers on the plain for an alien landlord, or moved up into the mountains in order to remain free sedentary farmers. There they remain today.

Another possible day trip from Marrakesh is the enchanting Atlantic town of **Essaouira**, a 4hr journey by bus. Here you can swim, wander through the town's souks, and eat at one of the many excellent fish restaurants.

The Tizi-n-Test

The **Tizi-n-Test pass** crosses the High Atlas to link Marrakesh and Taroudannt through 200km of mountain road. It can be closed by snow or made more dangerous by ice any time between December

Getting to the Tizi-n-Test

There are regular **buses** every day from Marrakesh to Asni (90 mins), which leave from Bab Doukkala bus station and call at the Bab er Rob stop on their way south. If you are heading farther up the valley you should take the dawn departure (either 5 or 6am) for Taroudannt.

A place in a *grand taxi* will get you to Asni or Zaouia-Moulay-Brahim in three-quarters of an hour for no more than 15dh. Or you could bargain with a *grand taxi* and hire him for between 200 and 300dh for a whole day trip.

and March, and each year some portion is destroyed by falling rocks or a swollen mountain stream.

Nevertheless, it is definitely worth venturing up here: you will have the opportunity to climb the highest mountain in North Africa, to visit one of only two mosques in Morocco (along with the Hassan II in Casablanca, see p.441) open to non-Muslims, and to admire a succession of ruined kasbahs. Or you might simply come for the clear air and to walk in the high valleys.

Tahanaoute

Thirty-one km from Marrakesh on the Taroudannt road, the S501, you pass the strikingly picturesque village of Tahanaoute on the far side of the riverbed. A cascade of *pisé* houses surrounds a great rock which shelters the **shrine of Sidi Mohammed El Kebir**, whose festival is celebrated at Mouloud. It was the subject of Winston Churchill's last painting in 1958. Tahanaoute proper is a kilometre further, an ancient marketplace on the border of the mountains and plains where a **souk** is held each Tuesday.

Zaouia-Moulay-Brahim

Beyond Tahanaoute the road twists up above the meandering course of the river as it flows past the five knuckles of black rock that protrude into **Moulay Brahim Gorge**. A cluster of cafés line the roadside and the riverbed just before the turning uphill to the village of **Zaouia-Moulay-Brahim**; they look out over a wooded hill on the other side of the river. This hillside *zaouia* is one of the most important centres of spiritual life in the region. A fortnight after Mouloud a great festival is held here. A camel is sacrificed at the gates of the town, and its head and skin are taken down to honour two nearby springs that are used for ritual washing by men and women. The 3hr trek to the *koubba* on the summit is an integral part of the pilgrimage. Gaily caparisoned horses stand patiently on the banks of the riverbed beside mounting stools for the use of pilgrims in need of a photographic souvenir of themselves in the pose of a cavalier.

Even outside the festival, Moulay-Brahim remains a popular day-trip destination for Marrakeshi families. The town is formed from a small maze of streets that extend in a confusion of levels, courts and paved passages around the central shrine. This has a distinctive green pyramid roof; a wooden bar has been placed below the minaret as a barrier to non-Muslims. The rest of the village, with its cafés, pilgrim trinket stalls, two surviving potteries and hill views, is open and the population is pleasantly welcoming.

Asni

This pleasant roadside village, 15km farther south, is the local administrative centre and the destination for most *grands taxis* from the Bab er Rob in Marrakesh. Apart from the opportunities for walking from the hotel here (Imlil, Zaouia-Moulay-Brahim and Ouirgane are all within easy reach), it could be worth a visit for the busy souk held here on Saturdays. From Asni a partly tarmacked road leads up to the hamlet of Imlil (6 hours drive), which is the centre for hill walking in the **Toubkal National Park**. The park is named after the highest mountain in all North Africa and embraces some of the most striking and awesome highland scenery in Morocco. If you want to walk in the park, you must make proper preparations and set aside several days. Maps and guides can be found in **Imlil**.

Ouirgane

Continuing on the main Tizi-n-Test road, the hamlet of **Ouirgane** lies 16km south of Asni. It mainly consists of two celebrated hotels, whose gardens face each other across a stream which drains the western face of Jbel Toubkal to merge with the river Nfiss just below the village. Four km south of Ouirgane there is the intriguing mass of drystone walls that forms the hilltop *agadir* at **Tagadirt-n-Bour**, to the right of the road. Possible strolls from the village include the two-hour walk up to villages such as **Tikhfist**, or to a mountain waterfall in the company of local guides.

Tin-Mal

Another few kilometres south, the Almohad mosque of **Tin-Mal** emerges high up on the opposite bank of the river, a fortress of the faith with its high walls and strong towers. It is usually empty of tourists, yet must be considered one of the most memorable sites of Morocco, the sole survivor of the 12th-century city of Tin-Mal and one of only three mosques in Morocco that a non-Muslim may enter. Its striking position, deep in the High Atlas mountains, is equalled only by its extraordinary history.

The mosque has been restored, and a small **museum** built to house various architectural fragments. The track from the road has also been repaired, and you no longer have to clamber across a broken bridge. Small boys lie in wait for visitors and will enthusiastically lead you to the custodian, who may be in the

Si Taieb, a Caid of the High Atlas

Si Taieb succeeded his father as *caid* of the Goundafa tribe in 1883 at the age of twenty. His father, after a lifetime of rebellion, had sued for peace with the government and sent a legendary gift to the palace at Marrakesh: a hundred male slaves, each leading a horse and a camel; followed the next day by a hundred slave girls each leading a cow and a calf. Once in power, the young *caid* launched a campaign of aggressive expansion. He had at his disposal a tribal force of 5,000 men and his own slave guard of 500. By 1900 he had trebled the size of his domain, a fact which increasingly drove the rival High Atlas *caids*, the Glaoui and M'Touggi, into an alliance against him. In the words of the latter, 'He is a hill man who has discovered the plains. It will not be easy to get him out.' R.B. Cunninghame Graham has left a description of Si Taieb holding court in 1901:

Forty years of age, thick set and dark complexioned...not noble in appearance but still looking as one accustomed to command; hands strong and muscular, voice rather harsh but low, and trained in the best school of Arab manners, so as to be hardly audible... His clothes white and of the finest wool...his secretaries never stopped opening and writing letters, now and then handing one to the caid*...slave boys, in clothes perhaps worth eighteen pence, served coffee.*

In 1906 the rival *caids* seized their chance, for Si Taieb had been called to Fez. Their combined forces descended to plunder the Nfiss valley and burn the kasbah of Talat-n-Yâkoub. Si Taieb returned to find his homeland in desolation, and for six years never left the valley. Lyautey, the French Resident-General, was the only man who could entice the warrior *caid* from his mountain realm. In 1912 the lowland kasbahs of Amizmiz and Aguergour were returned to Si Taieb, and at a stroke he was restored to his pre-1906 position. He was also given arms and money for the conquest of the Sous Valley. After the capture of Taroudannt in 1913 he was honoured by being created *naib*, representative of the sultan in the south. In 1917 he was appointed pasha of Tiznit, and for seven years he remained in command of this frontier of the desert war. In 1924 he retired to his mountain kasbahs, where he died four years later, aged 65.

After his death his feudal authority was dismantled and replaced by the even rule of French officials, while his lands were divided between his son, Lhassen, and two nephews. A pleasant white house of spacious courtyards can be seen attached to the end of the kasbah of Talat-n-Yâkoub. This is the house of the *caid*'s grandson, an electrical engineer from Casablanca.

company of his son or one of his three hazel-eyed daughters. You might add a tip onto the price of your admission ticket. The mosque may be closed to tourists on Fridays, when the village of Tin-Mal uses it.

The Mosque

You enter through a small but sturdy door in the corner of the main tower which used to be reserved for the imam, the leader of the prayers, and the *khatib*, the pronouncer of the Friday sermon. The mosque is now roofless but this increases rather than diminishes the splendour of its interior. Deep shadows cast by the surviving brick columns and horseshoe arches contrast with an expanse of sunbaked wall which reflects the mountain sunlight to give the whole of the interior an enchanted roseate glow.

The central tower has been placed immediately above the *mihrab*, the arched niche which indicates the direction of Mecca. The dome above the *mihrab* and the arches that link with the domes underneath the two corner towers were richly decorated to draw the worshipper's attention naturally in this direction. The

Ibn Tumert and Tin-Mal

Ibn Tumert was a religious reformer who desired to enforce his puritanical doctrine over the Muslim community. A Chleuh Berber, he was born in one of the small villages on the northern slopes of the Anti-Atlas mountains and travelled east towards Mecca to study in the intellectual centres of the Islamic world. He was a well-known and controversial figure before his return to Morocco, and by 1124 he had selected Tin-Mal to be the citadel of his theocratic state.

It became a place of total obedience where he trained the mountain tribes for war against all who would not accept his authority. Dancing, music and singing were banned, art placed under his severe direction and codes of dress established which denied any ornamentation. Ibn Tumert lectured the Berber tribes in their own dialect, but taught them the Arabic Koran in a characteristically authoritarian manner. Long lines of warriors would each be given a word of the Koran as their name and by obediently calling out their new names in turn could learn whole suras of the Koran. As a capstone to his authority, Ibn Tumert gradually led his community to recognize that he was the Mahdi, the prophesied successor of Mohammed.

After two years at Tin-Mal he led a series of expeditions that enforced his authority in the valleys of the High Atlas, and consolidated these victories in 1128 by a bloody forty-day purge of the tribes. In 1129 three Almoravid armies attempted a joint assault on Tin-Mal. Though these were beaten off, Ibn Tumert's own siege of Marrakesh that same year ended in a costly defeat. The death of Ibn Tumert in 1130 was kept a secret from his followers for three years while his chosen successor, Abdel Moumen, consolidated his authority. In 1148 he captured Marrakesh, which became the administrative capital of the empire while Tin-Mal degenerated into the Almohad cult centre, secure treasury and favoured burial ground.

In 1154 Abdel Moumen subtly shifted the Almohads from a movement of religious reform to a dynasty invested in his own family. The great mosque of Tin-Mal was finished as a triumphant cult centre in the same year that Ibn Tumert's own children, grandchildren and cousins were quietly disposed of.

central aisle would also have boasted more elaborate details. All the other aisles would have been supported by horseshoe arches, embellished by bas-relief columns of which a few survive. At the opposite end to the *mihrab* is the *sahn*, the open-air court for worshippers to wash themselves, which has its own entrance arch and would have once contained an elaborate marble fountain. Either side of the *sahn* are two prayer-halls which, screened and provided with their own entrances, could be used by women. The old gates piled up against the outside walls are from the Koutoubia Mosque at Marrakesh, rejected second-hand gifts from the sister mosque built by the Almohads.

In its prime the whole mosque would have been spotlessly white. Excavations unearthed not so much as a fragment of a green-glazed roof tile or a single piece of *zellij* mosaic, otherwise ubiquitous elements in any Moroccan shrine. Almohad Tin-Mal remained true to its puritanical origins, and was composed of just bricks, wood and white plaster. The three brick towers are an unusual feature in that they are built above the actual prayer-hall of the mosque. Most minarets are quite free-standing and rarely aligned with the *mihrab*. The corner minaret towers were crowned by lanterns, but the central one did not reach much higher than it does today. You can climb up its staircase and look south down the Nfiss Valley to the Goundafa kasbah of **Agadir-n-Gouf**, which crowns the central hill.

Tin-Mal Village

There is a ruined kasbah at the centre of the village, as well as a mosque, a Koranic school and an old water tank which produces a regular crop of edible frogs. Past the village (a kilometre north on the main road) the old city walls of Tin-Mal lead up from the riverbank to the heights above. Tin-Mal was both the first and the last bastion of the Almohads. It was finally stormed in 1276 by the Merenids, who, though they respected the great mosque, left no house standing, no tomb undefiled, and no citizen of Tin-Mal alive. However, the historian Ibn Khaldoun, who visited Tin-Mal a generation later, found Koranic reciters had returned to the mosque. When they entered the valley in 1924 French administrators found the area around the mosque covered in old shrines of which there is now no trace.

On one side of the village square stands an olive press which was built from one family's savings accumulated in 16 years' emigrant labour in France. The owner is usually happy to show you the mill and explain the process, finishing off by selling you a litre or two of his Tin-Mal olive oil.

Where to Stay and Eat in the Tizn-n-Test

Luxury

Résidence La Roseraie, Km 60 Taroudannt Rd, Ouirgane Valley, t 0443 2094, *www.laroseraiehotel.ma*. This is made up of some two dozen apartments scattered around an extensive riverside garden (a fusion of raw Morocco and bourgeois France) which also contains two swimming pools and a stunning mass of rose beds, all confined within a horizon of wooded mountains. There is a restaurant and bar, where a portrait of Caid Goudafa by E. Varley hangs. A health centre has also been established above the mineral stream, although the pseudo-medical nature of spa life compares unfavourably with the joys of walking or riding in the magnificent hinterland. The hotel is one of the best places from which to ride in Morocco, and can organize anything from an hour's tuition within the grounds of the estate to a week-long expedition into the surrounding mountains.

Inexpensive

Au Sanglier Qui Fume, t 0524 485707, *www.ausanglierquifume.com*. One of Morocco's surviving colonial institutions, described by Paul Bowles in 1959: 'Lunch outside in the sun at *Le Sanglier Qui Fume*. Our table midway between a chained eagle and a chained monkey, both of which watched us distrustfully while we ate...Madame is Hungarian and lives in the hope that people coming through Ouirgane will speak her language or at least know Budapest...obviously disappointed in us.' It is still run by the same family that established it in 1945.

Ksar Shama, Ouirgane, t 0524 430101, *www.ksarshama.com*. A fabulous terrace with mountains in the background, this hotel restaurant has a reasonably-priced three-course meal with Moroccan mains and international starters and desserts.

The Ourika Valley and Oukaïmeden

The Ourika is a narrow valley that cuts deep into the High Atlas. As you intrude south down the valley, the mountains rise ever more precipitously and the area of cultivation diminishes further. At the head of the valley, constricted terraced gardens, their walls constructed from round river boulders, their bright crops shaded by slender almond trees, appear like some vision of the Promised Land. The gardens are productive throughout most of the year, since the Ourika stream which drains the northeastern face of Jbel Toubkal seldom runs dry.

In the summer, when Marrakesh can feel debilitatingly like a furnace, the Ourika Valley has a gentle trickle of cool, clear water, a breeze in the trees, trout in the river and oleanders that have just burst into flower. Small pottery workshops are found off the road and flour mills operate above the riverbed, fed by irrigation ditches that double as a source of power. For this constancy of supply the valley can pay an occasional but high price. Sudden fierce rainfall, especially in winter, carries a flood downstream which can rip out the sides of hills, bury houses in mud and boulders, and sweep all away in a great torrent of water.

In the past the people of the Ourika Valley were in a powerful position: they controlled the water supply to the city and gardens of Marrakesh, for old Moroccan law did not acknowledge the rights of any user downstream. In practice this meant that no ruler of Marrakesh could afford to have a hostile power in control of the valley, which has always been closely associated with the affairs of Marrakesh. This is still true today, and the lower reaches of the valley are lined with the villas of the richer Marrakeshis. It is a traditional place to relax, with a good selection of licensed restaurants beside the road.

Aghmat Rhmate

Twenty-eight kilometres from Marrakesh, a signposted tarmac road leads off to the hamlet of Aghmat Rhmate. This was, until the arrival of the Almoravids in the 11th century, the principal town of the region. Now it boasts a café and the elegant **tomb of El Mutamid**, the poet prince of Seville. He was exiled here by the great Almoravid Sultan Youssef ben Tachfine, who accused him of conspiring with the Christians. The *koubba*, restored in the 1960s, is a copy of the Almoravid Koubba Ba'Adiyn in Marrakesh, with the dedication inscription replaced by one of El Mutamid's verses.

Tomb of El Mutamid
adm free; tips accepted

The Ourika Valley

At the entrance to the Ourika Valley, 33km from Marrakesh, you pass through the Monday **souk of Tnine-de-l'Ourika**, which has for

Getting to the Ourika Valley and Oukaïmeden

A fairly continuous stream of buses and *grands taxis* plies the road from the Bab er Rob in Marrakesh to Ourika. A place in a full *grand taxi* should cost 25dh, though you might have difficulty in finding a taxi to Oukaïmeden in the summer months. Hiring a *grand taxi* should cost 300–400dh one way. Note that in the winter there is a direct bus service to Oukaïmeden (also from Babe er Rob) daily.

---

that one day each week become a destination for coach tours. On the opposite side of the valley, across a bridge, is the settlement of **Dar-Caid-Ouriki**, the house of the *caid* of Ourika. The ruins of the kasbah and its garden are approached through the encroaching hamlet of farms. Dramatically placed below a geological fault, the ruins retain a certain aura. Abdallah, *caid* of the Ourika in the 19th century, was an early ally of the Glaoui, an alliance confirmed by his marriage to one of Madani's six daughters. This relationship did not, however, stop Madani's brother Si Thami el Glaoui from removing Abdallah and appointing his own brother, Mohammed el Arbi, to the influential caidship.

The village of **Irhef** is 5km farther up the valley. This used to be an entirely Jewish community, but only a few Jews remain and the Jewish charity school is now full of young Muslims.

Setti Fatma, at 1500m, and nearly 20km farther, is the virtual edge of human habitation in the Ourika Valley. The last kilometre of road to Setti Fatma takes the form of a washed bank of gravel, which is continually being swept away. Across the stream from the hamlet, a path crosses below a group of café-restaurants and continues up to a system of seven waterfalls. Getting up to the first fall with its plunge pool, sunbathing rocks and tiny café is a quarter of an hour's stroll partly under the shade of walnut trees (raided by Barbary apes), but it does include the odd rock scramble. The other, higher falls demand some experience of rock climbing, or at least a good head for heights.

Following a path above the eastern bank of the main river you reach the green-tiled *koubba* of **Setti-Fatma** (*not accessible to non-Muslims*), a popular burial ground as the telltale head- and foot-stones indicate. The window grilles of the shrine are covered in a web of cloth knots left by supplicants. This is the centre of a four-day *moussem* held in August which attracts Berber farmers and shepherds from all over the High Atlas.

Oukaïmeden

Getting to Oukaïmeden, 'the meeting place of the four winds', provides at least half of the excitement of the place. Ten kilometres south of **Tnine-de-l'Ourika**, at the village of **Arhbalou**, a right turn takes you 30 twisting kilometres, up to the foot of **Jbel Oukaïmeden**. The road mostly climbs within sight of a mountain stream, the Asif Aït Leqaq, which has cut a series of steep canyons and waterfalls in the side of the mountain. Along the way you pass a string of stone and *pisé* Berber hamlets, perched way up but still surrounded by carefully tended terraced gardens, bramble hedges and orchards, even above suicidal cliffs.

As you climb up to Oukaïmeden, at 2600m, you pass through a whole series of altitude belts that gradually dispose of olive trees, almonds, henna and walnut, leaving you in a barren area of windswept rock. Providing there is no cloud cover, there is a continual and magnificently changing view over the valleys of the High Atlas to the east and west or away to the north to the distant blur of Marrakesh.

The settlement of **Oukaïmeden** itself is no more than a fairly ugly assortment of skiing chalets and associated huts and services sheltered by a rising platform of barren rock. The face of the mountain is scarred by the pylons that support the half-dozen ski lifts. As you arrive you pass a small reservoir lake, well stocked with fish, and a barrier at which you must pay an admission charge (*10dh*) to enter the resort. In winter this provides the best skiing in the country, and in summer it makes a good, well-supplied base for walking in the high valleys. What is more, around the town there is the most accessible collection of prehistoric rock carvings anywhere in Morocco.

There is no view from Oukaïmeden, but a superb one from the Tizerag TV relay station, atop a peak at 2,740m, which is at the end of a road that winds up for another 2km beyond the resort.

The Rock Carvings

There is a map in the Club Alpin Français (CAF) hut in Oukaïmeden that shows the location of the carvings, but the club is often locked up. Ask to be guided by any of the locals to the half-dozen sites.

The French, in their efficient way, built protective shelters around them, which have all now rusted down to a few inches. You can, if you don't like being guided, look for these telltale signs just to the right of the road above the reservoir as you enter the town; there are also some near the **Angour hotel**. Among the rocks you will find a collection of images that includes representations of shafted stone knives, Aztec-like ritual knives, some circular or stellar-solar shapes with rings, snake-lightning bolts, a male hunter beside a small deer, and an elephant with mouse-like ears and a penis but no tusks. They have all been dated to the 9th century BC.

Where to Stay and Eat in the Ourika Valley and Oukaïmeden

Ourika Valley

Hotels get gradually seedier and accommodation cheaper as you proceed up the Ourika valley. Most give Aghbalou as their address, but despite this they are easy to find, strung along the road.

Auberge Le Maquis, Km 45 Aghbalou, Ourika, t 0524 484531, *www. le-maquis.com* (€€). This is a family-friendly spot set in gardens not far after the Oukaïmeden turning. There's a pool, guided hikes and tours can be arranged, and the tranquil licensed restaurant serves a reliably delicious *tagine*. It is run by Saida and Jean Pierre Blanc.

Auberge Ramuntchko, Km 52 Aghbalou, Ourika, t 0524 482541 (€€). Tucked away up a drive to the right of the road (at km 52) and in its own garden, this is moderately priced and beautifully located. There's a fire-warmed dining room for winter, and an elegant terrace shaded with white umbrellas in summer. The rooms are filled with the sound of the river and the inns basks in a magnificent view of the mountains.

Bab Ourika Hôtel, t 0661 252328, *www.babourika.com* (€€). First along the road, up a turning to the right, this has a good view, a bar and good cooking, but a slightly soulless air.

Dar Elysha, Sidi Fattma (€). This is a good place to lay your head for the night and wake up to the mountains and a full English breakfast.

Dar Piano, Km 52 Aghbalou Ourika, t 0524 484842, *www.darpiano.com* (€). Near neighbour to the Auberge Ramuntchko, this welcoming French-run guesthouse is its equal in cuisine. Again, the views are extraordinary. *Closed June, July and Aug.*

Ourika Garden, Km 50 Aghbalou Ourika, t 0524 484441, *www. ourika-garden.com* (€). This has a charming garden, a pool and plenty of mod cons. Reasonably priced and a decent breakfast to boot.

The cheapest places are all at **Asgaour**, where the tarmac road gives out. One of the best of these is the **Tafoukt Hôtel** (which is more comfortable than its dour exterior might suggest, €), though the village cafés such as the **Asgaour** are good for meals, as well as advice on walks and introductions to possible mountain guides. In Setti Fatma itself, the **Café les Cascades** and its neighbours prepare meals to order.

Oukaïmeden

There are a number of places open in Oukaïmeden which tend to be filled with unbearably hearty mountain types and the smell of their boots and socks. The **Club Alpin Francais**, (t 0524 319036, *www.caf-maroc.com*) offers cheap beds for around 100dh a night in their *refuge*, but note that these are offered to members first.

Hôtel Chez Juju, Station du Ski Oukaïmeden, t 0524 319005, *www. hotelchezjuju.com* (€€). Probably the best choice in the area; a great wood-lined mock-Alpine chalet, with cosy rooms decorated with flowery prints.

Hôtel Courchevel, t 0524 319092, *www.lecourchevelouka.com*). Towards the smarter end, this a good spot with a lovely restaurant and will cost you less than €80 for a double. From Marrakesh, you can organise your trip through Riad Akka (*see* Where to Stay in Marrakesh, p.146).

Sports

The **National Ski Centre** at Oukaïmeden is open from November to March. The best conditions are usually in January and February – and often coincide with an impassable road. The skiing is Scottish: icy in the morning, wet in the afternoon, with some potentially surprising patches of rock. There are half a dozen button lifts and a 1660m chair lift. Day passes and ski hire are available from the local shop (it currently costs 90dh for a half-day pass including ski hire). If you hire a guide, choose well – there are plenty of chancers.

The Tizi-n-Tichka

The Tizi-n-Tichka pass crosses the High Atlas from Marrakesh to Ouarzazate and, like the Tizi-n-Test, can be blocked any time between December and March. It is an exciting and memorable journey, on a perfectly safe road that climbs twisting up through forests to the treeless summits of the pass. Just beyond the summit is the turning for the **kasbah of Telouèt**, the chief attraction of the journey.

To the Tizi-n-Tichka Summit

Aït-Ourir, 30km southeast of Marrakesh off to the left of the main road, is one of the string of market towns that nestles at the foot of the High Atlas. Good farm land stretches below, and the Tuesday souk is usually busy and empty of tourists. A well-built Glaoui residence can be seen to the south of the town, but it is inaccessible as it now houses an orphanage. You could eat at the reasonably priced **Le Coq Hardi** (38km from Marrakesh on the route d'Ouarzazate, **t** 0524 480056, *www.coqhardimarrakech.com*) a charmin g motel which has a garden and a licensed restaurant. It stands right beside the bridge over the River Zate, and can be filled at lunchtime with passing tour groups.

Beyond Aït-Ourir the road climbs quickly up into the foothills, after a few kilometres passing below the prominent *koubba* of Sidi Lahoussine. Just before the *koubba* a dirt track leads almost due south to the village of **Tidili-des-Mesfioua**. The Mesfioua, alone of the Berber tribes, succeeded in resisting the Arab tribes of the plains and held on to their area of the fertile plain of Haouz, centred on this village. They also preserved their traditions of tribal democracy and, up to the 20th century, suffered no autocratic *caid* to rule over them.

Twelve kilometres east of Aït-Ourir a tarmac road turns right up the Zate Valley, passing through a series of Mesfioua villages where the timeless, tireless pace of subsistence farming continues undisturbed by tourism. The road ends at **Arba-Talatast**, overlooked to the southwest by the twin peaks of **Jbel Yagour** (2723m) and **Jbel Meltsene** (3588m). The slopes of Yagour have some of the best-preserved prehistoric rock carvings in the area, while the summit of Meltsene is still rumoured to be used for the old Berber sacrifices celebrated on the equinox and solstices.

Back on the main road, the P31, you climb up through dramatic mountain scenery, the slopes covered in mixed woods of oak, pine and juniper. Perhaps the best view of these Mesfioua mountains is from the pass of **Tizi-n-Aït-Imguer**, at 1470m, where there is a particularly good view southeast to Jbel Tistouit, a summit looming up at 3224 m.

Getting to the Tizi-n-Tichka

There are three buses daily crossing the pass from Marrakesh to Ouarzazate, but just one (leaving from Bab Gehmat) which makes the trip along the dead-end side road to Telouèt. Telouèt Kasbah also has an odd local status and most taxi drivers would prefer not to go there, and try to dissuade you from going. The only option for the day trip to Telouèt is really hiring a car (for car rental agencies, see p.101).

Taddert is a roadside village poised below the last 15km of twisting road that climbs to the Tizi-n-Tichka summit. Though unpromising at first sight, it makes a pleasant stop, with its line of cramped cafés, and the licensed but inexpensive Auberge Les Noyers can – despite its roadside position – be a good place to eat, with its terrace overlooking a mountain stream. (You can stay there too but do not expect much heat.) A number of paths lead away from the sound of grinding truck gears to pisé farmhouses placed idyllically beside the terraced banks of mountain streams.

The **summit of Tizi-n-Tichka**, 'the gate to the pastures', is 2,260m high. From this central point in the High Atlas, a windblown, desolate expanse extends in all directions, though the immediate environment is ringed by the now customary mineral stalls. Four kilometres farther on there is a left turn for the kasbah of Telouèt.

The Kasbah of Telouèt

Telouèt is 21km east from the main road on a tarmac lane that leads past stunted pines and mineral-stained soil, which has given the ground a sanguinous hue in keeping with its reputation. Eventually you glimpse a minaret that rises from the low village of El-Khémis Telouèt, separated from the sprawling extent of the kasbah by the river Mellah. Above the kasbah, overlooking a prominent *koubba* in the centre of the cemetery, there is a simple hotel, the Auberge Telouèt, which provides meals.

Three generations of *caids* of the Glaoui tribe built extravagant structures out of wood and *pisé* to form this kasbah. Most of Telouèt is consequently an area of leached and shapeless mud banks. Broken spars and wattle frames protrude like the bones of some decaying leviathan. This area of ruin is screened from immediate view by the most recent, stone-built White Kasbah, with its numerous layers of towers, buttresses, crenellations and curtain walls, built by Caid Brahim, Thami el Glaoui, between 1934 and 1955.

The road skirts the village to approach the kasbah from behind. Melted forms of old walls grow stronger where a few families squat with their chickens, dogs and children in the more weather-resistant corners. A gateway directs your approach through narrow walls that open into a large paved courtyard. Even the minaret of the kasbah mosque has been infected with the universal crumbling.

The Making of the Lords of the Atlas

The Glaoui first rose to fortune by aiding Sultan Moulay Hassan in completing a late crossing of the High Atlas in 1893. Moulay Hassan, the last of the great pre-colonial rulers of Morocco, rewarded them with a gift of munitions which was later followed by a position at his court. The Glaoui prospered in the service of the sultans: Madani el Glaoui served Sultan Abdul Aziz as minister of war, before advancing to become grand vizier (prime minister) to Sultan Moulay Hafid, while his brother Thami was appointed pasha of Marrakesh. The brothers used their new wealth and great position gradually to enlarge their influence over the Berber tribes of the High Atlas. The kasbah of Telouèt grew in stature with each new conquest of a village and submission of a tribe.

By 1907 the Glaoui had become key national figures, but their greatest hour came in 1912 when they became the sworn allies of the French. They undertook the expansion of French rule south of the High Atlas, and created an empire within an empire for themselves in the process. Thami succeeded his brother Madani in 1918 and inherited Telouèt on his cousin Hammou's death in 1934. Only the collapse of French power in 1956 toppled this aged but still avaricious warrior who, at his peak, had 600,000 souls under his care. Within a year of Independence the Glaoui chiefs were either dead, in prison, or in exile, their lands confiscated and their tribesmen disarmed. Each year their kasbah moves closer to its sentence of complete decay.

The amiable custodian conducts tours of the main reception rooms of Caid Brahim's White Kasbah (*tips accepted*). The haphazard evolution of the palace becomes apparent in the eccentric route to these rooms, affording tantalizing glimpses of dark corridors, subterranean staircases and obscure sun-baked terraces. The dusty, long, echoing corridor to the reception rooms provides an astonishing contrast to the massive assertive confidence of these halls. The vulgarity of display mixes with detailed Moorish craftsmanship of the highest order to silence the visitor.

An ornate grille-window frames a significant view of the old kasbah of Telouèt on the edge of the village, with barely two of its walls left standing. The old kasbah is the size of a traditional fortress of a mountain *caid* and would have boasted little decoration beyond crenellated towers and motifs embossed into the *pisé* of the exterior walls. Inside, the rooms would most likely have been small, dark and infested. The halls of the White Kasbah of Telouèt are of another order and, though now empty of furniture, the absence of rich cloth, carpets, worked metal and wood seems merely to enhance the grandeur of the interior. The roofs above are still secure and you are allowed up to enjoy the excellent view. They were once decorated with great expanses of green glazed tiles, but these now lie in shattered heaps at the foot of the outer walls.

On the way out the custodian may point out a large windowless room, the cinema. Edward G. Robinson was Caid Brahim's brother-in-law. The screening of the latest fantasies from California seems bizarrely appropriate in this last outlandish product of feudal grandeur.

The rest of Telouèt is not officially accessible and is securely locked up. Every year the buildings become more dangerous, but the custodians can sometimes be encouraged to take visitors around. For the brave, the route to the kitchens, Hammou's Kasbah and the *harem* runs through another delightful maze of passages. The kitchens are vast, and recognizable chiefly by their blackened walls. The mixture of soot, melting *pisé* and exposed beams is impressive only in its size and the imminent danger of final collapse. Telouèt was entirely staffed by slaves except for one salaried French chef. Over a thousand slaves fled overnight when the news of the death of Si Thami el Glaoui reached the kasbah.

At the heart of Telouèt, physically and emotionally, was Hammou's Kasbah, a stark, square keep formed from massive walls, dark and featureless inside. Hammou was the cousin and brother-in-law of Madani and Thami, but remained violently opposed to the French, whom he would not permit to enter his feudal domain. He was the *caid* of Telouèt and ruler of the traditional mountain territory throughout the period of phenomenal growth in Glaoui power until his death in 1934. Stories of his occult powers blended with the grim truth of his violent, xenophobic and sadistic nature. *Sloghis* – hounds that could each kill a wild boar by themselves – trailed behind guests in the kasbah like some canine thought police, while the final bloody resolution of a tribal feud too often ended at the hands of Hammou in his labyrinthine cellars. These have long since collapsed to bury the evidence of this grim underworld.

The *harem* courtyard is beyond Hammou's Kasbah and is approached through a number of rooms. The central courtyard was equipped with large pools of water which have now cracked and drained. The cool rooms that open from this internal space, thanks to a trick of design, are not overlooked by any battlemented tower. Two ornamental fruit trees survive, and in spring still fill this breezeless space with the scent of cherry and apricot blossom. After the initial pleasure of discovery, the languid introspection and sterility of the *harem* creep back to repossess the spirit of the place.

Beyond these identifiable features you can wander freely among the curtain walls and acres of complete ruin. Banks of *pisé* now and then astonish you with their tremendous range in height, which hints at some past extravagant architectural form. Fragments of carved cedar, carved foliate arabesques and shattered tiles can be glimpsed buried deep in what appears at first to be nothing but bleached soil.

It may seem extraordinary that such a place as Telouèt should not be better preserved but, for a Moroccan, Telouèt is a monument to treason on a vast scale. The Glaoui were totally identified with the most extreme French colonial ambitions right up to 1956. Si Thami el Glaoui was deeply involved in the deposition of Mohammed V, and his officials had extorted and stolen for years. Allied with the French, they had hunted down those who worked for Independence and fought against the Liberation Army.

If you have come in your own vehicle and have some time, the unforgettable medieval town of **Aït Benhaddou** is another 30 kilometres along from Telouèt on the road to Ouarzazate. There are a couple of simple hotels in the town, which is a UNESCO World Heritage Site. *Jesus of Nazareth* and *Lawrence of Arabia* were both filmed there.

Essaouira

This is the most enchanting Moroccan town on the Atlantic, and perhaps on all the coasts of Morocco. The old town and port, encircled by 18th-century battlements, overlook a scattering of barren, wave-worn islands. A great sandy bay sweeps out to the south, while wooded hills dominate the skyline to the east. The old parts of the town – the medina, the kasbah and the Mellah – express the exoticism of Morocco: the dark alleys are broken with frequent arches, and the women of the town are mysteriously concealed under their enveloping *haiks*. At dusk the call to prayer echoes across the silhouetted skyline, unchallenged by the distracting sound of traffic. Only the city's famous and noisy coastal wind has had as much impact on Essaouira as the faith proclaimed from its minarets.

History

Es-saouira, 'the little ramparts', has been known over the millennia as Amougdoul, Migdol, Mogdoul, Mogdoura and Mogador. The offshore isles are still collectively known as Mogador, a name that probably derives from the Phoenician *migdol*, a look-out tower. Phoenician sailors used these islands from at least the 7th century BC, while archaeological evidence suggests that the principal villa remained in occupation for a thousand years from 500 BC to AD 500.

In the 11th century the bay opposite the islands formed the chief port of southern Morocco. King Manuel of Portugal seized Essaouira early in his campaign to dominate the whole trade and coast of Morocco, and built a fort here in 1506. This fell to the Saadians even before Agadir, the main Portuguese base, was recovered in 1541, but the Saadian dynasty (who originated from the far south) preferred to use the port of Agadir.

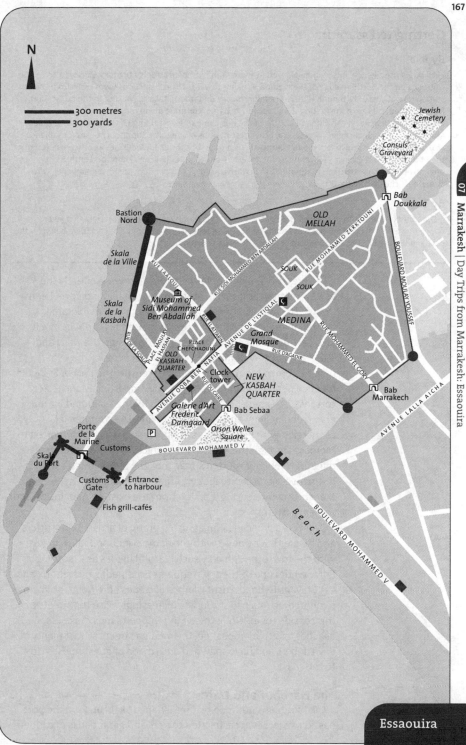

Essaouira

Getting to Essaouira

By Bus

All buses use the new bus station, plonked in some drab pot-holed streets about a 1½km walk from Bab Doukkala on the northern edge of the medina. Walking towards the conspicuous town walls from the bus station is relatively easy, though if there is a *petit taxi* around (10dh), take it. Walking to the bus station from Bab Doukkala, take the first right and second left, then continue along for 500m until you reach an assortment of cafés and the different booths of the bus companies, including CTM. There are buses daily to Marrakesh, Casablanca, Agadir and several other destinations besides. For Supratours buses (Casablanca, Marrakesh), head just outside the Bab Marrakesh. As a rule, stick to scheduled buses as otherwise you may tire of the regular sequence of local stops. Marrakesh is 2hr 30 away (with no traffic and enthusiastic driving) and the bus fare there is around 65 to 80 dirhams (plus 5dh per item of stowed luggage), with Supratours cheaper than CTM.

By Taxi

Grands taxis operate from the west side of the bus station (80dh per person to Marrakesh if you're happy to wait for it to fill up) but will usually be happy to deposit arrivals on the open square between the port and the medina. A car one way to or from Marrakesh should be 450dh.

The present shape and character of the town is entirely the achievement of Sultan Sidi Mohammed. Agadir had never been loyal to the Alaouite dynasty, and Essaouira was deliberately created to replace it. In 1760 the sultan used his captive French architect-engineer, Théodore Cournut, to design the walls and street plan of the medina, which helps account for their unaccustomed regularity. By the 19th century the port of Essaouira handled nearly half of Morocco's trade: importing Manchester cottons and exporting bales of ostrich feathers, almonds, gum arabic, ebony, ivory and dried camel skins. The commercial connection with Britain was strong, and tea was first imported to Morocco through this port, a drink which, with the addition of mint and French-imported sugar, took the nation by storm. The distinctive Moroccan teapot was first manufactured in Manchester by creating a fusion from the existing Andalucian and Yemeni patterns.

Over the last decades, an assorted group of artists, windsurfers and hippies have put up with the damp winds and fallen in love with the town, though only such cultural heroes as Orson Welles (after whom one of the town squares is named), Jimi Hendrix and Cat Stevens (who, as Yusuf Islam, still comes here frequently) are remembered much. But tourists increasingly pace the streets of this seaside town. While the wind-whipped sands make Essouira's beaches less than appealing, the medina streets attract plenty of day-trippers and have spawned an armada of guest houses close to the coast.

The Harbour and Gates

The harbour is guarded by the L-shaped **Skala du Port**, the port bastion, where two castellated towers and great banks of cannon once commanded the northern and western approaches. Two land gates still control admission to the enclosed quays of the harbour. Do not be put off by the guards standing around by these gates: despite appearances you are perfectly free to join the rest of the town and take a leisurely stroll through the docks, in order to admire the massed nets, flag-fluttering floats and busy decks of the fishing boats. The sardine-fishing fleet, the third largest in Morocco, provides a great spectacle of activity in the early morning or after dusk, as does the daily mid-afternoon fish auction by the port gates. The southern edge of the quay is occupied by ship builders, working on a line of emerging wooden hulls that illustrate every stage of the fascinating process of construction.

The main entrance to the harbour is through the **Porte de la Marine,** which you may occasionally find shut. It is one of the town's most famous structures. Its 18th-century architect, Cournut, achieved an equable fusion of traditions – details from a classical gateway combine with the green-tiled pyramid roof of a *koubba*. It is, like most of the town, a forerunner of 20th-century neo-Moorish public architecture, achieved at a time when Morocco was assertively independent. The three crescents of the Moroccan navy – a device borrowed from the Ottoman Turks – stand proudly carved into the limestone by an inscription that records that the gate was erected by Sultan Sidi Mohammed in 1769, year 1184 of the *Hegira*.

Place Moulay Hassan

The best place to get the flavour of Essaouira is Place Moulay Hassan. The square is lined with elegant, tall white houses picked out in blue that help give it a tranquil and intimate atmosphere. The cafés seem to break down the strongest reserve: the travellers who have arrived for a day but stayed for a few weeks are quick to offer an exchange of books or some tedious but well-meaning advice. Do not ignore the beggars, like most of the other tourists, but befriend them immediately with a silver coin. They are a feature of the place, and there is nothing more rewarding than earning their salute in the morning rather than trying (ineffectually) to avoid their unremitting attention.

The Woodcarvers' Souk

In the casemates and pebble-paved courtyards below the north bastion of the **Skala de la Ville** battlements (lined with bronze cannon cast for Philip II and Philip III of Spain), some of the skilled joiners and carvers of Essaouira have their workshops. The rich, resinous smell of the wood is a great attraction and the craftsmen are usually happy to demonstrate their skills. Acacia and ebony are both dark woods that are contrasted very successfully with the pale wood of the lemon tree and the rich chestnut of thuja wood. Shells, mother of pearl, strips of silver and copper are also inserted to create astonishingly inlaid tables, chests and cabinets. Essaouira also has the best selection of trays, chessboards, dice cups, thuja boxes and backgammon sets. Similar work seen in other cities is likely to have come from Essaouira, and be more expensive. You should bargain in the bazaars, but the cooperatives in town and the casemate workshops have less time for negotiations and generally offer a reasonable first price. Any hinges and locks should be examined carefully – skill with wood is seldom matched with much love for metalwork.

The Museum of Sidi Mohammed ben Abdallah

Museum of Sidi Mohammed ben Abdallah
Rue Laâlouj,
t 0524 475300;
open Wed–Mon
8.30–6;adm

The ethnography museum of Sidi Mohammed Ben Abdallah is found on the southern side of Rue Laâlouj, the street which leads from the Skala de la Ville back to the centre of town. Originally constructed in the early 19th century as the town house of a pasha, it was transformed into the town hall during the French Protectorate, with the unfortunate addition of a monolithic central staircase that now completely dominates the central courtyard. The museum has been overhauled and extended, to become a delightful repository for the traditional crafts, textiles, carpets, clothing, jewellery and weapons of the region, as well as of some early maps, engravings and sketches of the town.

The Medina Thoroughfare

From the main square outside the port, the high red archway with its green-tiled roof (sometimes used to house art exhibitions) leads to the old *méchouar*, now the tree-lined Ave Oqba ben Nafia. This attractive broad avenue was originally an assembly place, where the garrison paraded and processions were marshalled. Avenue du Caire leads from the old *méchouar* to the strongly guarded Bab Sebaa. The triangular patch of open ground just to the south of the gate has been named **Orson Welles Square** and provided with a plaque to commemorate that fantastic polymath who was producer, director and principal actor of the film *Othello*, which was mainly shot here in 1949. Though his financial backers deserted him he won the affection of the town, who for a mere 2dh each a day provided him with all the craftsmen and extras he wanted, while everyone was fed on sardines.

The eastern side of Avenue Oqba ben Nafia is lined with hotels and a growing number of art galleries, led by **Galerie d'Art Frédéric Damgaard**, which acted as midwife to the city's recent rise to artistic renown. The fortified western side of the avenue (once the city walls) is dominated by a distinctive clocktower beneath which is an archway leading into the small killim-lined and café-overlooked **Place Chefchaouni**. Pass under the second archway (occupied by Damgaard's famous framing workshop and galleries) to twist past more intriguingly furnished bazaars and inviting cafés before passing beneath the old kasbah and returning to Place Moulay el Hassan.

Alternatively, take the archway at the northern end of Ave Oqba ben Nafia, which leads to the civil area of the old town and the central thoroughfare of Ave de l'Istiqlal. To the right, on the eastern side, rises the minaret of the **grand mosque**, its spacious prayer-hall mostly tucked out of sight. The 200m-long avenue is largely devoted to kitchen and hardware stalls, piled high beneath the green-tiled overhang and framed by blue shutters.

The heart of the town's trading is reached at the central crossroads. The central souk area, known as **Souk Jdid**, lined with an arcade of short stone arches, is enclosed by twin gateways. Off to the west are courtyards housing fish, chicken and spice markets. To the east the *fondouqs* house old metalware and other secondhand goods, *jellabas* and killims, and the densely packed network of jewellers' booths. North of these souks, Avenue de l'Istiqlal, now lined with a blue-tiled arcade, becomes devoted to the vegetable and grocery trade.

The Beach

The beach to the south of the town, protected from the full force of the Atlantic surf and current, is one of the safer bays on this coast in which to swim. The area nearest the town is often occupied by football games and piles of seaweed, but as you walk farther out towards the **ruined fort** the sand gets cleaner and the beach emptier. This ruin is a remnant of Sultan Sidi Mohammed's defence system. Built on a rocky promontory, the fortress's compact walls have split but not disintegrated, despite being washed daily by the incoming tide.

Back from the beach, and screened slightly by the dunes, is the town's stumpy lighthouse, built beside the koubba of one of the town's patron saints, **Sidi M'gdoul.** There is a story about the origin of this saint which claims that he was a Scottish merchant called McDougall who saw the error of his hard-hearted ways and, having converted to Islam, settled down in a hermitage on the shore to help the poor of the town. The more historically minded will recall that Essaouira used to be known by its old Carthaginian title of Migdol, which gives the saint an even more venerable link to another widely scattered trading nation.

Tourist Information and Services in Essaouira

ⓘ **Essaouira >**
10 Rue du Caire,
t 0524 783532;
open 9–12 and 3–6.30

The **tourist office** has leaflets aplenty, and the staff are amenable. The multi-lingual tourist website (*www.essaouira.com*) is useful for skimming through local events and finding out what's on when.

There are **banks** around or just outside Place Moulay Hassan (with bureaux de change) and another just shy of the Mosque Sidi Ahmed on Ave de l'Istiqlal. There are a couple of **bookshops**, including Jack's Kiosk on Moulay Hassan, which sells a good map as well as Anglophone newspapers. For the **internet**, try the Rue du Caire or the Place Moulay Hassan. There is a **pharmacy** on Ave de L'Istiqlal and the **hospital**, a little outside the Bab Marrakech, is on the helpfully-named Boulevard de l'Hôpital. The **post office** is on Ave Lalla Aicha.

⭐ **Riad Baoussala >>**

Where to Stay in Essaouira

Luxury

Palais Heure Bleue, Rue Ibn Battuta, t 0524 783434, *www.heure-bleue.com*. Just inside the Bab Marrakesh (once you are inside, take a right off the main thoroughfare) is Essaouira's slickest hotel. The Heure Bleue is a super-riad, with an idyllic central courtyard surrounded by colonnades, rooms filled with Moroccan crafts and an elegant rooftop swimming pool with one of the city's best views. Animal skins, a grand piano and a private cinema complement the wood-and-leather interior, a mix of old-world European gravitas and Moroccan artistry, although the service might be better given the heady price.

Expensive

⭐ **Hotel Villa Maroc >**

Hotel Villa Maroc, 10 Rue Abdellah Ben Yassine, t 0524 473147, *www.villa-maroc.com*. This is one of the most delightful hotels in Morocco, discreetly tucked away on the edge of the medina. To find it go through the archway beside the clock on Ave Oqba ben Nafia, turn left and walk down beside the wall for about 60m. A traditional house with beautifully furnished rooms, a *hammam*, breakfast terrace and attractive central courtyard, the Greco interior (decorated with Moroccan crafts) has been used in countless photo shoots and dinner is an elegant affair. It also offers special honeymoon and sporting packages (quad bikes, camel rides, among other activities). Details on the website.

Moderate

Riad Al Madina (once Hôtel du Pasha), 9 Rue Attarine, t 0524 475907, *www.riadalmadina.com*. It snakes around a splendidly restored 18th-century courtyard. The hotel has fine views from the terrace and, though the decorator responsible for the renovation has at times tried much too hard to make an effect, especially in the bedrooms, the staff are cheerful and willing.

Riad Baoussala, t 0524 792345, *www.baoussala.com*. An exceptionally picturesque and well-run hotel, this has an idyllic pool and offers excellent and inexpensive meals. It lies a little south of Essaouira (its one drawback) and northwest of Mogador airport. But, as Essaouira grows into ever more of a tourist hive, Baoussala's only drawback may increasingly become one of its strengths.

Maison du Sud, 29 Ave Sidi Mohammed, t 0524 474141, *www.riad-maisondusud.com*. An attractive, centrally-located riad with attentive staff and much-praised breakfasts, The Maison du Sud receives the early morning call to prayer loud and clear but the attractive interior, expansive terrace and the tall ceilings of many of the bedrooms more than make up for it. Just remember to pack your ear plugs.

Inexpensive

Hotel Sahara, Ave Okba Ibnou Nafiaa, t 0524 475292. Breakfast is simple fare and the plumbing and facilities are unpredictable, but the Sahara is well-run, clean and excellently placed near the ocean. Good for the price, especially if you plan a late night out.

Check your room (and its bathroom) before deciding to stay.

Des Remparts, 18 Rue Ibenou Rochd, t 0524 473535, *www.riadessaouira-palaisdesremparts.com*. This medina hotel sits opposite a bakery and is run by friendly staff. It sits next to the beach, the staff are voluble and the views exceptional, especially from the terrace. Recently refurbished and blessed with an excellent chef (and a jacuzzi). Go for the sea views and air – not the décor – and try to get a west-facing room.

Le Méchouar, Ave Oqba ben Nafia, t 0524 475828, *www.lemechouar.com*. The rooms are comfortable, if slightly humdrum in terms of décor, but Le Méchouar is easy to find, and wonderfully central. Both terrace and restaurant are attractive but be aware that the bar may be noisy into the early hours.

Hotel Tafraout, 7 Rue de Marrakesh, t 0524 476276, *www.hoteltafraout.com*. In style more spartan Mexican *estancia* than glittering Moroccan riad, the Tafraout was once the home of Jewish traders. Close to the beach and in the medina, the rooms are very reasonable and this makes for a pleasant base, although the basic furnishings may transport you back to those visits to IKEA in the 1980s.

Residence El Mehdi, 15 Rue Sidi Abdesmih, t 0524 475943, *www.residenceelmehdi.com*. A surprisingly modern place with televisions in every bedroom, a central courtyard with a parrot, a restaurant and a very homely, domestic feel. Terrace, patio and a heroic attempt at English on the website make this a good-all-round local choice.

Riad Nakhla, 2 Rue Agadir, t 0524 474940, *www.essaouiranet.com/riad-nakhla*. Good breakfasts and simple rooms (check for damp first) make this a good deal, even though the fittings are a little worn and in need of repair.

Hotel Beau Rivage, 14 Place Moulay Hassan, t 0524 475925, *www.beaurivage-essaouira.com*. Above the Café de France, the Beau Rivage is clean and scrupulously honest, with some rooms overlooking the sea and others overlooking the square.

Cheap

Cap Sim, 11 Rue Ibn Rachid, t 0524 785834. A stone's throw from Essaouira Beach, Cap Sim is good value. Basic, friendly and well-run. It is not stylish and you should check your mattress first, but the terrace has good views and it's in a pleasant neighbourhood.

Hotel Smara, 26 Rue de Skala, t 0444 472344. A wonderful terrace view and not much besides. Expect simplicity and brusque staff and hope to find a towel and uncover occasional spots of cleanliness. The Smara is a good place to rough it out by the ocean, drink rum and pen your masterpiece.

Eating Out in Essaouira

Expensive

Chez Sam, port's end, t 0524 476513. Follow Ave Mohammed V northwest as it hugs the coast and bear left once you arrive in the port. On the seafront is what looks like a stranded boathouse. Chez Sam sits in a phenomenal location and serves excellent seafood. Be prepared for capricious, inefficient staff and you will have a good afternoon.

Le Coquillage, Essaouira port (just before Chez Sam), t 0524 476655. Another excellent fish restaurant in the port with good views over the harbour and hearty portions.

Le Chalet de la Plage, 1 Blvd Mohammed V, t 0524 475972. This restaurant stands on the seafront opposite the Hôtel des Iles (best avoided), with a terrace directly washed by the tide. It serves alcohol and has a seafood menu and a range of cheaper local dishes. At lunchtime it can be rather busy.

El Minzah, 3 Ave Oqba Ibn Nafia, t 0524 475308, *www.leminzah.com*. A classic in Essaouira, justly famous for its *pastilla* with lobster, and other fine seafood dishes.

Moderate

Lalla Mira, 14 Rue d'Algérie, t 0524 475046, *www.lallamira.net*. A good

★ Des Remparts >

★ Chez Sam >>

★ El Minzah >>

★ Hotel Beau Rivage >

place for fish and with plenty of vegetarian options, Lalla Mira has a bright if slightly twee dining room and a licence. You can stay here too but it is the food that makes it a draw – its central medina location is noisy by night.

(★) **Dar Loubane >**

Dar Loubane, 24 Rue de Rif, **t** 0524 476296. This is a beautiful 18th-century palace with a courtyard restaurant, just a few yards from the clocktower arch in the centre of the old town. It is furnished with modern orientalist pictures, Mogador memorabilia, some intriguing junk, a fountain and the odd *gnaoua* musical ensemble, which can be very loud. It is licensed, and the competent menu embraces both French and Moroccan cooking. Try any of the curries, *tagines* and salads.

Inexpensive

Café L'Horloge, Place Chefchaouni. Perfect for crêpes, omelettes, tea and snacks. Quiet, friendly and reasonable. Occupies an old synagogue,

Café Essalam, 23 Place Moulay Hassan, **t** 0524 475548. No licence but the food here is tasty, the service good and prices on the light side.

Café Bab Lachour is only slightly more expensive, but calmer. You can eat outside on the café terrace, or upstairs in a first-floor dining room. An excellent deal.

Alternatively, try the outdoor tables of the fish grill-stalls in the port.

Fez

Fez is slung across two hillsides between the Rif Mountains and the Middle Atlas, surrounded by lush farmland. The city is a medieval labyrinth of earthen houses and it still has a mosque for almost every day of the year. Its medieval guild system survives too, populating its market streets with artisans who work with wood, metal or cloth.

But on many of those same streets, Fez seems almost ostentatiously reticent, only yielding up its treasures once you have passed through the simple wooden doors. On the inside, its houses are visions of grandeur and elegance, a legacy of extraordinary wealth and of an artistic vision enriched and codified by influence from Andalucía. There are few better places to lose your way.

08

Don't miss

⭐ **Palms and pools**
Dar Batha Museum
p.188

⭐ **Architectural marvel**
Bou Inania Medersa
p.191

⭐ **Weightless elegance**
The Attarine Medersa
p.197

⭐ **Painter's palette**
Tanneries p.201

⭐ **Medieval city**
View from Bordj Nord
p.208

See map overleaf

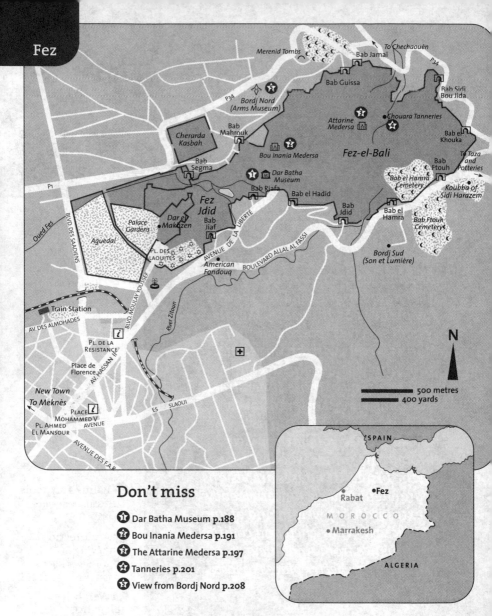

Don't miss

⭐ Dar Batha Museum **p.188**

⭐ Bou Inania Medersa **p.191**

⭐ The Attarine Medersa **p.197**

⭐ Tanneries **p.201**

⭐ View from Bordj Nord **p.208**

Fez is the most complete Islamic medieval city in the world. Its history has for a thousand years also been the history of Morocco's political, commercial and intellectual life, even though it is now superseded by the modern cities of Rabat and Casablanca, and to some extent by its own New Town (*ville nouvelle*), built by the French after 1912.

The first independent Muslim kingdom of Morocco was established here on the plain of Saïss, upon the shell of the old Roman capital of Volubilis, by a great-grandson of the Prophet

Mohammed, Moulay Idriss, at the end of the 8th century AD. The Idrissid state that was created by his son, Idriss II, stands at the core of Moroccan national identity. Idrissid Morocco declined as a political power after a mere century of rule, but it left behind a new city – Fez – where Islam, law, literacy, art, industry and skilled crafts had a safe refuge.

The citizens of Fez, the Fassi, became an urbane upper-middle class that were sufficient unto themselves. They paid lip-service to the current powers, but kept their true loyalty for the fallen Idrissid dynasty. In the heart of the city of Fez stands the ornate tomb of Idriss II, who, to be put in an Anglo-Saxon context, must be compared to some fallen Arthur descended from the family of Christ, and to whom many of the chief citizens can proudly trace their genealogical descent.

For all their pride and insularity the Fassi yet provided a vital pool of skills that were at the disposal of the Almoravids, the Almohads, and any dynasty that could unite the disparate regions of Morocco. Fez is most imperishably linked, though, with the Merenids, who through the 13th and 14th centuries presided over the most prosperous period of the city's history, as well as choosing it to be their capital. There was no love lost between the sultans and the Fassi, however, despite the plethora of Merenid buildings in the city. The former dwelt in a separate walled enclosure, the palace city of Fez Jdid, where all the instruments of government were located.

Much has perished in the long decline from this period, and it is chiefly the old mosques, tombs and religious colleges that have survived, respected by each dynasty, every mutinous regiment and pillaging tribe. The *medersas* are open to non-Muslims, but the rest of the vast heritage of religious architecture remains inaccessible. Visitors are left to concentrate on the street pattern, the style of life, the sounds and odours, which remain triumphantly unchanged.

History

Foundation Legend

At his birth in 791 Idriss II inherited his father's kingdom, centred on the two existing cities of Christian Volubilis and Jewish Sefrou. He and his loyal regent Rashid decided to create a specifically Muslim city, and one day while travelling between the two cities they rested halfway, at the Ras el Ma spring. The boy Idriss followed it downstream to discover a wide, well-watered valley fringed with hills. Greatly encouraged by this gorgeous vista, and the prophetic welcome of an aged holy man, they decided to establish a settlement on the right bank of the river that year, in 799. During the excavation for the foundation walls a golden axe, a *fas*, was unearthed. This fateful discovery helped settle the form of the human sacrifice required if each gateway of the new city were to be protected by a resident spirit, a tradition that was widespread in many parts of the world. A pair of Persian exiles, or Fars, were buried alive at each gate, and the city was known as Fez, its citizens as Fassi.

Idrissid Fez (799–1075)

Idriss II ruled his kingdom from a walled city, containing his El Aliya palace and barracks for his 500-strong Arab guard, on the left (northern) bank of the valley. This bare nucleus of a city was soon flooded with refugees from the turbulent politics of the more prosperous and Arabized Muslim states of Spain and Tunisia. In 818 a civil war in Andalucía drove 8,000 refugees to Fez; they were presented with the empty right (southern) bank by Idriss II. Seven years later another tide of refugees fled a revolution in the holy city of Kairouan and were given land on the left bank. This settlement pattern remained for the next 250 years. Fez-el-Andalous and Fez-el-Karaouiyne were two quite separate cities that faced each other across the riverbed, each enclosed in its own walls. The Andalucians were considered to have the prettiest women and the men were considered strong, brave, handsome and good farmers, but also just a little dull. The Kairouan men were considered more elegant, better educated but a bit over-partial to the luxuries of life. What they both shared was a strong Arab identity and an urban, literate, technical and intellectual culture far in advance of any mere Berber tribe. It was as if a fortified Manhattan were suddenly placed in the middle of the prairies.

Idriss II died in 828 and his tomb became the focus of the city's pride and identity, as it is today. His kingdom was divided amongst his squabbling sons, but the ruler of Fez was accepted as first among equals. During his grandson Yahya's reign the two grand mosques of Andalous and Karaouiyne were founded to give graphic evidence of the settlements' prosperity. In 917 Fez fell under the control of the Shiite Fatimid Empire, expanding west from its core territory of Tunisia. In 930 the Ommayad Caliphate of Córdoba took over, and ruled the city through a governor for over a century.

The Almoravid and Almohad Period (1075–1248)

In 1075 the Almoravid leader Youssef ben Tachfine captured Fez, just five years before he succeeded in uniting Morocco for the first time. The Fassi could not at first accept these unsophisticated Berbers from the Sahara, but they soon learned to benefit from their firm rule. Though Marrakesh was the political capital, Fez was better suited to act as the commercial hub of an empire that stretched from West Africa to the Pyrenees. The Almoravids dismantled the divisive twin walls and erected a single circuit to protect both districts. The endless bickering over river rights ended, for the Almoravids came from the desert and knew all about the efficient collection and distribution of water. Clean mountain springs were tapped and a network of pipes, sewers and mills prepared the ground for future expansion.

Water was also the tool by which the Almohads, based in Taza, at last seized control of Fez in 1146 after a long siege. Abdel Moumen built a dam upstream in order to collect a great head of water which he suddenly released; the resulting flood washed the walls around the valley clean away. The Almohads then marched in and demolished the remaining walls, declaring that 'only justice and the sword shall be our ramparts'. They also demolished any traces of Almoravid rule, on the flimsy basis that the architectural decoration of the previous dynasty had been impious. Later sultans ignored these early declarations and constructed a massive new perimeter wall. This still defines the extent of Fez-el-Bali, and some gateways and large sections, particularly to the north, are still in place.

Merenid Fez (1248–1465)

Abou Yahya, the chief of the Beni Merin tribe, captured Fez in 1248, the year that he had treacherously massacred the leaderless Almohad army. So important had the city now become that this date is taken to be the start of his reign. Though the period of Merenid rule was to prove the glittering zenith of the city's fortune, the Fassi never took to this dynasty, mere Berber chiefs of a nomad tribe from the eastern plains. They frequently rebelled against their new rulers, and in truth no dynasty has been able to win the city's affection away from the original Idrissid line. Abou Yusuf Yacqub reigned from 1259 to 1286 and firmly established Fez as the capital of Morocco. He did not, however, feel secure enough to dwell amongst his citizens. On 21 March 1276 he started work on Fez Jdid, 'New Fez', enclosing it in a double wall 750m away from the turbulent politics of Fez-el-Bali. It was known officially as El Medinat el Baida, 'the white city', and a portion of the river Fez served as a moat for its outer walls, which were crowned with crenellations and reinforced by square towers. The white city held the court and palace of the sultans, the mint, baths, markets, three mosques – the Grand, the Red and the Flower – an aqueduct and separate quarters for the sultan's mercenary guard. Abou Yusuf Yacqub was the first Moroccan ruler to build a *medersa*, a residential college for religious education. It was an archetype

Orientation

The city has a population of half a million and is divided into three parts. Fez-el-Bali (Old Fez) is the enigmatic and fiercely Muslim medina, a maze of hidden quarters, *fondouqs*, *medersas* and mosques, with narrow streets that remain inaccessible to cars; two of its streets, Rue Talaa Kebira, and Rue Talaa Seghira, form key arterial routes that can help you find your way. Fez Jdid (New Fez) is the 13th-century Imperial city to the west of the medina, still dominated by the royal palace and the Mellah, the old Jewish ghetto. The French-built *ville nouvelle* is even farther to the west, a separate entity with wide avenues and new developments which would be without interest but for its cafés, hotels, restaurants, and convenience.

Fez Jdid

This is the west of the medieval city and the site of the Kasbah and its inaccessible palace. The Grand Rue de Fez-Jdid bisects this corner of the city. It is home to the Mellah and the Danan Synagogue. To the west, the area is bordered by the Boulevard des Saadiens, which runs along the west wall of the Aguedal Gardens. As you approach Fes-el-Bali to the east, you will come across the Dar Batha Museum.

Fez-el-Bali

You are unlikely to remain aware of your location in the Fez-el-Bali, a maze of curved and jagged alleyways. The west part of this area is best handled by remembering Talaa Kebira and Talaa Seghira, two streets which run east–west past the Palais M'Nebhi and the House of Ibn Khaldun. Further east, and still a little to the north, Place Seffarine and the Karaouiyne Mosque, which flank it, form a centrepoint from which to explore that area. Heading southwest into the best of the Andalucian Quarter, where you will find the Andalucian Mosque, the Rue Sidi Youssef (and its other-named parts) is a useful navigating tool.

Ville Nouvelle

The new town is dominated by the broad Avenue Hassan II, which runs northeast to southwest. Off the south side of it comes Boulevard Mohammed V, leading to Place Mohammed V.

which his successors developed and embellished into one of the great glories of Fez.

In 1438 the barracks were enlarged and converted into the first separate Jewish quarter in Morocco. Wealthy Jewish merchants had long been convenient targets in urban unrest, and by placing them within the protection of the royal city the Merenids bound this community, useful for its many skills and taxable wealth, to their service. One of the more disagreeable services was the preservation of the heads of the executed in salt, before they were displayed on gates. The word for salt, *mellah*, soon became synonymous with a Jewish quarter.

The Decline of Fez after 1465

In 1465 the last Merenid sultan, Abdul Haqq, was dragged through the streets of Fez-el-Bali before having his throat cut like a sacrificial goat. A council of Idrissid sherifs had planned this bold insurrection, and they succeeded in ruling a republic for seven years. This political experiment was finished by the Wattasids, the hereditary viziers of the Merenids, who marched into Fez at the head of an army. Wattasid authority over the next century was slowly reduced to Fez itself, as the Portuguese seized control of the coast and tribal dynasties fought over the rest. An earthquake

Getting to and from Fez

By Air

The **Fez-Saïss airport** (**t** 0535 624800) sits 15km south of the city (or due south of the P24 road to Immouzer), it has just one terminal. Several airlines serve Fez-Saïss, including Royal Air Maroc, Atlas Blue, and Jet4You (*see* below for contact details). Within Morocco, Royal Air Maroc flies directly only to Tangier, Agadir and Casablanca but then flies to eleven different Moroccan cities from Casablanca.

Fez's half-hourly airport bus, no.16, leaves from Place Mohammed V, or pay 30dh for your own taxi, 5dh for a place in a *grand taxi*.

Airline Offices

Most airlines (Royal Air Maroc is the exception) do not have offices in Fez, but can be contacted by phone or email.

Royal Air Maroc: 54 Ave Hassan II, **t** 0535 625516, airport booth **t** 0535 624712, general information number **t** 089 000 0800, *www.royalairmaroc.com*.

Atlas Blue: **t** 082 009 090, *www.royalairmaroc.com*.

Jet4You: **t** 0802 044044, *www.jet4you.com*.

By Train

Travel by train whenever possible, trust no published schedule and buy your ticket and a seat reservation early and directly from the grand new **station** (**t** 0890 203040, *www.oncf.ma*), which is located on the Ave des Almohades on the northern edge of the *ville nouvelle*. It has a left-luggage office, plus a handful of shops and cafés. A taxi ride, in a licensed cab with meter on, from the station to any centrally placed Fez hotel will be 10dh or less. There are seven trains a day to Casablanca (8hrs), all of which also stop at Meknès and Rabat, and six to eight trains south to Marrakesh (8hrs) daily, including a sleeper connection. (There are considerably more services to Marrakesh from Rabat and Meknès.) To be sure of a seat, it is often worth buying a first-class ticket. If you want to buy it in advance, you could phone the national rail line (**t** 0890 203040), but it is easier to ask your hotel to arrange your ticket for you.

By Bus

Bus travel into and out of Fez can be slightly confusing as there are two bus stations. The busier and more convenient to get to is the **newer terminal** just north of Fez-el-Bali's Bab Mahrouk. It has its own café and is well served by *petits taxis*. Call **t** 0535 732992 for info.

The **CTM bus stop** (**t** 0535 438282) is just off Ave Hussein de la Jourdanie, close to Place Atlas, and, although more awkward to reach, is generally more useful. The most frequent bus connections are west to Meknès (one hour), Rabat (three hours), Casablanca (five hours) and south to Marrakesh (ten hours), with the latter served at least twice daily. Prices work out at about 15–20dh per hour.

By Car

Although a hindrance within the city, a car could be useful for day trips as well as for travelling further afield. For car hire ask at reception in big hotels or go directly to such agencies as **Avis** (at the airport or 50 Blvd Chefchaouni, both on **t** 0535 626969), **Europcar**, 41 Ave Hassan II, **t** 0535 626545.

---

shattered the town in 1522, and the Saadians, a dynasty from southern Morocco, occupied Fez 19 years later. They made no secret of their preference for Marrakesh, and their only constructive action was to build two artillery forts with which to intimidate the city. In 1666 Fez welcomed the first Alaouite sultan, Moulay Rachid, as a liberator, and he responded in kind by building another *medersa* here. This *rapprochement* was quickly reversed: Sultan Moulay Ismaïl detested the city and did everything in his power to humble Fez and vaunt neighbouring Meknès. Most of the later Alaouite sultans tended to alternate between Fez and Marrakesh, and it was not until the reign of Sultan Moulay Hassan (1873–94)

Getting around Fez

By Bus

Fez is one of the few Moroccan cities where local buses can be of real use to a visiting tourist. The route numbers are marked on the sides, not on the back or front as you might expect.

Useful routes include:

No.3 leaves from the train station and ends at Bab Ftouh
No.9 runs from the Atlas quarter (near the embassies) to Dar Batha
No.10 runs from Bab Guissa (the centrally placed northern gate to Fez-el-Bali) to the train station
No.16 runs from the train station to the airport
No.19 runs from the train station to Place des Alaouites
No. 29 runs from Ricif to the Atlas quarter.

By Taxi

Fez's red *petits taxis* use their meters and are therefore delightfully cheap and trouble-free. Taxi fares increase by 50 per cent after dusk or 9pm, whichever is earliest, and until around 6am.

In the *ville nouvelle*, you should be able to find taxis on Ave Hassan II (especially around the crossing with Blvd Mohammed V), at Place Mohammed V, the train station and in Rue des Normandes, off Blvd Mohammed V, which is a *grands taxis* park. In Fez Jdid try the Place des Alaouites, while in Fez-el-Bali they can usually be hailed outside all the principal transport gates: Place Baghdadi (between Bab Bou Jeloud and Bab Mahrouk), the northern Bab Guissa, southern Bab er Rsif, southeastern Bab Ftouh and Dar Batha-Place Istiqlal (just south of the Bab Bou Jeloud).

Grands taxis for Meknès and Rabat can be found at the bus station north of Bab Mahrouk.

By Car

A car is a hindrance in Fez. If you drive into the city from the west or south you will invariably find yourself escorted by motorbike-borne 'guides'. There is absolutely no way to shake them off (apart from revealing a deep knowledge of the city in colloquial Maghrebi), but treat them as a convenience, for they can lead you directly to your chosen hotel. It is as well also to be aware, though, that they are aiming for the greater prize of taking you round the medina and earning a commission from the bazaars and carpet shops. Once in Fez, get your hotel receptionist to recommend a secure parking place, then completely empty your car and forget about it.

Tours

It is possible to avoid both public transport and amateur cartography by hiring a guide for the day or even just a few hours. Most riads and hotels will offer to organise this and several have their own guide. But, to be really certain of quality, hire a licensed guide, since any number of children or young adults will offer to take you round anyway and expect payment later. Occasionally this is quite useful but, for longer tours, the hotels are more reliable. You can expect to pay around 250–300 dirhams for a guide for one day, perhaps less if you were a drama student.

---

that decay was decisively checked. He built three administrative palaces that physically and symbolically united Fez Jdid and Fez-el-Bali, and most of the substantial Fassi merchant houses date from his reign.

The grip of the European powers strengthened after Moulay Hassan's death, and on 30 March 1912 Sultan Moulay Hafid was forced by the French to sign the Treaty of Fez, which established the French Protectorate. The city reacted violently to the surrender of national sovereignty, and on 17 April the European population was hounded through the medina streets and lynched – over 80 mutilated bodies were stacked up before the palace gates. The sultan's army joined the rebellion and manned the city walls, but the following day a French force marched from Meknès and first shelled and then occupied the subdued city.

Sultan Moulay Hafid was removed to Rabat, where the government of Morocco has since remained, and Casablanca became the still-unrivalled mercantile metropolis. Here in Fez, the French built an ordered *ville nouvelle* (New Town) of regular avenues well to the west of the old city to house the European population in comfort and safety. Fez-el-Bali is now a unique medieval survivor, fallen far from grace but remaining one of the most distinctive cities of the world.

Fez Jdid

Though the most famous sites are in Fez-el-Bali, a walk through the simple street plan of Fez Jdid and a visit to the Dar Batha Museum make a good preparation for the heady and confusing alleys of the old town.

Place des Alaouites

From the Place de la Résistance in the *ville nouvelle*, Blvd Moulay Youssef leads directly to the Place des Alaouites, a kilometre away; or you can hop on the no.3 bus. This main entrance to the palace was created by King Hassan II between 1969 and 1971, as the ceremonial guard and great gates proclaim. On occasion this entire square is covered in a patchwork of carpets brought out by Fassis to honour some official guest. The gleaming brass doors were manufactured in the medina in 1971, and are kept clean by being rubbed with lemons.

The Royal Palace (Dar el Makhzen)

I believe this to be the finest single sight Morocco has to offer; one of the wonders of the world.

Traveller's Guide to Morocco, Christopher Kininmonth

The royal palace occupies half of Fez Jdid and covers over 80 hectares. Within its walls is an inaccessible city that holds 700 years of pavilions, squares, gardens and palaces. It includes a mosque, the *koubba* of Sidi Mejaed, and a *medersa* built by the Merenid Sultan Abou Said Othman in 1320. Sidi Mohammed built the Dar Ayad el Kebira palace in the 18th century; Moulay Hassan the present royal apartments in 1880; and in 1980 another palace was added, the Dar el Bahia, for the Arab summit held the next year. There are rumours that the king Mohammed VI intends to open it to the public.

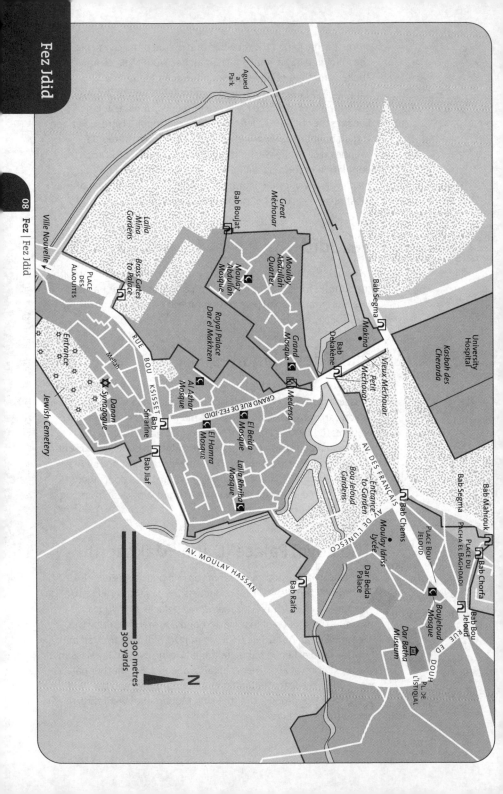

Fez Jdid

Agued a Park

Laila Mina Gardens

Brass Gates to Palace

Bab Boujat

Great Méchouar

Moulay Abdullah Mosque

Moulay Abdullah Quarter

PLACE DES ALAOUITES

Ville Nouvelle

Mellah

RUE BOU

Entrance

Danan Synagogue

Jewish Cemetery

Royal Palace Dar el Makhzen

Grand Mosque

Bab Dekakene

KSISSET

Bab Smarine

Al Azhar Mosque

Medersa

GRAND RUE DE FEZ-JDID

El Belda Mosque

El Hamra Mosque

Laila Rhriba Mosque

Bab Jiaf

AV. MOULAY HASSAN

300 metres
300 yards

N

Bab Segma

Bab Makina

Kasbah des Cherada

University Hospital

Vieux Méchouar

Petit Méchouar

Boujeloud Gardens

AV. DES FRANÇAIS

AV. DE L'UNESCO

Entrance to Garden

Bab Chems

Moulay Idriss Lycée

Dar Beida Palace

Bab Raifa

Bab Segma

Bab Mahjouk

PLACE DU PACHA EL BAGHDADI

Bab Chorfa

PLACE BOU JELOUD

Bab Bou Jeloud

Boujeloud Mosque

RUE ED DOUH

Dar Batha Museum

PL. DE l'Istiqual

The Mellah

The Grand Rue du Mellah runs from Place des Alaouites through the whole Mellah district. The Jewish community had to walk barefoot within the three royal cities (Marrakesh, Fez and Meknès) and in front of a mosque, but by the 18th century the Fassi Jews had acquired the right to wear sea-rush socks outside the Mellah. There are few Jews left, but a legacy of jewellers' shops, brocade, balconies, small windows with their tracery of iron grille work, and an air of business gives the quarter something of its old distinctive atmosphere. Tiny side streets lead off into a labyrinth of covered passages, underground workshops and timbered houses. A little way to the south is the Jewish cemetery, a great walled enclosure of whitewashed inscribed stones.

The Historic Synagogues of Fez

There are five historic synagogues in the Mellah, most found off small alleys leading from Rue Merin. The largest, oldest and most important is the **Synagogue Rabbi Shlomo Ibn Danan**, on Rue Derb El Feran Teati, which has been restored as a historic monument. This can be visited free of charge during reasonable daylight hours, though you will need a guide to point out the deliberately inconspicuous door. The synagogue was built by Mimoun Bou Sidan, a merchant from Zaouiat Ait-Ishaq village in the Middle Atlas, during the reign of Moulay Ismaïl and named after a 19th-century scholar-rabbi. The synagogue later passed into the ownership of the well-connected Bensoussan family. It is a dark, powerfully atmospheric place, built hard against the Mellah wall, with a subterranean *mikve* (ritual bath) and no space for women. Right next door is the **Synagogue Debada**, also on Rue Derb El Feran Teati, now a house and not normally accessible. **Synagogue Sabba**, Rue Derd El Wassa, is also a house, and the resident is unfortunately bored with visitors trying to see Morocco's most beautiful 18th-century synagogue. **Synagogue Dar El Ma**, 220 Rue Derb El Foukie, is tiny and tucked up two flights of stairs, but has elaborate wooden ceilings and cornices. It is also now a house, and its owners are friendly to interested visitors. **Synagogue El Fessaine**, Rue Derb el Fessaine, was the largest Jewish place of prayer built in the 17th century and is now in use as a sports hall.

Bab Smarine

As you approach the distinctive, crenellated, high gate of the Bab Smarine, restored in 1924, you pass through the glittering displays of the **jewellers' souk**. The Bab Smarine used to separate the

Mellah from the Muslim quarter, and before that marked the southern entrance of the city. Immediately beyond the arch is a covered food market which was established in an old granary built by the Merenid sultans. From the gate the Grande Rue de Fez-Jdid, lined with stalls and cafés, runs due north through the city to the outer walls. Along the way, on the right, is the **Hamra**, the red mosque, and then the **Beida**, the white mosque, built in the 13th century by the creator of Fez Jdid, Sultan Abou Yusuf Yacqub. The alleys to the left stop at the perimeter wall of the palace, beneath which is the pretty **mosque of Al Azhar**, built by Sultan Abou Inan in the 14th century, with a fine sculpted gate. The street opens out to form a small walled square known as the Petit Méchouar, under which the river Fez flows and in which is a gleaming back entrance to the royal palace.

Moulay Abdullah Quarter

A small arch to the left of the Petit Méchouar is the only entrance into the Moulay Abdullah district. This area is almost entirely enclosed by high walls and was chosen by the French as the *quartier réservé*, the red-light district, though there is little evidence of those days. Wandering through this calm residential area you soon pass the entrance of the **grand mosque**, which was built in just three years (1273–6) by Sultan Abou Yusuf Yacqub. Sultan Abou Inan was buried here in 1358 and a *koubba* was raised above his tomb beside the mosque. The main street leads after 200m to the **mosque of Moulay Abdullah**, with a conspicuous, slender minaret, built in the 18th century. The mosque has become a principal Alaouite tomb, full of the graves of princes and two sultans including Moulay Youssef (1912–27).

Petit and Vieux Méchouar

Back in the **Petit Méchouar**, at the northern end is the **Bab Dekakène**, sometimes known as the Bab es Siba. This massive, triple-arched Merenid gate served as the main entrance into the city and royal palace until 1971. Ferdinand, prince of Portugal, was imprisoned for six years in this gate after he had surrendered himself as hostage to allow his army to escape after a disastrous attempt to seize Tangier in 1437; his brothers refused to return Ceuta, near Tangier, to the sultan in exchange for his release. On Ferdinand's death his naked body, pierced through the heels like a butchered goat, was hung from the gate, where it swung for four days. His corpse was then gutted, stuffed with straw and put on show for a further 29 years.

On the far side of the arches there is the larger, walled **Vieux Méchouar**. On the left is the Makina, the old royal ordnance factory, built and run by the Italian 'Campionario Di Spolette' in the late 19th century. Although it now holds nothing more offensive than an export-orientated carpet factory, you will need permission from the tourist office to visit its huge vaulted halls. At the far end of the square on the left is the Bab Segma, a Merenid gate built in 1315. It was originally flanked by a pair of distinctive octagonal arches, like the gate to the Chellah in Rabat, although only one tower now survives. The smaller gate, the **Bab es Smen**, built in the 19th century, is the one that is used nowadays.

Bou Jeloud and the Gardens

The Avenue des Français leads due east from the Petit Méchouar 600m to the **Bab Bou Jeloud,** the main point of entry to Fez-el-Bali. For 500 years this area was a wasteland, caught between the cities of Fez Jdid and Fez-el-Bali, until it was developed in the 19th century by Moulay Hassan into the three palace gardens of Dar Batha, Bou Jeloud and Dar Beida. The old Bou Jeloud Palace, symbolically, was entered from either Fez Jdid or Fez-el-Bali. Only one of these palaces, the Dar Batha, is open, and now houses the **Museum of the Arts and Traditions of Fez** (*see* p.188). Otherwise the area remains dominated by high walls that hide gardens, palaces and pavilions, while less attractive administrative buildings are left exposed.

There is an entrance just east of the Petit Méchouar to the **Jardins de Bou Jeloud** (also known as the **Jnan Sbil gardens**) a delightful park with palm-shaded formal walks, cut through with ornamental watercourses that feed the round pond. First opened to the public in the 19th century, the 18th-century gardens were created by Sultan Moulay Abdullah and cover eight hectares. They were recently reopened after substantial restoration and make a very pleasant stop, especially for a pot of tea at **La Nouria café**. This is in the most famous and restful corner of the garden (also accessible directly from the road), and overlooks a mill race and its namesake waterwheel. This wooden watermill is sadly stuck solid, but it recalls a time when all the backstreet workshops of Fez were powered by dozens of such gently moaning creatures. Just outside the back door of the café is the pitch of a photographer, who continues to make use of an old box apparatus complete with cape and tripod.

Halfway along Avenue des Français toward Fez-el-Bali is a crossroads. To the left is the keyhole arch of **Bab Chems**; to the right the Avenue de l'UNESCO divides the public Bou Jeloud gardens from the walled park, pavilions and palace of **Dar Beida**, now occupied by a school, the Lycée Moulay Idriss, and so not open to visitors.

Place du Pasha el Baghdadi

A left turn opposite the entrance to the Lycée Moulay Idriss takes you to the Place du Pasha el Baghdadi. Idle buses now no longer take over this dusty triangle of land, where nut, fruit and cake hawkers and *petits taxis* collect. At dusk small groups gather around the odd musician, or haggle over temporary displays of second-hand goods, particularly on the side of the square by the solid-looking **Bab Mahrouk**, the 'gate of the burned'. This was built in 1214 by an Almohad sultan, Mohammed en Nasir. It was first known as the Bab ech Cheria, the gate of justice, as this was the execution square. It received its new name after El Obeidi, a leader of the heretical Rif Rhomara tribe, and Ibn el Khatib, a harmless 14th-century intellectual, were burnt alive here. This was a savage punishment designed to deny any chance of resurrection.

To the right of the Bab Mahrouk is the **Bab Chorfa**, a strong gate protected by two elegant towers that guards the entrance into the Kasbah en Nouar, the kasbah of flowers, also known as the Filali Kasbah. Though now just another residential district with a busy, stall-lined central avenue, it was once the site of the central Almohad fortress, which was occupied by the pasha of Fez under the Merenids and then renamed the Filali Kasbah to honour Moulay Rachid, of the family of that name, in the 17th century. The original mosque is just to the right inside the gate. Its façade was restored in the 18th century by Sultan Moulay Sliman, at the same time that he repaired the battlements.

The Dar Batha Museum (Musée des Arts et Traditions)

⭐ **Dar Batha Museum**
open Wed–Mon 9–5; adm

Through Bab Bou Jeloud, turn right and then right again along the comparatively broad Rue Ed Douh for 100m to the café-fronted Place de l'Istiqlal, where another right turn takes you to the entrance of the Dar Batha Museum. Alternatively, take a taxi or the no.1 bus from Place des Alaouites straight to the Dar Batha, or catch the no.18 from Place de la Résistance.

The palace of Dar Batha was begun by Moulay Hassan and finished by his son Abdul Aziz (1894–1909). A range of green-tiled pyramid roofs emerges above the red walls to cover the apartments and galleries that now house the exhibits and which have enjoyed some recent restorations. An amply sized **Andalucian garden** extends within the walls, its grid of blue and white raised paths lined by lush trees and swathes of shrub and bamboo. It's a delightful place, the tranquillity of the enclosed garden appealing as much as the exhibits. In September and May concerts of Andalucian music are held here.

Inside, the cases of exhibits follow no particular scheme: astrolabes, Middle Atlas carpets, stamps, illustrated Korans, pens, Berber jewellery, embroidery, guns, rural pots and coins from either the Idrissids or Alaouites are interspersed with blue geometric ware from Fez. The corner rooms contain the larger pieces of carved cedar, plaster or stone that have been recovered from restorations and excavations of Fassi tombs, mosques and *medersas*, some of them dated to the Merenid and Saadian dynasties. As ever in Morocco, the achievements of urban Andalucian culture appear timeless, as objects from the 10th to the 21st centuries have a great deal in common. The true contrast is with products from the Berber tribes, even ones stationed close to Fez. The city's former role as an oasis of technical skill and literate culture is revealed by this charming jumble of exhibits.

Fez-el-Bali

The four major accessible sites of Fez-el-Bali – the Bou Inania Medersa, Attarine Medersa, Fondouq Nejjarine and the tanneries – can be seen in half a day. The lesser *medersas*, the exteriors of the ancient mosques, the hidden bakeries, *hammams, fondouqs*, workshops and alleys of the medina could take weeks to find – to understand the city fully you have to have been born a Fassi. To arrive at the medina with no intention of buying anything is to miss out on the central life of the city, but see all you wish before making the rounds of the bazaars. Then you can savour the ritual of commerce without impatience, delight in the gift of mint tea, the opulent decoration of the large bazaars, and the loquacious salesmanship.

The Karaouiyne Quarter

The square in front of the main city gate, the Bab Bou Jeloud, is a bustling throng of cafés, cheap hotels, taxis, buses, bemused tourists and confident young guides. Originally it was the site of another Almohad kasbah, itself built over the ruins of an Almoravid fort which had defended this exposed western edge of the city. Some of the kasbah foundations were found a decade ago during building work on ground just to the west of the Bou Jeloud Mosque. The famous **Bou Jeloud triple arch** was built in 1913 by the French beside an earlier gate, just a year after they had occupied Fez. It served as a recognizable border between the native quarter of the medina and the administrative districts and the

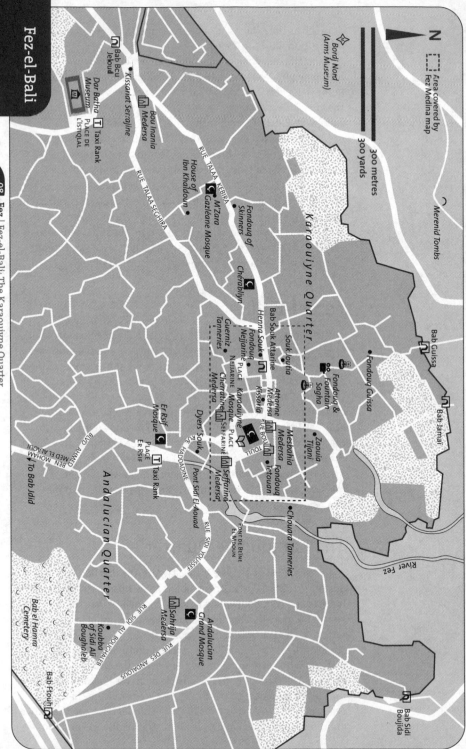

N

Bordj Nord
(Arms Museum)

Area covered by
Fez Medina map

300 metres
300 yards

Merenid Tombs

Karaouiyne Quarter

Bab Guissa

Bab Jamaï

Fondouq Guissa

Fondouq &
Fountain
Sagha

Souk Joutia

Bab Souk Attarine

Henna Souk

Attarine
Medersa

Kissaria

Mesbahia
Medersa   Fondouq
Tetouan

Zaouia
Tijani

Chouara Tanneries

River Fez

Fondouq
Nejjarine

Nejjarine
PLACE

Karaouiyne
Mosque   PLACE
SEFFARINE

Cherabliyn
Medersa

Seffarine
Medersa

Pont Sidi El Aouad

PONT DE BEINE
EL MDOUN

Guerniz
Tanneries

Fondouq of
Skinners

Cherabliyn

M'Zara
Gazléane Mosque

House of
Ibn Khaldoun

RUE TALAA KEBIRA

RUE TALAA SEGHRA

Bou Inania
Medersa

Kissariat Serrajine

Dar Batha
Museum

Bab Bou
Jeloud

PLACE DE
L'ISTIQLAL

Taxi Rank

Er Rsif
Mosque

Dyers Souk

PLACE
ER RSIF

Taxi Rank

RUE GADDADINE

BLVD AHMED EL ALAOUI

BEN MOHA
To Bab Jdid

Andalucian Quarter

RUE SIDI YOUSSEF

RUE DES ANDALOUS

RUE SIDI AL BOUGHALEB

Sahrija
Medersa

Andalucian
Grand Mosque

Koubba
of Sidi Ali
Boughaleb

Bab el Hamra
Cemetery

Bab Ftouh

Bab Sidi
Boujida

Guides

Arriving at the medina, usually at the Bab Bou Jeloud, accept the need for a guide for at least your first half-day. He or she can show you intimate parts of the old city where an unescorted foreigner would not be welcome.

Official guides can be found at the tourist office, outside all the major hotels, and from the tourist office on Place Mohammed V in the *ville nouvelle*. These official guides are a professional body but their talk and itineraries can become uninspiring through repetition. Unofficial guides charge less and may try harder to please, although their routes are often given an erratic twist as they try to avoid the police, since they are illegal – but that remains their problem, not yours.

resident-general's palace, which were established in the Dar Batha and Dar Beida in the first years of the Protectorate. The origin of the name of the gate is much discussed. It is thought to have started as Bab Abou El Jnoud, 'the soldier's gate', before being shortened and popularized to Bou Jeloud, 'the leather gate'. The gate frames the minarets of the Sidi Lezzaz Mosque and Bou Inania Medersa. The gold and blue tracery decoration represents Fez 'the blue'; the gold-green on the far side is for Islam.

Beyond the arch is an area lined by a few cheap hotels, food stalls and café restaurants, while straight ahead is the **Kissariat Serrajine**, a small courtyard lined with a glittering array of stalls selling embroidered leather, slippers and silverware. The medina's two major arteries appear here: Rue Talaa Kebira is down the narrow turning to the left, while Rue Talaa Seghira is to the right. They run roughly parallel to each other in a bow-shaped way, and are both lined with stalls, shops and bazaars. Periodically covered by arches and slats of bamboo, they later meet in the confused web of narrow streets known as the Kissaria.

The Bou Inania Medersa

②⑦ Bou Inania Medersa

open daily 9–6, except Fri am and at prayer times; adm

Taking Rue Talaa Kebira, you approach the Bou Inania Medersa, 100m along on your right under a covered archway. The Bou Inania Medersa is the finest and largest in Fez. The **prayer-hall** is in active use, which saves the spirit of the place from disappearing under the flow of visitors.

The entrance hall has a stalactite-domed roof; to the left is a room for the faithful to wash their feet. The main open-air court, paved in marble with a round, central pool, is surrounded by a carved cedar screen. There is a lecture hall at either side and a large prayer-hall at the end, across a marble-moated portion of the river Fez. The prayer-hall should not be entered by a non-Muslim, but it is fine to look at its *mihrab*, columned hall and *minbar*. The elegant **minaret** is clearly visible above the cedar-lintelled and green-tiled roof. The roofs offer an exciting view over neighbouring roof tops and a barrage of minarets.

The Golden Age of Fez

At the beginning of the 14th century, Fez-el-Bali had a population of 125,000. None of the houses was permitted to touch the city walls, which were lined with gardens and cemeteries and pierced by eight gates. Within the medina there were 785 mosques, 372 flour mills, 135 bakers' ovens, 93 public baths, 467 *fondouqs* and 80 fountains. Outside the walls, potteries, olive oil presses, sawmills, weavers' workshops, tanneries and smithies collected in three industrial zones around Bab Guissa, Bab Ftouh and along the riverbanks.

The medina was divided into 18 districts which each had a headman agreed upon by the chief residents. The *caid*, a magistrate learned in Koranic law, judged civil cases, with a deputy who specialized in marriage and divorce suits. There were 35 secretaries and accountants on the *caid*'s staff helping to supervise the financing of pious foundations, hospitals and baths. The *caid* also acted as rector of the university and censor of intellectual life. The various *medersas* lodged 2,000 students in Fez while they pursued their studies in the Karaouiyne University. Lectures were given in the grand mosques after morning prayers; the university library was housed behind the *mihrab* of the Karaouiyne Mosque, and the courts of the various *medersas* or the houses of professors were used for smaller teaching groups.

There was a hospital for the sick without family, and a leprosarium outside the ramparts housed lepers in isolation. The *muhtasib*, the prefect of manners, kept surveillance over the baths, the honesty of exchanges, weights and measures, and organized a weekly inspection of prostitutes by physicians.

There were 150 guilds each under the protection of a patron saint, such as Sidi Mohammed Ibn Attab for the shoemakers and Sidi Mimum for the potters. Numerically, the corporation of weavers was dominant – 500 workshops employed almost 20,000 workers – but the most powerful corporation was that of the semi-official water and drainage technicians. They and the water jurists alone understood the labyrinthine pipe system – the chief wonder of Fez. It filled fountains, public baths and mosque pools, drove 400 mills, and then '*the river doth disperse itself into manifold channels insinuating itself unto every street and member thereof to pass through countless conduits into sinks and gutters*'.

Above the urban hierarchy, the sultan appointed a pasha as governor of the city. He occupied the Almohad fortress at the western end of the medina, held enormous power and directly ran the police, and ordered criminal trials and executions.

The Bou Inania Medersa is a direct importation of 14th-century Andalucian techniques to Morocco. All the materials – the *zellij* mosaic, the plaster, marble and cedar – carry a range of patterns, in excellent condition, that threaten to overwhelm the architecture. But the geometric swirls hide a single point: the detail of the floral patterns illustrates a divine symmetry, and even the array of stalactites breaks down into an ordered span of interlocking arches. The cedar screen with its delicate weave of knots and stars seems to simplify into two dimensions, and invites a further reduction to the one-dimensional, single point. All can be seen as witness to the one God. The bands of Kufic calligraphy contain lines from the Koran.

Medersas were residential colleges for the learning of the Koran, and their endowments provided free board and lodging for students for six years, as well as the salaries of the administrative staff and the professors. This had an obvious political function, for the Merenid sultans could counter regional loyalties and divisive spiritual brotherhoods by educating future governors, judges and tribal chiefs near their side and within a state-approved orthodoxy. A little of this political dimension has crept into the Bou Inania. It was built by Sultan Abou Inan between 1350 and 1357 on an area of wasteland set apart and so removed from the independent spirit of the Karaouiyne University, which feared his intentions. This powerful sovereign (who had deposed his own father) strove energetically to enhance his new foundation and supersede the traditional university. The *medersa*'s sumptuous proportions and decoration were deliberately designed to eclipse its rival, and the sultan is remembered for his famously aestheticist response when presented with the costs: *'What is beautiful cannot be expensive at any price; what is enthralling is never too costly.'* It is no surprise that several lines praising Abou Inan and his munificent generosity have crept into the decoration of the main court, while the dedication stone declares him caliph, the successor to the Prophet.

The Clock and Sahn

The scaffolding opposite the *medersa* gate on the left hides, high up on a carved lintel of cedar, a dilapidated row of thirteen windows with some brass bowls on the sills and the odd water spout. This is known as the water-clock, though no description has survived and no satisfactory explanation of its working has been devised. It is considered to have been the work of a magician rabbi, and was finished in 1357 in time for the *medersa*'s inauguration. It may not have been a clock but a musical instrument of timed jets of tinkling water on brass, in celebration of the building, inside which is the *medersa*'s *sahn*, or courtyard for washing. Male tourists used to be able to enter this working portion of the *medersa* complex and admire the court with its central marble basin, stone closets and impressive flow of water. It is now closed, hopefully in order to repair its rich but precarious plaster and cedar carving.

Rue Talaa Kebira

Farther down the street is the *zaouia* of Sidi Ahmed Tijani, one of the two Fassi lodges of this widespread Sufi brotherhood. The street continues downhill into the intensity of the medina – bazaars, bakeries, grill cafés, *zellij*-decorated fountains and *hammams*. The heavily loaded mules of the Guir Valley porters pause for no man: listen for *'Balak!'*, the muleteers' look-out cry. The rich odours of olive oil, fresh mint, cedar shavings, leather, fat burnt on charcoal, *kif*, mule dung and human urine mix with the sounds of chanting from a Koranic nursery school, running water, hooves and the babble of business. Buy freshly squeezed orange juice, sweet cakes, fresh bread, or fried potato cakes to add another layer of sensual enjoyment.

As you begin to climb uphill you pass a row of blacksmiths, and beyond this, on the left, is an old **Merenid prison**, just like any other *fondouq* except for its noticeably heavier arches and colonnades where the prisoners would be chained. It is now the market for the butter and honey wholesalers. On the right, just before the **Gazléane Mosque**, an alley marked by a plaque leads to the house where Ibn Khaldoun (1332–1406), the great historian and sociologist, lived. Just beyond this turning is the **M'Zara of Moulay Idriss**, a monument that commemorates the place where the founder rested and envisaged the future city. On the left is the Derb bou Haj Mosque, and just beyond that the **skinners' *fondouq*** (*fondouq des peaussiers*), the yard where wet hides are scraped clean of fat and tissue. Some of the near-transparent, vellum-like finished products are then fitted here to ceramic drums and wooden tambourines. The oldest *hammam* in Fez is opposite the distinctive fountain on the right, but has been undergoing lengthy restoration for several years.

Cobblers' stalls increasingly dominate the street with their displays of slippers, and the second mosque on the right is the **Chérabliyn**, the slipper-makers'. This was founded by the Merenid Sultan Abou Hassan (1331–51), though only the minaret is original – which is all, apart from the gate, that a non-Muslim can see. Beyond the mosque there are a number of bazaars and then the **Souk Aïn Allou** area, where the fine leather-workers trade; their distinctive gold-stamped and decorated book-binding is still known as Morocco work, or *maroquinerie*.

Souk Attarine Gate

Beyond the Souk Aïn Allou look out for a modest gateway across the road marked by a rusty 'Souk Attarine' sign. The gate stands before a busy crossroad of paths and is a city landmark. It can be used as a starting point for short walks to the **Henna Souk**, to **Place Nejjarine** and to the *zaouia* of **Moulay Idriss II**, before heading farther along the main street to the **Attarine Medersa** and the great **Karaouiyne Mosque**.

The Henna Souk and Sidi Frej Maristan

Just before the Souk Attarine gate take the right turn and then, ten paces later, take the first left to bring you into the **Souk au Henné**, an intimate triangular *place* under the dappled shade of an old poplar tree. Here henna paste, hessian sacks of henna leaves, silvery blocks of antimony, rhassoul and dark, powdered kohl are weighed out and sold. More alarming is the display of the dried skins of lizards, snakes and small predators, with hutches of live hedgehogs and terrapins for magical pastes, aphrodisiacs and love potions. All the stallholders are happy to explain the use of their various products and can put you in touch with the local women who create the rich geometric patterns in henna with which hands and feet are decorated.

On the far side of the little *place* stands a normal-looking trading *fondouq* which occupies the site of the **Sidi Frej Maristan**, a mental asylum built in the reign of the Merenid Sultan Yacqub (1286–1307). A plaque on the wall proudly records this early example of enlightened medical care.

Fondouq Nejjarine Museum and Belghazi Museum

Take the second right turn down a narrow alley before the Souk Attarine gate, and after 25 paces turn right again to walk down a vine-covered alley lined with workshops to approach **Place Nejjarine** (the square of the carpenters). This is another of the medina's intimate places, which can be appreciated *en passant*, or at your ease in one of the small cafés. An elegant drinking fountain plays here into a basin of mosaic tiles, and cedar beams support a green-tiled canopy. On a weekday morning the carpenters can be found at work off any of the surrounding streets, adzing away at a twisted trunk, for instance, to carve a light, strong plough.

The 18th-century **Nejjarine Fondouq** dominates the place, with a great imposing ornamental gateway standing behind the fountain to frame one of the classic images of the city. The immaculate restoration of the *fondouq* has been paid for by Mohammed Lamrani, ex-prime minister and scion of an old Fassi family. It now houses the **Museum of Wood**, a state-of-the-art collection of tools, wood types and historic exhibits all beautifully displayed, labelled, securely dated and odiferous. Look out for the low dowry chests, high marriage chairs, ornate window grilles, prayer beads, elegant musical instruments, fairground wheels and the *karraka* – school boards by which the Koran was learnt. Continue through the three storeys up to the roof terrace for the views, a mint tea at the café, and a chance to sit and collect your thoughts.

Museum of Wood
t 0535 740580; open Wed–Mon 9–12 and 3–6; adm

If you take the alley beside the *fondouq* you will be heading towards the smell of the Guerniz **tanneries**, which are just before the Sidi Moussa Mosque. These are the oldest of the three Fez tanneries; tradition has it they were established by Idriss II. A short stroll brings you to the **Belghazi Museum**, a 17th-century riad with a splendid private collection of crafts and antiques, from rugs to jewellery and weapons. Some of the art is for sale. The courtyard café is a good spot for tea, and there are fine views from the roof.

Belghazi Museum
19 Derb Ghorba, t 0535 741178; open daily 9.30am–6pm; adm

The Zaouia of Moulay Idriss II

Non-Muslims are not allowed into the sanctuary here, but you can get an excellent view of the interior from the edge of the women's gate.

Take the right turn just beyond (east of) the Souk Attarine gate, and after about 80 paces you will pass under a gate. Bear left, up through a street dedicated to the selling of nougat, for 19 paces before turning left (having ducked beneath the wooden bar that hangs across the alley), from where it is about 70 paces, along a street dedicated to selling votive candles and trinkets, to the best view into the *zaouia* of Moulay Idriss II.

Within the darkened sanctuary the tomb can be seen heavily draped in a rich embroidered velvet cloth, the *ksaoua*, and surrounded by baroque brass, flickering coloured candles, glittering lamps, offerings, European clocks and praying women. It is strikingly similar to a saint's shrine in Spain, Naples, Sicily or Greece, and round the corner of the sanctuary a hole lined by well-worn copper allows the devotees to touch the tomb. As well as being the patron saint of the city, Moulay Idriss II is especially appealed to by boys before circumcision and women before giving birth.

It is not known if the reforming Almoravids or Almohads suppressed the cult, but Idriss II's tomb was re-identified during Merenid rule, in 1307, after an uncorrupted body was unearthed here. The present *zaouia* was constructed in 1437, but it was the Wattasid dynasty (1472–1554) that developed it into a major cult centre. Throughout August the numerous guilds of the city still go in procession to the tomb and offer decorative gifts, animal sacrifices, religious chants and *nubas* of classical Andalucian music before starting their festivals. In the 18th century Moulay Ismaïl restored the shrine, and until the 19th century it was hung with contracts by which the various towns and tribes tried to establish the exact terms upon which they accepted the rule of each new sultan. The right of sanctuary, *horm*, is still respected, and Sultan Abdul Aziz appalled the Fassi when he arrested the murderer of a European who had taken shelter beside the tomb.

The Kissaria

The Bab Souk Attarine is also the spice-sellers' gate that marks the entrance to the Kissaria, the dense network of traditionally expensive shops on an irregular criss-crossing grid of alleys and tiny shop-filled squares that cluster at the heart of the medina. This is a sublime area for shopping, a world away from the piles of tack in the enormous tourist bazaars. Here each proprietor sits in his own small booth with everything within reach. It fortunately remains an area dedicated to local needs – fine cloth, silk threads, jewellery, clothes, hats and blankets – and at night the whole Kissaria is locked.

On your first visit stay close to the main street. About 35 paces along the street (on your left) is the welcoming interior of the Dar

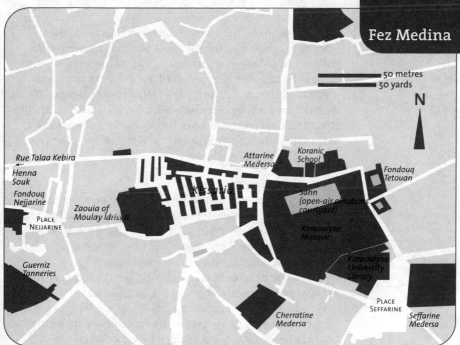

50 metres
50 yards

N

Rue Talaa Kebira
←

Henna
Souk

Fondouq
Nejjarine

PLACE
NEJJARINE

Zaouia of
Moulay Idriss II

Guerniz
Tanneries

Kissaria

Attarine
Medersa

Koranic
School

Sahn
(open-air ablutions
courtyard)

Karaouiyne
Masque

Fondouq
Tetouan

Karaouiyne
University
Library

PLACE
SEFFARINE

Cherratine
Medersa

Seffarine
Medersa

Saada café restaurant, while another 40 paces brings you past a quiet cul de sac (on your right) with a fine view of the minaret of the *zaouia* of Moulay Idriss.

The Attarine Medersa

**The Attarine
Medersa**
*open daily 9–6, except
at prayer time; adm*

A hundred metres (225 paces) past the Bab Souk Attarine, on the left just as you enter a vaulted and confusingly busy crossroads, are the distinctive bronze doors of the Attarine Medersa. Built by Sultan Abou Said Uthman (1322–5) within a confined space, it does not have the grandeur of the slightly later Bou Inania, but is a finer, more delicate structure. It is at least as rich in its *zellij*, plaster and wood decoration, but with a lighter architectural touch emphasized by reflecting pairs of arches seemingly supported by thin stone pillars.

The plan is familiar: an entrance hall with stairs to the upper floors (with 60 rooms for students), and a central fountain court with a prayer-hall beyond. There are no lecture halls as the Attarine was designed as an addition to the Karaouiyne University, not a rival. You may enter the prayer-hall; the *mihrab* is to the right, flanked by pillars and lit by coloured glass windows. A bronze chandelier hangs from the cedar ceiling.

The *zaouia* of Sidi Ahmed Tijani, 200m north of the *medersa*, is the main lodge of this influential Sufi brotherhood founded by Sidi Mohammed Tijani in Algeria in the 18th century. Persecuted by the

Turks, he fled to Fez. The brotherhood was a great ally of the Alaouite sultans, aiding them in religious reforms; when Moulay Hafid retired to Tangier in 1912 he wrote a scholarly work in praise of the order. Opposite the green-tiled minaret, go through an arch, then pass under another arch into a low and tight passage. Off to the left is the *fondouq* **of the weavers**, a dim, dilapidated but highly atmospheric old courtyard full of the noise of looms. The weavers are used to visitors, and you can buy a silk-cotton *haik* or bed cover for a couple of hundred *dirhams*.

The Karaouyine Mosque

It is perhaps appropriate that this grand mosque at the heart of Fez and Moroccan culture should remain such an elusive building. Its outer walls are so encrusted with shops and houses that its shape is lost, while the four main gates offer intriguing but baffling vistas of a succession of pure white colonnades and simple rush matting with a woven red design. They occasionally frame a turbanned lecturer sitting cross-legged against a far wall.

First built in 859 by Fatima bint Mohammed ben Feheri, a prosperous refugee from Kairouan, the mosque was improved by a Fatimid governor in 933 and enlarged by Abd er Rahman III, governor of the Omayyad Caliph of Córdoba, in 956. Rebuilt by the Almoravid Sultan Ali ben Youssef from 1135 to 1143, it was finished a few years before the dynasty fell.

It is a rectangular space sufficiently large for 20,000 to say their prayers simultaneously. The roof is upheld by spacious round-topped arches supported on 16 arcades of 21 spans. An open-air court, the *sahn*, of four spans' width, is at the opposite end from the *mihrab*. Within this open court the Almohads placed a marble basin and the Saadian Sultan Abdullah el Ghalib added two flanking pavilions modelled on those of the Lion Court in the Alhambra at Granada. The chief glory of the mosque remains the **central aisle**, which leads up from the centre of the court to the *mihrab*. This is embellished with increasingly elaborate floral and Kufic script carved into the plaster as you advance, while the domes that span the arches are raised higher and higher as they approach the *mihrab* and are ribbed or vaulted with bold stalactite decoration. The carving is in mint condition as it was covered by the Almohads two years after it was finished and only revealed in the restorations of 1950. The mosque also houses one of the richest libraries of the Islamic world.

The best view of the mosque available to a non-Muslim used to be from the roof of a restaurant on Rue Boutoil-Karaouiyne, but it has now moved premises. Instead, your best chance of a bird's-eye-view is to walk down the outer east wall of the complex and ask for the chance to see inside. You may find a family who will help for

An Ancient Centre of Learning

The great library of the university, to which there is no entry, is stored behind the white walls between the Place Seffarine and the mihrab. Considering the physical state of the city, the library has survived well. It boasts a 9th-century manuscript Koran and an original manuscript of Averroës (Ibn Rachid) amongst its 30,000 precious volumes.

The Karaouiyne University is one of the oldest in the world, dating from AD 850. Its origins lie in the teaching of the Koran in the mosque, just as Christian universities grew out of monastery and cathedral schools. Allied subjects such as grammar, theology and Koranic law were taught in informal lectures, with an accent on learning by heart rather than on debate or written papers. It is claimed that as a young French peasant boy the future Pope Sylvester II studied at Fez a century before Bologna, the first European university, was established. He certainly so astonished the European courts with his mathematical and astronomical knowledge that he was later accused of making a pact with the devil. In the 14th century 2,000 students, *tolba*, dwelt in the various *medersas* to be instructed by the ulemas, the doctors and professors. Averroes (Ibn Rachid), Ibn Khaldun, Leo Africanus and Ibn Battuta all participated in the intellectual milieu of Fez. In 1963 the university was 'nationalized', having been the single source of higher education until then.

a small tip. If not, ask for Osiama, the 6-year-old boy who kindly led me through a grand merchant's house (belonging to his family) and onto a platform on the roof. From here, you can see into the courtyard, but never as far as the central decorated aisle of the mosque itself. On your left you will pass the locked door of the **Mesbahia Medersa**, closed for restoration at the time of writing. It was built in 1346 by Sultan Abou Hassan, and nicknamed '*er rokham*', the marble, owing to his lavish use of the stone. The central white marble basin was brought over from a mosque in Algeciras.

Having turned the corner you pass on your left the *fondouq* of the Tetouanis (*Fondouq Tétaounine*), a fine 14th-century Merenid court used by Andalucian merchants from Tetouan. You are welcome to enter as there is a small carpet shop within. There is a less grand *fondouq* a few doors below.

The tall, distant minaret is that of the *zaouia* of Moulay Idriss II, while the lantern-less minaret on the grand mosque is the Trumpeter, from which Ramadan is announced; the nearest is the 10th-century white domed minaret that echoes the grand mosque of Kairouan, Tunisia. The mosque's internal court, the *sahn*, with flanking twin pavilions and dazzling blue and white floor, is also partly overlooked.

Place Seffarine

Shaded by fig trees, this is by the southeastern corner of the mosque, the direction of the *mihrab* and prayer. It has a pleasant fountain and is full of metalworkers tapping away at an impressive range of pots and kettles, including some really gigantic ones for weddings. This, like the Bab Souk Attarine, is a recognizable centre from which to explore this end of the medina – the Seffarine Medersa, Dyers' Souk and the Cherratine Medersa – or the tanneries, and the Medersa es Sahrija beside the grand mosque of the Andalucian quarter.

The Seffarine Medersa

A doorway on one side of the Place Seffarine leads into the Seffarine Medersa, which is still occupied by Islamic students, who will happily show a few affable visitors around (*tips accepted*); it is normally closed to groups and brusquer tourists. Established by Sultan Abou Yusuf Yacqub, the founder of Fez Jdid, in 1280, it was the first *medersa* in Morocco, and follows the design of a Fassi house, since professors used to lecture in their home when not using the mosque. *Medersas* had long been established in Egypt, Syria and Iraq, but with the additional gift of a library the sultan showed that he too was interested in education. The rooms and small pool arranged around the irregular courtyard have a simple domestic elegance, but the dilapidated central prayer-hall (offset from the irregular *medersa* courtyard) shows signs of the extravagance that would be unleashed in the Attarine Medersa 25 years later. It is good to see a *medersa* in use: the plain mattresses, heaps of books and notes and the normal squalor of student life add a vital missing ingredient to empty tourist-thronged halls. The *medersa* roof has an intriguing outlook over the river mills, houses and bridges.

The Dyers' Souk

Continue on past the *medersa* door and drop down into the Dyers' Souk, the Souk Sabbighin or *Souk des Teinturiers*, which is on the riverbank to the right of the bridge. The swatches of bright-coloured wool draped over the street to dry are perennially photogenic. The vats of dye and the grave, grey-clothed vat masters are more disturbing. If you are with a guide, ask to be shown the riverside mill where seeds and minerals are crushed to extract the raw dyes. The millers wade through the thick, pungent waters of the stream, raking aside mounds of garbage in order to direct enough water into the workings of the mill – a vision of mingled squalor, rancid steaming waters and skilled medieval use of water power.

The Cherratine Medersa

Standing in front of the library at the top of Place Seffarine, turn left and walk along Rue Haddadine (lined with displays of teapots, kitchenware and jewellery) for about 90 paces and then turn right up Rue Cherratine. Walk for about 130 paces and, having passed the Dar Sekka bazaar, you will reach the twin bronze doors of the **Cherratine Medersa**, a dilapidated but delightfully unvisited corner of the city. It is an extensive complex built by the first Alaouite sultan, Moulay Rachid, in 1670 to celebrate his reunification of Morocco. From the bronze doors on the street an ornamental passageway leads directly into the calm, quiet order of the spacious interior courtyard with its central pool. One side opens directly into a high-vaulted mosque, the orientation of which allows the whole courtyard to be treated as a *sahn*. No windows break the severity of the walls: instead, the residential blocks, each looking into its own lightwell, have been cunningly placed off the three corners, approached through passages. The fourth corner houses the ablutions courtyard – the only one in Morocco still in exuberant working order, with a fountain by the entrance and water-filled pool in the central courtyard, around which are ranged seven L-shaped closets. For its combination of privacy without prudery, and functionally inspired decoration mixed with a touch of grandeur, it is exemplary. It is no wonder that the Victorian closet-makers looked to the East for their inspiration.

Beyond the *medersa* there is a pretty triangular square, **Place Chemaïne**, where dried fruit is sold, and beyond that the Kissaria begins with several shops that specialize in lambswool hats and embroidered fezzes.

The Tanneries

⭐ Tanneries

The **Chouara** or Dabbaghin, the largest of Fez' three ancient tanneries, is on a terrace above the river Fez, a well-beaten 200m walk along Rue el Mechattine from the northeastern corner of Place Seffarine. The powerful, distinctive smell is enough to guide you. Once there, boys will take you to terraces and courts where you can see the operations without being too much in the way. There is a rush of guilt as you attempt to stifle your initial nausea and notice that you are part of a stream of foreigners who arrive, look repulsed, take photographs, tip and leave. The honeycomb of vats, their assorted colours, processes and levels, have an endless fascination. The neighbouring roofs and hills are flecked with drying skins, a tone down in colour from the livid vats of saffron, poppy, indigo, mint and antimony. The scantily dressed tanners appear like so many human storks, their long elegant legs working through the pools, bobbing down to worry a skin and then striding off to wash at the fresh-water standing pipes.

The tanneries are worked by a mesh of specialist and cooperative guilds with their own hierarchies of apprentices, craftsmen and master craftsmen. A whole range of processes are undertaken here: fresh animal skins are treated and pounded in alternating liquid and solid vats of urine and pigeon shit; they are then scraped, wet dyed, scraped, and perhaps dry-dyed, before being trimmed and sorted for auction. (If you were to continue down this alley you would enter a fresh food market, with fish, goats' heads, bowls of petals for scent, herbs and spices, ending in the happy mayhem of the square.)

Out of the Medina

From Place Seffarine a short walk downhill through the Dyers' Souk (avoiding the narrow bridge across the river into the Andalous side of the old city) and a right turn in the twisting street should drop you down into the sunbaked tarmac space overlooked by the green-tiled minaret of the **Er Rsif Mosque**. From here, local buses and *petits taxis* offer a quick means of leaving the medina. Alternatively, retrace your path, going uphill from the Bab Souk Attarine towards the Bab Bou Jeloud, or if you have the energy explore a different section of the old city by walking uphill to the Bab Guissa and Bab Jamaï.

From Bab Souk Attarine to Bab Guissa and Bab Jamaï

A turn north off the Souk Ain Allou, just after Bab Souk Attarine and 15m before the conspicuous Dar Saada restaurant, will take you into the **Souk Joutia**, the market for salt, eggs and fish. The Rue Hormis runs roughly north from this souk towards Bab Guissa. About 40m beyond the Joutia, and 20m to the right of the street, is an 18th-century *fondouq* and fountain, the central square of the **Es Sagha** district, which used to be a great haunt of jewellers. The elegant carved-plaster and cedar colonnades of the Fondouq Sagha are now one of the centres of the wool trade: raw spun wool is stored here, auctioned off and brought back from the dyers in bright-coloured batches to be sold to weavers and carpet-makers.

Back on Rue Hormis, bear left and climb uphill past a cinema, a local social centre that's surrounded by cheap grills and cafés. Off from here is another henna and spice market, the **Place Achabin**. The path snakes farther uphill, past a fountain on the left, to the area around **Fondouq el Yhoudi** or **Guissa**. In the morning there's a distinctive aroma of cedar wood and singed hooves from the workshops of farriers, joiners and wood-turners. Ask to be shown the original Fondouq el Yhoudi, high up on the left, where Jewish merchants were based in the 13th century before the Merenids moved them to Fez Jdid. Replaced several times since then, the *fondouq* is now used for the sorting, grading and auctioning of tanned and dyed skins.

Below the **Bab Guissa** is a complex of three buildings, a 14th-century mortuary chamber and a 19th-century mosque and *medersa*, none of which are open to non-Muslims. To the right of Bab Guissa are the more elaborate Bab Jamaï and Bab Ferdaous, where you can find a no.10 bus to speed you back to the Place des Alaouites on the western edge of Fez Jdid, or a taxi to take you to the *ville nouvelle* or on a tour of the ramparts.

The Andalucian Quarter

This half of Fez-el-Bali is a quieter, residential area. It has the Sahrija Medersa, no bazaars, lots of local shops and, as a direct consequence of there being hardly any tourists, a much friendlier and more courteous population. (See below for a suggested walk through the area.) It is likely to stay that way, for the quarter's great historical centre stands on the summit of a hill and has – even by Moroccan standards – a particularly elusive Grand Mosque (Jemaa el Kebir, to a local). To get to it, or to the partial view from the side doors, there are two main approaches. From the Chouara tanneries, cross the conspicuous **Pont de Beïne el Mdoun**, the bridge of the two cities, into the Andalucian Quarter and then follow the Rue Seffah for about 500m as it climbs the hill. Alternatively, cross the river Fez at the smaller **Sidi el-Aouad** bridge (by Place Er Rsif), which is just off the Dyers' Souk below Place Seffarine. From here it is probably easiest to keep to the fairly level Rue Nekhaline for about 300m, until you turn right onto the Rue Seffah and trudge uphill.

The Andalucian Grand Mosque

One of the best views of the mosque is from a side gate that looks straight across the elegant *sahn* courtyard towards the white minaret, which is capped with a stumpy dome. It was first built by Meriem, the equally pious sister of Fatima, the founder of the Karaouiyne Mosque, but was largely rebuilt by the Almohad Sultan Mohammed en Nasir in the 13th century. The Merenids gave it a fountain and built two nearby *medersas* for students. They presented an entire library to the mosque in 1415, but this never developed into a separate university.

The Sahrija Medersa

The Sahrija Medersa
Closed for refurbishment: check with the tourist office.

This *medersa* 'of the pool' lies southwest of the Grand Mosque. It was built by Abou Hassan between 1321 and 1323, while he was still heir to the throne. When he became sultan he built another in the Karaouiyne Quarter, the Mesbahia Medersa, and commissioned others at Taza, Meknès and Salé.

It is a dilapidated but enchanting jewel of the period, with a simple but harmonious plan. A rectangular pool fed from a marble bowl surrounded by a worn grid of tiled drainage rills dominates the centre of the small courtyard, with splendid carved plaster, cedar walls and *zellij* mosaics touched with the true serenity of age. On the outer face of the prayer-hall you can still see the hinges of those typical Moorish hanging gates which would later become associated more with secular than with sacred buildings. The prayer-hall, with simple coffered ceiling and comparatively austere central *mihrab*, retains a venerable dignity. On two sides of the courtyard, behind wooden grilles, are the former students' rooms, four of which have windows that overlook the pool.

Instead of retracing your steps, you could also continue south from the Grand Mosque/ Sahrija Medersa out of the medina down Rue Sidi Ali Boughaleb. The *koubba* of this saint is on the right just at the beginning of the cemetery. The saint is not actually buried here, but the shrine remains an important popular cult centre. The ill and the mad surround the *koubba* on Tuesday nights, and wait for the saint to appear in their dreams and suggest a cure. The cemetery of Bab Hamra on the right should not be entered by non-Muslims and has a local reputation as the resort of black magicians. At Bab Ftouh you can find a taxi to get round the ramparts, or take a no.18 bus back into the New Town.

Musée de la Musique Andalouse de Fès
Makhfia Derb Cheikh El Foket, **t** *0535 863281; www.musique-andalouse.com/musee. htm; tips accepted*

The **Musée de la Musique Andalouse de Fès** (Fez Museum of Andalucian Music) is exceptionally hard to find, about three or four minutes' walk from the Sahrija Medersa through a series of alleyways. You may want to ask directions to find it, perhaps at the Sahrija Medersa. The museum itself is set in a stunning riad at the end of a short cul-de-sac. There are only a few display cabinets which contain *rababs*, *ouds* and violins, with instruments made with horse hair or with intestines. On the wall you can find a photo of Bennani, a father figure for contemporary Andalucian music. The form remains popular in Morocco today and it is among the least Middle Eastern of the Arab-Muslim musical genres. Like so much of the architecture in Fez, it drew heavily on the influence of Iberia's south coast. Concerts still take place here from time to time and are very much worth attending (*see* the website for programme details). But you can still hear some of the traditions in the limpid, late-romantic guitar concertos of Joaquín Rodrigo Vidre (1901–1999), not least the *Concierto de Aranjuez* (the haunting piece written after his child was miscarried) and, as the name implies, the *Concierto Andaluz*.

A Short Walk

If you want to explore the area, the Fez tourist office has an excellent **walk** it suggests. This begins at the Idrissid Jemaa al-Anouar, or Mosque of Lights, now a ruin. It lies close to the eastern wall of Fez, about halfway up, on the western side of a large block a little northeast of the Andalucian mosque. From here, walk south to the Andalucian mosque and *medersa* (following the right-hand wall), before you come to the Sahrija Medersa (*see* p.203) under an enclosed corridor and, immediately after it, the **Jemaa al-Oued**, a pleasant 18th-century mosque (with ruins behind it). Now you must turn right, walk until the next main junction and turn right again and walk for five to ten minutes to the 11th-century Bin Lamdoun Bridge and Square, replete with artisans and hawkers. Continuing ahead, you then turn left, then right and finally right again as you pass through the craft market. At the end of these you will find the colourful **Chouara Tannery** to your right. The road begins to arc left and after a few minutes the *Zaouia* of Sidi Ahmed will appear on your left, the exquisite tomb of a major Fassi saint. Turn right and zigzag a couple of times before you are in the Herbalists market, or **Souk Al-Achabine**. As you leave the market, take a right and walk for five minutes until you reach the Bab Guissa, a northern gate out of Fez. Finally turn right and you are at the **Palais Jamaï**, now a luxury hotel worthy of a pit stop for cocktails.

A Tour of the Ramparts

Before leaving Fez try to witness dusk from the hills. Flame-coloured light plays on the ochre walls and flickers finally over the high minarets. The sky is full of pigeons and swallows enjoying the evening flight; smoke from thousands of kitchens floats upwards from the medina. Then you are hit by the call to prayer. A 15km circuit round the outer walls by taxi gives an excellent overview of the city. The surrounding hills, particularly at Bordj Sud and by the Merenid tombs, all provide magnificent views over Fez-el-Bali.

Fez Jdid

Starting from the southern tip of the Place de la Résistance in the New Town, take the exit for Taza, which descends into the river Zitoun valley. The outer walls of Fez Jdid rise to your left, enclosing the Mellah and the Jewish necropolis, which is entered through the Bab Jiaf. Schools and hospitals cluster around the Bab Jebala/Bab Riafa, which leads to the area that Moulay Hassan developed in the 19th century to unite Fez-el-Bali and Fez Jdid. An electrical sub-station on your right marks the site of an old aqueduct; opposite is the Bab el Hadid.

Below the walls a great artesian fountain ensures that there is a patch of bright-green grass around the splash pool. Near here are the discreet walls of the American Fondouq, a charitable hospital for animals. As the road swings closer to the walls you pass Bab Jdid, which provides direct bus and taxi access into the heart of the medina.

Bordj Sud

Crossing over the river Boufekrane here, the approach track to Bordj Sud can be seen to your right. This fort was built by Portuguese prisoners of the Saadian Sultan Ahmed el Mansour (1578–1609) as part of a system that was designed as much to intimidate the Fassis as to defend them. The fort is partly in ruins now, but it would have had a good field of fire over the Andalucian and Karaouiyne districts that rise either side of the now invisible river Fez.

Bab Ftouh Cemetery

Pass below the vast cemetery of Bab Ftouh, studded with the whitewashed *koubbas* of holy men – non-Muslims are not usually welcome on this hill. All the great professors of the Karaouiyne University are buried here, and on the summit there is an open-air mosque, a *msalla*, used for the great feasts of Aid el Kebir and Aid es Seghir. Around the *msalla* are the *koubbas* of the Sebatou Rijal, the anonymous seven saints who, according to local tradition, brought Islam to Morocco.

At the lower eastern corner of the cemetery is a *koubba* to **Sidi Harazem**, who came to Morocco from Arabia and, before retiring to a life of poverty and silence, taught at the Karaouiyne Mosque. He was so skilful a debater that he silenced the most agnostic and sophistic of *jinn*, and has become the patron of Koranic studies and students in general. The ancient festival of Sidi Harazem takes place in spring. An equivalent of the European Lord of Misrule is elected, and they process up to the Andalucian Grand Mosque to officiate as the student sultan for Friday prayers. Now a humorous affair, in the past it was a great occasion for political unrest. The final resting place of the Sidi's bones is a contentious issue: they are not claimed to lie here but in Marrakesh, or in the nearby spa of Sidi-Harazem. Below the cemetery is the Bab Ftouh, to the left of which behind the walls stretches the cemetery of Bab Hamra.

Beyond Bab Ftouh to the Potteries

The Potters' Quarter, with its distinctive chimneys belching black smoke from kilns still fuelled by orchard prunings and dried olive pressings, has been moved away from the medina and is now found 1km east of Bab Ftouh just off the main Taza road. Turn left by the blue-tiled tower of the Boissons Talounite café, and a left turn at the next dirt crossroads leads directly to the **Poterie Fakh-Khari**, well geared to receiving visitors, with a café and two showroom shops. In the compound you can watch apprentices kneading the raw clay, skilled potters working it on wheels, the stacking and unstacking of furnaces, and schools of fluent painters decorating plates, bowls and hotel ashtrays, while in other rooms teams of young boys cut glazed tiles to be the raw ingredient for the *zellij* mosaics made by the master craftsmen. There is no admission charge, prices are not bad and there can be an encouraging murmur of business from designers and exporters commissioning special pieces.

Otherwise, continue east of Bab Ftouh to pass the eastern gate, Bab el Khouka. An extensive suburb has here sprawled out beyond the old city to obscure most of the eastern walls. The next gate, **Bab Sidi Bou Jida**, is named after the *koubba* of that saint, which is on your right. He can be compared to St Jude, the patron saint of lost causes, and is greatly favoured by students before exams and women before marriage. Across the river Fez there is a new tiled auction yard outside the walls. The smells and sights here are intense: trucks unload raw, bloody skins direct from butchers and slaughterhouses. The great wet bundles are forked over by specialists, bought, packed on to mules and sent down into the medina for the first stage in the long tanning process.

The Jamaï

Next is the **Bab Jamaï**, which leads into the luxurious Palais Jamaï Hotel. This incorporates a few rooms and a magnificent Andalucian garden that belonged to a distinguished Fassi family, the Ulad Jamaï, which had a tradition of government service. The Jamaï brothers, Haj Amaati and Si Mohammed Soreir, served Sultan Moulay Hassan as Grand Vizier and Minister of War. After the death of their master they fell victim to the jealousy of the child-Sultan Abdul Aziz's Turkish mother and her ally the half-black chamberlain, Bou Ahmed. They were imprisoned in Tetouan, their property forfeit and their families persecuted. Haj Amaati died in prison but remained chained to his brother (in high summer) for eleven days. Si Mohammed survived the ordeal but was released only after 14 years. On his deathbed he requested that '*my chains and fetters are to be put back upon my limbs. I desire to appear before God...that I might appeal to Him for the justice my sultan refused me.*'

The Vista and the Merenid Tombs

The next gate after the **Bab Jamaï** is the 13th-century Almohad Bab Guissa, above which the road climbs up through the cemetery hill of the same name. Beside the turning down to the ugly Merenides Hotel, a long, wide garden terrace has been established which allows locals as well as rich tourists to enjoy this unsurpassed view over Fez-el-Ball. As you join the colourful mass of kaftans billowing in the breeze of the evening *paseo*, you see below, tucked behind its ribbon of ancient wall, virtually the complete extent of the Karaouiyne district. The *zaouia* of Moulay Idriss II is immediately recognizable by its high, green-tiled pyramid roof and accompanying tall minaret. Just to the left, and lower, a great expanse of green tiles marks the Karaouiyne Mosque, with its whitewashed minaret. This is crowned with a dome, not the usual Moroccan lantern, faithfully echoing the grand mosque at Kairouan, in Tunisia, founded by Uqba ben Nafi in 683. A lower, conventional minaret can be seen to the right: this is the Trumpeter's tower from which the end of the fast of Ramadan is announced. The city below remains defined by its 12th-century walls, the intense urban network in heady contrast to the hillside olive groves that overlook the medina to the north and south.

The Merenid tombs can be reached only by taking a goat track from the road. Most visitors seem content to enjoy them at a distance, surrounded by a crumbling mass of ruined walls, old quarries, caves and the odd melancholic figure. The tombs were originally established within the extensive walls of an old Merenid kasbah that defended this hilltop. Below it, but outside the city walls, was the medieval leper colony. The prominent arched cube among the tombs was once covered with a green-tiled pyramid roof, while a marble-columned interior court held a simple stone tomb carved with an elegant epitaph in a sea of coloured *zellij* mosaic. In the 14th century this patchwork of enclosed hilltop tombs must have equalled Rabat's Chellah in elegance. Now it is all dust. Well might Alexander have wept at the tomb of Cyrus, the greatest of all the great Persian Kings, when he saw that his mausoleum was neglected and covered in dust and rubbish less than a century after his death.

Bordj Nord

ⓘ Bordj Nord
open Wed–Thurs,
Sat–Mon 9–12
and 2.30–6.30, Fri
2.30–6.30; adm

Below the garden terrace viewpoint a series of neat paths takes you down to the star-shaped Bordj Nord. Built in 1582, this was the second of the Saadian fortresses designed as much to cover the city with a threatening field of fire as to protect it. A century and a half later, in the Alaouite period, the elegant lance-shaped corner redoubts were added; in 1964 the weapons collection from the Dar Batha Museum was moved here to form a separate **Museum of**

Arms (*Musée d'Armes*). A walk around the cool dark vaults and casements of this immaculately preserved old artillery fortress, however, is worth the price of the ticket by itself. The collection takes you through the whole history of armaments, with cases of prehistoric Stone Age tools, Bronze and Iron Age weapons, casts of rare medieval European devices and a comprehensive display of 18th-, 19th- and 20th-century weapons.

For a foreign visitor it is the vast array of Moroccan weapons stacked in an imposing mass in the three rear casements, which date from the 16th to the 20th centuries, that is most rewarding. They show clearly how far the souvenir swords in the bazaars have evolved from the original very serviceable military sabres with their characteristic 'snake-head' wooden handles and chased-steel hand-guards. This is also true of the daggers, with a practical grip given by their bone, metal and leather handles and the very slight curve of their blades. The *fusils Marocains* with their almost 2m-long barrels (made in Fez, Tetouan or Taghzout) alone live up to one's exotic expectations, with some of their stocks and powder-horn accessories so encrusted with carved ivory, raw coral and silver and gold that they become male jewellery. For the historian the two bronze cannon at the exit provide crucial evidence of Morocco's industrial sophistication in the 16th century, and the self-sufficiency that allowed her to keep both the Portuguese and the Ottoman Empire at bay. The Arabic inscription on the damaged five-tonne cannon reads 'made on the order of [Sultan] al-Walid ibn Zaydan in 1044 H' (AD 1634), while that on the vast 4.5m-long bronze cannon reads 'made by el Haj el Ghourg on the order of el Ghalib', the Saadian Sultan who ruled from 1557 to 1574.

The Cherarda Kasbah

The Bordj Nord fort overlooks the extensive square-walled Cherarda Kasbah, protected by towers and surrounded on almost all sides by a cemetery. It was built by Moulay Rachid in 1670 to house tribes in the sultan's service, notably the Oudaïa and Cherarda cavalry. It is now divided into hospital and university buildings and is therefore closed to tourists.

At the end of the long kasbah wall the Bab Segma, with a single remaining 14th-century octagonal tower, separates the kasbah from Fez Jdid. A kilometre of wall runs west from here to enclose the royal park and palace, and then a left turn before the sports park follows another monumental kilometre stretch of royal wall to arrive back at Place de la Résistance.

Information and Services in Fez

Tourist Information

ⓘ **Fez >**
Tourist Office
t 0535 624769

Tourist Board
Place de la Résistance,
t 0535 623460; both
open 8.30–noon
and 2.30–6.30

Fez has a **tourist office** in the *ville nouvelle* where Blvd Mohammed V meets Ave Mohammed Es Slaoui. They can help with monuments, hotels, restaurants and possibly guides too, as well as tourist maps. But Fez also has a **tourist board**, which can be found on Place de la Résistance, a few blocks (and only ten minutes' walk) to the north. They may supply what the tourist office lacks.

Tourist Police

Fez is less aggressively money-grabbing than Marrakesh but you should still expect the amateur dramatics of the Moroccan marketplace and its matinée idols. To ensure that this does not pass from being convincing to coercive there are the tourist police in their navy uniforms, who are also supposed to prevent pushy 'freelance' guides and even imprison them if they seriously overstep the line. On the latter, they are fighting a losing battle and it is worth being aware that people who offer to help you find your way usually expect money in return and can be quite insistent on accompanying you and then on pushing you for more money than you give them. Sometimes you might need them but, if not, you may need to be firm to prevent them 'guiding' you. Always ask shopkeepers or hoteliers for directions as they cannot leave their workplace and tend to be more amenable. The main office for the **tourist police** is at Bab Bou Jeloud. Older travellers sometimes report being treated with greater respect, thanks to a strong culture of respect for older heads.

Communications

Telephones

Maroc Telecom recently added an extra digit to all urban area codes in the country, meaning that Fez's area code was **t** 35 but is now **t** 535 (or **t** 0535 with the essential first zero). Some business cards and hotel brochures have not yet caught up, so you may need to supply the 5 after the initial 0. The number of Maroc Telecom's head office in Rabat is **t** 0537 719000. Always begin with a zero if making a call within Morocco.

Telephones are dotted around the streets (and most take coins), often outside petrol stations or by major crossroads if they are in the *ville nouvelle* or in small Maroc Telecom shops in the medina. For the latter, look out for the blue signs with orange lettering. But for long-distance calls you are usually better asking at a hotel where, though perhaps double the price, at least the line is clear.

Email and Fax

Internet cafes are dotted around the city although they are more common in the *ville nouvelle*. Most hotels have wifi these days as well as a computer you can use; if not, they can point you to somewhere nearby.

Occasionally you may see 'FAX' written in the window of a very small and rudimentary shop but for the most part you are best to find a hotel.

Post and Telegrams

The **Central Post Office** is in the *ville nouvelle* at the corner of Ave Hassan II and Blvd Mohammed V (*open summer Mon–Fri 8am–3.30pm and Sat 8am–12 noon; Oct–June Mon–Fri 8.30am–12 noon and 2.30–6pm*, **t** 0535 622400). The poste restante is to the left as you enter. The telephone section (open until 9pm) has its own side entrance when the rest of the building has closed up. Other branches include Place de l'Atlas, and Place Batha in Fez Jdid. Check *www.bam.net.ma* (in French) for branch details. Hotels will usually post your cards and letters for you but otherwise try to use the post office's own postbox.

For more details on telegrams, letters and parcels in Morocco, *see* p.88, Practical A–Z.

Courier Services

DHL: Hotel Sheraton, Ave des F.A.R. *Open Mon–Fri 8.30am–6.30pm, Sat and public hols 8.30–12.30pm.*

TNT: t 0522 276728. (No Fez branch, but one in nearby Meknès at 41 Rue Nehru.)

Chronopost: This operates out of the main post offices and is both cheaper and slower than its better-known global cousins; *www.chronopost.com*.

Emergencies

Police t 19

Fire Service t 16

Ambulance t 15

Telephone Enquiries t 160

Hospitals and Medical Care

Hôpital Ghassani in the east of the *ville nouvelle* (2 Rue Benzakour in Atlas district, **t** 0535 622777) is reasonable and the **Clinique Ryad** on Place Hussein de Jourdanie (**t** 0535 960000) is a well-run private clinic. It is likely you will have to pay up front despite having insurance. As a rule, it is best to avoid Morocco's ubiquitous dental practices.

Pharmacies are well-stocked and there is a good one next to the Bab Bou Jeloud and an **all-night pharmacy** on Blvd Moulay Youssef by the Place de la Résistance in the *ville nouvelle*, **t** 0535 623380.

Maps

Tourist offices often have the most recent maps, but they tend to deteriorate quickly. Fez's bookshops stock maps and so do plenty of stalls, especially in tourist zones like the Bab Bou Jeloud area. But medieval Fez is almost beyond the skill of cartographers.

One exceptional map is found in book called *Fez from Bab to Bab: Walks in the Medina* by Hammad Berrada, although it may be more readily available in French (*Fes de Bab en Bab: Promenades dans la Medina*). You might be able to pick one up at the **American Language Centre, t** 0535 624850, or *info@alif-fes.com*.

Money

Banks are mostly in the *ville nouvelle*. The **BMCE** on Place Mohammed V offers the most useful range of services, but there is also the **BMCI**, 10 Rue Assela, **Banque Populaire** and **Crédit du Maroc** on Ave Mohammed V. In the heart of Fez-el-Bali there is a branch of Crédit du Maroc uphill from the Cherratin Medersa for currency exchanges. All large hotels will change money and travellers' cheques for guests.

Festivals in Fez

The students' *moussem* of Sidi Harazem is held at the end of April, and the two major city festivals of Moulay Idriss II and Sidi Ahmed el Bernoussi are both in September.

Shopping in Fez

For most, shopping in Fez means haggling in the medina, where your most flamboyant acting skills may finally have some financial impact on your life. The trick is to outperform your salesman, displaying only the most desultory interest, reeling as he mentions his price, and employing grandstanding arguments wherever possible. Work out what you want to pay beforehand and try not to move your price until he's made some major concessions on his, if at all. At the end, shake his hand and congratulate him on what a tough negotiator he is.

Markets in Fez are redolent with ceramics, carpets, metalwork, leather, drums, tambourines, shoes and belts, pots and pans. They generally open at 8am and close at dusk, but some stay open for evening trading too. If you are looking for something a bit special try **Mohammed ben Abdeljalil's shop**, 35 Rue Talaa Seghira. Do not be content with his street-side stall but ask to be shown the rooms behind, which are laden with *objets d'art*.

For picnics, the **central market** is off Blvd Mohammed V, just across the street from the Café Zanzibar. Bookshops and market stalls alike sell the 1920s and 1930s French-language tourism posters which, with their broad areas of deep colour, make for striking hangings for your bathroom or loft conversion back home.

Books and Prints

There are a couple of bookshops that stock English titles, as well as the newsstands found in the big hotels. The **Librairie du Centre**, 134–5 Blvd Mohammed V, and the **Hôtel de Fez**, Ave des F.A.R., are worth a look.

Librairie Fikr al-Moassar, 15 Rue du 16 Novembre, has titles in English and French, including plenty of travel and photo books. Newspapers are sold at all these shops and along Blvd Mohammed V.

Carpets, Blankets, Weaving

As a rule, it is the Berber carpets that are most notable in Morocco, not the Arab ones. Rabat is the centre of this industry, but Fez has mountains of carpets too. The city's fabrics, textiles, embroidery and woven goods will also catch your eye. Fez has a warren of fabric shops just east of the **Karouiyne mosque complex**. For obvious reasons, it is also a good city to buy traditional Moroccan clothes, whether kaftans (wide-sleeved gowns), *burnouses* (hooded jackets) or *jellabas* (wizardish robes with pointed hoods.) If you are headed for the mountains, it might be a good idea to pick up a blanket or two.

Iron, Brass and Copper

The metalworkers of Meknès and Fez are exceptional, and widely renowned for their painstaking craft and outstanding expertise. If you have plenty of time and you like a particular craftsman's work, you may want to commission a piece. Even if you do not have the time, the most long-established artisans here are very reliable and many people simply give a foreign address to the craftsman and the product does arrive (with no postage cost, thanks to a special export system.)

Jewellery

There is plenty of jewellery to be had in Fez and there is a difference in style between the jewellery in the **medina souks**, which are usually made of metal and make use of multiple colours, and the jewellery available in the **Mellah**, the Jewish area. For more African, ornate jewellery, you may want to stay in the souks, but for the finer pieces, try the Mellah's own smiths.

Spices and Scents

Fez's **Souk El Attarin** (Spices Market) is a good place to shop for cumin, cinnamon, paprika or mint. You might even buy a *tagine* cooking pot.

Woodwork and Leatherwork

Fez's older mosques offer carved proof of how long Fez's **woodcarvers** have been producing exquisite work. Even if you buy nothing, the labour itself and the smell of orangewood and cedar make it worth exploring the area around **El-Nejjarine**. All sorts of ornaments are available but you may want to look out for a working courtyard, since you are then more likely to be talking to the artisan himself and seeing some of the process in action.

A visit to the **tanneries** is a wonderful experience, even though you can only peer down on them from a little distance. Set out in gulleys the tanneries look like a painter's palette and the colours are at least as rich. Jackets and belts are a good investment here.

Sports and Activities in Fez

Fez would be one of the best cities in the world for *parkour*, with its patchwork of closely packed roofs set at odd heights. But the old city is otherwise too close for sport to ever move beyond the occasional children's games of football down an alleyway or across a closing marketplace. (Footballs, incidentally, are the best present for young boys, as they cannot usually afford one.) But once outside the medina it is possible to go **riding** at the racecourse, improve your game at Fez's **Royal Golf Club**, or **hire mountain bikes** to explore some of the villages outside.

Football

Maghreb Fez, Complexe Hassan II, *www.massawi.com*. If you prefer to watch than participate, you might enjoy seeing the popular local team in their fine bumble bee strips. The stadium holds 45,000 people.

Golf

Royal Golf Club, Km 15 Route d'Imouzzer, **t** 0535 665210. An 18-hole course opened in 1924 and set amid parkland and lakes.

Riding

Domaine Equestre Aïn Amyer, 2.5 km, Route d'Imouzzer, **t** 0535 942118. Horse-riding excursions around Fez.

Swimming

Les Trois Sources, 3 miles from Fez on the P24 south to Immouzer. Here you can enjoy some rural swimming (as well as ping-pong and billiards). It's an an enjoyable day out for families.

Hammam

A mixed *hammam*, with attendant masseur, operates in the Palais Jamaï Hotel. Alternatively, use the serene *hammam* at the elegant Riad Laaroussa in the medina (*see* Where to Stay, below).

 Riad Fès >>

Where to Stay in Fez

Whatever your budget, stay as close to the heady sights, odours and sounds of the medina for as long as you can, since Fez will repay familiarity with a dramatic drop in hassle.

If you fly in, you could organize a hotel from the airport, or else head to one and, if rooms are lacking, ask the concierge to help you find one. Fez has a range of options and not all are easy to find, so try to get as much information about the route (and what sights are on the way) as you can. If you are staying in a riad, expect a full-scale investigation of the area before you arrive.

Hotels in the more expensive categories will have air conditioning, TV and probably a pool and *hammam* too. In the middle category, they may have any one of these. Many of the middle-category options are riads, which have their own particular strengths, offering a more Fassi experience but often with less comfort and privacy than a hotel. The limit on guest numbers in riads mean they are not the cheapest option, unless you can persuade them to let you sleep on the roof. Thus the bottom end tend to involve very simple hotels which may not even offer breakfast, or hostels where noise or shared rooms are the price you pay.

 Dar Roumana >>

Luxury

Palais Jamaï, Bab Guissa, **t** 0535 634331, *www.sofitel.com/gb/hotel-2141-sofitel-fes-palais-jamai/index.shtml*. This has by far the best position, just within the medina

ramparts of Bab Jamaï, and all the cachet. Established in 1930 in the enclosed 19th-century palace of a Fassi Vizier, it is the only grand hotel from which you can walk straight out into the medina streets. It also has an extraordinary tiled Andalucian garden, enormous heated pool, tennis court, tiled *hammam* and Moroccan restaurant. It is featured in many novels, not least Paul Bowles' *The Spider's House*.

Riad Fès, Derb Ben Slimane, Zerbtana, **t** 0535 947610. The first Relais et Châteaux property in Fez, this is an opulent hotel in the medina. It is set around a series of exquisite patios and terraces with *zellij* tiling, fountains and a profusion of plants. The rooms and salons are lavishly furnished with Moroccan art and antiques and the hotel is equipped with every luxurious amenity from a spa to a stellar restaurant. Dreamy terrace with wonderful views.

Zalagh Parc Palace, Lôtissement Oued Fes, Route de Meknès, **t** 0535 755454, *www.zalagh-palace.ma*. Sitting just near the Kasbah but outside the old city walls, this five-star option has exceptional facilities, including a bowling alley, fabulous pool, health club and *hammam*. Inside it is grand and the rooms are large although the decoration is fussy.

Expensive

Dar Roumana, 30 Derb el Amer, Zqaq Roumane, **t** 0535 741637, *www.darroumana.com*. Restoring the 'House of the Pomengranate' was a labour of love for Jennifer, the charismatic owner. Now a chic guesthouse, it is filled with exquisite Moroccan workmanship, including mosaic tiling and intricate ceilings, screens and doors. There are breathtaking views from the roof terrace. Some rooms are in the moderate price category. Cooking holidays can be arranged, and the outstanding dinners are a highlight. A delicious breakast and – wonderfully – afternoon tea are included in the price.

Riad Laaroussa, 3 Derb Bechara, Talaa Sghir, **t** 0674 187639, *www.riad-laaroussa.com*. Lavishly furnished with beautiful fabrics and antiques, this is a gorgeous and deeply romantic 17th-century riad. Superb cuisine, accommodating staff, and a fabulous location in the medina. The largest suites nudge up into the next price category. There's a luxurious *hammam* and spa which are also open to non-guests.

Riad Le Calife, 19 bis Derb el Ouarbyia, t 0535 762608, *www.riadlecalife.com*. A sumptuous riad in the heart of the medina, this has just seven rooms and suites all stylishly furnished with a mixture of traditional and contemporary Moroccan furnishings. They prepare delicious meals (and can even arrange cooking lessons), served out on one of the charming terraces. Book early, as it fills with repeat guests.

Riad Le Ksar de Fes, Route d'Ain Chgagg, t 0535 665018, *www.riad-leksardefes.com*. If you want to get away from the hubbub of the city, this is a good choice a few kilometres from the centre. Although it is a relatively new hotel (2009), it has been sensitively built in traditional style and is surrounded by luxuriant gardens which enjoy superb views of the Atlas mountains. The suites range considerably in size, comforts and price, and the gardens contain a pair of *douirias*, traditional Moroccan cottages which are ideal for families or couples looking for seclusion. Online offers mean that prices sometimes drop as low as €90.

Riad des Oudayas, 5–6 Derb el Hamia, Quartier Ziat, t 0535 636303, *www.lesoudayas.com*. A very attractive, leafy riad in the middle of the medina with a plunge pool and beautiful furnishings and mosaics. Rooms (from €100–120) and courtyard are the ideal serene foil to the hubbub of the souks.

Royal Mirage (formerly the Sheraton), Ave de la Menara, t 0535 930909, *www.royalmiragehotels.com*. This is a large, modern hotel with immense marble foyers, big bedrooms and magnificent pools and is tucked away in the *ville nouvelle* suburbs. Service is patchy and it could do with a revamp, but online deals means it regularly drops a price category.

⭐ **Dar Seffarine** >>

⭐ **Riad Tizwa** >>

Moderate

Batha Hotel, Place De l'Istiqlal, t 0535 741077. The hotel has an appealingly dated look, with cool rooms, a bar that feels like a railway carriage, a restaurant that used to be the British Consulate-General and an indecisively named 'Coffée Schop'. The double row of tiled bedrooms surrounds a long, open courtyard, and there are fountains, a small but welcome pool and a licensed restaurant and bar in the old block.

Dar Attajali, 2 Derb Qattana, Zqaq Roumane, t 0677 081192, *www.attajalli.com*. An attractive riad, sensitively restored, with a large pool, a very restful terrace and many beautiful, original architectural features. There's no a/c or television, and some rooms are plainer than others so pick carefully. At the top end of this category.

Dar Seffarine, 14 Derb Sbaa Louyate, Seffarine, t 0671113528. A spectacularly beautiful dar just off the Place Seffarine, this has been painstakingly restored and is now a chic and surprisingly modestly priced guesthouse. Narrow staircases wind up to a rambling roof terrace with medina views where communal dinners are served under the stars.

Hotel Ibis Mousaffir, Blvd Bahmad, Place de la Gare, t 0535 651902, *www.ibishotel.com*. This has a fabulous exterior on Avenue des Almohades just beside the train station on the northern edge of the New Town. It is part of a well-designed national chain of station-side hotels that all have efficiently plumbed bathrooms, pools, bars, licensed restaurants and garden areas. With rooms starting at around €50, it can rapidly get filled up, and is worth booking ahead.

Riad Tizwa, 15b Derb Guebbas, Douh Batha, t 0535 637874, *www.riadtizwa.com*. Well located close to the Bab Bou Jeloud yet in a quiet alleyway, this homely but classic riad has kept its understated beauty and charm, notably in its central courtyard. It has a comfortable roof terrace, a very friendly staff and a growing collection of Morocco travel books. Tastefully decorated, it looks especially idyllic by candlelight in the evenings, when you can eat dinner (with a few hours warning). Book it alongside its Marrakesh sister (*see* p.146) to save time.

Inexpensive

Grand Hotel de Fez, 12 Blvd Chefchaouni, **t** 0535 932026, at the southern end of Blvd Abdallah Chefchaouni in the *ville nouvelle*, is an 80-room hotel overlooking the gardens of Place Mohammed V. It has a history from French colonial times and keeps up appearances to maintain a profile from that age.

Hotel de la Paix, 44 Ave Hassan II, **t** 0535 625072. This is another useful budget hotel, with 40 bedrooms, right in the middle of the *ville nouvelle*. It does the job well and is well-priced but has little character.

Olympic, Blvd Mohammed V, **t** 0535 932682. Convenient as it lies close to the central market. It also has a restaurant, plain rooms and is kept clean and tidy.

Pension Campini Tazi, 15 Rue Campini Batha, **t** 0535 637342. A basic, irregularly painted guesthouse on a side street not far from Bab Bou Jeloud but just outside the wall. Roof terrace overlooks the gardens in the palace of the king's brother but also the Mellah. Rooms (which are around €20–30) are basic and bare. Good for larger groups as group rooms available for up to 7 or 8 people, which works out even cheaper. Also a very quiet corner of town.

Cheap

Showers are often not included in prices at this level, if indeed warm ones are available. Toilets are shared and there may be noise, given the likely profile of the guests (young travelling students).

Hotel Erraha, near Bab Bou Jeloud, **t** 0535 633226. It is tucked away above the two-corner café and entered from a side alley. Expect nothing for the price (€10) and you will at least enjoy the view from the terrace.

Pension Batha, 8 Sidi el Khayat, Batha, **t** 0535 741150. Very simple fare here but with a pleasant atmosphere, clean sheets and a decent terrace.

Pension El Kasbah, 5 Kasabat Nouar, **t** 0535 637889, *barnossi2006@ hotmail.com*. Apparently the only hotel in the kasbah, this is a fantastic location, though it may be suited only to hardier travellers, with spartan rooms and bottom-end furnishings. The rooms are perfectly adequate and clean, and larger groups have the option of taking a traditional four-sofa Moroccan room. The terrace is underwhelming.

Eating Out in Fez

Fez is famous for its cuisine but you can spend a few pennies on a good meal in the city too. Recommended guesthouses serving dinners (order in advance) include the Dar Roumana, Riad Fès and Riad Laarousa (*see above*, Where to Stay).

Expensive

Dar Saada, 21 Rue Attarine (in the medina), **t** 0535 637370, *www. restaurantdarsaada.com*. Dar Saada is where you go to lunch in earnest, with some empty time ahead over the afternoon. In the heart of the souks, this princely playpen returns you to a different era.

La Maison Bleue, 2 Place de l'Istiqlal, **t** 0535 636052, *www.maisonbleue.com*. Sumptuous decoration and furniture have turned this old family palace into a romantic dining *diwan* at which you lounge back on cushions while you listen to live music and wait for the dishes of the day to be brought. The menu here changes daily. Lantern-bearing staff will escort you out at the end of the evening. (La Maison Bleue is also a fashionable and very plush hotel.)

Palais Jamaï Hotel, Bab Guissa, **t** 0535 634331. The El Fassia restaurant here serves Moroccan food from its perch overlooking the medina. There is live Andalucian music played too but it is the *tagine*, *pastilla* and *mechoui* (*see* p.63) for which the restaurant is rightly famous. The restaurant is an orientalist's dream and was once inhabited by the Grand Vizier of Jamaï. Be sure to try its legendary *harira* (lentil and chickpea soup.)

⭐ **La Maison Bleue >>**

⭐ Palais M'Nebhi >

Palais M'Nebhi, t 0535 633893. This is one of the best and most reclusive addresses in Fez. It is about 450m east of the Bab Bou Jeloud on the northern side of Rue Talaa Seghira. It occupies a beautiful palace built by the famous Menehbi family that was later used by Marshal Lyautey, and also a language school. The couscous is exceptional but come here for the setting above all.

⭐ Café Clock >>

Restaurant Zagora, 5 Blvd Mohammed, t 0535 940686. This Franco-Moroccan restaurant sits in the *ville nouvelle*, indifferent to the medina because it has created a buzz all its own. Very popular, it is becoming an institution in the *ville nouvelle*. A good thing too, as the restaurant is beautifully kept and enjoys a modern edge in a city focused on its past. Try the tasty spicy dumplings.

Moderate

Kai Tai, 12 Rue Ahmed Chaouki, t 0535 651700. For tasty Japanese and Thai food in sleek surroundings, should you need a break from Moroccan fare.

⭐ Le Kasbah >

Le Kasbah, Rue Serrajine, t 0535 633430, This idyllic rooftop restaurant flanks the Bab Bou Jeloud, an ideal place from which to watch the day wind down and the evening develop as you sit under the wooden verandah. This is entirely Moroccan food, an excellent place for your main meal when you spend the day walking through the souks.

Palais de Fès, Dar Tazi, Place Er'cif, t 0535 761590, *www.palaisdefes.com*. Long an institution in the city, this is a very popular restaurant in a labyrinthine palace. There are regular theme nights and live concerts. It is also a small guesthouse and frequently receives very positive reviews for both.

Les Remparts, 2 Arset Jiar, t 0535 637415. There is a good atmosphere here and the belly-dancing undoubtedly helps, but the food is not paramount. Come here for a fun evening and a good feed, not for fine dining.

Inexpensive

Chez Vittorio, 21 Rue Brahim-Redani (sometimes known as Rue Nador),

t 0535 624730. This is found just south of Ave Mohammed es Slaoui, a block east of Place Mohammed V. It is a small, efficiently run Italian restaurant, though both staff and customers are predominantly and animatedly Moroccan. You can choose pasta, pizza or meat dishes from the menu, while picking over some antipasti as you sip your wine.

San Remo, 3 Ave Allal ben Abdellah, t 0535 944656. Another good Italian, recommended by locals.

Café Clock, 7 Derb El Magana, t 0535 637855. Walk east along Talaa Kebira and very soon there will be a sign above your head and to the right saying 'Café Clock'. Turn left down a narrow alleyway then left again up some stairs. Café Clock is an idyllic café with a series of roof terraces, which is named for the old water-clock tower next door. It does a mix of Moroccan and western food and it makes an excellent stop-off for a while. They also run excellent cookery lessons, which include a visit to the market followed by a feast of the dishes you have prepared.

If you are looking for street food, wander through the souks and stop at a kitchen wall or a small café or barbecue. Rue Hormis, in the heart of Fez-el-Bali, is especially good for this. Just east of Bab Bou Jeloud, if you follow the alley round to the right, you will see a row of small restaurants popular with foreign students. Among them are **La Baraka** and **Des Jeunes**, both to be recommended for good cheap fare.

Entertainment and Nightlife in Fez

Nightlife is quiet in most of the city but one or two clubs are open in the *ville nouvelle* if you need to dance. In the medina itself public drinking remains rare. Scratch the surface a little and you will discover that many of the tiny grills in alleyways across the old town are used to selling kif or alcohol because, as so often in Fez, appearances deceive. But that is for the locals, so your best bet is to head for the *ville nouvelle* instead, where a few options await you. There are, of course, the hotel bars, one or two of which are quite good.

Bars and Cafés

Café Firdaous, opposite Hotel Batha. Many foreigners prefer this one.

Clock Café, 7 Derb El Magana, **t** 0535 637855. A deservedly popular hang-out, with an eclectic crowd. Great mocktails, as there is no license.

Jnan Palace Hotel Bar, Ave Ahmed Chaouki. This often has live music.

Mezzanine, 17 Kasbah Chams. Very popular restaurant and lounge bar opposite the Jnan Sbil gardens.

Mirador, 1 Dhar Lakhmiss, **t** 0535 665623. Lively spot with good views.

★ La Nouria Café >

La Nouria Café, near Bab Mekina. This has been going for some time and has a wonderful garden location.

Palais Jamaï, Bab Guissa, **t** 0535 634331. If all else fails and you need a view, this ultra-luxurious hotel will oblige – at a price.

Riad Fès, Derb Ben Slimane, Zerbtana, **t** 0535 947610. Part of the luxury hotel (*see* above). Lovely and atmospheric.

Clubs

Palais Jamaï, Bab Guissa. This has its own club on the premises.

Jnane Palace, Ave Ahmed Chaouki. Le Phoebus is perhaps the best disco in Fez.

Zalagh Parc Palace, Lôtissement Oued Fes, Route de Meknès. Another option.

Music Festivals

For the last few years a festival of sacred music has been held in Fez around the end of May and beginning of June, with two or three concerts daily for a week in the garden of the Dar Batha Museum, the Old Méchouar or the governors' palace. Musicians from all over the world may perform, as well as Jewish, Muslim and Christian musicians from Spain and Morocco who share the common inspiration of Andalucía.

Day Trips from Fez

Moulay-Yâkoub

Moulay-Yâkoub is just 20km northwest of the city, across gently rolling hills. It is a pleasant holiday resort, a favourite sketching-ground of Maghrebi artists and much loved by Moroccan families, who can all indulge in some quiet hypochondria there. It's built on terraces above a hot sulphurous spring which fills a series of natural *hammams* and enclosed pools. In the past it enjoyed a reputation as a haunt of prostitutes and a cure for venereal disease; now the waters are modestly claimed only to cure 'renal and urinary' diseases. There is a small admission charge for the warm sulphurous pool and for the *hammam*, which has separate enclosures for men and women. Swimming trunks are worn in the baths; souk stalls sell a selection of these as well as soap, beads, towels and candles. You can eat at a number of cafés or at the restaurant just above the baths. There are a couple of hotels with licensed restaurants. Opposite the village is the rounded hill of Lalla Chafer, with a few pine trees growing on its slope. Walking up the hill to the café on the summit is all part of the cure, while lower down the hill an all-new spa has been constructed (see the website for details, *www.moulayyacoub.com*).

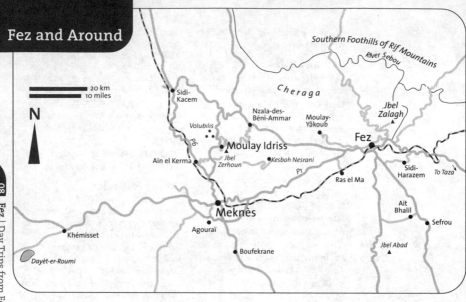

Sefrou

Famous for its waterfalls, walking, caves, views, hot baths and mineral water, the countryside of Ifrad (south of Safrou) is especially beautiful and the town's narrow streets are good for exploring. The **June cherry festival** is a big draw for outsiders. Sefrou is 35 kilometres southeast of Fez. There are *grands taxis* and buses that serve it daily.

Meknès

Meknès is at the centre of a rich agricultural region where olives, grain, vegetables and grapes are successfully grown by the thick-set Berber farmers who seem to characterize this area. Despite its splendid imperial past as the capital city of Sultan Moulay Ismaïl, its present population of around half a million, its army base and its university, Meknès remains more of a large Berber town than a cosmopolitan urban centre. Meknès is divided into three distinct areas: the *ville nouvelle*, with its neat, French-built, tree-lined avenues, cafés, bars and hotels, is to the east of the Boufekrane river valley; the walled medina, its skyline a confusion of green, white and gold minarets, perches on the western hill; to the south of the medina, through the Bab Mansour, stretches the Imperial City, a bewildering, only partially occupied enclosure surrounded by over 25km of massive *pisé* walls.

Seeing everything Mèknes has to offer would take several days. If you have just one day, start with the Imperial City and then, if you

Getting to Meknès

By Rail

The most useful **train station** is on Rue Emir Abdelkader, **t** 0535 522763, a little east of Avenue Mohammed V. This lands you directly in the *ville nouvelle* and at the western end of a large semi-circular rail loop. The main train station is a kilometre to the east on Avenue de la Gare, not far from the CTM bus station. (The medina's northeastern wall is around 1.5 km west of Abdelkader station.) There are trains to and from Fez eleven times a day (serving Meknès Abdelkader) with the first one before 3am. There are almost twice the number serving the main station in Meknès. The same trains serve Rabat too.

By Bus

There are two **bus terminals**. The most useful and efficient is the new CTM coach station on Avenue de la Gare, just west of the main train station. There are almost hourly departures to Fez (50mins) starting at dawn and ending in the mid-afternoon.

Other private coach companies and local buses use the new consolidated terminal outside Bab el Khemis/Bab el Mellah on the western edge of the medina. A shuttle service of buses, nos. 2 and 7, connects the medina and *ville nouvelle*.

By Taxi

You will find *grands* and *petits taxis* just west of Place el Hédime in the medina, and on the northern side of the Place Istiqlal (Batha), beside the post office, in the *ville nouvelle*. It is a short 40min/25dh hop to Fez by *grand taxi* and still less (in time and money) to Moulay Idriss. The best spot to pick up a taxi in the *ville nouvelle* is across the main road from the police station (to the right as you approach Avenue Moulay Ismail to cross to the medina).

By Air

Royal Air Maroc's office is at 7 Avenue Mohammed V, **t** 0900 00800 (call centre).

---

still have time and energy, visit the Dar Jamaï Museum or the medina souks and the Bou Inania Medersa.

History

The origins of Meknès are exclusively local and Berber, in direct contrast to the foreign and Arab birth of Fez. The city originated as a hilltop kasbah that won renown as one of the principal bases of the Khajarite Berbers, who overthrew the rule of the first Arab conquerors in AD 741. By the 10th century it had grown into the principal market of the Meknassa Berber tribe, which dominated the region.

The power of the Meknassa was shattered by the great Almoravid general Youssef ben Tachfine in 1069, when he first united the country, but their name survived in the town of Meknès. It was rebuilt on a generous scale a century later, during the Almohad period, within a rigid square grid of walls. Its neat street plan was focused around the central mosque; Bab El Jdid is a survivor from this period. A later reconstruction under the Merenids is recalled by the 14th-century Bou Inania Medersa.

A new period in the city's fortunes dawned in 1666 when the ruling Alaouite sultan, Moulay Rachid, appointed his younger brother, one Moulay Ismaïl, to be its governor. He proved to be a loyal and efficient servant who happily involved himself in

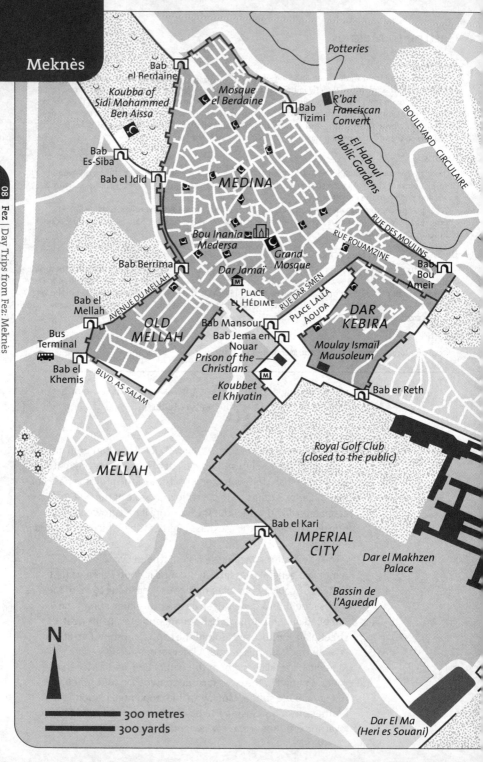

Meknès

Potteries

Bab el Berdaine

Koubba of Sidi Mohammed Ben Aissa

Mosque el Berdaine

Bab Tizimi

R'bat Franciscan Convent

BOULEVARD CIRCULAIRE

Bab Es-Siba

El Haboul Public Gardens

Bab el Jdid

MEDINA

RUE DES MOULINS

Bou Inania Medersa

RUE ROUAMZINE

Bab Berrima

Grand Mosque

RUE DAR SMEN

Bab Bou Ameir

Dar Jamaï

DAR KEBIRA

Bab el Mellah

AVENUE DU MELLAH

PLACE EL HÉDIME

PLACE LALLA AOUDA

Bus Terminal

OLD MELLAH

Bab Mansour

Moulay Ismaïl Mausoleum

Bab el Khemis

BLVD. AS SALAM

Bab Jema en Nouar

Prison of the Christians

Bab er Reth

Koubbet el Khiyatin

NEW MELLAH

Royal Golf Club (closed to the public)

Bab el Kari

IMPERIAL CITY

Dar el Makhzen Palace

Bassin de l'Aguedal

N

300 metres
300 yards

Dar El Ma (Heri es Souani)

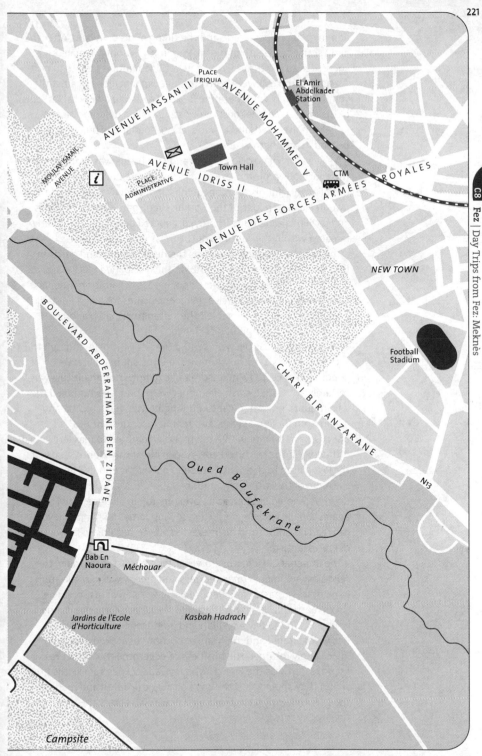

administration, local trade and the tilling of his own land. After the early, accidental death of his brother in 1672, Moulay Ismaïl succeeded to the throne, which he retained until his death in 1727. Fez and Marrakesh were both embroiled in rebellions against the young monarch, who therefore decided to create a new capital out of the loyal city of Meknès. The existing walled medina was left largely undisturbed, and a brand-new Imperial City built just beyond its southern walls.

A slave army of 50,000 Berbers and Europeans was employed on the enormous project. Dozens of palaces were built for Moulay Ismaïl's court, for his 500 concubines and four wives, and his few favoured children (out of the 800 he sired); gardens, parks, ponds and pavilions were built, improved, knocked down and constantly replaced within the confines of the massive external walls.

The Imperial City also served as the headquarters and garrison for a standing force of 25,000 Abids, the disciplined black slave army which the sultan employed to impose his arbitrary rule. Vast storehouses, stables, exercise fields, enclosures for allied nomadic cavalry and armouries enabled the sultan to dispatch a force quickly at the first sign of dissidence.

Moulay Ismaïl has been presented to history (mostly through the accounts of ex-slaves, missionaries and the snubbed literate population of Fez) as a megalomaniac tyrant. Though his rule was certainly arbitrary, his achievements were sound. He humbled the wild mountain tribes, recaptured Tangier, Mehdiya, Larache and Asilah from foreign powers, and rebuilt mosques, shrines, bridges, kasbahs and whole towns. He attempted to reassert orthodoxy in the confused, cult-ridden life of the country, and was the last sultan to treat the European powers as equals. His offer for the hand of Louis XIV's illegitimate daughter, Marie Anne de Bourbon, should be seen as an overture for an alliance with France against Spain, while in his letters to King James II of England you can read his sound and disinterested advice, arguing in favour of Protestantism.

The Imperial City did not, however, long outlast its founder: the Abid slave regiments grew reckless and greedy without the stern hand of their master, and deposed a succession of his sons. The Lisbon earthquake of 1755 shattered the palace compounds and, while his son Moulay Abdullah and grandson Sidi Mohammed (1757–90) altered and maintained portions of Meknès, they increasingly returned the business of government to either Fez or Marrakesh. It was the French who revived Meknès, for like the great sultan they appreciated the city's strategic position and made it their central army base, building a new town across the river for their regiments.

Bab Mansour

The best place to begin exploring either the medina or the Imperial City is **Place el Hédime**. To get there from the New Town, follow the main road across the valley, Avenue Moulay Ismaïl, to enter the medina through the Bab Bou Ameir. Then turn right to climb 400m up the busy **Rue Rouamzine**, turn left by the post office onto Rue Dar Smen; the *place* is at the end of this street.

Bab Mansour separates the central square of the medina, **Place el Hédime**, from Moulay Ismaïl's vast, enclosed Imperial City. It has come to symbolize Meknès: it is reproduced in countless books, articles, postcards and posters. It is difficult to see it at its best during the day, for the sun shines into your eyes from the east and leaves the gate in shadow. The softer evening light picks out the details, but even then the gate appears ponderous and over-decorated, and the relief too bold. The pillars, a mixture of Ionic and Corinthian columns torn from the classical ruins of Volubilis, appear misplaced, empty gestures that distract from the overall harmony. It succeeds as architecture in a way that the sultan might have been content with: powerful, looming, appearing obsessively strong and rigid, its top panel of carved Koranic script a reminder of the strong Muslim orthodoxy of the Alaouite dynasty. It is too squat and beefy to move you and it is poorly framed by a river of traffic flowing past. The beginnings of more elegant detail appear in some of the panelling the form of the keystone arch and the scalloping. Note the **Magasin Artisanale Damascenerie Sa'ad** beneath and within, which showcases the city's intricately decorated metalwork.

The less obtrusive but altogether more agreeable gate, to the right looking from the square, the Bab Jema en Nouar, was built in the same period; it now leads to a school housed in an old mosque and the gate apartments. Both gates were designed by Moulay Ismaïl's court architect, the renegade Christian known as Mansour el Aleuj, and completed in 1732 during the reign of the great sultan's son, Moulay Abdullah.

Place el Hédime

This square was created in the mid-17th century by Moulay Ismaïl, who required a grand entrance before the Imperial City, the traditional area in an Islamic city for the public execution of justice, the issuing of proclamations, the jostle of petitions, the emergence of the royal procession to the grand mosque and the distribution of charity. In modern times it degenerated into a dusty car park, but a few years ago it was transformed once again into an elegant public space complete with new fountains. These are in pleasing harmony with the original 17th-century enclosed fountain (on the far side of the square), with its dazzling glimmer of *zellij* mosaic circles. The square itself hosts occasional wandering performers and musical acts too, often drawing enormous crowds where Marrakshis crossing the Jema al-Fna might not even notice.

The food market running along the southern side of the square is screened by a long row of barbers and pottery shops. It is a wonderful place to gather a picnic: choosing from the glistening cones of flavoured olives, pats of goat's cheese, prime fruit and fresh vegetables from the farms that surround Meknès. Here even the dates look polished. At the northwestern corner of the square an alley leads directly to the grand mosque, passing on the left a 14th-century town house, the **Maison Merenide**, which has been turned into a tourist bazaar.

The Imperial City

I have built these buildings – let those who can destroy them.
Sultan Moulay Ismaïl

We have never seen anything equal to it, neither among the modern buildings nor among the ancient.
Temim, a 17th-century French ambassador

The extent and past grandeur of the Imperial City can best be appreciated in a 5km walk broken halfway at the Café Heri es Souani. Most of the city is in ruins and has been built over by village communities, and the royal palace is not open to the public. The little pavilion of Koubbet el Khiyatin, the nearby underground store rooms, Moulay Ismaïl's mausoleum, the Dar el Ma and the Aguedal Tank are the highlights of the Imperial City, though inevitably the abiding image left at the end of the day is of a bewildering series of massive walls.

The Dar Kebira

The first thing you come to through the Bab Mansour is the large **Place Lalla Aouda**, the formal processional square of the old Dar Kebira, or enclosed palace quarter, which, like the Place el Hédime, has been renovated with fountains and trees. None of the palaces has survived, though, and it is now just another residential area of the city.

The Dar Kebira was finished in 1677 and opened by the sultan, who sacrificed a wolf under the full moon at midnight and set its head above the gateway to the palace. According to the chronicler ez-Zayyani, the Dar Kebira contained 24 separate palace compounds, gardens and barracks, and two mosques. Most of these were destroyed by the sultan's son Moulay Abdullah, and the mosques alone have survived. Called the **Lalla Aouda** and **Chaouia**, they face the square, where only eunuchs were permitted to make the call to prayer. The palace museum (now the National Jewellery Museum) in the Oudaïa Kasbah at Rabat (*see* p.259) was also originally built as a palace by Moulay Ismaïl, and gives some indication of what must have been the varied splendours of the Dar Kebira. It would have been decorated with columns extracted from Volubilis, and ornamentation looted from the great Saadian palace of El Badi at Marrakesh.

Comparisons with the palace of Moulay Ismaïl's great contemporary, Louis XIV, continue to be made. However, Versailles, with its radial axes of parkland, its draughty uncomfortable interiors and the exterior splendour of its façade, could hardly be further removed from Moulay Ismaïl's secretive, heavily enclosed pavilion gardens. The sultan could not have begun Meknès in any spirit of competition with the French – he is known to have started work ten years before he received the first reports of Versailles. In any case he is much more likely to have looked east to Ottoman Istanbul for his exemplar. What Meknès and Versailles share is a roughly equal consumption of material and human lives.

The Koubbet el Khiyatin

If you go through the Bab Filala at the southwestern corner of Place Lalla Aouda, you will find yourself in a small square that has the pavilion of Koubbet el Khiyatin in the far right corner. This was an audience chamber used for the reception of foreign ambassadors and the interminable bargaining over the ransom of slaves. It literally means 'the hall of the tailors', a poetic Arabic image for the role of an ambassador, who, like a tailor, joins two opposing pieces of cloth (or nations) together with delicate, time-consuming stitch work. The decorated carvings on the walls endlessly repeat in Kufic script 'All jell' – glory to God. You may notice that the carving is not of the highest quality, for this 17th-century *koubba* was restored in the 1950s.

Beside the Koubbet is the entrance to the **'prison of the Christians'**, a misleading title for a massive vaulted underground network of storerooms, an impressive and mysterious acreage of damp stone lit by skylights. Intriguing bricked-up passages disappear to other decayed sections of the old underground city of cellars. The Christian slaves of Meknès were actually never housed here, but it is known that the sultan moved prisoners here before receiving ambassadors so that the subterranean cries for help would undermine their composure during negotiations.

The right-hand arch of the two ahead leads to the exclusive, walled and guarded **Royal Golf Club**, which has been created out of the central palace garden. Moulay Ismaïl kept a delightful menagerie in this garden: four wild asses from Guinea ran wild, two white dromedaries allowed themselves to be washed in soap every morning, and wounded storks were cared for. Royal Arabian horses that had completed the pilgrimage to Mecca remained unridden and free for the rest of their lives; beads and scrolls from the holy city hung from their necks and any criminal was assured of sanctuary if such a horse allowed him to approach. On its death, each horse was reverently buried in shrouds and a *koubba* raised over its tomb.

Moulay Ismaïl's Mausoleum

Moulay Ismaïl's Mausoleum
open Sat–Thurs 8.30–12 and 2–6; adm

Through the left-hand arch, opposite half a dozen bazaars, is the long white mausoleum of Moulay Ismaïl. The actual prayer hall of the mosque remains closed to non-Muslims, but the tomb can be approached providing you are respectfully dressed and tip the guardian. The sanctuary was completely restored by King Mohammed V in 1959. As you progress through the three admirably austere courtyards with serene tiled floors and walls, you progressively shed the distractions and the noise of the outside world. The rectangle of blue sky framed by the high walls itself works as a form of meditation on the absolute. At the central fountain court, remove your shoes and enter through the door on the left into a lavishly gilded and decorated Moorish hall with a high-vaulted ceiling capped by a pyramidal *koubba*. From here you may look onto the marble tomb of the great sultan, flanked by two clocks (the gift of Louis XIV mentioned above), but do not advance into the room, which is used by pious pilgrims for prayers.

The Dar el Makhzen

Beyond the mausoleum is the **Bab er Reth**, 'the gate of winds', which opens on to a kilometre-long passage below a stretch of massive double walls. The Sultan used to ride along this road in a chariot drawn by his plump concubines. The *harem* had a precarious status, for Sultan Moulay Ismaïl cared for few of his children (most of his adult sons were exiled to the oasis of the Tafilalt, near Er Rachidia) and even less for his concubines. His official wives were, however, forceful characters. Moulay Ismaïl's first wife, Zidana, who was black, was a fearsome witch who was even allowed out of the *harem* when escorted by a suitable chaperone. Her ally was his third wife, the English sultana. She had been captured in 1688, aged 15, en route to Barbados with her mother. Moulay Ismaïl returned this surprised mother-in-law to England with presents and a letter for the king.

The wall on the left of the passage is the exterior, defendable perimeter of the Imperial City; that on the right defines a particular palace enclosure, the enormous **Dar el Makhzen**, or chief palace of the sultan, which was finished in 1697 and refurbished by Moulay Hassan in the late 19th century. Today it is in royal use again and the inside is therefore inaccessible.

A right turn at the end of this long walk, below the Water Fort, Bordj el Ma, will take you into the ***méchouar***, a colonnaded space where rulers could receive the ovations of their people. The gate on the right is the guarded main entrance to the palace, whilst a stroll to the left, through an enclosed hamlet clustered around a mosque and out through a gate, will allow you to admire the extent and width of the outer walls. To the east, stretching inside these walls, is the **Kasbah Hadrach**, the old barracks of the Bukharis, the crack guards regiment of the sultan's black slave army. This old kasbah quarter is protected by two gates, Bab en Nouar and Bab Lalla Khadra, next to the mosque of that name.

Beyond the *méchouar*, an arboretum has been established in the pavilioned **Jardins de l'École d'Horticulture** (Ben Halima Park) on the left of the road, while on the right a squatter village nestles beside the royal palace in the ruins of the **Kasbah Bab Merrah**. Storks nest on decaying *pisé* buttresses and towers, a few cows graze in a paddock that once held a delicate pavilion, and a young cripple shelters in a cardboard hut.

The Dar el Ma

A further 500m walk beside the *pisé* walls that partly hide these areas brings you to the Dar el Ma, also known as Heri es Souani. This is the most accessible and impressive remnant of the Imperial City, a massive warehouse where silos held provisions for the court and standing army. There is a café selling coffee and cold drinks, surrounded by a garden of olive trees growing on the massive roof. From here you can see miles of walls, modern villages and ruins stretching in every direction, surrounded by open farmland enclosed in turn by distant mountains.

To the south a campsite, racecourse, arboretum, military academy and two schools partly fill the enormous enclosed area of the old Aguedal gardens. To the west stretch the four hectares of the **Aguedal Tank** (*Bassin de l'Aguedal*), constructed by Moulay Ismaïl to supply water for the palace gardens and orchards, now often surrounded by groups of picnicking families. Inside the Dar el Ma there are impressive arched chambers and cascades of creepers hanging illuminated from skylights in the roof. In two of the corners, round chambers surround a well where water could be drawn up 50m by machinery worked by circulating mules. A large, roofless area of vaulted rooms – 15 rows of 21 broken arches – extends southwest, partly overgrown with fennel, to create a famously impressive vista. It is thought to have been used as a stable, where some of the sultan's thousands of horses were housed in the cool shade.

Most visitors have tired legs by now and are content to walk beside the Aguedal Tank back towards the medina from the Heri es Souani. At the far end of the tank a left turn brings you into the Beni M'Hammed district, and a right turn along the central avenue takes you out of this modern settlement through the **Bab el Kari**.

Below this gate is one of the most impressive stretches of external wall, the 'wall of riches'. A road leads from this gate across empty ground west to the new mellah, while a right turn climbs up past a taxi rank towards the medina. A left turn along the Blvd As Salam will take you to the most beautiful gate in Meknès, the towered **Bab el Khemis**, or you could continue uphill and go through the Bab Zine el Abadine to re-enter Place el Hédime.

The Dar Jamaï Museum

The Dar Jamaï Museum
t 0555 530863; open Wed–Mon 9–12 and 3–6.30; adm

The Dar Jamaï, which has an unobtrusive entrance on Place el Hédime, is a 19th-century vizier's palace that now houses a collection of Moroccan arts and crafts (the *Musée Régional d'Ethnographie*). Like every Moroccan museum, it is a disordered presentation of often undated Andalucian-influenced products from urban craftsmen together with the traditional crafts of the Berber tribes of the Middle Atlas.

The palace is an attractive, calm building, and the worn ceramic floors and graceful patina of age greatly contribute to your enjoyment of the exhibits. It belonged to the same brothers who built the Palais Jamaï (now a luxury hotel, *see* p.213) in Fez. They were powerful officials in the court of Sultan Moulay Hassan and were descended from one of the Arab tribes that had taken service under the Alaouite sultans, the Oulad Jamaï, and become hereditary servants of the government. At the centre of the museum is a mature **Andalucian garden**, well planted with shrubs and often buzzing with birds.

The contrast as you enter through the cool, dark, twisting entrance passage of the palace emphasizes the domestic sanctity of an enclosed Moroccan house. Along this passage are some examples of Andalucian painted wall tiles, their foliate patterns familiar from woodcarvings but rarely seen in this form in Morocco. Even more surprising is the small collection of miniature paintings, all of which were produced here in Meknès.

In the few rooms off the central garden you can see the silk banner used by Sultan Moulay Hassan for his campaigns, dated 1874 to 1887 in the Gregorian calendar, and a small display of brilliantly bound, compact Korans. The collection of elaborate keys is entertaining, and the other items of wrought ironwork, splendid door bosses and supporting hinges, show how much the Gothic borrowed from the Moorish taste.

The **vizier's reception room** upstairs is fully furnished, and a useful antidote to the false impression of Moorish domestic style given by the serene interiors of *medersas* and empty palaces. For here there is a riot of familiar 19th-century clutter – coloured glass, debased workmanship, painted wood and conflicting plasterwork. The display of 19th-century Fez and Meknès ware is more pleasing: these **ceramics** have a gentler line, and warmer, more fluid shapes than seen in today's merely capable, rigid geometricism. The contrast with rural domestic pottery is always strong; though geometric in intent, the gourd-like shapes of the vessels and the black lines on red show Berber design at its most primitive and conservative.

The collection of **Berber jewellery** makes for an interesting comparison with that offered in today's souks, although the universal style of much native Islamic jewellery holds few surprises. The metalwork has a solidity that one hardly expects today, for these were collections of disposable wealth, while nowadays jewellery concentrates on display. For more on this, pick up a copy of Jean Besancenot's informative *Bijoux Arabes et Berbères du Maroc* (Ed de la Cigogne, Casablanca).

There is a fine mixed collection of Moroccan **carpets and killims** from the indigenous Berber tribes of the High and Middle Atlas. The tendency was to produce woven and embroidered killims rather than a true knotted carpet. The carpet collection also clearly shows why few Moroccan carpets have survived from any period further back than the 19th century: the large, thinly spaced knots tied to inadequate backing will not last more than a century unless the carpets have been used as wall hangings. Consequently, the admirably warm and simple diamond-lozenge original designs are difficult to find today. The Zayan/Zaian carpet is a good example of this, while the carpet from Aït-Bousba opposite shows the origins of the pictogram, or 'message carpet', though it is splendidly random and primitive compared with the over-busy pattern-book designs found in today's bazaars. All the killims here show a natural restraint in embroidery, with designs based on harmonious stripes of colour, interspaced with geometric lozenges, diamonds and triangles. The products from Zemmour and the Beni Mguild tribal confederation are most attractive, and are still being created.

The Medina Souks

If you turn left in front of the museum (while facing it), a 200m walk along Rue Sekakine will take you to **Bab Berrima**, a busy junction of streets. On the left is the old Jewish quarter, the **Mellah**. A 300m walk from the Bab Berrima along Souk Bezzarin on the outside of the medina wall – a local shopping street which is a mass display of Tupperware, kitchenware and jeans – will take you to the brick-built **Bab el Jdid**. This translates as 'the new gate', somewhat contrarily since it is the oldest gate in Meknès – with arched vaults dating from the 12th-century Almohad city. In front of the Bab el Jdid there is a good selection of grill-cafés, and a row of tent-makers will probably be busy in their shops cutting canvas and sewing awnings together on their pedal-operated Singers.

Beyond the Bab el Jdid, if you keep to your right the wall that surrounds the vast cemetery of Sidi Aïssa and follow it to the Bab es Siba, 'the gate of dissidence', an avenue on the right leads up to the distinctive green-tiled pyramid roof that covers the venerated **koubba of Sidi Mohammed ben Aïssa**, built by the Sultan Sidi Mohammed (1757–90). You should not approach too closely, nor wander through the cemetery, which is decorated with the domed tombs of many revered Islamic saints.

If, on the other hand, you enter the old town through the Bab el Jdid, a right turn will lead you to the **Souk Seraria**, the blacksmith's souk, populated by an assortment of knife-grinders, charcoal salesmen and tool-makers. On the left you can enter the sultan's *fondouq*, a delightful 18th-century brick courtyard established for the use of armourers.

As the street narrows you enter the centre of the jewellery trade. A right turn lets you out by the Bab Berrima, while a left turn brings you into the covered **Souk Khiatine el Najjarine**, the central thoroughfare of the medina, lined with the shops of metalworkers, tinkers and carpenters. You soon pass on the right the **Najjarine** ('the carpenters') **Mosque**, which follows a 12th-century Almohad plan even though the visible work is all 18th-century restoration. Beyond the mosque, again on the right, is the **Dlala Kissaria**, one of a number of interior courts lined with carpet and killim booths that stock the products of the Middle Atlas tribes. It is one of the easiest and most accessible places in which to bargain for killims – there is a good range of stock and the merchants are jovial.

A right turn by the Kissaria can take you down the old dyers' street, passing the **Sebbarine Mosque** on your left, to re-emerge in Place el Hédime by the Dar Jamaï Museum.

If, on the other hand, you continue along the main covered thoroughfare, known at this point as **Rue Sebat**, you will enter the richest and most tourist-oriented area of the souk. A hundred metres farther on your right are the ornately decorated gates of the **Grand Mosque**. The mosque is at the heart of the medina, and has five elaborate entrances; it occupies the same area as the 11th-century Almoravid grand mosque, replaced by the Almohads and then again in the 13th century by the Merenids.

The Bou Inania Medersa

The Bou Inania Medersa
Rue Najjarine; open July–Aug Mon–Fri 9–5; rest of the year 9–12 and 3–6; adm

The *medersa* is directly opposite the Grand Mosque (the latter is closed to non-Muslims); its entrance is below a cupola in the main street, and protected by enormous bronze decorated doors. It was begun by Sultan Abou Hassan, creator of the Salé *medersa*, but finished by and named after Sultan Abou Inan, who reigned from 1351 to 1358. The entrance passage leads through a gate in a cedar screen with the Barakat Mohammed symbol carved above, which could be translated as 'the chance for faith'. The tall, rectangular court paved with black and white marble squares surrounds a central pool.

A band of *zellij* mosaic runs beneath bands of Koranic script that are carried upwards by all the decorative materials – carved plaster, glazed tile, marble and carved cedar all conspire together to carry the word of God. Around three sides of the court runs a gallery above which are two storeys of students' rooms. The solid, angular pillars of the gallery are saved from stolidity by columns that reach up towards the tiled cornice, and restrain the tracery design of the plaster walls. The fourth side of the courtyard opens into a spacious prayer-hall tiled in green and yellow, with a carved peacock fan set above the *mihrab*.

The beauty and sophistication of the Arabic script entwined in the decoration can mislead modern visitors on the depth of the education that was undertaken in a *medersa*. There was little emphasis on formal literacy: generations of students simply learned to recite the classical Arabic poetry of the Koran. Even centuries ago the language of the Moroccan street, Maghrebi Arabic, not to mention the three Berber dialects, was already far removed from the language of 7th-century Mecca.

The communal life of the *tolba*, the student reciters, is revealed in the ground-floor washroom with its long shared sink, although the upstairs rooms include an individual and very European-looking WC. Do not miss the view from the roof across the green-tiled Grand Mosque and prominent minarets of the medina. The double lancet windows of the Touta minaret can be seen almost due west, with the minarets of the Ahmed Chebli and Sidi Kadour el Alaoui mosques to its right.

Leaving the *medersa*, the rich clothes shops and bazaars of the kissaria stretch ahead, but a sharp right turn beside the Grand Mosque will take you down Rue Sabab Socha, passing on the left the **Filala Medersa**, built by Moulay Ismaïl in the 17th century. This is a smaller and cruder version of the Bou Inania, and is not open to the public. From there a right turn down Rue ez Zemmour will eventually return you after a few twists and bends to Rue Dar Smen and Place el Hédime.

Meknès ›
Tourist Office
Place Istiqlal (Batha),
t 0535 524426

Regional Council of Tourism, Complexe
Artisanale,
t 0535 531733

Information and Services in Mcknès

The regional **tourist office** distributes the usual attractive town map leaflets and can arrange for the hire of guides. The building is south of the *place* on the Esplanade de la Foire, inside a big yellow gate. Failing that, the **Regional Council of Tourism** is in the Complexe Artisanale on the left as you head west along Blvd Moulay Ismail to leave the *ville nouvelle*.

Banks in the *ville nouvelle* include the BMCE, 98 Av des F.A.R., t 0535 514835, and the Banque Al Maghrib, 10 Avenue Mohammed V. There is a branch of the Banque Populaire along

Rue Dar Smen near Place el Hédime. There's a bank on Place Istiqlal too.

Where to Stay in Meknès

Hotel Menzeh Dalia, RP N6 (Rabat road), **t** 0535 468578, *www. hotelmenzehdalia.com* (€€€€). Pool, sauna, *hammam* and elegant luxury make this ideal if you want ease and facilities. It's not in the centre though.

Hotel Rif, Rue d'Accra, **t** 0535 522591, *www.hotel-rif.com* (€€€). A well-kept hotel in the centre, with a pool, a popular bar, the Bahia nightclub and two restaurants.

(★) Ryad Bahia >

Ryad Bahia, 13 Tiberbarine Medina, **t** 0535 533092, *www.ryad-bahia.com* (€€€). This much-loved riad is close to the medina's central Place El-Hédim and has been wonderfully restored. The charming staff look after guests very well too. The rooms on the roof terrace are especially enchanting. Prices (which start at around €60) include breakfast.

Riad D'Or, 17 Rue Ain El Anboub/Rue Lalla Aicha Adouia, Hammam Jdid District, **t** 0641 078625, *www.riaddor. com* (€€€–€€). Attractively decorated and lying in the heart of the medina, the Riad D'Or has attentive staff and a restfulness you will welcome after a day pounding the streets. There's a delightful central courtyard, with beautiful tiles and plants. Double rooms from €40.

Bab Mansour, 38 Rue Emir Abdelkader, **t** 0535 515967 (€€). All that you need and a decent restaurant too. Nothing spectacular but a reasonable option and vey convenient. Rooms from €30 per night.

Hotel Majestic, 19 Ave Mohammed V, **t** 0535 522035 (€€). Seven decades' worth of guests have dined and slept in this Art Deco institution, although its days of splendour are long gone. The rooms are plain and the furnishings a tad threadbare, but as a bonus there's a roof terrace.

Hotel Palace, 11 Rue de Ghana, **t** 0535 511260 (€€). Handy for the station and the medina, the Palace is a good budget bet, with knowledgeable staff

and clean, functional rooms starting at about €30.

Maroc Hotel, 7 Rue Rouamzine, **t** 0535 530075 (€€). A very reasonable budget option that is clean and presentable and has an attractive and restful terrace. This is perhaps the best of serveral basic hotels on Rue Rouamzine and nearby Rue Dar Smen.

Camping Aguegal, **t** 0535 551828 (€). Close to the Royal Palace, this is a good central location but also a pleasant spot and the prices (17dh per adult, 12dh per child) are very reasonable.

Eating Out in Meknès

In the medina there are some delightful café-restaurants by the Bab Berrima and Bab el Jdid that are well placed for a quick lunch, and a good selection along Rue Dar Smen and Rue Rouamzine. In the *ville nouvelle*, try Avenue Mohammed V.

La Case, 8 Blvd Moulay Youssef, **t** 0535 524019 (€€€). In the *ville nouvelle*. This is the place to head to if you want to enjoy sophisticated, rich French cooking, accompanied by a superb selection of wines. *Closed Monday*.

Restaurant Le Dauphin, 5 Ave Mohammed V, **t** 0535 523423 (€€€). One of Meknès' best offerings, this medina restaurant has an surprisingly unassuming entrance which leads into an atmospheric dining room and garden. French food and a licence to boot. A good place for fish.

(★) Restaurant Le Dauphin >>

Le Collier de La Colombe, 67 Rue Driba, **t** 0535 565041 (€€). Centrally located and with exceptional views, Le Collier also serves up lovingly prepared Moroccan fare. Try the famous house speciality – freshly baked *pastilla* stuffed with all kinds of local delicacies.

Oumnia, 8 Ain Fouki Rouamzine, **t** 0535 533938 (€€). A delightful Moroccan restaurant in intimate, traditional surroundings. The service is amenable and the food is excellent local fare. Superb value.

Restaurant Zitouna, 44 Jemaa Zitouna, **t** 0535 530281/532083 (€€). Located near the Bab Tizimi, this occupies a traditional 19th-century

Moroccan house. A perfect choice for a palatial, traditional Moroccan meal in the medina.

Riad Meknès, 79 Ksar Chaacha Dar Lakbira, t 0535 530542, *www. riadmeknes.com* (€€). This is one of the best places to eat Moroccan food in Meknes and the prices are reasonable. Take your swimming trunks. Book in advance by emailing *riad@iam.net.ma* and book an outdoor table.

La Coupole, 2 Ave Hassan II, t 0535 522483 (€). Serving French and Moroccan food at reasonable prices. Licence and very attentive service. Try the bar next door when you've finished dinner.

Marhaba, 23 Ave Mohammed V, no tel (€). A wonderfully under-priced canteen at which to buy all the local favourites. A classic in the city.

Pizzeria Le Four, 1 Rue Atlas, t 0535 523423 (€). Good *ville nouvelle* choice for pizza and a few drinks into the late hours.

Le Pub, 20 Blvd Allal ben Abdallah, t 0535 524247 (€). A vibrant spot for Moroccan and international food as well as for drinks.

Festivals

A Fantasia festival is held in the Imperial City in September, the same month as the *moussem* of Moulay Idriss and Sidi Bouzelm. It involves traditional forms of riding-as-performance accompanied by music and sometimes dancing.

Moulay Idriss and Volubilis

About 40km west of Fez stand the twin sites of Islamic Moulay Idriss and Roman Volubilis, just 4km apart on the edge of the limestone, olive-covered hills of Jbel Zerhoun.

Moulay Idriss

Moulay Idriss is the principal and most famous of the villages on Jbel Zerhoun, and a national pilgrimage site as it holds the tomb of Moulay Idriss, the holy founder of the first indigenous Islamic kingdom of Morocco. As an indication of its high status it is governed by its own pasha, and is home to the *caid* of the whole Zerhoun region. It is an astonishingly dramatic site. The two distinct quarters of the town, Tasga and Khiber, are piled up, around and between two massive exposed outcrops of volcanic stone. The landscape around the town – hills where ordered olive groves alternate with rough forests – is in harmony with the spiritual atmosphere, for the Jbel Zerhoun is a centre both of orthodoxy and ecstatic cults.

The First Idrissids

The tomb of Moulay Idriss ibn Abdulla, 'el Akbar' – the great – is the venerated heart of the town. He was a sherif, a descendant of the prophet, who fled to Morocco from Arabia to escape the slaughter ordered by the Abbasid caliphs, who had destroyed his family at the fateful battle of Fakh in AD 786. Accompanied only by his loyal slave Rashid, he journeyed through Egypt and headed west to escape from the area of Abbasid rule. He had arrived at

Getting to Moulay Idriss and Volubilis

From Fez, your only transport options are hiring a car, and hiring a *grand taxi* for the day (ask your hotel receptionist what sort of price you should be paying). Volubilis is 4km from Moulay Idriss off a loop road, the 3312, to the left of the P28. You can also reach Moulay Idriss by *grand taxi* from Meknès (Avenue Moulay Ismail), leaving hourly during working hours.

Volubilis (known as Walila in this period) by 788, when he was welcomed by the prominent Arab Auroba tribe as their imam. He was assassinated by a secret agent of the Abbasid caliph in May 791, but the posthumous birth of a male heir in August, from a local Berber concubine, allowed his holy dynasty to continue. The slave Rashid exercised authority until he himself was assassinated (this time by an agent of the Aghlabid dynasty of Tunisia), at which time the 11-year-old Idriss II was proclaimed leader in the mosque at Volubilis. Idriss II later went on to expand his authority greatly and found the city of Fez, in which he was buried. The tombs of both father and son were rediscovered in the 15th century, in the Merenid period, after centuries of neglect. It was a period when Morocco was threatened by strong external enemies, and these new shrines helped provide a focus for a politically expedient orthodox nationalist cult. The present town and sanctuary of Moulay Idriss are mostly 18th century, for Moulay Ismaïl piously and sympathetically restored the shrine, including some of the pillars from Volubilis. The entire town was closed to Jews and Christians until 1912.

Your first experience of the holy town is likely to be of a busy and dusty bus and car park. Above and ahead, a line of stalls leads to the triangular wedge of souks that points towards the sanctuary **mosque of Moulay Idriss**. To the right of the sanctuary stretches the Tasga quarter of the town; the higher Khiber quarter is to the left. The souk stalls are lined with eyebrows of green tiles that contrast well with the rising white mass of the double village beyond. Curious woven reed plates, rosaries, golden scarves, grilled food, religious trinkets and embroidered cloth are displayed for the pilgrims. As you near the sanctuary, masses of coloured nougat and enormous green candles predominate. An unmistakable wooden bar halts non-Muslims before the outermost courtyard, while within stretches a whole complex of halls, fountains for washing, prayer-halls and the holy tomb of Morocco's first legitimate Islamic ruler. Pilgrims are allowed to stay in the courtyards, but in summer the chants and collective enthusiasm seldom allow much sleep. To the right of the sanctuary entrance is the royal guesthouse, to the left the offices of the Habous, the ministry that administers religious endowments. Most of the olive groves in the region are leased annually by the **Habous** to farmers, the rents being used to maintain the shrine, mosque and schools.

If you go back to the bus park and follow the tarmac road up a steep hill, turn right past the post office and climb some stone steps, you will come to a famous cylindrical **minaret** encased in blue and white Koranic script, built in 1939 from stone and faïence. Later the path splits under the shadow of a great vine, and there is a good view down onto the glazed roofs and white courts of the secretive sanctuary of Moulay Idriss. Both paths lead downhill towards the sanctuary **souk**. The **medina** is small enough to allow you to wander freely along its erratic climbing alleys, their secrecy interrupted by surprising views, lone cafés and a generally friendly populace.

Just above the river is a complete, round, open-air **Roman bath**, the stones worn by use. It's still connected to a hot sulphur spring that oozes up through healing mud, and is particularly good for rheumatism. Farther on, a bridge built by Moulay Ismaïl spans the river Khoumane; on the other side a path climbs up past a few cottages, deteriorating rapidly into a goat track. If you scramble up this slope of rocky undergrowth, you'll reach a ruined 18th-century **pavilion**, with a fine view over the back of the twin rocks and houses of the Tasga and Khiber quarters.

Volubilis (Oualili)

Volubilis (Oualili)
www.sitedevolubilis.org
open daily from 8pm to
dusk; adm

The gorgeous ruins of the Roman city of Volubilis, ancient capital of the province of Mauretania Tingitana, sit below the escarpment of Jbel Zerhoun. At dusk it is a magical place and, though I have now trod through the stones for decades, I am constantly surprised by its delicate, melancholic beauty. It is the finest archaeological site in Morocco and fully equal to any of the more famous Roman North African ruins that can be seen in Tunisia, Algeria or Libya. The site's most distinctive feature is an astonishingly well-preserved basilica, though the complete triumphal arch, the columns of a Capitoline temple and a dazzling series of mosaic-floored villas are equally memorable. It is an exposed, largely shadeless site, so try to avoid the midday sun. It is at its best in the morning or evening, when the sun gives a warmer colour to the stones. Volubilis is known locally as Oualili, the Berber for oleander, which covers the riverbed on the southern edge of the town.

History

The physical remains of Volubilis, like so many of the great Roman sites in North Africa, largely date from the golden period of the empire. This stretched from the reign of Trajan to the end of the Severi dynasty (of North African origin) – AD 97–235. The city has, however, a richer and more complex history that symbolically unites the two great Middle Eastern cultures that

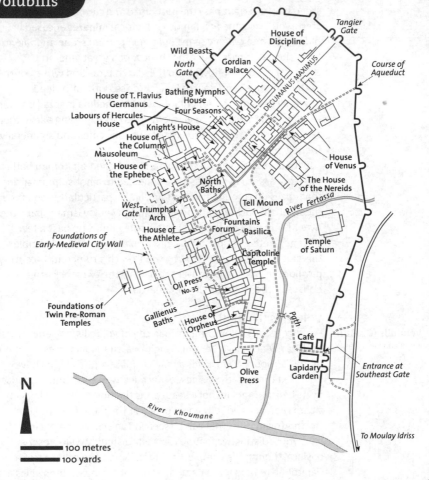

have had a fundamental influence on Morocco: the Phoenicians and the Arabs.

Excavations into the mound of ruins at the site's centre hint at a past that extends back into a Neolithic culture that came early under Phoenician influence, as ruins found here of an old temple to Baal attest. This inland market town covered 15 hectares and is believed to have served as the western capital of Juba II of Mauretania (25 BC–AD 23). Juba, though of North African blood, was a Roman client-king educated in the household of the Emperor Augustus. His wife was not some native princess but Cleopatra Silene, the child of Mark Anthony and Cleopatra. He became increasingly dependent on Roman support to govern his kingdom, so that in all practical matters it was absorbed into the empire long before Claudius' formal annexation in AD 45. The city stayed loyal to Rome through the testing years of Aedemeon's revolt in northern Morocco (roughly contemporary with that of Boadicea in Britain) and was rewarded with grants of citizenship and a ten-year tax holiday. The actual capital of the province was fixed at Tangier, but the presence of the basilica court house hints that Volubilis may have functioned as the centre of the hinterland.

Volubilis was also the centre of a rich agricultural region (over 50 villas have been found in the immediate area) which exported corn, wild beasts and oil to the coast. It was, however, on the vulnerable southeastern edge of the province, and was defended by a ring of five forts at the modern hamlets of Sidi Said, Bled el Gaada, Sidi Moussa, Tocolosida and Aïn Schkor. There was no road east to the city of Oujda, then ruled as part of Mauretania Caesarensis (Roman western Algeria), for the sternly independent Baquates tribe occupied the area around Fez and Taza. Increased frontier tension at the end of the 2nd century is evident in the decision during the reign of the Emperor Marcus Aurelius to construct a 2.5km circuit of city walls, pierced by eight gates and buttressed by forty towers. This period also witnessed the peak of prosperity, with a population estimated at over 20,000.

The near collapse of central government by the end of the period of military anarchy (235–84) – when over 30 generals had seized control of the Imperial throne in a debilitating succession of coups – resulted in the fall of the city to tribal attack in around 280, a disaster evidenced by the hidden caches of coins and bronze statuary found by archaeologists beneath some of Volubilis' villas. This partial collapse of the frontier (Banasa and Thamusida, north of Rabat, had also fallen at this time) was confirmed during the reign of the Emperor Diocletian (284–305) for, although a Roman army was based in Tangier in the 290s under the command of a co-emperor, it was decided that it was too expensive to undertake the reconquest of much of Morocco. The province was reduced to just the northern hub of the ports of Lixus-Tangier and Ceuta, and henceforth governed as if it was part of Spain.

After the initial trauma of the sack, a reduced form of urban life seems to have continued in Volubilis, boosted by refugees escaping the heavy taxes and persecutions of the late Roman Empire. Records from the Arab conquest speak of an independent trading community, now known as Oualila, ruled by a council of Christian tribal chiefs. The location of this city was downhill, beside the oleander-strewn banks of the river Khourman. A wall fenced off the old Roman town centre, which was used as a cemetery. A new intact *hammum*, built over a Roman bathhouse by the riverbank, provides a lone standing testament to this era.

It was to this city that Moulay Idriss fled at the end of the 8th century, and here that his son Idriss II was first proclaimed imam. Idriss II's foundation of Fez deliberately removed the capital from this ancient town with its traditions of oligarchy and religious pluralism. The new capital quickly drained the old of vitality, and by the 11th century Volubilis was a deserted shell.

The city was only reduced to ruin in the 18th century by Moulay Ismaïl's architects, who used its stones to build the Imperial City of Meknès, and by the Lisbon earthquake of 1755. Fortunately, an English antiquarian, John Windus, had sketched the site in 1722. These drawings were of great use to the French archaeologists who began work here in 1915, their digging assisted by Marshal Lyautey's loan of thousands of German prisoners of war.

The Olive Presses

The arch by the ticket office is the old southeastern gate of the Roman city. There is an open-air collection of sculpture and inscriptions next to the office, and a shaded café which sometimes serves lunch. From here a path leads across a largely unexcavated area of the city to cross a stream, the river Fertassa. Beyond this stream, on the left, squats the first of many classical stone olive presses with their associated drains, storage and separation tanks. The construction of a replica press here is a delightful addition to understanding the site.

The extraction of olive oil was of primary importance to Volubilis, as it still is to the villages of Jbel Zerhoun, where techniques have remained unchanged. The olive flesh and stones are first crushed by a large millstone, then shovelled into woven grass-reed sacks that look like a deflated tyre. These are then packed on top of each other on a pole (or poles) and compressed by a heavy cross beam which is gradually tightened. Liquid oozes out from the sacks and is caught by a circular drain which feeds off into a number of tanks where the oil, watery fluids and solid vegetable matter separate naturally. It is an easy matter to add more water and float the olive oil off into jars for export or domestic use.

Olive oil was an essential part of ancient urban life: it was a basic ingredient of cooking; used for bathing and medicines; and was the preferred fuel for lamps. The residue from the presses was put to good use – it was either fed to livestock, or the dried cakes were used as fuel to power the bathhouses. Throughout the city you will find that even the grandest houses had their own olive press. Commerce and manufacture were forbidden to the Roman senatorial class, but anything remotely agricultural, even making bricks, could be done to your heart's content without losing status. It is refreshing to imagine this grand provincial capital surrounded by piles of crushed olives, and the back doors of mansions reeking of discarded black tarry oil. The river Fertassa, joined by the river Khoumane from Moulay Idriss, flowed outside the southern city walls and served as a combined moat and sewer.

The House of Orpheus

The House of Orpheus stands by a conspicuous clump of three cypress trees. This is the largest house in the southern part of the city, named like all the mansions of Volubilis after the subject of their principal mosaic. It is a palatial building divided, in the eastern tradition, into public and private quarters, each with its own entrance.

The first, private entrance leads to a room with a **dolphin mosaic** on the floor. The diamond lozenges, interlocking circles and airy curls which surround the central figure echo traditional carpet designs. There is also a **kitchen** with its niche for statuettes and lamps dedicated to the household gods, the *genius*, the *lar* and the *penates*. The *genius* can be thought of as a guardian angel, the *lar* as a representative of dead ancestors, and the *penates* as twin benevolent spirits who stopped food and drink going off and looked after the sanctity of the family hearth. To the right of the kitchen is an intimate paved bath with its adjacent boiler room.

The second entrance leads directly into the **atrium**, a lavish open-air court decorated with a mosaic floor showing the sea goddess Amphitrite pulled by a seahorse and surrounded by sea creatures. The courtyard is surrounded by the main living rooms, a similar arrangement to contemporary Moroccan houses. The large southern room, the *triclinium* or dining room, has the magnificent **Orpheus mosaic**. The U-shaped plain area of flooring would have been covered by couches, leaving the central circular panel free to be admired from a number of angles. It shows Orpheus playing his harp, encircled by a ring of trees which, like the mammals and birds, are seduced by his music – even the sphinx and griffins look tranquil. It is enclosed by a disciplined decorative pattern with two delightful infills that show a pair of mallards feeding from an urn, and a pair of Barbary partridges at a bird table. Orpheus (amongst other musical triumphs) descended to hell in an attempt to rescue his wife Eurydice and '*to the music of his strings he sang and all the bloodless spirits wept to hear...and Sisyphus sat rapt upon his stone. Then first by that sad singing overwhelmed, the Furies' cheeks it's said were wet with tears*' (Ovid).

Next door, to the left of the path, lie the ruins of the **Gallienus Baths**, an extensive *hammam*, notable now only for one section of broken and faded mosaic amongst a series of gaping holes. These public baths were redecorated by order of the Emperor Gallienus (AD 260–68), who turned them into the most lavish in the whole city. Gallienus is otherwise known for his military reforms. He divided the army between reserve forces and highly trained mounted regiments, who could rush to any trouble on the border.

The Forum, Basilica and Capitoline Temple

Passing another, smaller public bath on the right, the path climbs a flight of steps to enter the paved public square of the city, the **forum**. This formal centre was usually ringed with market courtyards, official temples and the offices of civic government. On the western side, the *macellum*, a small butcher's souk, has been identified. Archaeologists have also discovered that it was built over a number of ancient temples. The southern face of the forum is dominated by the long arcaded outer wall of the **basilica**, the Roman courthouse, which was completed in the early 3rd century AD. It is one of the finest examples in North Africa of one of the most determinedly Roman of all civic buildings. The walls are substantial enough for the original shape of the building to be easily imagined, though you will have to fill the central nave with two double rows of columns. These ran down the entire interior length to frame the two apses at either end of the building. In the centre of each of the two apses would sit a presiding Roman magistrate, usually the governor and his deputy, surrounded by his legal staff and secretaries. The administration of justice was a very public affair, and the citizens of Volubilis would freely wander in and out of the forum to listen to part of a case, view a prominent litigant or assess the character of a new Roman official. The plan of the building may call to mind that of a church, and rightly so, for the first state-built churches of the 4th century took the basilica, not the existing religious architecture of the temples, as their direct model. In front of the basilica stand various plinths that bore monuments to commemorate officials, generals and emperors.

The raised **Capitoline temple**, with its elegant Corinthian columns, stands to the right of the basilica. Now very obvious, it would have been less so when the area was enclosed in an arcaded courtyard. Within this enclosed court an altar can be seen, from which thirteen steps advance up to the terrace of the temple, which, like the ancient temple in Rome, was dedicated to the trinity of gods, Jupiter, Juno and Minerva. There were two classes of Roman gods, those who protected the state and those who protected the family. The Capitoline triad were the chief divinities of the state. A council would assemble below the Capitol to declare war, generals appeared before setting out to battle, and after victory they would return here to offer crowns of gold and booty. Juno and Minerva, like the Virgin Mary, were appealed to on all manner of occasions, but in their Capitoline role they watched over the health and population of the whole province.

At sunset the view through these pillars east to Moulay Idriss is triumphantly photogenic. This would have been the usual orientation for a temple, but instead it stares mysteriously at the back of the basilica. It makes little sense, unless the whole complex was built over a pre-existing shrine.

The **House of the Athlete**, labelled '*Maison au Desultor*', stands at the northwestern corner of the forum. It contains a crude mosaic of a sportsman who has won a cup for vaulting over a grey horse. Beyond this stand the ruins of some fashionable shops and, opposite on the right, one of two public fountains that surround the ruins of the city's third and largest public bath, which covered an area of 1,500 square metres. This, the **north baths**, and the fountains were probably built on the orders of the Emperor Hadrian, and fed by an aqueduct that channelled fresh spring water from the Zerhoun hills.

The Triumphal Arch

The path now leads across the principal avenue to the magnificent triumphal arch, raised in AD 217 by the governor Marcus Aurelius Sebastenus in honour of the Emperor Caracalla and his mother Julia Domna, whose defaced medallion bust can be seen on the right. Julia Domna, a Syrian intellectual and a princess in her own right, accompanied her husband, the Emperor Septimius Severus, on his campaign in Britain from 208 to 211, where she became known as the 'mother of the camp'. After Septimius' death at York she was later the unhappy witness of the fratricidal murder of her son Geta, who had tried to take refuge in his mother's lap from his brother and co-emperor Caracalla's murderous rage. For all this, the family may have been genuinely popular in Volubilis, for they were North African by origin and had achieved a remarkable legal reform by extending Roman citizenship to all provincials. By the time the arch was finished, however, Caracalla and Julia Domna had already been murdered by an usurper. The arch remains an impressive monument, built from local Zerhoun stone and with little evidence of the reconstruction by French archaeologists in 1933. It was originally capped with a bronze six-horse chariot and nymphs who cascaded water into carved marble bowls below. It carried an inscription which thanked the province for this symbol of loyalty and remitted all outstanding debts to the Imperial exchequer, though there was a broad hint that the emperor would be happy to accept a free gift of soldiers and elephants.

From the arch, the broad **Decumanus Maximus** leads to the Tangier gate. This central street was faced with a columned arcade which would have been lined with small shops and craft stalls.

Tucked discreetly behind this screen were the large residences of officials, landlords and merchants. Just south of the arch is a house that is sometimes pointed out to visitors as a brothel, though the penis carved on to a stone lintel that now stands alone in a room was probably nothing more than a good-luck sign.

The Grand Houses

The **House of the Ephebe**, named after the fine bronze head found here (now in the Archaeological Museum in Rabat), is immediately north of the arch. It has an impressive interior courtyard with a central pool, around which are arranged public rooms ornamented with mosaics. The most elegant of them, second on your right, has Bacchus being drawn in his chariot by leopards. On the northern side of the house there is an old mausoleum which seems to have been incorporated into the house as a cellar. Next door to the west is the House of the Columns, which sports a circular pool in the atrium, beds of geraniums and a famous spiral, fluted column which was carved in the early 3rd century AD.

In a back dining room in the next-door house, known as the *Maison au Cavalier* – **the Knight's House** – there is a mosaic of a lascivious Bacchus, aided by Eros, discovering Ariadne, neglected by Theseus, asleep on the shore at Naxos. The figures are crude but the god's prurient eyes are alive and the flesh glistens with colour. Ariadne subsequently bore Bacchus six children, and her bridal chaplet was placed in the stars, where it forms the Corona Borealis or Cretan Crown. Next along, staying on the left side of the road, is the **Labours of Hercules House**, named after the crude mosaic found in the dining room. Here, in oval frames, are strip-cartoon images from the life of Hercules – as a child strangling snakes; the capture of Cerberus; the Cretan Bull; cleaning the Augean stables; the Stymphalian birds; wrestling with Antaeus; the Erymanthian boar; the Lernean hydra; Hippolyta's girdle; and slaying the Nemean lion. It is thought the mosaic might have been made in the reign of the Emperor Commodus, who had a Hercules obsession, but Hercules was always a popular hero in Morocco due to his identification with the Phoenician Melkarth and the number of his achievements that occurred here. Another room has Jupiter and his boyfriend Ganymede in the centre, with the four seasons depicted in the corners. There are the usual private quarters behind the public rooms, with bath and frescoed panels painted to imitate marble. The arches in front of the house provided space for eight shops. The house was entered from a side street, guarded by a porter's lodge.

Beyond is a row of five smaller but still grand houses. The first held an inscription that has identified it as the **House of T. Flavius**

Germanus; the second has a well-preserved and amusing mosaic of Dionysis and the four seasons; the third, marked by one crude pillar, is known as the **Bathing Nymphs House** (*Maison des Bains des Nymphes*) after a mosaic which shows three nymphs undressing and dancing beside the Hippocrene spring, overlooked by Pegasus, an ancient cult tree, and a horned wild-man (presumably Actaeon half-metamorphosed into a deer). Directly behind this house is the northern gate, which opens out into the extensive western cemetery, while opposite, across the street, is the **House of the Nereids**. If the restorations have been completed, the poolside mosaic here is well worth a look, as is the disturbing mosaic of four wild beasts – a bull-baiting scene, a lion, a lioness and a leopard eating heads.

Back on the left-hand side of the main street, beyond the smaller houses, is the **Gordian Palace**. With its imposing exterior of a dozen Ionic columns, this is believed to have been the governor's seasonal residence, rebuilt during the reign of Gordian III (AD 238–44). Two houses were combined to give a total of 74 rooms, including courtyards with pools and bathhouses. Inscriptions found in the palace record a series of agreements between the Roman governor and the chief of the Baquates tribe. The frequency of new treaties in the 3rd century suggests a troubled frontier. The last pact, made just a few years before the fall of the city, refers wishfully to a '*Foederata et ducturna pax*', a federated and lasting peace. To those in the know, the wording of the treaty – which treated the Baquates kingdom almost as an equal entity to the Roman Empire – must have spelt trouble. Though the palace is strong in atmosphere, its decoration is restricted to a few columns and some simple geometric mosaics. The large villa complex next door known as the **House of Discipline** is one of the most recent areas to have been excavated. It is believed to have served as a place of detention.

A single cypress tree about 100m east of the Decumanus Maximus marks the **House of Venus**. Renowned for its mosaics, this was also where the superb bronze busts of Juba II and Cato (now in the Rabat Archaeological Museum) were discovered, buried in a protective bed of sand. The house is currently undergoing stabilization and is not accessible to the public, although a platform has been built to one side to allow a good view of the two most famous mosaics.

The central courtyard has an I-shaped pool, decorated with a damaged mosaic of a series of racing chariots drawn by rival teams of peacocks, geese and ducks, which includes accurate period details of a hippodrome. The large dining room straight ahead used to house a mosaic of Venus being carried through the waves (now displayed in Tangier). From the raised platform one can see the naked Hylos captured by nymphs, a colourful composition dominated by rippling muscles and erotic curves; the two side panels show scenes of guilty *erotes* being chastized. Hylos was an Argonaut who joined Jason's crew as the darling squire of Hercules. He went ashore but was seized by two nymphs, Dryope and Pegae, who dragged him away to live with them in an underwater grotto. The next-door mosaic shows chaste Diana with a nymph surprised by Actaeon at her bath, her bow hanging from the branches of a cult tree. Actaeon is already sprouting horns, for the goddess – in revenge for being surprised – changed him into a stag, and he was then chased and devoured by his own hounds.

Returning back to the forum, you get a brief look at pre-Roman Volubilis as you pass an ancient mound composed of fragments of past temples and burial chambers. Across the river Fertassa are the foundations of the **Temple of Saturn**, where over 600 carved stone offerings have been discovered. This was established centuries before the Roman period as the Phoenician temple of Baal, a Semitic horned male deity of the mountains and streams, whose rites and worship continued unchanged under the Roman label of Saturn.

Festivals in Moulay Idriss and Volubilis

The massive national festival is held in late summer or autumn. Five visits to the festival used to be considered, by locals at least, to equal a pilgrimage to Mecca.

Where to Stay in Moulay Idriss

⭐ Buttons Inn >

Buttons Inn, Dar Zerhoune, Moulay Idriss, t 0535 544371 (€). A pristine and welcoming guesthouse, with just a handful of pretty rooms and a panoramic roof terrace filled with plants. Fayssal and his family can arrange guided tours, hikes and horse rides into the surrounding hills, prepare picnics, and organize cookery lessons.

La Colombe Blanche, 21 Rue Zouak Tazgha, Moulay Idriss, t 0535 544596, *www.maisondhote-zerhoune.ma*. This guesthouse is tucked away next to the town walls, and has simple, well-priced rooms overlooking a traditional tiled patio. Dinners on request.

Eating Out in Moulay Idriss and Volubilis

This area is almost perfect for a picnic, taken either in the olive groves of Jbel Zerhoun or by the tree-shaded, ruin-skirted river Khoumane, which trickles just south of Volubilis. Provisions can be bought in Moulay Idriss. There is a café inside the Volubilis site entrance, several café-restaurants in Moulay Idriss and a licensed restaurant at the Volubilis Hotel (t 0535 544408, €€) overlooking the Roman ruins (although this is not recommended as a place to stay). Both the guesthouses listed above offer dinners on request.

El Baraka de Zerhoun, 22 Aïn Smen-Khiber, t 0535 544184. On the left of the tarmac hill road that climbs directly through Moulay Idriss. It is a delightful restaurant that offers meals that can consist of bowls of local Zerhoun olives, hot pastries, an excellent spiced vegetable salad and a good local *tagine*. It has no drinks licence.

Rabat

Rabat overlooks the Bou Regreg river where it runs into the Atlantic Ocean. On the opposite bank sits Salé, quieter and less immediately eye-catching. The physical peak of Rabat is the idyllic Oudaïas Kasbah, or royal city, which sits like a stork's nest overlooking the estuary. Beneath it, the medina spreads southeast and, beyond it, the ville nouvelle *(new town)* built under the French.

The city has a glamorous history, although less as a capital (as the French appointed it in 1912), and more as a jumping-off point for pirates (or corsairs) who attacked European ships and ports in Spain and France. That maritime history has always defined Rabat, with its towering defensive walls providing protection against the ocean. Its face remains turned towards Europe and even North America, but this is nothing new: on the southeastern side of the city lies Chellah, the old Roman city of Sala Colonia.

09

Don't miss

❶ **Rugs and wares**
Medina souks p.251

❷ **The fortress village**
Oudaïa Kasbah p.256

❸ **Medieval landmark**
Hassan Tower p.260

❹ **Ancient bronzes**
Archaeological Museum p.264

❺ **Roman and Muslim remains**
Chellah p.265

See map overleaf

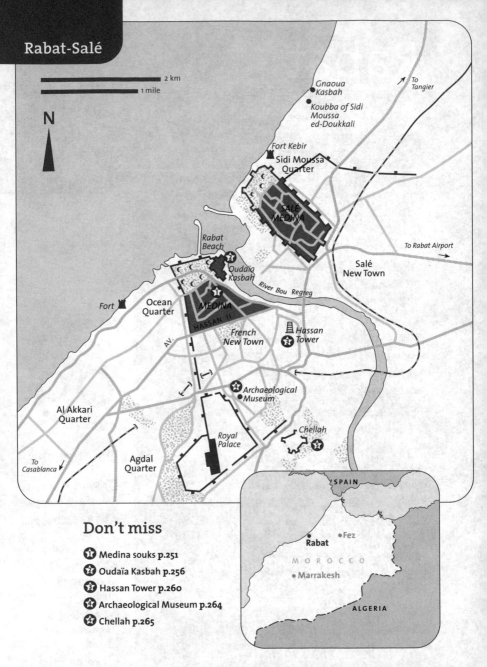

2 km
1 mile

N

To Tangier

Gnaoua
Kasbah

Koubba of Sidi
Moussa
ed-Doukkali

Fort Kebir

Sidi Moussa
Quarter

SALÉ
MEDINA

To Rabat Airport

Rabat
Beach

Oudaïa
Kasbah

Salé
New Town

River Bou Regreg

Fort

Ocean
Quarter

MEDINA

HASSAN II

French
New Town

Hassan
Tower

AV.

Archaeological
Museum

Al Akkari
Quarter

Royal
Palace

Chellah

To
Casablanca

Agdal
Quarter

SPAIN

Don't miss

1 Medina souks p.251
2 Oudaïa Kasbah p.256
3 Hassan Tower p.260
4 Archaeological Museum p.264
5 Chellah p.265

Rabat · Fez

MOROCCO

· Marrakesh

ALGERIA

The Atlantic coast was known by the French as 'Maroc Utile' –
'useful Morocco'. The industrial, commercial and political
heartland of the country is concentrated in the three neighbouring
coastal cities of Rabat, Kénitra and Casablanca; the fertile coastal

provinces of the Rharb, Chaouïa and Doukkala have long been prized as the grain-bowl of the nation. For a visitor the comparatively prosperous and Western-influenced Atlantic coast serves as an excellent bridge to the more striking and aggressive culture of the interior.

Rabat wears the well-ordered urban architecture of the 20th century: broad tree-lined avenues, a central park, apartment blocks and suburban quarters for the ministries, officialdom and foreign diplomats. The conurbation now has a population of 1.8 million (including Salé), and an impressive air of activity by day. Brisk men armed with briefcases stride to their appointments along the broad avenues of the city centre. The main streets are lined with newsagents, bookshops, cinemas and cafés, but this familiar core of a modern capital city also contains striking monuments from the past.

The twin cities of Rabat and Salé, on opposite banks of the Bou Regreg estuary, have a long history. Rabat, the city on the southern bank, has known greater extremes of fortune, while its northern twin has had a steadier if less glamorous past. Half an hour's walk from the city centre, Salé is now really a suburb of Rabat, but it still retains its own traditional identity.

The 12th-century city walls still dominate 21st-century Rabat. The more intimate achievements of the Merenid dynasty can be found in the 13th-century medina of Salé and in Rabat's royal necropolis – the walled garden of the Chellah. The Rabat Kasbah, in its strategic position above the estuary, has been at the heart of the city's long Islamic history. It has a celebrated Almohad gate, an Andalucian urban interior and a garden palace from the 17th century now transformed into a delightful museum. For rarer insights into the Phoenician and classical achievements there are the Archaeology Museum and the ruins of Sala Colonia inside the Chellah walls, to reward you with haunting views and art of the highest order.

History

All the civilisations of Morocco have been drawn to the safe harbour of the estuary of the Bou Regreg, where the river has cut access to the sea through a forbidding line of Atlantic cliffs. For Rabat the wheel of fortune has in 2,500 years twice turned to elevate it as an imperial capital, and twice as an important maritime trading power; in between these glories it has been reduced to a humble village.

Ancient Sala Colonia and the Orthodox Rabat

Like Tangier and other cities of the Moroccan coast, Rabat was first Phoenician, then Roman. It was the southernmost urban centre of the Roman province and, as Sala Colonia, given the privileges of a *colonia* or self-governing city by Trajan. Though Roman rule was withdrawn in the 3rd century, it remained a trading centre, identifying with the Muslim Kharijite heresy in the mid-8th century. Protected by the powerful Berber Berghouata confederacy, it survived until the 10th century, when a garrison of orthodox Arabs established a *rabat*, a religious community of warriors, on the site of the present kasbah. The Almoravids took up the struggle against the heretic Berghouata and lost their first two leaders to it, but their deaths were avenged by Youssef ben Tachfine, celebrated founder of the Almoravid Empire.

The Imperial Capital

The first Almohad sultans, in the 12th century, found the site useful as a combined military and naval base, but it was not until the reign of Yaacoub el Mansour, the third Sultan, that it was decided to turn Rabat into an imperial capital. He raised the vast Grand Mosque of Hassan, the series of impressive gateways, and built the enormous and still-surviving extent of city walls for his Rabat el Fath, the Rabat of Victory. Work stopped the day Yaacoub died; his successors neglected this empty but magnificent encampment on the Atlantic coast, and chose to rule from Seville or Marrakesh. The Almohad walls of Rabat were only to be occupied fully in the 20th century. In the 14th century the Merenid sultans, with their exquisite taste, selected the backdrop of the near-empty city as the site for their royal necropolis. They enclosed the Roman ruins of Sala Colonia in high walls pierced by a magnificent gate that hid a complex of fine gardens, delicate mosques and sanctuaries, the Chellah. Commercial life was then concentrated in Salé – Leo Africanus, who passed through Rabat in 1500, reported that it sheltered a scattering of a mere hundred houses.

The Pirate Republic

Recovery came in the early 17th century when Muslim refugees, expelled from Andalucía by Philip III of Spain, were offered the empty city of Rabat by the Saadian Sultan Zaidan. Because the original Almohad walls enclosed far too large an area, the Andalucians built the dividing wall that still separates the medina from the New Town. The principal business of Rabat and its sister city of Salé then became organized piracy and, due to the collapse of Saadian authority, from 1627 the two cities were able to establish themselves as an independent entity, the Republic of the Bou Regreg. The Republic was governed by an elected council or *divan* of sixteen members, which met in Salé. Each year the *divan* in turn elected a *caid* and an admiral.

Orientation

Rabat and Salé have spread enormously in recent decades, but all the places of interest remain within walking distance of each other. Rabat itself could hardly be more convenient for the traveller. Ave Hassan II conveniently divides the medina from the new city: to the east it leads to the Pont Moulay Hassan, the bridge across the Bou Regreg to Salé, and to the west (having passed through the Almohad walls) it takes you to the main bus station and the road to Casablanca. Ave Hassan II is crossed by Ave Mohammed V, which leads you north right through the medina, or south, as Ave Yacoub al Mansour, past the Royal Palace to the Chellah. The pavements of Ave Mohammed V are the heart of the city, and here you can find the impressive exteriors of the post office, the train station and the major banks. Cinemas, cafés, hotels and restaurants are also all concentrated on this boulevard or on the side streets that connect it to the Ave Allal ben Abdallah, which runs parallel, to the east.

Medina

Ave Mohammed V processes unbroken from the *ville nouvelle* to cut through the western end of the medina, providing a useful way across to the coast as well as a landmark. Ave Hassan II runs along the outside of the southern medina walls, while the Grand Mosque is nestled just inside. While the south and west of the medina have straight boundary lines marked by the walls, the north and east end at the meandering coastline, making the medina more a triangle than a square, with the markets largely in the centre and the south. On a small promontory at the medina's northernmost point sits the Oudaïa Kasbah.

Ocean District

There is little reason to visit this area but it sits southwest of the medina and reaches to the coast. Continuing southwest out of the area, you reach the road to Temara Plage (Beach), 13km south, and, ultimately, Casablanca.

Ville Nouvelle

The spacious and well-ordered Ave Mohammed V runs down through the *ville nouvelle* from the medina, with the train station and parliament on its western side. Embassies are generally in the eastern corner of this area, just south of the Mausoleum of Mohammed V, which is a stone's throw from the bridge to Salé. Smart hotels, bars, restaurants and state buildings are dotted throughout. Ave de Toumerte forms its western limit and the Rue du Chellah runs south through the area's centre.

Méchouar and Chellah

Southeast of the *ville nouvelle* sits Chellah and a little to the west of that is the Royal Palace, which is inaccessible to the public. The *méchouar* is the enormous square just north of the palace, traditionally used as a place for swearing allegiance to the monarch.

Agdal

West of the royal palace is Agdal, a residential area with plenty of small shops and restaurants, as well as Rabat Agdal (the second train station) and Agdal University on Place Mamoun. The grid-like streets make it easy to find your way around but the Mosque Badr (beside the station) and the square beside it are useful landmarks.

Jan Jansz, a German renegade who took the name Murad Reis, was the first and most successful pirate admiral of Salé. In one of his raids he took 237 captives from the village of Baltimore outside Cork in Ireland, before proceeding to attack fishing fleets off Iceland. Five years later, in 1636, he raided the south coast of England, and then sent his captives across France by land to Marseille, where they were shipped to the slave markets of Algiers. In 1640 he was back in northern waters again, and St Michael's Mount in Cornwall lost 60 villagers to the 'Sallee Rovers'.

Getting to and away from Rabat-Salé

By Air

Rabat-Salé **airport** (**t** 0537 809090) is 8 km outside the city centre and serves Paris, Lyon, Tripoli and other destinations in Morocco with Royal Air Maroc and Air France. There are trains to Rabat-Ville from the airport, or a taxi to the centre of Rabat should cost 100 dirhams.

By Train

Rabat's new **railway station** (**t** 0535 736060) sits on the main trunk line from Casablanca to Fez, and is located just up the road from the parliament. Trains run almost continuously (every 30 minutes) to Casablanca and there are fast services to major cities like Fez, Meknès and Marrakesh and overnight services to long-haul destinations. Check *www.oncf.ma* for more details.

By Bus

There are buses between Rabat and all the major cities in Morocco. The main bus station is on Place Zerktouni and the CTM is on the same road out of town – the Casablanca road to the southwest. However, given the inconvenient location of the bus stops, you are best to arrive by train when possible.

By Car

There is no need for a car in the city itself, but it can be useful for exploring the region. For car hire offices, *see* Getting around Rabat p.253.

The European renegades were usually employed only in the navigation and the technical handling of the corsair ships. It was the Andalucian refugees under their captain who acted as the fighting force. They spoke a *lingua franca* that was a mixture of French, Italian, Spanish and Portuguese. On return to Salé, 10 per cent of the prize money was awarded to the *divan*, which increasingly became an oligarchy of successful captains and merchants. The Republic of the Bou Regreg was never a homogenous entity, and only constant external pressure from the European powers at sea and rival Muslim warlords by land kept the inhabitants from pursuing faction fights and civil wars to their full conclusion. The sand bar across the estuary and the savage cliffs prevented any European fleet from seriously threatening the pirate craft, although a subtle mixture of bombardment, blockade and bribes from the English and Dutch led to the release of some slaves and a variety of 'protection' arrangements with some of the European powers.

The golden days of anarchy, profit and adventure ended when Sultan Moulay Rachid took possession of Rabat in 1666. The sultan assumed a controlling 60 per cent stake in the corsair business and profits nose-dived for the other shareholders.

New Rabat

The period after Sultan Moulay Ismaïl's death in 1727 saw a rapid decline in Moroccan trade and widespread destruction by warring heirs to the throne. Locally this conflict was intensified by rivalry between Rabat and Salé. During the wise rule of Sultan Sidi Mohammed (from 1757) an attempt was made to discourage the remaining pirate activity, even before the French bombardment of Rabat in 1765. After this attack the Sultan allowed a French consul to settle in Rabat, established a new administrative palace on its present site – safely out of range of European cannon – and encouraged the town to develop its now-renowned carpet trade, as well as building two new mosques and laying out a park. Unofficial coastal piracy and wrecking continued, though, until the navy of the Austrian Empire took savage revenge for the loss of one ship in 1829 by shelling all the coastal cities of Morocco.

Rabat enjoyed reasonable prosperity as one of the towns under the firm control of the government during the 19th century, though it was increasingly superseded as a trading centre by Casablanca, with its large harbour. Rabat's future was radically altered in 1912 by France, who, wary of the old cities of the interior, selected Rabat as the new political centre for the administration of the country. The fiction that the French Resident administered Morocco for the sultan was vigorously maintained, and Sultan Moulay Youssef was duly installed in the palace of Rabat.

French rule from 1912 to 1956, while rapidly developing a glittering new town, made few changes to the traditional pattern of life in the old city. The Protectorate was a colonial regime interested in ruling a conquered Islamic nation with the minimum of expense. This necessarily involved ruling through traditional power structures, and avoiding any unnecessary social, moral or political interference. As part of this policy the native quarters were left as sanctums of traditional custom, while separate modern quarters for Europeans were built outside them. This policy, defensible on aesthetic grounds as well as that of convenient security, was initiated in Rabat by the first French Resident, Marshal Lyautey. After Independence, Mohammed V and his son, the late King Hassan II, developed the palace of Rabat from a mere symbol into the actual seat of national authority.

Rabat

The Medina

🔟 The Medina

The Rabat medina was built by the Moriscos, those Spanish inhabitants of Muslim descent who were expelled by Philip III in 1607. They built the Andalucian wall (*Rempart des Andalous*), a long rampart reinforced by rectangular towers that enclosed the northerly fortifiable portion from the excessive 5km perimeter wall constructed in the Almohad era. The Andalucian wall stands on the northern side of Avenue Hassan II, its flat top furnished with narrow gun slits in keeping with its 17th-century origins and in

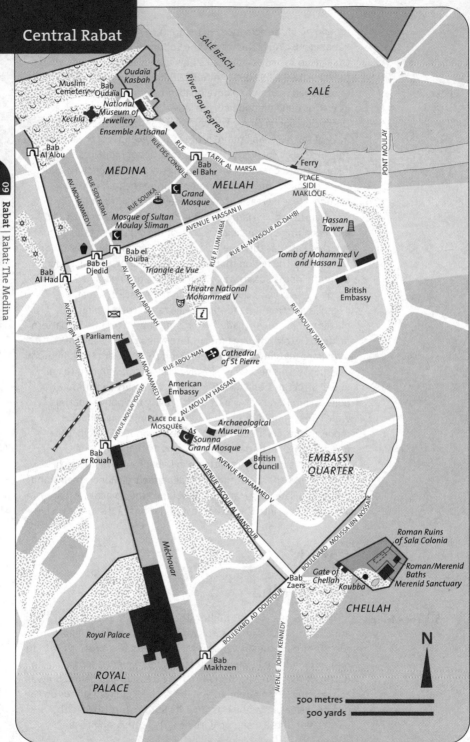

SALÉ BEACH

River Bou Regreg

SALÉ BEACH

SALÉ

PONT MOULAY

Muslim Cemetery
Oudaïa Kasbah
Bab Oudaïa
National Museum of Jewellery
Kechla
Ensemble Artisanal

Bab Al Alou

MEDINA

RUE DES CONSULS

RUE SOUIKA

RUE

TARIK AL MARSA

Bab el Bahr

MELLAH

Ferry

PLACE SIDI MAKLOUF

AV. MOHAMMED V

RUE SIDI FATAH

Grand Mosque

Mosque of Sultan Moulay Sliman

AVENUE HASSAN II

RUE P. LUMUMBA

RUE AL-MANSOUR AD-DAHBI

Hassan Tower

Bab el Bouiba

Bab el Djedid

Bab Al Had

AV. ALLAL BEN ABDALLAH

Triangle de Vue

Tomb of Mohammed V and Hassan II

British Embassy

AVENUE IBN TUMERT

Theatre National Mohammed V

i

RUE MOULAY ISMAIL

Parliament

RUE ABOU-NAN

Cathedral of St Pierre

AV. MOHAMMED V

American Embassy

AV. MOULAY HASSAN

Bab er Rouah

AVENUE MOULAY YOUSSEF

PLACE DE LA MOSQUÉE

As Sounna Grand Mosque

Archaeological Museum

British Council

EMBASSY QUARTER

Méchouar

AVENUE YACOUB AL MANSOUR

AVENUE MOHAMMED V

BOULEVARD MOUSSA IBN NOSSAIR

Roman Ruins of Sala Colonia

Bab Zaers

Gate of Chellah

Koubba

Roman/Merenid Baths
Merenid Sanctuary

CHELLAH

Royal Palace

BOULEVARD AD DOUSTOUR

AVENUE JOHN KENNEDY

ROYAL PALACE

Bab Makhzen

500 metres
500 yards

N

Getting around Rabat

Buses are useful for getting between some of the main areas, particularly if you are headed to Agdal or Salé, but taxis are easy and inexpensive. Within the medina it is always quickest to walk (or cycle) but in the *ville nouvelle* the long boulevards can make wheels more worthwhile, especially in the heat of the day.

By Taxi

Rabat's taxis are blue and a ride anywhere in town should cost no more than 20 dirhams. Taxis are found at the railway station, near the main entrances to the medina, like Bab Chellah and Bab El-Bouiba, or on Ave Mohammed V. In Agdal, try Place Al-Mamoun or next to the Badr Mosque; in the embassy district, the Place Abraham Lincoln. If you are going to Chellah, be sure to take a taxi, thereby avoiding a long, dull walk, and ask them to take you to the gate. Coming back, catch one on the main road.

To catch a *grand taxi* anywhere east (Salé, Meknès, Fez etc), head along Ave Hassan II but for Casablanca or Bouknadel (Plage des Nations) go to the taxi rank outside the bus depot at Place Zerktouni.

By Car

A car is not needed in Rabat and Salé, unless you also want to explore the region; even then, *grands taxis* and buses are all you need. In the *ville nouvelle*, many of the hotels have parking spaces and the *ville nouvelle* and Agdal are generally easy for parking. It is impossible to drive in the medina itself and the orientation of the city (with water on two sides) is such that a wrong turn can cost you quite a bit of time.

You can hire from **Avis** (7 Rue Abou Faris El Marini, **t** 0537 721818; also at the airport: **t** 0537 831677), **Europcar** (29 bis Rue Patrice Lumumba, **t** 0537 722328; also at the airport: **t** 0537 724141) or **Hertz** (467 Ave Mohammed V, **t** 0537 707366).

By Bus

Buses are a good way to travel substantial distances within the city but less good for short distances. Useful routes include the no. 3 (from the town centre to the train station and cathedral before entering Agdal and then finishing at Hay Riad). For Salé, take no. 12 or no.13 from Place Melilla. For Temara Plage (beach), take the no.30 or no.33 from the Bab El-Had.

Boats

A fun way to travel to Salé is by rowing boat. Try near the Mausoleum of King Hassan.

---

contrast to the comparatively light-hearted crenellations that decorate the medieval Almohad walls to the west.

Two gates pierce the western Almohad wall of the medina: the northern **Bab Al Alou** and the southern **Bab Al Had**. The latter was the principal entrance and is protected by a pair of protruding five-sided towers cut with gun ports. The handsome entrance gate is formed from three superimposed horseshoe arches and was rebuilt by Sultan Moulay Sliman in 1814. It was decorated with the heads of the executed until the early 20th century. Since the hole was punched through the walls by the nearby Avenue Hassan II, it has functioned as an entrance into the vegetable market that stretches beyond this gate. In its shadow, a row of clerks armed with typewriters sits ready to assist the less literate through the formal paths of bureaucracy, something that has been going on in Morocco for decades and which the French travel-writer Antoine de Saint-Exupéry recorded seeing in Fez in the 1930s. Around the market are ranged all the cheaper *pensions*, as well as a tempting assortment of grill-cafés that provide some of the best cooking in the city.

Guides

It is probably not worth hiring a guide in Rabat since the medina is not too difficult to navigate and the number of sights is limited. In many ways, the best parts of a visit to Rabat are the walks through the medina and its kasbah, along the coastal walls or through the *ville nouvelle*. But a guide is useful at Chellah, and several are usually available on site (and in several languages).

Just behind the bustling market area, with its artisans' stalls, bazaars and intimate little cafés, are the tranquil residential quarters of an Andalucian town. Houses of stone are barred by old stained and riveted doors, their walls half-plastered and painted with lime with details picked out in azure or ochre yellow. Each quarter has a local mosque for daily prayers, a communal bakery, a fountain and usually a bathhouse. Its ordered 17th-century Andalucian foundation has given the medina a regulated street pattern. It is easy to explore, in contrast to the tortuous mystery of the medieval medina in Fez.

Beginning in the southwest, at the crossing of the Rue Souika and Rue Sidi Fatah, is the **mosque of Sultan Moulay Sliman**, which he founded in 1812. Farther along Rue Souika, past intriguing displays of domestic goods – mostly bolts of cloth and kitchen ware – is the **Grand Mosque**, entirely rebuilt in the late 19th century, although it was founded by the Merenids. Opposite the mosque, on the right-hand side of the road that leads down to the Bab Chellah, there is a 14th-century **fountain** that is the sole surviving remnant of the Merenid mosque. The three broken arches with their fading decoration were placed here around 1370; they now provide an impressive façade for an Arab and Islamic bookshop.

The market booths around a Grand Mosque traditionally hold more expensive merchandise (their rents help in the upkeep of the mosque). The covered **Souk es Sebat** was once a famous centre for Moroccan workmanship: the intricate gold-stamped leatherwork which can still be found amongst the glittering array of embroidered slippers, filigree belts and ornamental hats. There are a number of specialist courtyards off the main market. A reconstructed arch leads into Rue des Consuls. Across this medina thoroughfare, a street passes through a small square colonized by fishermen and cheap grill-cafés to twist down past pavements dressed with the pathetic objects of the flea market and pop out through the low walls of the **Bab el Bahr**, the old port gate, to meet the thundering traffic on the coastal highway. From this gate an alley leads south up to the **shrine of Lalla Qadiya**, where returning pilgrims from Mecca spend their first night home in prayer. Here a charming trader has set up a tea shop in the street which has a fine view up the estuary. Follow this alley into the old Mellah (Jewish quarter), or a short walk upstream along the main road will take you to the boat crossing to Salé.

Rue des Consuls

This is where the larger carpet dealers and bazaars are found. Between the French bombardment of 1765 and the Protectorate of 1912, all Euopean consuls and merchants were obliged to live on this street. No.62 was the house of the consul Louis Chénier, father of the celebrated French poet André Chénier. There Is a series of splendid old **fondouqs**: No.109, the Fondouq ben Aicha, is the grandest; No.93 is the Tailleurs' Courtyard; No.141 the Kissariat Moline; Nos.31–2 are the Fondouq Ben Aïssa; and at 232 Rue Souika is Fondouq Daouia.

National Artisan Museum
open Wed–Mon 9–12 and 3–6; adm

Ensemble Artisanal
t 0537 730507; open 9–12 and 2.30–6.30

A right-hand turn on to the main coast road, Rue Tarik Al Marsa, takes you to the **National Artisan Museum** (Artisanat du Maroc) with a display of traditional crafts in two old shops. On this street also is the **Ensemble Artisanal** which is a good place to gauge prices and perhaps even pick up a gift. There is a carpet souk just next door.

The Souk el Ghezel

At the end of the Rue des Consuls in front of the kasbah is the Souk el Ghezel, now no more than a tree-shaded car park with a whitewashed *koubba* at its heart. This was the wool market for the carpet-weavers of Rabat, a space that was also convenient for the auction of Christian captives from the 16th to the 18th centuries, when speculation over the size of the eventual ransom played a large role in the bidding.

The **wool market** hasn't moved far: it can be found about 140m to the west, spread down half of the length of Blvd Al Alou. The shops in this area are home to the best joiners, wood-carvers and painters in the medina, as well as to a number of profusely stocked antique-bazaars.

The square whitewashed **Kechla**, also known as *Château Neuf*, was built by Sultan Moulay Rachid in the 17th century to keep a check on the Andalucian population of the kasbah and medina, and has served as a prison, slave pen, arsenal and garrison in its day. It is surrounded by an extensive Muslim cemetery; these hug the coast in both Salé and Rabat. An underground tunnel connects the Kechla to the kasbah, but neither this secret entrance nor the Kechla fortress itself is open. The cemetery is enlivened once a year by the *moussem* **of Lalla Kasba**, when young girls pray for help in finding a good husband. At the western end of the boulevard is a collection of shops such as Himmi's, which can provide everything on hire for the great day: tents fit for *caids*, vast couscous pots, and a fantastic assortment of bridal litters that range from traditional painted boxes to peacock and conch-shell floats of glittering glass.

Rue Sidi Fatah

There is no need to carry on west to the Bab Al Alou – it is not one of the city's great gateways. About 150m down the Rue Sidi Fatah, near the Mosque el Qoubba, are the 'new' baths, **Hammam el Jedid**, a 14th-century Merenid building whose income is partly devoted to the maintenance of the Merenid tombs at Chellah. Farther down Rue Sidi Fatah a splendid high porch shelters the gates to the **mosque and tomb of Moulay Mekki**, an 18th-century saint. The painted geometric design of the porch includes wreaths of flowers, a very rare detail in the strictly image-less religious art of Morocco. It hints at Ottoman influence and has now faded into a charmingly harmonious fusion of light blue and green. The mosque's elegant octagonal minaret is decorated with small arches and stalactites under the windows. Beyond it there is also the *zaouia* of **Sidi ben Aissa**, on the right before the Rue Souika.

The Mellah

This, the old Jewish quarter of the medina, can be entered through its own gate in the Andalucian wall, opposite Place du Mellah. After 50m, a right turn off Rue Ouqqasa (the southern continuation of Rue des Consuls) leads to the central passage of the Mellah with its many dead-end alleys extending off from both sides. The Mellah is now very low-rent, where it has not crumbled completely, and the cramped, claustrophobic atmosphere is intensified by the street vegetable and meat stalls with their accumulated refuse. Somewhere within this area are over a dozen synagogues, all now closed – some carefully locked and preserved, some the haunt of squatters. It is not, though, a particularly old Mellah: the Jews of Rabat were constantly being moved around by different sultans, and this cramped but defensible quarter was allocated to the community by Moulay Sliman only in 1808. At the far extremity of the Mellah is the **mausoleum of Sidi Maklouf**, a Jew who converted to Islam. He was venerated for his piety and spectacular miracles, not least of which was parting the waters of the Bou Regreg to enable a student, stranded in Salé, to visit him.

The Oudaïa Kasbah

⊘ Oudaïa Kasbah

The Oudaïa Kasbah is at the heart of the military history of Rabat. This was the site of the original *rabat* from which generations of cavalry issued to bring the heretic Berber tribes into obedience to successive sultans. It has also been a government bastion against a recurring enemy that came to destroy by sea. Garrisons of Almoravid, Almohad, Merenid, Andalucian and Alaouite troops have stood on guard here ready to repel raiding fleets, which from the Vikings of the 11th century

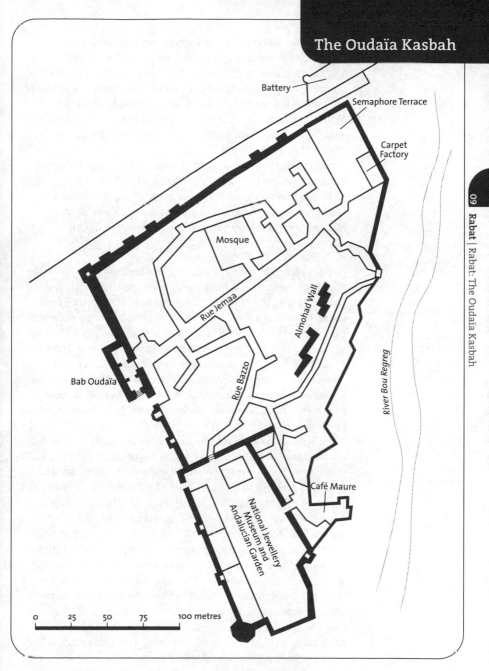

Battery

Semaphore Terrace

Carpet Factory

Mosque

Rue Jemaa

Almohad Wall

River Bou Regreg

Bab Oudaïa

Rue Bazzo

Café Maure

National Jewellery Museum and Andalucian Garden

0   25   50   75   100 metres

through to the marines of 20th-century France have all come from Western Europe. The kasbah walls are consequently 10ft thick and 30ft high. Built by the Almohads, they have been constantly reinforced, most noticeably by the Andalucian refugees and the Alaouite Sultans in the 17th and 18th centuries.

The name Oudaïa is a comparatively recent innovation. The Oudaïas were one of the Bedouin Arab tribes that entered southern Morocco in the 13th century. They became clients of the Alaouite sherifs from the Tafilalt, and were an important source of strength in the meteoric rise of Moulay Rachid to the throne. Moulay Ismaïl sent part of the tribe to the Rabat kasbah to keep an eye on the Andalucians and to campaign against the Zaer, a truculent Berber hill tribe.

Today some thirty families inhabit the kasbah, among them a handful from the US and Europe. Many of the houses are painted a light blue to protect against mosquitoes, giving the village a strongly maritime flavour. The area is usually cleared of non-Muslims on Friday afternoon before the Muslim Sabbath.

Bab Oudaïa

The approach to the Bab Oudaïa is up a broad stairway from the Souk el Ghezel to the kasbah. The gate was constructed in the late 12th century by the Almohad Sultan Yaacoub el Mansour. Though capable of defence it has an obvious ceremonial purpose and this side of the kasbah is not a first line of defence: the city walls screen the land to the west and the coast to the north. Instead, the Bab Oudaïa overlooks the medina, and formed the entrance to the original Almohad palace complex in the kasbah. The sultan's gate had a role in Moorish society not far removed from an ancient forum. Here petitioners would wait, assemblies and meetings take place and justice be seen to be dispensed.

The Bab Oudaïa is one of the accepted masterpieces of Moorish architecture. The puritanism and self-confidence of the Almohad creed, rather than restricting artistic expression, encouraged a triumphant return to first principles. The powerful impression that you receive from the gate is not achieved by either great size, expensive materials or lavish decoration but by an instinctive sense of balance, proportion and inner tension. At one level you have the simple, clear, strong form of a horseshoe arch cut through a stone wall and flanked by two rectangular towers. At a second level the veneer of exuberant decoration seems to float out from the stone in an abstraction of pure form. The traditional Islamic decorative design has been cut into the same strong ochre-rose stone as the gatehouse, the bold-cut reliefs casting dark, contrasting shadows against the evening glow of burnt gold. Two bands surmount a false circular arch, with the corner spaces balanced by two stylized scallop-shell palmettes surrounded by bevelled serpentine forms. The false outer arch is decorated with a distinctive band of *darj w ktarf*, that ubiquitous leaf-like profile of interlocking arches. The superior bands each continue the shell motif, one with a calligraphic layer and the upper band with a shell-studded relief line of stalactite arches. The genius of the whole is in the subtle relation of decoration to form. The decorative arch discreetly indicates with its diffuse edge the circumference of a circle whose diameter is exactly half the width of the square formed by the top lintel that includes the two flanking towers. A few minutes spent absorbing this tension, pursuing the clean form defined by the decorative skin, is to enter into a form of meditation. The **gatehouse** is composed of two halls, with the inner gate set at a right angle to its more celebrated brother. It is often used for exhibitions and may at other times be closed, but at such times an arch to the right serves as the entrance to the kasbah. The Bab Oudaïa is one of the few spots in Rabat where young men importune you to be your guide. This must be a hard task, as the Kasbah is small, safe and easy to find your way around.

Inside the Kasbah

The kasbah interior is a delightful whitewashed Andalucian village built by the refugees from Hornachos, who also fortified the gatehouse roof in their feud with their fellow Andalucian refugees in the medina.

The central street, the Rue Jemaa, passes the kasbah **mosque**, La Jamaa el Atiq, founded by Abdel Moumen in 1150, and the oldest in Rabat. The minaret was restored in 1700 and the mosque repaired by Ahmed el Inglizi, an English renegade who worked for Sultan Sidi Mohammed (1757–90). Farther on is the semaphore terrace (*plateforme du sémaphore*), a signal station that now provides an intriguing view over the entrance to the Bou Regreg estuary and across to Salé. A storehouse on the right built by the mad Sultan Moulay el Yazid at the end of the 18th century now houses a carpet factory. Below the platform there are further defensive walls and a round tower refortified in 1776 by Sidi Mohammed after the French bombardment. The chief defence of Rabat-Salé remained the estuary sand bar, which sealed the harbour from any deep-keeled sailing vessels. The Atlantic swell, the savage cliffs and outlying rocks made naval bombardments in the age of sail a difficult operation. Walk down from the high walls of the kasbah to the beach and there are a couple of restaurants overlooking the ocean. But, for a drink, you would be best to go to Café Maure in the former Palace Museum (*see* below).

National Museum of Jewellery and Andalucian Garden

open Wed–Mon 9–4.30 (closed half an hour for lunch); closed Tues and national hols; adm

The National Museum of Jewellery and the Andalucian Garden

The former Palace Museum is now the National Museum of Jewellery. Its former highlights – geometrically-patterned ceramics, a cartload of richly-coloured rugs and several wardrobes' worth of armour, robes and blankets – all remain in storage, and their future remains uncertain. The galleries of the old palace now gleam with glittering treasures spanning several centuries.

The exhibits are in rooms around the Andalucian Garden, which can be approached from either of two archways below the Bab Oudaïa, and also from the kasbah. Rue Bazzo, the second turning on the right from the central Rue Jemaa in the kasbah, takes you downhill by a beautiful twisting path to the museum. You pass by the Café Maure, enclosed in a secretive terrace between the museum garden and the estuary ramparts. It is a delightful place, with tiled benches and rush mats, where you can sip mint tea and consume plates of sticky cakes as you watch the estuary traffic.

Sultan Moulay Ismaïl built this palace between 1672 and 1694. It is a walled enclosure within the kasbah area, the delightful garden it contains cut through by a number of traditional pebble-paved paths. The museum is housed in two rooms on the western side of the garden as well as in the palace apartments. At the heart of the palace stands a cool courtyard paved in terracotta and green tiles, filled by the sound of a central marble fountain gently trickling into a basin. This is enclosed within a whitewashed arcade to form a heavenly vision of Moorish taste.

Some of the jewellery on display is exceptional and it begins with prehistorical and then Roman pieces before a room off to the right showcases lustrous 19th-century jewellery from Fez and more striking, robust examples from the Sahara. The waterfall necklaces are especially impressive. The room off to the left displays fabulous ivory-inlaid guns, bejewelled daggers and a 19th-century diadem.

The Hassan Mosque

Hassan Mosque
open 8am–dusk; free; daily guard ceremony at 5pm. Modest dress required.

For eight centuries the unfinished Hassan Tower has loomed above Rabat. It is the minaret of the Almohad Grand Mosque, the truncated pillars of which stretch out in a great rectangular field below. The mosque had fallen into disrepair and was a bramble-covered ruin when Leo Africanus visited Rabat in 1500, but it was not until the great earthquake of 1755 (the same one that shattered Lisbon) that the arches and pillars of the mosque were thrown down. More recently, on the southern edge of the site a white **mausoleum**, **mosque** and **library** have been built on a raised terrace to the memory of King Mohammed V.

The Hassan Tower

🛈 **Hassan Tower**

Poised on the high escarpment above the river the tower looks particularly magnificent as you approach Rabat by the bridge from Salé. It has great solidity, a lordly purpose and, in its unfinished state, a noble flaw that does not distract from the beauty of its proportions or the decoration of boldly carved tracery.

The tower was built between 1195 and 1199 by the Almohad Sultan Yaacoub el Mansour as the centrally aligned northern pivot of his grand mosque. It was to be the conclusion of a building programme that included the Koutoubia in Marrakesh and the Giralda in Seville. The floor of the mosque was raised and levelled from the surrounding ground so that the tower has two heights: 50m from the natural level of ground on its northern wall and 44m from the raised mosque floor of the southern wall. Each face of the tower is different, with a subtle movement of relief arches and interlaced decoration that is based on two classic designs brought to Almohad Morocco from the sophisticated culture of Andalucía. Inside, a ramp rather than a staircase ascends through six chambers that become more ornately decorated the farther you climb. This ramp deliberately echoes the Samarra Mosque in Iraq, which was acknowledged to be the biggest in the world. It was built in AD 850 and allowed the caliph to ride up to the summit on horseback on an external ascending ramp and call his army to Friday prayers. Behind the tower there is a staircase that leads down to a tomb for the unknown warrior, and a small additional mosque dedicated jointly to all the many previous ruling dynasties of Morocco.

The Mosque Ruins

The ruins of the Hassan Mosque and that of Samarra in Iraq are still among the largest in the world. Yaacoub el Mansour, who ruled over the entire western half of the Islamic world, with an empire that stretched from Spain to Libya, deliberately attempted to build a mosque that would vie with the finest efforts of the great cities of the East.

The rectangular plan of the mosque measures 183m by 139m, and was crossed by a forest of aisles: 21 longitudinal spans and 28 laterals that multiply into 312 marble columns and 112 stouter arch-bearing pillars. Three arcaded courts open to the sky broke this massive roofline. The open court nearest the tower, the *sahn* or washing area, had rows of fountains that played into marble basins and were fed from eleven huge cisterns hidden beneath the floor. There were four doors in this northern wall and six on the eastern and western sides. The central 'nave' leading up to the *mihrab* was designed to be significantly wider, to draw the worshippers' attention to the direction for prayer. It is just possible now to imagine the splendour of the interior, by ignoring the irritating modern paving and transforming the truncated remnants into the shifting vistas of columns, flooded with arcaded pools of harsh sunlight and the mass of genuflecting warriors that filled it for just a few years.

The Mausoleum

King Mohammed V's tomb has a traditional and distinctive green-tiled pyramidal roof capped with a triplet of golden spheres. A broad ornate staircase leads up to it from the southern end of the old mosque. Royal guards in scarlet with a white burnous patrol the arcade of Italian white marble, with its four arches leading to the balcony of the royal *koubba*. The sarcophagus is a block of white onyx from the mountains of the Hindu Kush set in a sea of polished black marble. A scholar mutters verses from the Koran in one corner, or dozes. Heraldic banners from all the provinces and towns of Morocco are suspended in serried ranks under the balcony, and a bronze chandelier, which weighs one ton, hangs from the roof. The decoration of the ascending ceiling must be the last word in gilded ornate. The king's sarcophagus has been accompanied by that of his youngest son, the genial Prince Moulay Abdullah, since his death in 1983.

The mausoleum was designed by a Vietnamese architect, Vo Toan, and finished in 1971. Aesthetically it must be considered something of a disaster. It is impressive only in the lavish use of luxurious materials, which expresses the Moroccan people's great regard for the king who led them in their struggle for independence. He has already assumed an almost holy status, and it is traditional in Morocco that the interiors of saints' shrines should be decorated as richly as a community can afford. On a lower level of the terrace a mosque has been constructed, its three handsome doors and *mihrab* arranged on the same axis as the ancient mosque. The colonnade of finely sculpted white marble from Carrara stands atop a library dedicated to every aspect of the reigning Alaouite dynasty.

The *Ville Nouvelle* (New Town)

The Boulevards

The major French-designed public buildings of Rabat are all found along or around the Avenue Mohammed V, the grand boulevard that connects the medina with the royal palace. Their architecture combines Egyptian, classical and Moorish elements to create an impression of order and stability. The PTT ministerial building contains a small **postal museum**, mainly a stamp collection, which is open during office hours. Rue al Mansour ad Dahbi leads off to the Théâtre National Mohammed V, opposite which is the **Triangle de Vue**, a pleasant, restful urban garden created in 1920. The northern corner contains the walls of a ruined 18th-century mosque and a number of tombs.

Postal Museum
open during office hours

Farther down Avenue Mohammed V is the terracotta-coloured and U-shaped **parliament building** (*Chambre des Représentants*). Opposite the station, Rue Abou-Nan leads to Place Sahat al Golan and the striking **Catholic Cathedral of St Pierre.** Two palisade-like towers emerge from a totally white nave; the windows and lintels have been decorated with geometric shapes in brick in a deliberately Islamic borrowing.

The Walls and the Bab er Rouah

The 5km **Almohad wall** encloses the kasbah, medina, palace and *ville nouvelle*, and has five city gates surviving in some form: the Bab Al Alou, Bab Al Had, Bab er Rouah, Bab Makhzen and Bab Zaers. The section between the Bab Al Had and the Bab er Rouah on Ave Ibn Tumert provides a pleasant 1km walk; the ochre battlements are decorated with flowering plants and clusters of palm trees.

The **Bab er Rouah**, 'the gate of the winds', was built in the same era as the Bab Oudaïa, and is the only true surviving Almohad structure that is comparable with it. Set above Place An Nasr, isolated from the traffic flow, the two massive surrounding stone bastions still allow you to envisage its central defensive role. The stone carving in this exposed position is still carefully balanced and controlled, with a ring of concentric engaged arches rippling out from the gate and enclosed by an ancient scroll of the Koran in Kufic script. The eastern face of the gate has an even lighter cut of stone with a delicate bed of floral and vegetable tracery supporting a palmette. The blend of elegant fantasy, tension of design and the gate's purpose in defence are reinforced by the interior chambers. Four rooms with elegant cupolas inevitably force visitors into a series of dizzying turns. The rooms are open periodically for **exhibitions** and for the moment are as close to a national gallery of art as there is in Morocco. If they are open at all the hours will be 8.30–12 and 2–8.

Going back into the city from the gate you face the **As Sounna Grand Mosque**, the minaret of which dominates the skyline of the New Town. It was built by Sidi Mohammed in the 18th century and has been the victim of frequent restorations.

The Royal Palace

The southeastern corner of the Almohad defences was selected as the site for a new palace in the 18th century, and a park was enclosed behind the Grand Mosque. Constantly altered and improved, the palace was almost entirely rebuilt by the late King Hassan, who also extended the grounds behind the main block to include a private golf course, enclosed by a new stretch of the city wall. Many of the chief offices of state are housed within the walls and it is very much a working palace. You can go into the grounds, but don't wander off the central avenue.

Through the ornamental northern gate, on the left, is the **Lycée Moulay Youssef** and a small suburb for past and present employees of the king. On the right are the stables, an exercise paddock and the princes' school, and then the open *méchouar*, or assembly place. The building on the right is the Ministry of the *Habous* (responsible for religious foundations). The outer wings of the main block contain the house of the president of the council and cabinet offices. A mosque, the supreme court, an oratory and the central **mausoleum of Moulay Hassan** coexist with the various royal apartments. The mosque on the left, Ahl Fas, is used for the official Friday royal prayers when the king as imam rides the short distance from the palace in a carriage and returns riding on a horse, his brow shaded from the sun by a crimson parasol of state. This procession, a weekly ritual for past sultans, is now rarely performed, and the 12.30pm cavalcade will be advertised well in advance. The southern gate leads into the Blvd Ad Doustour. If you turn left, the southern Almohad wall leads to Bab Zaers, from where you can return to the New Town or take the turning right to go into the Chellah.

The Archaeological Museum (Musée Archéologique)

🌟 **Archaeological Museum**

open Wed–Mon 9–4.30; adm

This small but excellent museum is the major attraction of the *ville nouvelle*. To reach it, take the Rue Moulay Abdul Al Aziz from the As Sounna Grand Mosque and turn right on to Rue al Brihi. The museum is the low, modern building on the corner. It has more archaeological remains than any museum in Morocco.

The **central hall** contains a large marble statue that was discovered at Sala and has been identified with King Juba II or his son Ptolemy. The handsome marble torso beside it was recovered from Volubilis and considered to be from the 2nd century AD. Around the walls are the results of the excavations at the microlithic site of Taforalt, and Neolithic child burials from Skhirate and Harhoura from about 4000 BC.

The **first floor** has a chronological collection of artefacts extracted from Sala Colonia, in four cases. The first contains bronze fragments of sculptures, a little bust of Juba II, an ivory cylinder with four carved scenes and a representation of Apollo; the second contains ceramic shards and coins from the excavations; the third holds funerary objects from the classical period; and the fourth contains objects from Islamic Chellah. The next exhibits demonstrate the often overlooked survival of the classical sites into recent history, with Christian and Jewish cult objects and relics of Islamic occupation up to the 14th century.

Recent archaeological digs reflected in the museum have concentrated on old Islamic sites. Finds from two towns opposite the Spanish coast, Ksar-es-Seghir and Balyounesh (between Tangier and Ceuta), show the high state of Islamic civilization that these foundations of Ommayad Córdoba enjoyed from the 10th century. There is also pottery from Sijilmassa (south of Er Rachidia), from the 8th century, and fragments from the medieval sugar mill at Chichaoua (between Marrakesh and Essaouira). Going back down to the central hall, a small open-air courtyard on one side is lined with a random selection of carved stones from different epochs.

The greatest treasures of the museum are its **bronzes**, displayed in a special side hall (*no photography allowed*). The finest pieces are the 1st-century AD **bust of Cato the Younger**, probably modelled from the death mask of the orator, who preferred to die free under the Republic than live under an emperor, and the **bust of the young Berber man** with his hair bound by a fillet, which is another sculpture thought to be King Juba II, who married Cleopatra Selene, daughter of Anthony and Cleopatra.

The **Lustral Dionysius** is a superb full-length statue, a Roman copy of the original carved by the Greek master Praxiteles. The fisherman casting his net and the rider with his missing leg are further 1st- or 2nd-century Roman works. The bronze guard dog from Volubilis was discovered in 1916, and probably made during the reign of Hadrian in the 2nd century. In the glass cases further small bronzes can be seen – a horse and rider from Volubilis, a snake discovered in Banasa, a head of Oceanus from Lixus, and figurines of Eros and Bacchus. There are fine marble heads of Diana and of a Berber youth. In the extensive collection of classical objects, the military diploma given by the Emperor Domitian to the cavalryman Domitius, found at Banasa, adds a poignant personal touch.

Chellah

 Chellah
open daily
9am–5.30pm; adm

One of the most beautiful of Morocco's many striking historical ruins, Chellah is not distinguished architecturally but has a wistful atmosphere of antiquity. The walled enclosure has bred strange beliefs – such as those of the buried treasure of Sultan Yaacoub, guarded by a prince of the Jinn, and of a fleeting visit from the Prophet Mohammed – but the factual narrative is fanciful enough. Freshwater springs flow out from this hill less than 500m from the brackish estuary of the Bou Regreg, and human settlement probably always clustered on this slope even before the Phoenicians founded Sala. This city, after a millennium of

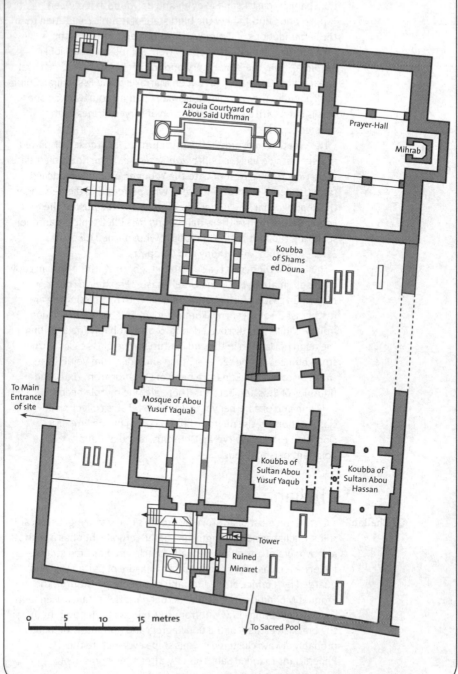

Zaouia Courtyard of
Abou Said Uthman

Prayer-Hall

Mihrab

Koubba
of Shams
ed Douna

To Main
Entrance
of site

Mosque of Abou
Yusuf Yaquab

Koubba of
Sultan Abou
Yusuf Yaqub

Koubba of
Sultan Abou
Hassan

Tower

Ruined
Minaret

0   5   10   15 metres

To Sacred Pool

existence, was reduced to a ruined mound in the 10th century, but continued to be used as a revered burial ground. The first Merenid Sultan, Abou Yusuf Yaqub, chose to build a tomb and mosque here, burying his wife, before joining her in his own grave in 1286. Later, the Merenid sultans enclosed it for the use of their own dead. Now their shrines are also reduced to picturesque ruin, and Roman Sala Colonia has been re-exposed by excavation. A lush growth of garden is established beside the path that leads down to the sacred spring, the Merenid tombs and along to the corner tower that looks over the meandering turns of the Bou Regreg river.

The Walls

The Merenid Sultan Abou Said Uthman (1310–31) began the walls, which were finished by his successor, Abou Hassan, in 1339 and embellished by Abou Inan (1348–59). The Zippoun Berber tribe were appointed as the hereditary protectors of Chellah, a duty which they continued for centuries after the fall of the dynasty.

The simple arch of the gate is enclosed by half-octagonal towers, their lean, twisted battlements supported by a delicate tracery of dripping stalactites. The Kufic script on the gate reads, 'I take refuge in Allah, against Satan, the stoned one', a useful invocation for the biers of dead sultans to pass under. The gate enforces a double twist before you enter the Chellah through a more orthodox Islamic horseshoe arch decorated with flanking shell motifs. A stairway descends steeply through the well-watered, luxuriant gardens, a confused mass of palm, bamboo, banana, hibiscus, fig and the drooping handkerchief leaves of the datura. On your right as you descend the flocks of storks have utterly colonized the trees and bushes. As the path opens out to reveal the sights, it is the feathered guardians you first notice, their nests perched on the top of old walls and minarets.

The Roman Ruins of Sala Colonia

To the left are the excavations of the Roman city. They occupy the northern half of the enclosure and border the Merenid necropolis. It is a confusing site because of the different levels of terraces. The heart of the excavation is the broad main street; look out for the foundations of the triumphal arch that crossed the thoroughfare. Immediately south of this are the intriguing remains of a bath complex with an elegant circular hall. The rest of the complex survives as the *hammam* restored by the Merenid Sultan Abou Inan.

Immediately above the arch stood the temple to Jupiter, though less than half of the 45m by 28m ground plan survives. This once overlooked the forum (the irregular plaza) at the end of the main street. Fragments of columns can be found which once enclosed this space with a shaded colonnade. Look around the inscriptions for there is one here dedicated to the Emperor Constantine (AD 306–37). This late date came as some surprise for it was believed Sala had fallen, like the other Roman cities in Morocco, to the barbarians in AD 280. The Limes frontier stood just south of the city, connecting the Ouad Akrach to the Atlantic, watched over by a fort on the Sidi Khalifa cemetery. The city was defended by walls from AD 144, but somehow survived as an isolated coastal outpost of Empire until the 5th century.

The Sacred Pool

A cluster of *koubbas* sit on a mound above a walled pool. Stubs of gutted candles can be found within. The venerated saints, though wrapped in Islamic green shrouds and familiar whitewashed shrines, belong to pre-Islamic cults of great antiquity. The pool is surrounded by old brick vaults, and drains out through a gravel stream that runs through an enclosing grove of drooping banana plants. Sacred black eels swim up to lurk in shaded recesses of the pool; infertile women peel boiled eggs (once sold by two boys who slept on the floor of the shrine above) to offer to them and an old lady sells charms and trinkets as well as food for the eels. Unmarried women still come too, eager for a *Baraka* (blessing) that will provide them with a husband. The scene is so strongly archetypal, such a graphic pagan survival in the shadow of ruined cities and royal tombs, that you instinctively check twice to discover if you are dreaming. That barren women should offer eggs, the universal symbol of fertility, to be devoured by phallic eels as emissaries of an ancient deity calls any visitor to compose a few lines of verse.

The Merenid Sanctuary

The sanctuary is easily recognized: its two locked minarets, of the mosque and *zaouia*, are invariably topped with a ponderously balanced pair of storks adding to their nest. Enter into the *sahn*, the small introductory courtyard, and proceed into the ruined **prayer-hall**. This and the adjoining tomb were the first structures built by Abou Yusuf Yaqub, in 1284. The *mihrab* is straight ahead, by the four columns of the pillared mosque. The ruined minaret is conspicuous to your right, near a pool. Pass either side of the *mihrab* to enter the necropolis.

This larger complex was designed by Sultan Abou Hassan (1331–48). Leo Africanus counted 32 Merenid graves here in 1500, but the number that can be distinguished today is very much less. The grave of the 'Black Sultan', Abou Hassan, lies against the outer wall to the right, within a *koubba* decorated with arches and tracery. The facing *koubba* is that of Sultan Yaqub, known locally as the 'Commander of the Jinn'.

The tomb of Chems ed Douna, 'the Light of Dawn', can be seen in the southeastern corner (bottom left as you stand by the *mihrab*) under a recess. Her long tombstone has been carved with verses celebrating the magnificence of her funeral. A Christian convert to Islam, she was a concubine of Abou Hassan and mother of Abou Inan, who eventually deposed his father. Abou Hassan was chased into the High Atlas and died an exile in the winter of the following year, but was buried decently, as you can see, in the Chellah in 1352 by his son. Abou Inan would himself choose to be buried on the heights overlooking Fez.

The sanctuary also contained a *zaouia*, a religious college which, though damaged, is in a better state than the mosque. The minaret is on the left, with the wash basins and latrines directly below. The court lined with cells faces a central rectangular pool with two sunken white marble shells for water jets that drained into the pool. The bases of the thin white marble columns can be seen with some surviving mosaic tilework. The Roman influence here is unmistakable.

A much smaller prayer-hall faces the *mihrab*, with a passage behind that allowed pilgrims to make the seven circuits that were believed by some to be equal to the pilgrimage to Mecca.

The beautiful soft red glow of the sanctuary wall shields a tranquil and formal garden formed by a double line of orange trees, fed with water from the sacred spring. From here you can look out over the walls to inspect tidy and fertile vegetable plots.

Information and Services in Rabat

ⓘ **Rabat >**
Regional tourist office,
22 Ave d'Alger, Hassan

ONMT
corner of Rue Oued El
Makhazine and Rue
Zalaga, **t** *0537 674013,*
www.onmt.org.ma

Rabat has a regional **tourist office** hidden away in Hassan (the embassy district) but you are unlikely to glean much more than a smile from the man on the front desk and will need to seek out signs of life upstairs, which may or may not lead to further enlightenment.

The **ONMT or national tourist office** is a little more helpful and can at least provide a map. It is open from 8.30am until 6.30pm Monday to Friday but takes an impressive three-hour lunch break from midday.

Communications

Maroc Telecom recently added an extra digit to all urban area codes in the country, meaning that Rabat's area code (formerly **t** 037) is now **t** 0537.

Public telephones are dotted around the streets but Maroc Telecom shops are generally easier and quieter and you'll find a few around town: on Blvd Mohammed V in the *ville nouvelle*, in Agdal and in the medina. For long-distance calls you are best to use your hotel and get a clear line.

Email and Fax

Internet cafés are especially common in Rabat and the easiest place to find them is in the *ville nouvelle*, if you do not have internet access in your hotel. Rue Tantan in the *ville nouvelle* a block east of the parliament is one option, so too is 44 Rue Abou Derr in Agdal or Interplanet at 6 Rue Ibn El-Yasmine, Ave de la Victoire. But your best bet is to try any of the better hotels.

Faxes can be sent from many hotels, the main post office on Blvd Mohammed V and from plenty of smaller – though less reliable – outlets too.

Post and Telegrams

The fabulous Central Post Office (*Mon–Fri 8am–4.30pm and Sat 8.30am–12pm*) is in the *ville nouvelle* on Ave Mohammed V next to Ave Soekarno. As well as all the usual post office services, it has a Western Union booth inside for money transfers.

Courier Services

DHL: 40, Ave de France, t 0537 779934. *Open Mon–Fri 8.30am–6.30pm and Sat 8.30am–12.30pm.*

Chronopost: 29 Rue Michlifen, Agdal, t 0537 673939.

FedEx: 23 Ave Tariq ibn Ziad Hassan, t 0537 661166.

TNT: Lôtissement Riad Old Mtaa, Secteur 1 no. 585, t 0522 276728, *accueil@tnt-maroc.com*.

Post Office: Ave Mohammed V (*see also above*). This is your easiest option as it has courier services on site.

Emergencies

Police t 19
Fire service t 16
Ambulance t 15
Telephone Enquiries t 160

Hospitals and Medical Care

Hospital Avicenna (or Ibn Sina), Place Ibn Sina in Agdal, t 0537 672871.

SOS Medecins, 6 Rue Moulay Slimane, t 0537 204914. A useful 24-hour clinic.

Polyclinique de Rabat, 8 Rue du Tunis, Hassan district, t 0537 204914. Another 24-hour clinic,although slightly inconveniently located in the embassy district.

Clinique des Orangers, 6 Ave Pasteur, t 0537 732424. In the Orangers district,

Pharmacies are all over town, particularly in the *ville nouvelle*, and several offer an all-night service should an emergency arise. Ave Moulay Rachid has a *Pharmacie de Nuit* (night pharmacy) and there are plenty more pharmacies on the streets of the *ville nouvelle*, including Ave Mohammed V.

Pharmacie Oudayas, Rue des Consuls, t 0537 727770. In the medina.

Pharmacie Souk Tahti, Rue des Consuls, t 0537 711290. Also handily located in the medina.

Maps

It is easier to track down maps in Rabat than in many other Moroccan cities – but a fairly simple map will do. Some of the bookshops are well-stocked (*see* under Books below) but the **Division de Cartographie** (*www.acfcc.gov.ma*) is exceptionally good, stocking a range of maps of the city. You generally need to order them two or three days in advance. The most recent is generally the annual **Carte Touristique** produced by the ONMT tourist office (*see* details above). But if you want a map with the medina streets in detail you may have to look harder. The Royal Geographical Society in London has done good Rabat maps in the past and it is worth checking their website for re-publication or reprinting plans.

Money

Banks are largely concentrated in the *ville nouvelle*, particularly along the Ave Mohammed V. This wide street boasts numerous banks, including Société Generale, BMCE (with a bureau de change) and Attijariwafa. Cashpoints (ATMS) remain the easiest way to get cash in Rabat. In the medina, Hotel Dorhmi (close to the medina's southwest corner) has a **cashpoint**. The larger hotels will exchange money and travellers' cheques for guests, although commission rates are generally high.

Shopping in Rabat

There are plenty of good reasons to go shopping in Rabat, especially if you are looking for the specialities of the region, notably **carpets** and **ceramics**. Prices are less negotiable in Rabat than in Fez or Marrakesh, so you can give your acting skills a rest.

Books and Prints

There are a couple of bookshops that stock English titles, as well as the newsstands found in the big hotels.

American Language Center, 4 Rue de Tanger, **t** 0537 767103. The bookshop attached to the language centre has a good range of books, most imported from the USA, but several featuring Moroccan themes. *Closed Mon*.
English Bookshop, 7 Rue el Yamama, **t** 0537 706593. A useful and central bookshop (not far from the train station) with a wide selection of books in English.

Carpets and Embroidery

Carpets are one of Rabat's specialities. While Berber rugs are less common than in Marrakech, the Arab rugs here are more plentiful and more likely to be locally produced. As ever, you might begin at the **Ensemble Artisanale**, Rampe Tarik-al-Marsa, on the coastal road just south of the Andalucian gardens. The best area to buy carpets is **Rue des Consuls** just next door: there is still a twice-weekly **carpet auction**, held Mondays and Thursdays, on this street.

Rabat has a colourful tradition of embroidery and the best area to hunt down shawls, linen and the like is the **Souk es Sebat**, which runs off from the south side of the Rue des Consuls.

Jewellery

There is jewellery to be had in Rabat but you are much better off looking in Fez. The **Souk es Sebat** is, again, the place to try. You can still buy more 'African' jewelry this far north and it might be worth trying the Mellah for some finer pieces.

Iron, Brass and Copper

The best of Moroccan metalwork lies further east in Meknès and Fez but you can pick up good deals in the main souks here. Lanterns, bowls, paperweights, daggers and more are all available. **L'Art Moderne** on Rue des Consuls offers a more modern take by recycling used metal to make traditional products.

Musical Instruments

Souk es Sabat has a couple of shops where you can find ouds, *darbuka* drums, tambourines and more. Although not a place to buy anything high quality, these market stalls and shops offer up all sorts of good musical instruments to take home in your luggage as presents, especially for children.

Woodwork and Leatherwork

As with so many traditional Moroccan goods on sale in Rabat, the leather and wooden goods on sale in the souks here are from other parts of the country. Nevertheless, the range is impressive and there are still good deals to be found, especially for basic leather goods like belts, wallets or colourful slippers (*babouches*).

Sports and Activities in Rabat

Health Clubs

Hotels are going to be your easiest option for this but beyond them you have two choices. Either there are the inexpensive and basic iron-man gyms with music blaring as young men tone themselves despite the heat or there are the luxury health and spa centres. For the former, there is one on the main coastal road just as it swings west from the Andalucian gardens (before it turns south down the coast next to an attractive hotel). For the smarter clubs, the **Ritz Carlton**, **Sofitel** and **Splendia** hotels all offer health clubs and spas which are available to non-guests for a fee.

Running

Rabat is a good place to run thanks to the coastline, which you might follow south from the kasbah. Running through the *ville nouvelle* is fairly easy too. There's an attractive **park** for running off Blvd Ad Dostour with a popular 2-mile circuit. Another good place for a jog is the forested area by the Dar Es Salaam golf course (beyond the Chellah).

Surfing and Swimming

There are a couple of surf clubs below the northern wall of the medina if you want to try the waves but you are best to head out of town to the attractive **Temara Plage** 13km southwest. The locals prefer the popular **Plage des Nations** (*see* p.281) to the north of Rabat, which is better for swimming than surfing.

If you prefer not to take to the sea, the **municipal swimming pool** is on the coastal road about a mile and a half southwest of Rabat-Agdal train station. Several of the hotels have pools, including Le Dawliz (see p.280) in Salé and the Sofitel (see below) in Rabat, close to Ave Mohammed V and the Royal Palace.

Where to Stay in Rabat

Hotels and riads fill up quickly throughout the year in Rabat and it is advisable to find a room early in the day or book in advance. Rabat is a fairly hassle-free city to walk around and so there is no need to buy the protective shelter of a top-class hotel. Anywhere clean and central should do for all but the most luxury-addicted travellers. In general, ease and comfort are the virtues of the *ville nouvelle* hotels, while the medina and kasbah hotels offer a better location and sometimes a fabulous view. But if you were going to stay in the *ville nouvelle* in any one of Morocco's cities, you would be best to choose Rabat, with its grand French colonial administrative buildings, broad boulevards and gracious familiarity with the needs of visiting diplomats and politicians.

Luxury

Sofitel Rabat Jardin des Roses, PO Box 450 Souissi, **t** 0537 675766, *www.sofitel.com*. West of Chellah and the Royal Palace, the Sofitel (formerly the Hilton) is a few minutes by taxi from the centre of town but un-doubtedly a place to escape and be pampered. It is set amid Andalucian-style gardens, with pool, spa and fitness centre.

La Tour Hassan Méridien, 26 Rue Chellah, **t** 0537 239000, *www.latourhassan.com*. Founded in 1914, and recently expensively renovated, this occupies a central streetside position in the heart of the city. It has an elegant enclosed garden courtyard, the Moroccan La Maison Arabe restaurant, a bar and the contented hum of a busy social and business centre.

Villa Mandarine, Rue Ouled Boussba, Souissi, **t** 0537 752077, *www.villamandarine.com*. Surrounded by orange groves, this is less convenient

⭐ Riad Oudaya >>

for the sights but an undeniably gorgeous hotel, not least thanks to its palm-shaded gardens and swimming pool.

Expensive

Dar El Kebira, 1 Impasse Belghazi, Ferrane Znaki Medina, (just west of the Rue des Consuls), **t** 0537 724906, *www.darelkebira.com*. This is an elegant Andalucian-style riad with an attractive terrace and sensitive interior decoration. It lies not far from the kasbah and the staff are exceptionally accommodating.

The Golden Tulip Farah, 10 Place Sidi Maklouf, **t** 0573 237400/734747, *www.goldentulipfarahrabat.com*. This has everything you could ask for from a modern, international hotel, with a superb position on Place Sidi Maklouf, overlooking the estuary, medina and the Hassan Tower. This 193-bedroom, 8-suite hotel has plenty of rooms overlooking the Bouregreg River and a wonderful terrace. On a spare but elegant roof terrace is a pool and a range of excellent views.

Riad Dar Baraka, 26 Rue de la Mosquée, **t** 0537 730362, *www.darbaraka-rabat.com*. This is unimaginably well-placed at the top of the Kasbah and has a terrace overlooking the last stretch of the river and Salé beyond. Fig trees and *zellij* mosaics add to the appeal but you will need to book well in advance, as Baraka has just two rooms. The meals are worth staying in for.

Riad Dar al Batoul, 7 Derb Jirari-Laalou (in the medina), **t** 0537 727250. A beautiful courtyard and two terraces make this 200-year-old riad an appealing medina option. Original mosaic and geometrical designs enrich the romantic setting still further. Breakfast is the only meal served here.

Riad Oudaya, 46 Rue Sidi Fateh, **t** 0537 702392, *www.riadoudaya.com*. Location and décor make this an exceptional riad, set around an elegant courtyard with open fires. Food is excellent, service less so and mod cons in short supply.

Soundouss, 10 Place Talha, Agdal, **t** 0537 675959, *www.soundousshotel.ma*. The Art Nouveau design makes this a stunning building and worth a night, even if the service is variable at best and the wifi elusive.

Moderate

There is a good selection of moderately priced hotels (with bars and restaurants). Those that are not riads are often more popular with Moroccans than with tourists.

Balima, Ave Mohammed V, t 0537 707967, *www.hotel-balima.net*. Very well-equipped for its price, as Balima has a restaurant, bar, disco, garden and terrace, as well as offering connecting family rooms. Charmingly dated and probably swarming with the ghosts of French politicians past, the former *grande dame* of the *ville nouvelle* overlooks the parliament and is close to the station.

Hotel Bou Regreg, Ave Hassan II and Rue Nador Rabat, t 0537 724110, *www. hotelbouregreg.ma/presentation-ang. htm*. This may not be the best offer in town and its staff may not run a famously tight ship but the Bou Regreg has excellent views and lies just opposite the medina walls. It has a restaurant, piano bar, terrace and even a disco.

Le Pietri, 4 Rue Tobrouk, t 0537 707820, *www.lepietri.com*. A pleasantly renovated modern hotel with a very friendly staff. The price is good value for the services and comforts on offer.

★ Royal Hotel Rabat >

Royal Hotel Rabat, 1 Rue Amman, t 0537 721171, *www.royalhotelrabat. com*. A great budget option, with a central location, spacious – if plain – rooms, and delightful staff. The décor is a little dated, but it is spotless throughout. There is also a simple restaurant, offering good value set menus.

Inexpensive–Cheap

There are several cheaper options in the medina, mostly around the market inside the Bab el Had, the medina's central western gate. Some of these offer rooms for little more than 10 dirhams a night, and can be found mostly just to the east and north-east of the market.

The following hotels are a notch or two up the price scale, and offer a commensurate level of service and facilities.

Hotel Majestic, 121 Ave Hassan II, t 0537 722997, *www.hotelmajestic.ma*. A well-liked budget option as it has large rooms, is centrally located and is kept well by amenable staff. Book well in advance.

Hotel des Oudaïas, 132 Blvd El Alou, t 0537 264043. This sits at the northwest corner of Rabat. Across one road is the kasbah, across the other the Atlantic. A colourful place with a gym next door (not part of the hotel), this offers a good deal in a convenient spot, especially for medina shopping, surfing or a visit to the Andalucian gardens opposite. Try for a room with a view.

Hotel Splendid, 8, rue Ghazza, Ave Mohammed V, t 0537 723283. Another good choice for less spendthrift travellers, the Splendid is clean, central and is centred on a courtyard. Exceptional value.

Eating Out in Rabat

Some of the best options for dining out in Rabat are found in hotels and riads. For example, a very pleasant afternoon can be spent at the Sofitel (*see* above) garden and you might choose to enjoy a buffet lunch while you are there.

Expensive

Borj Eddar, Plage de Rabat, t 0537 701500, *www.borjeddar.com*. Overlooking the sea, Borj Eddar is a wonderful place to eat seafood and enjoy the Atlantic breeze.

Dinarjat, 6 Rue Belgnaoui, t 0537 704239, *www.dinarjat.com*. Close to the kasbah and boasting exceptional Moroccan cooking, the Dinarjat offers tables draped in white tablecloths in the sun-drenched 17th-century courtyard, or restful, shaded dining areas decorated in rich, muted colours flanking it. Best accessed from the car park on Ave El-Alou (where you should find the restaurant's flunky), entering the medina (as you walk northeast) two or three lanes after Rue Sidi Fateh.

Le Grand Comptoir, 279 Ave Mohammed V, t 0537 201514. A resoundingly successful French affair, stylish and sleek, with live jazz a

★ Dinarjat >>

★ Le Grand Comptoir >>

regular feature in the upstairs bar but the real highlight the excellent food. Stick with the old French favourites. The restaurant itself is attractive and well cared for.

The Koutoubia, 2 Rue Pierre Parent, **t** 0537 701075. This is one of the oldest restaurants in Rabat, with a gaily painted interior and separate bar. It has been living off its reputation for decades, but can still throw some memorable evenings and is good for the traditional Moroccan favourites.

Moderate

The greatest concentration of bistro-like French restaurants licensed to serve alcohol is just south of the train station on or just off Ave Moulay Youssef. If you choose the *menu du jour* this can work out very reasonably at around 50dh, though you can spend much more.

La Bamba, 3 Rue de Tanta, **t** 0537 709839. A good Middle Eastern menu with low prices, La Bamba is close to Ave Mohammed V and makes for a hearty stop. It's also good for paella and tapas.

Le Crépuscule, 10 Rue Med El Jazouli, **t** 0537 732438. This medina stop is where to buy tasty crêpes.

⭐ **Dar Naji** >

Dar Naji, Rue Jazirat Al Arab, *www. darnaji.cn.ma*. This wonderfully conceived restaurant is a good place to stop for lunch or simply for tea, since it functions as both a restaurant and a tea house. Located next to the fabulous Bab Al Had.

La Mamma, 6 Rue Tanta, **t** 0537 707329. An excellent choice of all your favourite Italian dishes and pizzas is available at La Mamma, which has been going for four decades and remains very good at what it does.

Paul, 82 Ave des Nations Unies, **t** 0537 672000. A pâtisserie and bakery in the *ville nouvelle*, this makes an attractive place for a pit-stop.

Riad Oudaya, 46 Rue Sidi Fateh, **t** 0537 702392, *www.riadoudaya.com*. With a beguilingly hidden location, this is a wonderful place to enjoy an excellent Moroccan dinner. (See also under Where to Stay, above.)

Tagine wa Tangia, 9 Rue Baghdad, **t** 0537 729797. Close to Rabat-Ville

train station, TwT is inexpensive, family-run, broad-ranging and thoroughly Moroccan. Throw in the live music and alcohol licence and you have a good night ahead.

Inexpensive

As ever in Morocco, some of the most rewarding eating is to be found not in a formal restaurant but in the cheap café-restaurants scattered around the market area in from the Bab Al Had. These you can sniff out for yourself, but there are in addition a few specific café-restaurants nearby that are worth finding. The **El Bahia** is built into the Andalucian walls of the medina, approached along Ave Hassan II, halfway between the entrances to Rue Sidi Fateh and Ave Mohammed V. Take the cheap fixed menu or order a chicken or *kefta tagine* in the upstairs Moorish dining room or in the courtyard. Try Ave Mohammed V also, where you will find several local eateries just inside the medina gates. Be sure that you are not eating display food here.

Cafés and Bars

No visit to Rabat is complete without a visit to the **Café Maure**, tucked between the National Jewellery Museum of Oudaïa and the estuary. Amongst the cafés strung along Ave Mohammed V, **Le Petit Poucet** rates highly, and an evening spent 'people watching' in the café and bar of the **Balima Hotel** remains one of the city's chief entertainments. The **Café 7eme Art** on Ave Allal ben Abdallah is a lively place for a drink in the afternoon sun.

Just behind the Balima on Rue Tanta there is a more intense drinking scene in **La Dolce Vita**. The glass-fronted lobby of the **Terminus Hotel**, near the train station, is another good observation post for street life. Just up from here, along Ave Moulay Youssef, there is a string of busy bars: that of the **Hotel d'Orsay** as well as the ground floor of restaurants. On Place des Alaouites, opposite the train station and beneath the 'Siemens' sign, there is the wood-lined and overwhelmingly male **Henry's Bar**. **Le Puzzle** (79 Ave Ibn Sina) is a good bar to try in Agdal.

Salé

Salé has long maintained a separate identity from Rabat. Its great period of prosperity was under the Merenid sultans, who rebuilt the walls and constructed the *medersa* and other buildings. These medieval achievements still seem to express the spirit of the town, which consciously maintains a low-key and pious Islamic identity in contrast to the secular bustle of its neighbour.

History

The very name of Salé proclaims a past different from that of its neighbour. Local traditions assert that the citizens of the ancient city of Sala Colonia settled the headland of Salé after their venerable home had been destroyed by the orthodox *rabat* garrison stationed in what is now known as the Oudaïa Kasbah of Rabat. Salé grew into a prosperous port city, until one terrible night Alfonso X of Castile descended like a wolf on the fold, attacking during the feast night of Aid es Seghir in 1260. The booty the Castilians captured was immense, the city was sacked and most of its citizens were killed or enslaved. Abou Yusuf Yaqub, the brother of the founder of the Merenid dynasty, hurried to the rescue of the city and reached Salé in one heroic day's ride from Taza. He was too late to rescue the city but succeeded in expelling the raiders, and in an emotional scene vowed to rebuild it. His actions helped establish the Merenids as credible rulers of Morocco, and Salé consequently became a cornerstone of Merenid pride. The sacked city was rebuilt with an energy and elegance which still marks its identity. While Rabat shrank to a village raided by the Portuguese in the 16th century, Salé according to Leo Africanus had '*all the ornaments, qualities and conditions necessary to make a city civil, and this in such perfection that it was visited by several generations of Christian merchants*'.

Old Salé maintained a troubled supremacy over the Andalucian settlements in Rabat in the dazzling days of the pirate Republic of the Bou Regreg, from 1629 to 1666, but then stagnated. The Alaouite sultans who came to power from 1668 preferred to live and build in Rabat. Salé has remained enviably unchanged over the years although a slew of new housing projects beyond the medina have brought many of Rabat's middle class across the Bou Regreg. But the old city centre seems impervious.

The Medina

Three streets, Boulevard Touil, Rue de la Grande Mosquée and the central Rue Souïka/Kechachin, provide sinuous crossings of the length of the old town, an under-visited network of twisting and

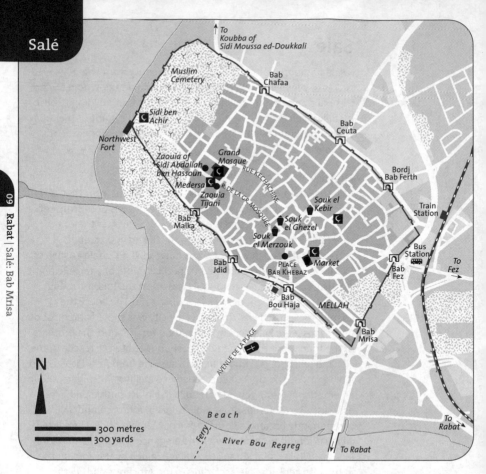

irregular streets. The streets wind past the white façades of houses that have little ornamentation other than strongly reinforced doors. The medina is entirely enclosed by walls and roughly rectangular in shape, 800m wide and 1,500m long; the northern coastal third is occupied by a large cemetery. Outside the walls Salé has grown greatly to the north and west, in a fairly dismal style, since Independence.

Bab Mrisa

This unmistakable massive arch is flanked by two elegant towers and decorated with floral tracery and sculpted inscriptions. It was built by Sultan Abou Yusuf Yaqub between 1260 and 1270, after the Castilian sacking of the city, in a similar style to the Almohad gates of Rabat. A reinforced canal led from the estuary through this water-gate into a basin within the city walls. Here the fleet moored in complete safety, surrounded by arsenals and dockyards.

Getting around Salé

There is hardly anywhere to stay in Salé, so most visitors base themselves in Rabat. A **fishing boat** will take you from the wharf below the Rabat medina across the Bou Regreg for a couple of dirhams. The Jaich el Malaki, also known by its old name of Avenue de la Plage, leads straight up from the Salé wharf to the medina through the Bab Bou Haja.

Grands taxis (*petits taxis* are restricted to either Rabat or Salé) or **buses** (**no.12, no.13** and **no.14** from Rabat's Place Melilla) will drop you farther along at the Bab Fez, which gives swift way to the Bab Khebaz.

The Mellah

The Jews were given this area after the canal had become hopelessly silted. They were moved, over the road to the north, when Moulay Ismaïl required this corner for a garrison of Abids, but expanded back again before the exodus after Independence.

The Souks

The **Bab Fez** is a natural point of entrance, with taxis, train and bus station clustered outside it. Stalls of grilled kebabs, and tables full of nuts, sweets and fruit are clustered in and around the portals. To the left a few streets down, Rue Dar Reghai takes you in a natural flow of pedestrians to the heart of the town. The stalls along the way are full of products for the local rather than the tourist market, for Salé has remained largely aloof from the world of hassles and quick sales. A number of tempting kitchens exist along this street and its extension, Rue Souïka. Here, as well as absorbing the colour and sounds, you can also taste the medina.

On the right is the tomb and mosque of Sidi Ahmed Hadji, a respected 17th-century *marabout*, venerated with gifts of tall green candles. The triangular **Souk el Kebir,** partly shaded by trees, is the main market in Salé. Piles of second-hand clothes are sorted through at the back whilst carpenters, leather-workers and slipper-makers create a delightful cacophony of sound and activity.

Christian slaves captured by the 'Sallee Rovers' of Rabat and Salé were often sold here. In spite of the many salacious-Orientalist tales that have circulated ever since, Christian women were commonly treated with a certain care and respect. Whether or not these rules were always adhered to is of course another matter, but in theory any proof of sexual interference from the captors gave automatic liberty to the captive, and married women – or those who, despite beatings, refused to embrace Islam – were occasionally returned. Barbary piracy was a business activity, which had its code of conduct.

To the left of the Souk el Kebir, just before some gates, a right-hand turn leads to Rue Haddadine, the blacksmiths' and tinkers' street that leads directly north to cross Rue Bab Sebta. To your left Rue Kechachine takes you on west past the workshops of the sculptors in wood and stone, and joiners' shops turning out headboards for beds and footboards for the wall benches that are found in most Moroccan homes.

Taking the left turn from the Souk el Kebir takes you to the kissaria, a small pocket of alleys where the most skilled artisans have their stalls. The **Souk el Ghezel**, the wool market, is an open space lined by shops where early in the morning, under the protection of canvas and a few trees, bales of wool are weighed from tripod stands and gently haggled over. The adjacent **Souk el Merzouk** is the quarter for the tailors, cloth merchants and embroiderers, whose young assistants create long trails of twisting silk. After the fountain on the right, look out for the door of the *Fondouq* **Askour**, the hospital and school founded by the Merenid Sultan Abou Inan in the 14th century. The courtyard is functional but the elaborate door is covered in a cascade of carved stalactites.

The Medersa and Grand Mosque

The main mosque is 300m on down Rue de la Grande Mosquée. Tailors' shops with their array of kaftans give way to the larger walled houses of the merchants, decorated with their Andalucian-style doorways. A small white-washed square has stairs leading up to the Grand Mosque and, on the left just past an 18th-century fountain, a gate into the *medersa*. The mosque was built in the reign of the Almohad Abou Yaacoub Youssef (1163–84). The clear lines of the doorways and the simple elegance of the carving contrast with the gates of the **Merenid** *medersa* built by the Black Sultan, Abou Hassan, in 1341. Here there is rich cedar- and plaster-carving, vivid paintwork and an overhanging roof over the arch.

Merenid medersa
open 9–12 and 2.30–6; adm

The building is much smaller than the great *medersas* of Fez, though the details are as lavish and exciting. In the central court a gallery of columns, decorated with contrasting designs and coloured faïence mosaics, leads your eye up to the area of delicately carved cream plaster that gives way to the crowning walls and hanging gallery of sombre carved cedar. The prayer-hall has a finely painted ceiling and the *mihrab* has some fine carved decoration. The courtyard is designed to sit in rather than pace around. A few minutes can be spent spotting the recurring motifs of Islamic decoration drawn entirely from the natural world – plants, flowers, fruit and shells.

The foundation stone introduces the one distracting secular tone, '*Look at my admirable portal, rejoice in my chosen company, in the remarkable style of my construction and my marvellous interior.*

The workers here have accomplished an artful creation with the beauty of youth...' Arabic poetry does not always translate well. The courtyard pillars would perhaps present a more serene interior if their distracting decoration were removed. Two galleries of cells can be explored, and do not miss the opportunity to get out on the roof with its view over the rooftops of the Salé medina across the estuary to Rabat, slipping the warden a tip for the privilege.

The Zaouia of Sidi Abdallah ben Hassoun

Through an arcade just to the left of the grand mosque is the door of the *zaouia* of Sidi Ahmed el Tijani decorated with geometric mosaics and carved plaster. At the back of the mosque is the *zaouia* of Sidi Abdallah ben Hassoun. A window allows you to look into the mausoleum, which was rebuilt in the 19th century. Each year on the afternoon of Mouloud, the Prophet Mohammed's birthday, a collection of large candles and complicated wax lanterns is escorted through the town in a great procession guarded by the guild of boatmen dressed as Turks or corsairs, and the saint's descendants and devotees carrying candles decorated with filigree and silk. The entire retinue deposit their offerings at the shrine, where they remain until the new year. Sixteen days later, Sidi Abdallah, Salé's patron saint, is venerated by all the religious brotherhoods, who sing chants, psalms and mystical exercises in his honour. Sidi Abdallah came from the south of Morocco but moved to Salé in order to avoid the distractions of tribal politics. He was respected during his lifetime and attracted many pupils before his death in 1604. The Sidi was adopted by sailors and travellers, who continue to visit the shrine for auguries to indicate the safety of their voyage.

The Cemetery

The cemetery extends west from Sidi Abdallah's shrine and a dirt track winds out across the large expanse of graves to the Northwest Fort, Borj Nord-Ouest, an 18th-century redoubt containing a number of bronze English and Spanish cannon. At the end of the bastion there is a good view across the estuary to Rabat. The track passes a number of simple whitewashed *koubbas*. The shrine nearest the fort is that of Sidi ben Achir, an Andalucian scholar and mystic who died in 1362. He has a great reputation for curing the sick and the mad, and in 1846 Sultan Abder Rahman built a series of lodgings for pilgrims to stay in as they await their cure. The reputation of the saint has not diminished, particularly among women. The old ladies will be upset if you walk too close, perhaps for your own benefit – the saint also has the power to wreck Christian ships along this coast.

Beyond the Walls

The Koubba of Sidi Moussa ed-Doukkali

The cliffs along the coast at Salé do indeed look evil to shipping. The Boulevard Circulaire that runs along the edge of the cemetery takes you out through the Bab Chafaa, from where the road continues above the sea. Patient men with long bamboo fishing poles perch above these high and dangerous cliffs. A 3km walk beside the shore will take you to the Koubba of Sidi Moussa ed-Doukkali, which Moulay Ismaïl carefully restored. This Sidi is greatly loved by the poor, who hold an enormous celebration in August in his honour. He voluntarily chose an ascetic life, grubbing along this shore for edible roots and sorting driftwood and debris to sell in order to buy fresh bread for the poor. He was also a skilled magician, and humbled the arrogant rich by miraculously flying to Mecca each year for the pilgrimage. Today the shore is lined with refuse, while shantytowns extend inland from the road.

The Gnaoua Kasbah

Just beyond the *koubba* is the kasbah of the Gnaoua, a *pisé* fortress built by Moulay Ismaïl to house his Abid troops – black Africans from Guinea, as the name still proclaims. The wind and the salt spray have etched weird patterns into the walls, and graffiti left by the Abid regiments or renegades with their captives can still be seen etched into the less-eroded sections.

Oulja Pottery

A rich deposit of clay has been discovered on the northern bank of the Bou Regreg estuary and there are now two dozen kilns at work in the pottery hamlet of Oulja, a 2km *petit taxi* ride from Salé. Rabat-Salé was a pottery-producing centre in the 17th, 18th and 19th centuries, and this function has re-emerged in the form of the **Complexe des Potiers**, open when the sun is out. This craft centre follows some of the traditional influences, as well as striking out in new directions. You can find the potters at the rear of the centre.

Where to Stay and Eating Out in Salé

You are best to stay the night back in Rabat as Salé only merits a morning of a traveller's time. The following options, all of which serve food:

Dawliz Hotel, Ave du Bouregreg, t 0537 883277, *www.ledawliz.com*(€€€). Smart, well-located, with a pool.

 The Repose >

The Repose, 17 Zankat Talaa, t 0537 882958, *www.therepose.com* (€€€). A beautifully restored riad in the medina, with hospitable owners who will arrange everything from splendid dinners to massages.

Riad Albahaca, 1 Rue Sidi Bel Achir Hassouni, t 0666 084919, *www.riadbahaca.com* (€€€). An elegant guesthouse, with wonderful sea views from the terrace.

Riad Dar El Mouhit, 12 Rue Lemfedel, t 0664 935869 (€€€). A charming riad, with obliging staff and local cuisine.

Day Trips from Rabat

Bouknadel Jardins Exotiques and Plage des Nations

It's a 1km drive off the Rabat–Kénitra highway to the most attractive and tranquil beach on this area of coast – the **Plage des Nations**. Coming from Rabat, stay on the old P2 road – not the new motorway – and it is 18km north of Salé. The beach's name is due to its status as a haunt of Rabat's diplomatic community, and it still retains a certain cachet, with the late-1960s Hôtel Firdaous sitting perfectly alone on the Atlantic shore (day visitors may use the facilities for a small charge). To get to the beach from Salé, there is a no.28 bus that leaves about every 20 minutes from Bab Mrisa and drops you beside the road for the beach or gardens. A place in a *grand taxi* will cost around 10dh, and take you right to the beach.

Musée Dar Belghazi
*on the Kénitra road,
t 0537 822178,
www.museebelghazi.
marocoriental.com;
open daily 8.30–6; adm*

The **Musée Dar Belghazi** stands close to the Plage des Nations turning, near the 17km milestone to Salé. This private museum, opened in 1995, was created by an architect, antique dealer and decorator with an eye for the more sumptuous elements of Moroccan culture: rich embroideries, metal gilt, splendid coffers and cascades of jewellery. The exhibits change as they are sold or lent to various other exhibitions and museums.

Bouknadel Jardins Exotiques
open daily 9–6; adm

The **Bouknadel Jardins Exotiques** are on the western side of the road, 12km from Rabat. Even if you are not wild about plants, the cool, shaded, intimate bamboo benches, the flowers, smells and tranquillity make this a whimsical and restful place. The gardens were created by the ingenious horticulturist and ecologist M. François in the 1950s, and at their peak held over 1,500 species. His verse thoughts on ecological principles and on his love for Morocco are found at the entrance, before a mass of hibiscus and red-hot pokers. The garden originally contained a zoo and an aquarium but

Around Rabat

Getting to and around Mohammadia

Mohammedia is most easily approached by train, with trains every half-hour from Casablanca and from Rabat (and a few super-early services too). The **station** looks out over a small square on Ave Hassan II which is also used by **taxis** and **buses**. This is directly behind the kasbah, and a one-kilometre walk north along Ave Abderrahmane Sarghini and Blvd Moulay Youssef will lead you directly down to the beach.

the cages are thankfully now empty, leaving a delightfully profuse series of gardens inhabited by birds, turtles and frogs. The site extends in a long, thin belt of four hectares between the road and the coastal dunes. There are three sections: an indigenous collection of Moroccan flora, a formal Islamic Andalucian garden and a collection of exotica from all over the world. The lush ecosystems of America, Japan, China, the Pacific, the Caribbean and southeast Asia have all been skilfully re-created in delightful confusion on this dry, sandy coastal plain. The network of bamboo bridges, stone walkways, root passages, ruined temples and pagodas is magnificently eclectic, definitely bizarre and saved from being kitsch by rapid weathering and luxurious overgrowth.

Mohammedia

Mohammedia does a surprising double act. It is on the one hand the centre of Morocco's oil business, with a refinery and an oil terminal on the western side of town, and on the other a swish summer beach resort with a 3km seafront promenade, casino, racecourse, a pretty kasbah quarter, a yacht marina and a terrific golf course. From June to September the town is full of families from Casablanca on holiday. If you are a golfer looking for a relaxed resort, without tourists and with a strongly Moroccan flavour, Mohammedia is probably made for you.

Though the oil terminal was opened only in 1960, Mohammedia has a long history as a port. It was known as Fédala to the medieval merchants of Europe. Their common trading pitch was taken over by the Portuguese, who briefly occupied the place at the turn of the 15th century. Local opposition soon forced them out, though they have left a memorial – the kasbah looks indigenous enough but was actually built by the Portuguese. It has been restored in recent years (although badly battered by floods in 2002) and now contains a pretty residential quarter whose neat pavements and window boxes are at happy variance with the usual medina street scene. Mohammedia was renamed in 1960 in honour of the king who brought independence to the country, Mohammed V.

The town has taken a battering in the last decade or so – literally, in 2002, when it øwas badly damaged by floods. There plans to construct a glossy marina and clean up the threatened coastline.

Where to Stay and Eating Out in Mohammedia

The best restaurants are congregated at the western end of town near the port. There are surprisingly few hotels, and none which can currently be recommended. Your best bet is to stay in Casablanca, which is only a 20-minute train ride.

Restaurant du Port, 1 Rue du Port, t 0523 325895 (€€€). Located, naturally, by the harbour, is easily the most famous place to eat in town; you can gorge on fresh fish simply grilled on charcoal in the garden courtyard.

Sans Pareil, Rue Farhat Hached, t 0523 322855 (€€€). Equally popular as the above (despite the name), this serves French food.

Frégate, Rue Oued-Zem, t 0523 324447 (€€). Another good option.

Casablanca

This city is a surprise for those who have been fed with picturesque images of Marrakesh and Fez. For it is a modern city, with a skyline dominated by towering office blocks, and sprawling suburbs ringed in the approved metropolitan style by a motorway ringroad. The streets are jammed with cars and the five-storey apartment block is the dominant housing form. The pavements are filled with besuited figures and women dressed in international styles such as you would find in any southern European city.

Casablanca dominates the national economy: it is the chief port, the financial, industrial, commercial and manufacturing centre of the kingdom. This was all achieved within the 20th century – from a town of 20,000 in 1900, the Casablanca conurbation is now home to 3,500,000. In North Africa, only Cairo can compete with Casa in growth, verve and vibrancy, but it is this city facing out to the Atlantic that seems the more orientated to the international pattern of trade and sympathetic to Western influences. At times, as you cruise down a palm-fringed, car-packed boulevard to catch glimpses of the sun setting in a western ocean, you could be forgiven for thinking yourself in California. The French administration must be credited with much of this achievement. They carefully planned the new Atlantic face of Morocco in their own image, while allowing the xenophobic cities of the interior to wither into mere historical monuments.

If Casa is a source of fascination to the political observer and speculation for the businessman, it has tended to be dismissed by far too many travellers. A pleasant day can be spent taking a taxi out to the vast Mosque of Hassan II, the only working mosque in Morocco open to non-Muslims; or a stroll through the grand streets of the French-built *ville nouvelle* and the stone arcades of the suburban Nouvelle Medina, Morocco's most elegant and hassle-free souk. No one with an eye for colour or street theatre should miss a stroll through the packed streets of the Ancienne

Getting to and around Casablanca

By Air

Many international flights to Morocco, and most domestic flights, use the **Mohammed V Airport** (*www.onda.ma*), 30km out of town on the main P7 route to Marrakesh. By far the easiest way to get there is on the direct **train** link that takes you from either the Port or Voyageurs railway stations in Casablanca to the main airport concourse in half an hour. There are trains every hour, running from 6.38am until 10.38pm (and from 6.50am to 10.50pm the other way). CTM also run a connecting bus service that takes you direct from the airport to the central CTM station. In addition there is a *grand taxi* rank, though the taxi fare, at around 200dh, compares badly with a train ticket of 35dh.

By Rail

Arriving by train you can get off at the port station, Casa Gare du Port, or Casa Gare des Voyageurs. The Gare du Port is admirably sited by the main coast road and fronts on to Blvd Houphouët-Boigny (formerly Blvd Mohammed el Hansali, and still shown as such on many maps), which leads 500m straight to Place des Nations Unies (formerly Place Mohammed V). This is the hub of the city and the nexus of its major avenues, as well as the main entrance to the medina. The Gare des Voyageurs leaves you with a half-hour walk or a taxi ride into the centre of town. Most, but not all, trains from Rabat (1hr) arrive at the Gare du Port. There are 18 a day, the last one leaving from Rabat for Casa Port at 9pm.

By Bus

The **CTM station**, t 0522 541010, *www.ctm.ma*, with its café and separate luggage check-in, is at 23 Rue Léon Africain, in between the central thoroughfares of Ave des F.A.R. and Rue Allal ben Abdallah. Buses leave for Rabat (1hr 30) every half hour (same fare as the train) and almost every hour for Fez (5h 30) and Marrakesh (4 hours).

By Car and Taxi

Walking around the city centre is one of the major charms of Casablanca. It is only worth catching a taxi for a trip out to the Grand Mosque of Hassan II, the Nouvelle Medina or the Gare des Voyageurs. *Petits taxis* can be caught on Place Mohammed V and the Ave des F.A.R. They usually have meters, but if the meter is switched off the fare, per person, should be around 10dh for the Gare des Voyageurs or the Nouvelle Medina.

You can catch a *grand taxii* to Rabat or Fez from just east of the CTM bus station on the main road. Trains are best, though.

If at all possible try not to drive in Casablanca, due to the poor street signs, competitive traffic, packs of scooter-riders and the usual indomitable Moroccan pedestrians who maintain a courageous indifference to cars.

Medina. It is true that as a mere 18th-century construction it cannot stand comparison with any of the medieval cities, but if you have spent any time in Morocco there is an almost unearthly satisfaction in walking through a medina without so much as a whiff of a bazaar, carpet shop or a guide. Casa also has some fabulous fish restaurants, while its humbler bars and cafés offer the opportunity to dive through the external distractions of tourism and meet some of the people of Morocco on common ground. My abiding image of the city is of two old women walking hand in hand down a street, one typically French, one unmistakably Moroccan. This could and should happen anywhere, but only in Casablanca did it feel commonplace.

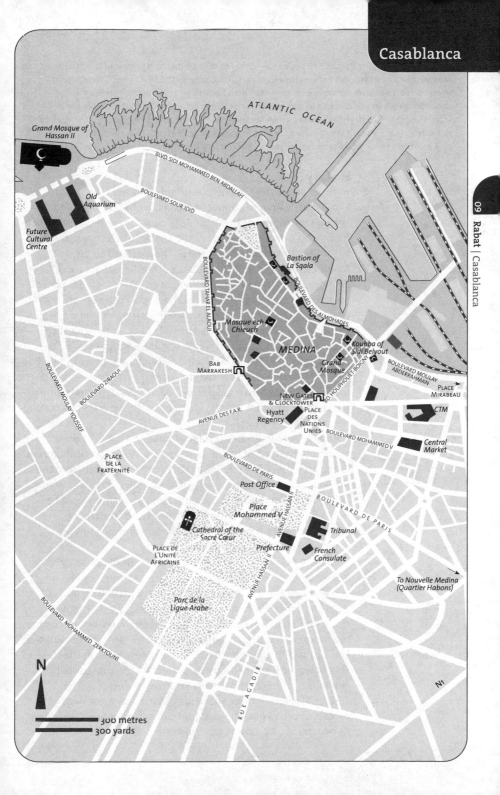

ATLANTIC OCEAN

Grand Mosque of
Hassan II

Old
Aquarium

BLVD. SIDI MOHAMMED BEN ABDALLAH

BOULEVARD SOUR JDID

Future
Cultural
Centre

Bastion of
La Sqala

BOULEVARD TAHAR EL ALAOUI

BOULEVARD DES ALMOHADES

Mosque ech
Chleuch

MEDINA

Koubba of
Sidi Belyout

BOULEVARD MOULAY
ABDERRAHMAN

BOULEVARD ZIRAOUI

Bab
Marrakesh

Grand
Mosque

BD. HOUPHOUET BOIGNY

PLACE
MIRABEAU

New Gates
& Clocktower

CTM

BOULEVARD MOULAY YOUSSEF

AVENUE DES F.A.R.

Hyatt
Regency

Place
des
Nations
Unies

BOULEVARD MOHAMMED V

Central
Market

PLACE
DE LA
FRATERNITÉ

BOULEVARD DE PARIS

Post Office

BOULEVARD DE PARIS

Place
Mohammed V

AVENUE HASSAN II

Cathedral of the
Sacré Cœur

Tribunal

PLACE DE
L'UNITÉ
AFRICAINE

Prefecture

French
Consulate

To Nouvelle Medina
(Quartier Habons)

Parc de la
Ligue Arabe

AVENUE HASSAN II

BOULEVARD MOHAMMED ZERKTOUNI

N

N1

RUE AGADIR

300 metres
300 yards

Orientation

History

The smart western residential suburb, Anfa, was the site of a Phoenician trading station founded in the 6th century BC. It became the capital of the great Berghouata confederacy of Berber tribes who, under the banner of the Khajarite heresy, resisted the authority of the early Islamic states. The Almohad Sultan Abdel Moumen finally broke the resistance of the Berghouata and destroyed Anfa in 1149. The port remained in use for the export of corn, but by the 15th century it also housed a flotilla of corsairs who raided the Portuguese coast so effectively that the kings of Portugal were forced to send an armada of 50 ships against this threat in 1468, and again in 1515. In 1575 the Portuguese commander of El-Jadida closed the corsair base for ever by building a fort at Anfa which also served to guard the northern approach road to El-Jadida. This citadel remained in European hands until the Lisbon earthquake of 1755 shattered both the walls of Anfa and the treasury of Portugal.

Sultan Sidi Mohammed reclaimed Anfa, and built the present medina to the east of the ruins in 1770. The walls, fortifications and Grand Mosque of the medina all date from this period. From the previous era only the Portuguese name for their fort, Casa Branca, 'white house', remained in use, although strangely it would be neither the Arabic translation, Dar el-Beida, nor the French equivalent of Maison-Blanche, but the Spanish version, Casa Blanca, that would pass into general usage.

Sultan Moulay Sliman closed the port as part of his policy of isolating Morocco from Europe, but it was reopened by his successor in 1830. The tempo of trade increased with exports of wool and corn to Britain, whose merchants sold tea, teapots, clothes and paraffin candles through the city in return. In 1907 the town exploded in anger against the predominant influence of the Europeans, and nine French port workers were killed in the streets. This, however, furnished a useful pretext for the subsequent landings by the French army in Morocco. The energetic French Resident-Governor from 1912 to 1925, Marshal Lyautey, began the process of urban planning and port extension that soon produced its own tempo of commercial dynamism and growth. Morocco's mercantile élite from Fez were quick to move to the coast, and join in the colonial city's development and property boom.

A generation later the new city was at the forefront of agitation against French colonial rule. Casablanca still is the centre of contemporary political protest. In Western minds it is linked to three rather spurious events – the landings, the conference and the film. The Casablanca landings of November 1942 had no military significance, as the result had already been pre-arranged between the supposed opponents, the American and Vichy French generals. Seasick American troops were in fact landed with great confusion at Safi, Mehdiya and Fédala (Mohammedia), but not Casablanca. The Casablanca conference was held two months later in January 1943. It had no significance for Morocco: Roosevelt and Churchill spent their days planning the invasion of Sicily from a suburban villa in Anfa.

The Grand Mosque of Hassan II

Grand Mosque of Hassan II
Blvd Moulay Youssef; admission by guided tour only; hour-long tours (120dh) leave Sat–Thurs 9am, 10am, 11am and 2pm.

The 200m-high minaret of this vast new mosque floats above the skyline of Casablanca, the sun glancing off its façade of pale marble and glazed tile and from the three gilded balls at its summit. The tower is aligned to the points of the compass, not the direction of prayer, and so it is offset from the enormous rectangular 22-acre prayer hall, three times the size of St Paul's Cathedral. Vast titanium and steel doors guard the glimmering interior, a palatial expanse of polished marble floor, granite columns, carved stone and plaster Moorish arches with more than 70 cedar-panelled cupolas, which is lit by vast Venetian chandeliers of pale-green crystal. The roof is richly carved, painted and gilded and the size of a football pitch, but can slide open automatically in just three minutes to flood the hall with sunlight. As well as the cool marble ablution fountains beneath the prayer-hall, on important feast days the water rill in the middle of the mosque flows too. A mezzanine level, wrapped in a carved wooden screen, seems to float on a floor of coloured tiles and provides an area exclusively for female worshippers.

Perhaps the most astonishing aspect of the mosque is its position. It has been built out from the natural shoreline on a reclaimed embankment. This is in deliberate fulfilment of a Koranic verse, 'the throne of God was built on the water'. It is also a careful piece of symbolism: the wedding of late 20th-century Morocco to its new but ever more influential Atlantic identity. Moroccan culture has long been concentrated in the cities of the interior and has virtually ignored the Atlantic coast, which is still littered with the monumental evidence of medieval invaders,

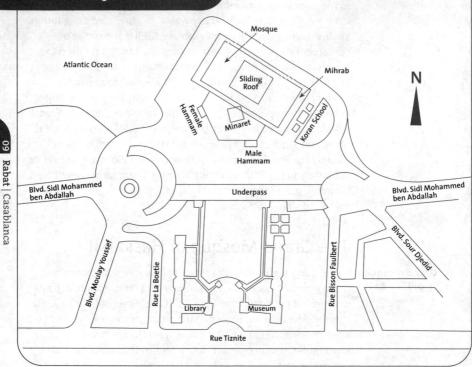

colonists and foreign merchants. For a long time the Arabs felt insecure about the Atlantic (known to them as the Sea of Obscurity), a coastline that was the final refuge of weak tribes driven from the good grazing of the interior. Only the most desperate stooped to the dishonourable occupation of living from the sea. This vast mosque is an attempt to correct a long cultural imbalance, its towering minaret a beacon to draw the faithful seawards. The mosque is one of the late king's most extraordinary, extravagant but ultimately successful building projects. Its cost has been estimated at US$800 million, entirely funded by donations from the people of Morocco, as the ubiquitous certificates displayed in every café, hotel, shop and home proudly attest. The immense plaza opposite is being enclosed by an arcade of shops and cafés that incorporate a cultural complex with a museum, school and *medersa*. About 3,000 people use the mosque on a normal Friday, and it only reaches its 20,000 capacity at the great festivals.

Nothing To Do With *Casablanca*

No scene of the film *Casablanca* was shot in Morocco, nor does the finished film bear much relation to the city of the past or the present. The film was released in the winter of 1942 and was lucky to gain from the enormous free publicity generated by the Casablanca landings and the Allied conference here. It was also fortunate in a last-minute change of cast: Ronald Reagan and Ann Sheridan were replaced by Humphrey Bogart and Ingrid Bergman, and as an inspired afterthought the director Michael Curtiz added Dooley Wilson singing 'As Time Goes By'.

The Old Town (Ancienne Medina)

There is an enormous and continual charm in exploring the old medina of Casablanca, where the crumbling 18th-, 19th- and early 20th-century houses conjure up an almost Neapolitan vision of street animation. Noon and mid-afternoon are the worst times to explore here. Owing to the late date of the medina's construction, it is relatively easy to pick your own route through the streets, which are comparatively wide, well labelled and without the labyrinthine intensity of Fez or Marrakesh. It is also quite without carpet shops and bazaars (which are all neatly laid out by the southern exterior wall) and so is empty of guides and multilingual commission men. Instead the narrow streets are packed with street stalls with exuberant displays of vegetables, fruit, groceries, cooked food, Tupperware and clothes.

The old Jewish quarter, the **Mellah**, stood just to the north of Place des Nations Unies (old Place Mohammed V). A dusty car park a few years ago, the old back entrance to the medina here has now been completely reconstructed, with an ornamental clock tower (the third in a succession of such towers to stand here) in front of the elegant walls and a gate worthy of Anfa's Almohad period. The area behind it is filled with an open-air market selling tourist bric-a-brac and freshly squeezed orange juice. You might also visit the impressive **Jewish Museum**, which tells the story of Morocco's Jews. To get there, take a taxi southwest down Avenue Hassan II. A few minutes later and just before you reach the Gare Oasis, turn right down Blvd Abderrahim Bouabid. Take the 10 o'clock turn off the second little roundabout down Rue Ahmed Akkad and follow the road as it turns left. The museum is on the right.

Jewish Museum
81 Rue Chasseur Jules Gros, t 0522 994940, http://casajewish museum.com; open Mon–Fri 10–6

On the northeastern side of the medina is the 18th-century **bastion of La Sqala**. This prominent artillery terrace is dominated by a handsome gatehouse, from where the battery commander once directed the range and elevation of cannon fire that last opposed a European fleet in the mid-19th century. Today there are only four cast-iron cannon, their muzzles pointing towards the rattling masts of the yacht harbour, while on either side the white houses of Casa stand suspended above the sand-yellow city walls.

The postern gate, which once led directly to the old port but now gives access to the wallside gardens, is usually locked.

Opposite the Gare du Port sits the *koubba* **of Sidi Belyout** (a name derived from Abou el Louyou, 'father of the lions', the title of a great commander of a jihad), set reclusively amid a stand of trees within whitewashed walls. Non-Muslims are not allowed to enter, but you can peer through the gateway and admire the constant succession of Casa babies brought by their mothers to pay their respects to one of the principal patrons of the city.

The *Ville Nouvelle* (New Town)

The 500m length of Blvd Mohammed V is lined with some delightful Art Deco apartments and hotels, as are the two parallel streets, Rue Allal ben Abdallah and Avenue Houmane el Fetouaki. The **market square**, a splendid Moorish courtyard, is your principal objective. The arcaded interior is lined with a dazzling display of the full range of Moroccan fruit, vegetables, meat, shellfish and flowers. It is a wonderful vision of the freshest and ripest products of the land, with one or two tourist stalls for visitors. The surrounding streets have a large choice of bars, cafés and licensed restaurants. Stop to have a coffee in the cool arcade, or a drink in the unreconstructed 1920s interior of **Le Petit Poucet**, 86 Blvd Mohammed V. This is the ideal place to imagine the lost world of French North Africa immortalized by Albert Camus. It was the favourite haunt of Antoine de Saint-Exupéry, the pioneer poet of flight and philosopher of aviation. Though better known for *The Little Prince*, his classic work *Wind, Sand and Stars* is partly based on the heroic days of flying mail across the Western Sahara (see Further Reading, p.303).

Place Mohammed V

Heading south from Place des Nations Unies, the broad Avenue Hassan II leads towards Place Mohammed V, the dry administrative heart of Casablanca. In the 1920s Henri Prost and Robert Marrast were employed as the architects for most of the official buildings that surround the square. They helped define the neo-Moorish style of French colonial architecture, which remains very influential. They took details hitherto reserved for the interior of a Moorish house and used them to create an impressive monumental exterior. Behind the traditional decorative elements – the green-tiled roofs, horseshoe-arch arcades, interior courtyards and the free use of *zellij* mosaic – the functional subdivision of the building into corridors and offices followed Western traditions. The central fountain operates on Fridays and weekends; to its east rises the mass of the **Palais de Justice** or **Tribunal**. Next door, tucked into the corner, is the **French Consulate** with a statue of Marshal Lyautey to the fore, neatly protected by a high fence. The **Prefecture** to the south is easily recognizable, with its famous modernist clock tower striking a jarring note amid the principles of the neo-Moorish style. The post office and the Banque du Maroc sit very solidly on the northern face of the square.

To the south of the place stretches the flat expanse of the **Parc de la Ligue Arabe**, with neat promenades and a number of elegant cafés, in the half-shade along Blvd Moulay Youssef. On the western edge is the School of Fine Arts, across the street from the old **Cathedral of the Sacré Coeur**, designed by Paul Tornon in 1930. The ferro-concrete nave washed with a creamy yellow is currently used for temporary exhibitions (there are longstanding plans to convert it into a cultural centre). It is a striking structure, the exterior dominated by three rows of descending buttresses and gargoyles. The long narrow apertures are filled with a geometric arrangement of glass that deliberately recalls the marquetry and *zellij* mosaic traditional to a religious building in Morocco.

The Nouvelle Medina (Quartier Habous)

Created as a showpiece of colonial paternalism, this new quarter for Muslims was built to the southeast of the then-European city centre. It was directly modelled on the surviving 18th-century quarters of Casablanca, and on the elegant town of Essaouira to the south. A few of the inhabitants of the shantytown slums were transferred to these elegant narrow streets, with wider connecting roads lined with stone arcades.

The Nouvelle Medina now has Casablanca's largest concentration of bazaars and craft shops. It is the cleanest, most ordered **souk** in Morocco, lacking vitality but with a fine selection of all the national crafts. The most attractive arcades are in the area north of the railway and south of Blvd Victor Hugo. The high walls of the royal palace, which enclose a secretive and elegant garden, line the boulevard to the north. A street surmounted by three picturesque arches leads to **Place Moulay Youssef**, with a central garden and a mosque built by the present king's great-grandfather in 1938. Two arcaded and arched streets on the left of the square lead to the larger **Place de la Mosquée**, with well-kept shaded gardens and the mosque of Mohammed V on its southern side. To the north are the imposingly high outer walls of the **Mahakma du Pasha**, the combined residence of the Pasha of Casablanca and tribunal of the Islamic courts, finished in 1952 by the French. The interior is a maze of courts decorated in traditional Moorish style with carved plaster and wood.

Mahakma du Pasha

open Mon–Sat 8–12 and 2–6

A bridge, the **Sidi Jdid**, leads south across the railway line to the main residential area of Nouvelle Medina. The vegetable and spice market of the **Balilida Quarter** is off the Rue du Rharb, a delightfully animated court full of the competing colours and odours of the souk. A terrace that runs parallel to the market above, the Rue Taroudannt, contains the stalls of herbalists and enchanters. Hedgehogs and turtles are sold live, and there are curtains of dried animal and bird skins from which to make charms and love potions. The small cones of green dried leaves from the henna tree are sold as the base for the henna paste used throughout Morocco for decorating hands and feet, and for invigorating and dyeing hair.

The Atlantic

To the west of the centre, **Boulevard de la Corniche** forms a beachfront popular with the young and fashionable Casablancais. To escape the mayhem of the street, find one of the beach clubs, which cost around 100 dirhams for the day.

Alternatively, try leaving the city. If you don't feel the need to swim, hop on a train to **El Jadida** to the south and then catch a cheap taxi (8dh) to **Azemmour**, an attractive fishing port full of art and with magnificent views. But if you really need to take the plunge or go surfing, you might want to wait until the famous **Temara Plage**, 13km south of Rabat.

ⓘ Casablanca >
Tourist Board (ONMT)
55 Rue Omar Slaoui,
t 0522 279533

Tourist Office
98 Blvd Mohammed V,
t 0522 221524

Information and Services in Casablanca

The **tourist board (ONMT)** and the **tourist office** both supply city maps and booklets.

Communications

Post and Telegrams

The main **post office** (*open Mon–Fri 8am–6pm*) is at the junction of Blvd de Paris and Ave Hassan II. There is a smaller branch at 116 Ave Mohammed V and one in the medina on Place Ahmed al-Bidaoui.

Money

There are plenty of **banks**. Three of the most convenient are Banque Populaire, 101 Blvd Mohammed Zerktouni, BMCI, 26 Place Mohammed V and SGMB, 2 Ave des F.A.R. but, unsurprisingly for the city that consumes almost a third of the country's electricity and is home to most of its businesses, there are

banks and ATMs dotted all through the city centre and in several of the smarter hotels.

Shopping in Casablanca

The **market** off Blvd Mohammed V and the streets of the Nouvelle Medina make a memorable shopping trip: for antiques and decorative pieces get a taxi to **Le Riad des Antiquaires** on the corner of Ave Lalla Yacout and Rue Mustapha el-Maami.

There are a number of well-established commercial **art galleries** in Casa that have exhibitions of Moroccan artists, decorative art from other Islamic countries and works from France and Belgium: **Galerie d'Art Moderne**, 5 Rue Manaziz, the **Galerie Alif**, 46 Rue Omar Slaoui, and **Galerie Bassamat**, 2 Rue Pierre Curie.

If you need to buy more up-to-date items, the **Casablanca Twin Center**, located in a pair of skyscrapers, is bound to have what you need. Morocco's largest shopping centre is on the crossroads of Zerktouni and Al Khadra boulevards. The shops take up the lower five floors, and there is also a five-star hotel.

Try **Ateliers d'Ailleurs** (t 0672 812046, *www.ateliersdailleurs.fr*) if you'd like to see local craftsmen and cooks at work. These tours are popular for the close-up interaction they provide, as well as the buying opportunities.

Where to Stay in Casablanca

Casablanca has a number of moderately priced hotels, solidly built during the Protectorate, which are concentrated in the city centre. They have spacious, comfortable bedrooms and are largely undamaged by improvements. There is not much interest or economy to be enjoyed by staying in the medina. If this is your first night in Morocco, give yourself a bit of extra comfort while you slowly adjust. This is especially relevant for Americans and Canadians who have just flown in.

Luxury
The Hyatt Regency, Place des Nations Unies, t 0522 431234, *http:// casablanca.regency.hyatt.com*. This stands behind sound-proof windows right in the centre on Place des Nations Unies and has everything but a nightclub.

⭐ **Royal Mansour >**

Royal Mansour, 27 Avenue des F.A.R, t 0522 313011, *www.leroyal mansourmeridienmaroc.com*, Much-loved and with excellent service, the Mansour may be the city's best top-end hotel. Marble and neo-Moorish interiors.

Expensive
Hotel les Saisons, 19 Rue el Oraïbi Jilali, t 0522 490901, *www. hotellessaisonsmaroc.ma*. A peaceful and comfortable hotel, with large rooms and attentive service. With rooms between €73 and 120, it offers good value.

Sheraton, 100 Ave des F.A.R., t 0522 439494, *www.sheraton.com/ casablanca*. A centrally placed and reliably efficient 280-room hotel with a swimming pool and car parking. Smart, light and comfortable. At the top end of this price category.

Hotel Toubkal, 9 Rue Sidi Belyout (2nd left off Ave des F.A.R. from Place des Nations Unies, opposite the Mansour), t 0522 311414, *www.bestwestern.com*. It has an unexceptional exterior but this hotel is a model of calm efficiency within. An intimate alternative to the vast hotels, and less than half the price (rooms from €100). There is also a swimming pool, small bar, restaurant and popular nightclub within the building.

Moderate
Barceló Casablanca, 139 Blvd d'Anfa, t 0522 208000, *www. barcelocasablanca.com*. A reliable if unexciting choice, the Barceló has decent restaurants. It lacks extensive facilities but the staff is friendly, it is in a pleasant, central area and the price is reasonable.

Dar Itrit, 9 Rue Restinga, t 0522 360258. This little guesthouse is located on the outskirts of town, about 15 minutes by taxi to the centre. Comfortable rooms, hospitable hosts, and superb home cooking make it a good mid-range alternative to the chain hotels in the city centre.

Hotel Maamoura, 59 Rue Ibnou Batouta, t 0522 452967, *www. hotelmaamoura.com*. Room furnishings are a touch drab but comfortable, while the food, mod cons and service are very good for the modest price.

Hotel Yto, Rue Taoufik al Hakim, t 0522 429870, *www.hotelyto.ma*. Not particularly central, but impressive at the price, with pleasant, comfortable, clean, large rooms. There's a good *hammam* nearby.

Ibis Moussafir, Rue Sidi Belyout, t 0522 466560. A reliable bet, this huge chain hotel is just beside the Gare des Voyageurs on Blvd Bahmad. It has its own garden, bar and restaurant.

Riad Des Plages, B50, Plage Essanaoubar Bouznika, t 0522 158289.

About 10km from Casablanca, but with an enviable beachside location, this is charming guesthouse sits amid gardens and palm trees. There are eight elegant suites decorated with traditional local crafts and textiles, and delicious dinners are available. If the pool doesn't tempt you, the beach is just 50m away. Perfect for a romantic break.

Inexpensive

Excelsior, 2 Rue el Amraoui Brahim (ex-Rue Nolly), **t** 0522 200263. For something dignified, colonial and dead central, with a comfortable touch of shabbiness, head for the Excelsior, which looks on to Place des Nations Unies.

Hotel Guynemer, 2 Rue Mohammed Belloul, **t** 0522 275764, *www.guynemerhotel.com*. A well-loved hotel with good food and an attractive interior, the staff at the Guynemer will pick you up from the airport.

⭐ Le Port de Pêche >>

⭐ Hotel Guynemer >

Cheap

Hotel Foucauld, 52 Rue Araïbi Jilali (formerly Rue de Foucauld), **t** 0522 222666. Plain and simple but reliable – and capacious too.

Hotel Mon Rêve, 7 Rue Chaouia, **t** 0522 311439. A good cheap option in a convenient spot with clean rooms. Noise is sometimes a problem so try for the top floor.

Where to Eat in Casablanca

Casablanca has the reputation of having some of the best cooking in Morocco.

Expensive

La Maison du Gourmet, Rue Taha Houcine, Maarifv (just south of Blvd d'Anfa), **t** 0522 484846. A mix of French and Moroccan food and a wonderful place for a celebration dinner. Expensive but the food is exceptional.

Restaurant A Ma Bretagne, Blvd de la Corniche (out of town), **t** 0522 362112, André Halbert's celebrated eaterie was once considered the best French restaurant in Africa. It occupies an

unusual modernist building with a stunning view over the sea. Prices are worthy of a Maître Cuisinier de France, but remain a bargain by European standards. Try the fish

Moderate

Al Mounia, 95 Rue du Prince Moualy Abdullah, **t** 0524 222669. Al Mounia does excellent Moroccan fare and is a charming place to boot. *Closed Sun.*

La Corrida, 59 Rue el Arrar, **t** 0522 278155. This long-standing establishment was the most fashionable spot in town during the 1960s. It's still good for grilled fish and tapas. *Closed Sun.*

Le Port de Pêche, **t** 0522 318561. For a reasonably priced French fish restaurant, walk 150m past the Gare du Port along Blvd Moulay Abderrahman, turn left at the dock gates and after another 150m walk through another set of dock gates to the restaurant ahead of you. This friendly place has a large busy upstairs dining room with napkins and waiters in matching red, a full seafood menu and a happy mix of Moroccan families, Franco-Maroc businessmen and travellers.

Rick's Café, 248 Blvd Sour Jdid, Place du Jardin Public, **t** 0524 274207, *www.rickscafe.ma*. One of the many Rick's in the city, with décor, music and setting just as you would expect, this one has the edge thanks to its fabulous original 30s setting. The food is very good.

Taverne du Dauphin, 115 Blvd Houphouët-Boigny, **t** 0522 221200. Bustling, friendly tavern. Fish seldom tastes this good, particularly the grilled prawns.

Inexpensive

L'Étoile Marocaine, 107 Rue Allal Ben Abdallah, **t** 0522 314100. A small restaurant decorated in the Moorish taste and serving traditional food (but no alcohol) at a reasonable price.

Le Petit Poucet, 86 Blvd Mohammed V, **t** 0522 275420. This was one of the smartest centres of urban life in Casablanca before the Second World War, when Albert Camus used to eat here. It has a reasonably priced restaurant, but for a cheaper meal use the snack bar next door.

Alternatively, there are some good fish bars across the road. **Le Buffet** at no.99 is one of these.

The market is also home to **Brasserie Bavaroise**, a pricier but good French restaurant.

Pâtisseries and Glaciers

The most famous Moroccan pâtisserie in Casablanca is **Bennis**, 2 Rue Fikh el Gabbas, **t** 0522 303025. Along Blvd Mohammed V you will find **La Normande** at No.213. Blvd du 11 Janvier boasts **L'Igloo**, where the most exotic combinations of fruit, sherbets, ice-creams, whipped cream, flavoured milks, juices, teas and coffees can be ordered. The Boulevard is just east of Place Mohammed V (old Place des Nations Unies). Finally, **Palais des Glaces** on Boulevard de la Corniche is long-standing and makes a good stop.

Entertainment and Nightlife in Casablanca

Most bars are sorry affairs with prostitutes often the only women but the smarter hotels like the **Hyatt** or **Transatlantique** are usually good bets. Or try **La Trica** on Rue el-Moutanabi.

The **Ain Diab district** is where partying enters the early hours. Dress smartly, take plenty of cash and head for Avenue de la Corniche.

Chronology

1100 BC Phoenician merchants from the Near East establish a network of coastal ports trading with the indigenous Berber tribes, ruled from 550 BC by Carthage.

202 BC Control of the region passes to the Mauretanian kings.

AD 44–303 A period of growing influence leads to the outright annexation of 'Mauretania Tingitania' by the Roman Empire.

303–682 The northernmost ports of Tangier and Ceuta pass from Roman to Vandal then Byzantine rule.

682 Uqba ben Nafi brings Islam to Morocco, just 50 years after the death of the Prophet Mohammed.

705–40 The Caliphate: the Arab Empire extends west to Morocco, allowing for the conquest of Spain in 711, but is expelled after the Tangier Mutiny of 740.

789–921 Moulay Idriss and his posthumous son, Idriss II, found Fez and establish the first independent Moroccan kingdom.

1042–1147 Almoravid Empire: Morocco is united by a fundamentalist reform group drawn from the nomadic Berber tribes of the Sahara, and in 1071 their leader Youssef ben Tachfine founds Marrakesh.

1147–1248 Almohad Empire: a second Islamic reform, drawn from the Berber tribes of the High Atlas, brings Morocco to its glittering zenith.

1248–1554 The Merenid dynasty rules from Fez, its glorious first century recalled by a number of supremely elegant mosques and *medersas*.

1554–1668 The Saadian dynasty: the growing power of Portugal in the 15th century Is repelled at the Battle of the Three Kings in 1578.

1668–1727 Anarchic 17th-century Morocco is re-united under the first Alaouite sultans: Moulay Rachid and Moulay Ismaïl.

1822–73 Relentless growth of European influence, partly checked by the energetic reign of Moulay Hassan (1873–94).

1912 Treaty of Fez. French and Spanish Protectorates formally established.

1912–56 France introduces technical, industrial and medical improvements and subdues all areas of tribal dissidence.

1956 Independence: Mohammed V leads the struggle and re-establishes royal authority.

1961–99 Reign of Hassan II. After the coup attempts of the early 1970s, the king becomes popular due to his re-occupation of the Western Sahara.

1999 Mohammed VI succeeds to the throne, proclaiming the ideals of political and economic freedom as well as the rule of law and human rights in his first speech to the nation, then releases political prisoners and sacks the former Minister of the interior, Driss Basri. Two years later he allows Amnesty International to set up an office in the country.

2000 Diplomatic relationship with Israel annulled in the wake of pro-Palestinian demonstrations in Morocco.

2002 Morocco's first elections to be recognized internationally as free are held. Thirty of the parliamentary seats are reserved for female candidates.

2003 Series of suicide bombs hit Casablanca, killing 26 people and tarnishing Morocco's claims to have managed to bridge Islam and modernity. The attacks are linked to an extremist Moroccan Islamist organization but also to al-Qaeda. The bombings cause widespread outrage.

2003 Mudawana introduced, a legal code recognising the equal status of women within marriage and giving them other crucial rights in the areas of marriage, divorce and custody of children.

2003–4 Morocco signs free trade agreements with the EU and USA, and is granted 'major non-NATO ally' status by the USA.

2004 A series of train bombs in the Spanish capital of Madrid kills 191 people. The Moroccan Islamic Combatant Group is implicated in the bombings and several Moroccans are eventually jailed for their part in the attacks.

2007 Parliamentary elections see the conservative, nationalist Istiqlal Party gain more seats than any other party and its leader, Abbas Al Fassi, appointed prime minister.

2010 The first EU-Morocco summit takes place, the first such meeting to be held between the EU and an Arabic country. Morocco's signicant efforts at political, economic and social reform are lauded and aid is promised in return.

Glossary of Terms

Abassids the 2nd dynasty of caliphs who ruled the Muslim world from AD 750–1258

abd (sing.), *abid* (plural) a slave; by inference a black slave, and used to distinguish the black regiments from the tribal ones in the sultan's army

Agadir principal city and port of south-western Morocco; literally the fortified communal hilltop granaries of the Berber tribes, also known as *ighrem*, *igherm* or *irherm*

aid holy day or feast, as in Aid es Seghir at the end of Ramadan

aïn (sing.), *aïoun* (plural) spring or water hole

aït child of, as used in the creation of a tribal identity, such as Aït-Atta

Aït-Atta Berber tribe from Jbel Sarhro who dominated the south from the 16th century to 1934

akbar 'the Great', as in *Allah Akbar*

Alaouite the present ruling dynasty of Morocco who, from their base in the Tafilalt Oasis, replaced the Saadian sultans in 1666

Ali cousin and son-in-law of the Prophet through his marriage to Fatima, and father of Hassan and Hussein. Ali succeeded Othmann as 4th caliph in AD 656 but his reign was punctuated by disputes which split Islam into the Sunni, Shiite and Kharijite camps

Almohad 'the unitarians'. An Islamic reform movement founded by Ibn Tumert in the High Atlas which replaced Almoravid rule over Morocco; the Almohad Empire, AD 1147–1248, was a peak period of Moroccan history

Almoravid 'the warrior monks'. An Islamic reform movement founded by Ibn Yaasin in the Sahara which, under his successors Abu Bekr and Youssef ben Tachfine, controlled an empire that stretched from Spain to West Africa (AD 1060–1147)

arabesque general adjective describing the architecture and the calligraphic, floral and geometrical decoration of Islam

argan hard oil-producing thorn tree that grows only in southwestern Morocco

asif river that flows throughout the year

Averroes/Ibn Rushd Muslim scholar born in Córdoba in 1126 who originally enjoyed the patronage of the Almohad sultans; his translation of Aristotle and philosophical works was of great influence to the Christian universities, though the orthodox of both Islam and Christendom condemned his rationalism

azrou rock, and the name of a town in the Middle Atlas

bab gate

beni 'the sons of', often used in the description of a tribe, such as the Beni-Merin

Berghawata/Berghouata heretical Berber tribal group who occupied the coastal region from Salé to Casablanca until conquered in the 12th century by the Almohads

bit room

cadi judge of Muslim law

caftan/kaftan formal outer garment, though it increasingly refers to an embroidered cotton robe

caid magistrate who in the lawless areas was often a tribal chief recognized by the sultan; now the chief magistrate of a commune

caliph the successor of the Prophet to the rule of the Muslim community

caravanserai defensive lodgings on a caravan route

Chleuh one of the three Berber tribal groupings who occupy the western High Atlas, the Sous and the Anti-Atlas. They are also known as Soussi or Masmuda and speak a dialect known as Tachelhait

cursive the familiar style of flowing rounded Arabic script

dakhla an entrance to a gorge and the name of a town of the Western Sahara, known under Spanish rule until 1976 as Villa Cisneros

dar house, building or palace; city quarters are often named after the most distinctive house of the quarter, like Dar Sejene in Meknès

daya lake

dirham the Ommayad caliphs based the first Muslim silver coinage on the Byzantine drachmae; the name and style was in turn copied by Moroccan mints

drâa arm; the river Drâa flows south from Ouarzazate into the Sahara

emir 'he who commands': originally the military deputies of the caliph, and transformed into a title of sovereignty

erg dunes or region of dunes in a desert

fantasia a display of horsemanship featuring small charges, dramatic halts and musket firing

Fassi an inhabitant of Fez. It can also refer to the rich merchant class in Morocco

Fatima only surviving daughter of the Prophet, wife of Ali and mother of Hassan and Hussein; the central female cult figure of Islam: the Hand of Fatima is an ancient good-luck talisman

Fiqh the Islamic legal code: there are four traditional codes acknowledged by the orthodox Muslim: the Malekite, Hanefite, Chafiite and Hanbalite; the Malekite is favoured in Morocco

foggara/khettara underground irrigation canal

fondouq/fondouk a courtyard surrounded by rooms which takes on a great range of functions.

gandoura a simple cotton tunic with sleeves and plain collar, mostly worn by men.

garum peculiar fish paste made of salt and mashed tuna intestines, beloved by the ancient Romans and manufactured for centuries on the Moroccan Atlantic coast

Gnaoua/Gnawa/Gnaiwaya black religious brotherhood from West Africa and also the name of their spirit music

habous religious foundations

hadj a pilgrimage to Mecca; the honorific title for those who have made the journey is Hadji

haik large cloth used by women to cover themselves in the street

Hammada the flat pebbly plateau of the Sahara

hammam steam or Turkish baths.

Haratine black serf caste in the south, having no tribal loyalties but often attached in a share-cropping arrangement to a nomadic warrior group.

harmattan hot dry winds which blow from the Sahara.

Hassan II King of Morocco 1960–99; born in 1929, he was educated in Rabat and Bordeaux, where he read law; he accompanied his father into exile from 1953 to 1955 and on Independence was put in command of the new royal army

Hegira The Islamic era which began with the flight of the Prophet from Mecca to Medina in July 622; the Muslim calendar is based on a lunar rather than a solar year, and each year is therefore 11 days shorter than each Gregorian year.

Hilali a nomadic Bedouin tribe that with the Sulaym left the Arabian peninsula in the 11th century to advance west along the North African coast

Ibn Battuta travel writer who was born in Tangier in 1304 and died at Fez in 1377; trained as a cadi, he travelled, worked and married throughout the Muslim world from Timbuktu to China

Ibn Khaldoun celebrated historian and sociologist who was born in Tunis in 1332, his parents having fled from Andalucía; he obtained positions in a number of Muslim courts and lived in Fez before settling in Egypt as the Malekite Mufti of Cairo

Idriss I/Moulay Idriss great-grandson of the Prophet and founder of the first Muslim kingdom of Morocco in 788; his tomb at Moulay Idriss is the pre-eminent national shrine

Idriss II posthumous son of Idriss I; creator of the city of Fez, where his tomb is venerated; his descendants, the Idrissids, have been a numerous and influential clan throughout Moroccan history.

Ighrem see Agadir

11 Glossary of Terms

imam leader of prayers and by implication also a political leader

Islam 'Submission to God': Mohammed is the best known and the last of a long line of prophets who taught submission to God, giving rules for the conduct of life and threatening unbelievers with divine punishment

Istqlal Independence party founded by Allal al Fasi in 1934, which took a leading role in the civil resistance to the French Protectorate. It held a strong position in post-Independence government from 1956 to 1962, subsequently held an important role in several coalition governments, and was returned to power in 2007.

jbel/djebel mountain; the Djeballa are a specific group of Arabic-speaking tribes that occupy the western Rif; it is also a city dweller's label of contempt for the unsophisticated, the hillbillies

jdid/djedid new, as in Fez Jdid, new Fez, the 14th-century royal extension to the city

jellaba/djellaba large cotton or wool outer garment with sleeves and a hood

jihad holy war against the enemies of Islam

Kaaba a meteorite venerated from antiquity in Mecca and situated on the spot where, according to tradition, Abraham erected his altar; Muslims pray towards the Kaaba and circle it seven times before kissing it as the culmination of the Hadj

kasbah the citadel of a town or a rural fortress

khaima grand tent of a tribal leader, now much reproduced for use at fêtes and as restaurants

khettara see foggara

killim a woven carpet

kohl ground powder of the metallic-looking sulphur of antimony; applied to the eyes, it stimulates an attractive watery sheen that is useful protection against soot and dust

Koran the word of God dictated to the Prophet Mohammed by the archangel Gabriel in Arabic

kouba women's room

koubba dome; by extension a *koubba* is the shrine of a saint's tomb which is usually covered by a small white cupola; they often form the object of a pilgrimage and are at the centre of female spiritual activity

ksar (sing.), *ksour* (plural) an Arabic noun derived from 'Caesar' that describes a fortified village

kufic angular style of Arabic script, named after the city of Kufa in Iraq, which is chiefly used in stone and plaster carving

Leo Africanus born in Granada in 1483, El Hassan ibn Mohammed el Fasi was enslaved by Christians, but when recognized as an intellectual was presented to the pope; he was freed, baptized and awarded a pension by Pope Leo V, who encouraged him to write his famous description of North Africa; having completed the great work, he died a Muslim in Tunis in 1554

litham veil

Lyautey, Marshal Hubert one of the most important commanders of the French Colonial Army, he served in Madagascar and Indo-China before taking charge of the absorption of eastern Morocco from Algeria; as Resident-General from 1912 to 1926 he set the shape and objectives of the French Protectorate

Maghreb 'the land of the setting sun or furthest west', containing the three nations of Tunisia, Algeria and Morocco

makhzen government, or government district

maksoura/maqsar wooden screens in a mosque that protect rulers from assassination

Malikite/Malekite the most widely practised school of judicial practice and Koranic interpretation in North Africa. It was formulated by Malik ibn Anas, a judge from Medina who died in 795

marabout holy warrior, ascetic or the chief of a religious brotherhood who has won the respect of the people; his tomb may be covered by a dome

Mauritania the two Roman provinces of Mauretania Caesariensis and Mauretania Tingitania, whose boundaries approximate those of modern Morocco and Algeria. It now refers to the Saharan country south of Morocco on the Atlantic coast

Mecca sacred town of the Muslims, 8km inland from the Red Sea, on the old caravan route from Syria to Yemen. Mosques are all oriented towards Mecca, 45° east and 12.5° south from Fez

méchouar a square adjoining a palace in which the population can assemble to pay homage to the ruler

medersa residential schools for the study of the Koran and religious law; they were introduced into Morocco in the 12th century, though the earliest surviving buildings date from the 14th

medina walled city or old city, in distinction to the new European-style quarter. Named after the city to which Mohammed fled to avoid persecution in Mecca

mellah Jewish quarter; the name derives from the word *melh*, meaning salt, as the Jewish community used to perform the task of salting the severed heads of the sultan's enemies in order to preserve them

mendoub agent or representative of the sultan, as found in Tangier from 1927 to 1956

Merenids dynasty who originated from the Beni-Merin nomadic tribe who dominated the eastern plains of Morocco and replaced the Almohads in 1248

midha fountain for ritual washing before prayer

mihrab a niche in a place of prayer which indicates the direction of Mecca

minaret the tower of a mosque used for calling the faithful to prayer; the pinnacle is crowned with domes representing the daily prayers, and a blue or green flag flying indicates Friday, the Muslim sabbath

minbar a pulpit-like staircase in mosques used for the noonday Friday sermon, the *khutba*

minzah In a palace, a garden pavilion, especially one enjoying a fine view

Mohammed the Prophet, the last in the succession of Noah, Abraham, Moses and Jesus who have called man to worship the one God

Mohammed V the popular monarch who led the struggle for Moroccan Independence and was exiled by the French; after Independence in 1956 he initiated a new era by ruling as King Mohammed V

Mohammed VI King of Morocco, who succeeded his father Hassan II in 1999, aged 36

mosque place of prostration, the place of reunion, the place of prayer.

moukarnas/muqarnas stalactite-like decorations chiefly of carved wood, stone or plaster

moulay honorific title, approximately 'lord', used in Morocco by the descendants of the Prophet.

Mouloud the great feast day celebrating Mohammed's birthday on the 12th day of the Muslim month of Rabi at-Tani

moussem originally an annual popular pilgrimage to the tomb of a saint, but now by extension any festival or outdoor entertainment

msalla prayer area; open-air mosque

muezzin the call to prayer, also the prayer caller

oasis An island of life in the desert supported by a water-gathering system

Omayyads the first dynasty of caliphs who ruled the Islamic world from 660 to 750 and were descended from Muawiya, the governor of Syria, who was proclaimed caliph after the assassination of Ali

oued river

pasha provincial governor, or the governor of a city

pisé packed wet clay, naturally baked by the sun; widely used throughout Morocco for the construction of walls, kasbahs and roads.

Protectorate Period of French colonial rule of Morocco (1912–56); administered by the Resident-General under the pretence that the sultan had contracted his authority to France by the 1912 Treaty of Fez.

Rabat/r'bat a *r'bat* is a fortified monastery; Rabat is a city founded by the Almohads on the site of an old *r'bat*; it has been the capital of Morocco since 1912

Ramadan Muslim month of fasting in the ninth lunar month of the year; no food, drink or sex is allowed during the hours of daylight; travellers, the sick, the old, the pregnant and pre-pubescent children are exempt.

Reguibat a desert Berber tribe.

Rehamna Arab tribe that dominated the arid plains north of Marrakesh from the 16th century

Resident General (Résidents Généraux) the French rulers of Morocco from 1912 to 1956: Lyautey, Steeg, Saint, Ponsot, Peyrouton,

11 Glossary of Terms

Nogues, Puaux, Labonne, Juin, Lacoste, Grandval, Boyer de la Tour and Dubois.

rharb/gharb west; the Rharb is the fertile coastal region between Larache and Kénitra

rogui a pretender to the sultanate

roumi Roman, Christian, foreigner

Saadian Moroccan dynasty which replaced the Wattasid sultans in the 15th century and repulsed the Portuguese; they originated as sheikhs from the Drâa Valley and established their first capital at Taroudannt

sabil public drinking fountain

Sanhaja one of the three great groupings of the Berber people occupying the Sahara and parts of the Middle and High Atlas. Their dialect is known as Tamazight

sebka decorative repetition of interlaced arches, as were often used on the stone gates and walls of the Almohads

sebkha lake or lagoon

seguia irrigation canal

sheikh leader of a religious brotherhood

sherif/shorfa descendant of the Prophet

sidi male honorific title, always used to denote a saint but also more widely used

souk market

sufi general description for mystical Islamic brotherhoods

sultan ruler; a word of Turkish origin which implies a single, paramount ruler

Sunni the orthodox Muslims, and the preva-lent Moroccan form of Islam. The dispute between the schismatic Shiites and Sunni has never been of importance in Morocco.

tagine traditional Moroccan stew

taibia brotherhood

Targui (sing.), **Tuareg** (plural) the Sanhajan Berber tribe that occupy the central Sahara and dominated the caravan routes; they alone have retained a Berber alphabet, known as Tifinagh, and speak a Berber dialect known as Temajegh

tizi a mountain pass

Ulema the council of professors of Islamic law who since the 12th century have been consulted by sultans for the approval of new laws; they must also formally approve the accession of each new ruler

vizier chief minister of an Islamic ruler

wadi dry riverbed

Wahabbi puritanical reforming Muslim sect from Arabia who were active from the 18th century

Wattasid cousins of the Merenid sultans who first became hereditary viziers and from 1472 ruled directly until replaced in 1554 by the Saadians

zaouia/zawiya (sing.), *zouawi* (plural) the sanctuary or college of students that often collects around the tomb or sanctuary of a *marabout*

zellij geometrical mosaic pattern made from chipped glazed tiles, usually seen on the lower portion of a wall

Zenata one of the three great divisions of the Berber people, whose homeland is the northeast, the Rif and the eastern plains. Their dialect is known as Riffi or Tarifit

Further Reading

Travelling Companions

Bidwell, Margaret and Robin, *Morocco, The Travellers' Companion* (Tauris Parke, 2005). An absorbing anthology of travel writing where each chapter takes a different Moroccan theme.

Rabinow, Paul, *Reflections on Fieldwork in Morocco* (University of California Press, 2007). An almost painfully honest account of an anthropologist's attempt to find a Moroccan friend he can trust.

Rogerson, Barnaby, *The Traveller's History of North Africa* (Windrush Press, 2000). The only one-volume history in English of the Maghreb from the Stone Age to the present day.

History and Mythology

Abun-Nasr, Jamil M., *History of the Maghreb in the Islamic Period* (Cambridge, 1987).

Africanus, Leo, *A Description of Africa* (1600).

Barbour, Nevill, *Morocco* (London, 1965).

Blunt, Wilfrid, *Black Sunrise, The Life and Times of Moulai Ismaïl, Emperor of Morocco, 1646–1727* (Methuen, 1950).

Bovill, E. V., *The Golden Trade of the Moors* (Markus Wiener, 1995).

Dunn, Ross E., *Resistance in the Desert, 1881–1912* (Croom Helm, 1977).

Fix, Philippe, *Moroccan Myths and Legends* (Ragged Bears, 2003). This slimline hardback is a wonderful book to read aloud to your children. A handful of short, well-chosen Moroccan myths.

Forbes, Rosita, *El Raisuni, The Sultan of the Mountains* (Thornton Butterworth, 1924).

Hodges, Tony, *Western Sahara, Roots of a Desert War* (Croom Helm, 1983).

Ibn Battuta, *Travels in Africa and Asia, 1324–54* (RKP). An especially good abridged edition of Ibn Battuta's diaries is *The Travels of Ibn Battuta* by Tim Mackintosh-Smith (2003).

El Idrisi, *Description of Africa and Spain* (1866).

Julien, C.E., *History of North Africa* (London, 1970).

Le Tourneau, R., *Fez in the Age of the Merenids* (1961).

Lewis, Bernard, *The Jews of Islam* (Princeton, 1984).

Maxwell, Gavin, *Lords of the Atlas, The Rise and Fall of the House of Glaoui 1893–1956* (Eland, 2004). One of the finest Orientalist scholars examines Morocco's past.

Mayne, Peter, *A Year in Marrakesh* (Eland 2003). Mayne lived a local life in Marrakesh, learning the language and embroiling himself in the lives of his neighbours and acquaintances. A wonderful and sympathetic portrait.

Meakin, Budget, *The Moorish Empire, The Land of the Moors,* and *The Moors* (London, 1899, 1901, 1902).

Montagne, R., *The Berbers* (London, 1973).

Pennell, C., *Morocco: From Empire to Independence.* (Oneworld, 2003). Useful overview history.

Perkins, K. J., *Quaids, Captains and Colons in the Maghreb* (New York, 1981).

Porch, Douglas, *The Conquest of Morocco* (Cape, 1983); and *The Conquest of the Sahara* (Cape, 1985).

Thompson, V., Adloff, R., *The Western Saharans, Background to Conflict* (Croom Helm, 1980).

Woolman, David, *Rebels in the Rif* (Stanford University Press, 1968).

Anthropology

Chimenti, Elisa, *Tales and Legends of Morocco* (New York, 1943). Folk tales collected by the daughter of a royal surgeon.

Crapanzo, Vincent, *Tuhami, a Portrait of a Moroccan* (University of Chicago, 1986). An academic study of an illiterate artisan.

Deshen, Shlomo, *The Mellah Society* (University of Chicago, 1989). A study of pre-colonial Jewish life.

Dwyer, Kevin, *Moroccan Dialogues* (Johns Hopkins, 1982). Interviews from the Sous Valley.

Gellner, Ernest, *Saints of the Atlas* (Weidenfeld & Nicolson, 1969). A justly celebrated study of a holy dynasty in the High Atlas.

Mernissi, Fatima, *Doing Daily Battle: Interviews with Moroccan Women* (Women's Press, 1988); *Beyond the Veil: Male-Female Dynamics in Modern Muslim Society* (Al Saqi, 1985), *Islam and Democracy: Fear of the Modern World* (Virago, 1993, reissued with a new introduction in 2002). A hard-hitting assault on Muslim political culture in the wake of the Gulf War and 9/11.

Munson, Henry, *The House of Si Abd Allah* (Yale University Press, 1984). Conversations with a family outside Tangier.

Peets, Leonara, *Women of Marrakesh, 1930–79* (Duke University Press, 1988). Acute social observations by a long-resident Estonian doctor.

Waterbury, John, *North for the Trade* (Berkeley 1972).

Westermarck, Edward, *Ritual and Belief in Morocco* (London, 2 vols, 1926); and *Wit and Wisdom in Morocco* (London, 1930).

Travel Writing and Autobiography

Bowles, Paul, *Their Heads Are Green*, and *Points in Time* (both Harper Perennial, 2006)

Canetti, Elias, *The Voices of Marrakesh* (Marion Boyars, 2002). If you read just one book, make it this one.

Cunnighame Graham, R. B., *Moghreb el Acksa* (Nabu, 2010). An insight into Berber culture

by a late 19th-century traveller imprisoned in the mountains as he searched for the forbidden city of Taroudannt.

Eberhardt, Isabelle, *The Oblivion-Seekers* (Peter Owen, 2010). A wonderful and haunting account of Moroccan personalities and themes, from *kif* addicts to mystics. Eberhardt (1877–1904) died at 27 but this is a well-written legacy with plenty of insight. Try also *In the Shadow of Islam* if you can weather her attitudes to Jews and black Africans.

Frankopan, Peter, *Marrakesh: Through Writers' Eyes* (Eland, 2007). Orwell, Wharton and Freud all feature in this unforgettable collection of writings on the Red City.

Harris, Walter, *Morocco That Was* (1921, Republished Eland 2007). Walter had special access to the sultan and writes evocatively. *The Land of an African Sultan* (London, 1889), and *Tafilet* (Blackwood, Edinburgh, 1895) remain out of print.

Landau, Ron, *Kasbahs of Southern Morocco* (Faber & Faber, 1969).

Lewis, Wyndham, *Journey into Barbary*, first published as *Filibusters in Barbary* (London, 1932; republished Black Sparrow Press, 1984).

Lindqvist, Sven, *Desert Divers* (Granta, 2002). An expertly penned journey through the Sahara reflecting on the writers who went before him and on themes of colonialism, race and liberty. A must.

Mackintosh-Smith, Tim, *Travels with a Tangerine* (Random House, 2004). A coruscating travelogue-history which begins in Morocco as the author follows the travels of Ibn Battuta.

Oufkir, Malika, *Stolen Lives: Twenty Years in a Desert Jail* (Miramax, 2001). Long banned in Morocco, this book describes the twenty-year imprisonment of Malika's privileged Moroccan family following a 1972 coup attempt by her father, General Oufkir. An extraordinary tale.

Saint-Exupéry, Antoine de, *Wind, Sand and Stars* (Mariner, 2006). The pioneer poet of flight flying mail across the Sahara.

Shah, Tahir, *The Caliph's House: A Year in Casablanca* (Bantam, 2006). Shah moved to the city with his family and found a ruined (and haunted) old Caliph's house to live in. Darkly comic tale by an accomplished travel writer.

Weiss, Walter, *Morocco: In the labyrinth of dreams and bazaars* (Haus, 2006). A journey through modern Morocco digging up its past and its present.

Wharton, Edith, *In Morocco* (General Books LLC, 2010). Wharton spent much of 1917 travelling through Morocco, documenting her trip with customary wit and perspicacity.

Moroccan Writing Translated into English

Maghrebi fiction is at its best in novella or short-story form. It is distinguished by its fast narrative and plots, its violence and recurring theme of betrayal by friends and lovers.

Ben Jalloun, Tahar, *The Sand Child* (Hamish Hamilton), *Sacred Night* (Quartet), *With Downcast Eyes* (Little, Brown, USA). Three novels by one of Morocco's most fêted and literate of novelists, a long-time resident of Paris.

Abdesalam Boulaich, Mohammed Choukri, Larbi Layachi, Mohammed Mrabet and **Ahmed Yacoubi,** *Five Eyes* (Black Sparrow Press, 1979). A collection of short stories translated by Paul Bowles.

Choukri, Mohammed, *For Bread Alone, an Autobiography* (Telegraph Books, 2007). A celebrated description of a harrowing childhood on the outer edge of society.

Chraibi, Driss, *Heirs to the Past* (Heinemann 1972), *Mother Comes of Age* (Three Continents Press, 1984), *The Butts* (Passeggiata 1983). Three novels, of which the first is a classic not matched by its successors.

Layachi, Larbi, *A Life Full of Holes* (Harper Perennial 2008), *Yesterday and Today* (Black Sparrow Press, 1985), *The Jealous Lover* (Tombouctou Books, California, 1986).

Mrabet, Mohammed, *Love With a Few Hairs* (Arena, 1986), *M'Hashish* (Peter Owen, 1988), *The Beach Café* and *The Voice* (Black Sparrow Press, USA, 1980), *The Chest* (Tombouctou Books, California, 1983), *Marriage With Papers* (Tombouctou Books, California, 1988), *Look and Move On* (Peter Owen, 1989), all translated by Paul Bowles. Start with the 1960s collection of ten tales, *M'Hashish*, which could be translated as 'bombed out of your mind'.

Serhane, Abselhake, *Messaouda* (Serpent's Tail, 1993). A rite-of-passage novel about a young boy growing up in Azrou and about Morocco shedding the paternalism of the French Protectorate.

Western Fiction Set in Morocco

Barea, Arturo, *The Forging of a Rebel* (Flamingo, 3 vols). Vol 2, *The Track*, deals with the Rif war.

Bowles, Paul, *The Sheltering Sky* (Harper Perennial, 2005), set in the Algerian Sahara; *Let it Come Down* (Harper Perennial, 2006), on Tangier; *The Spider's House* (Harper Perennial, 2006), and *Collected Stories, 1939–1976* (Library of America, 2002), the most complete collection; though there is a host of rivals such as *The Delicate Prey* (1950), *A Hundred Camels in the Courtyard* (1962), *The Time of Friendship* (1967), *Things Gone and Things Still Here* (1977), *A Little Stone* (1950), *Call at Corazon* (1980).

Burgess, Anthony, *Enderby* (Penguin, 1995). Scenes from Tangier clublife.

Burroughs, William, *The Naked Lunch* (Grove, 2009). To those who know them the silhouettes of Tangier and Gibraltar emerge through the dazzling, distorted static of this fantasy.

Busi, Aldo, *Sodomies in Eleven Point* (Faber, 1992). In the words of the blurb, 'a journey of the heart and soul through Literature, Life and Homosexuality'. Morocco and its men treated on pp.37–129.

Chirbes, Rafael, *Mimoun* (Serpent's Tail, 1993). The tale of the breakdown of a young Spaniard in Sefrou, in which every object, each moment is rendered mysterious.

Freud, Esther, *Hideous Kinky* (Harper Perennial, 1999). Warm evocation of the joys of Morocco, as seen in the life of an English hippy mother by her five-year-old daughter.

Gray, Pat, *Mr Narrator* (Dedalus, 1989). An unpublicized modern classic that 'portrays with documentary accuracy a Morocco... colonized by surrealism'.

Grenier, Richard, *The Marrakesh One-Two* (Penguin, 1984). A comic adventure that takes its humour from the clash between Western and Muslim culture.

Gysin, Brian, *The Process* (Overlook Press, 1987). *Kif*-induced adventures in 1960s Tangier and the Sahara.

Hughes, Richard, *In the Lap of the Atlas* (Chatto, 1980). This is set in a fictional Telouèt.

Maugham, Robin, *The Wrong People* (Inland Womensource, 1986). Gay adventures among the smart British expatriate set of Tangier. First published in 1967.

Journals, Letters, Diaries from Tangier

Bowles, Paul, *Without Stopping* (Peter Owen, 1972). An autobiography nicknamed *Without Telling*, a failing not much corrected in the unauthorized biography by C. Sawyer-Lauccano, *An Invisible Spectator* (Bloomsbury, 1989).

Other Bowles-iana include *Paul Bowles by His Friends*, ed. G Pulsifer (Peter Owen); Bowles' slim *A Tangier Journal, 1987–89* (Peter Owen, 1990); and Jane Bowles' *In and Out in the World, Letters 1935–70* (Black Sparrow, 1985).

The Tangier scene has been well covered in: Green, Michelle, *The Dream at the End of the World: Paul Bowles and the Literary Renegades of Tangier* (Bloomsbury), and Finlayson, Ian, *Tangier, City of the Dream* (Harper Collins, 1992).

Entertaining memoirs include Croft-Cooke, Rupert, *The Caves of Hercules* (London, 1974); Edge, David, *Harem*; Herbert, David, *Second Son* (Peter Owen, 1972) and *Engaging Eccentrics* (Peter Owen, 1990); Stewart, Angus, *Tangier, A Writer's Notebook* (London, 1977); and Joe Orton's *Diaries* (London, 1986).

Art and Architecture

Besancot, Jean, *Costumes et Types du Maroc* (Paris, 1942), and *Bijoux Arabes et Berbères du Maroc* (Casablanca, 1954).

Burkhardt, Titus, *Art of Islam, Language and Meaning*, and *Moorish Culture in Spain*.

Damluji, Salma, *Zillij: The Art of Moroccan Ceramics* (Garnet, 1993). Expensive but definitive examination of the ceramic tradition in Morocco.

Dennis, Lisl and Landt, *Living in Morocco* (Thames & Hudson, 2001). An illustrated handbook on using traditional crafts in modern interiors.

Humbert, Claude, *Islamic Ornamental Design* (Faber & Faber, 1980).

Jacques-Meunie, D. J., *Greniers Citadelles au Maroc* (Paris, 1951), *Architectures et Habitats du Dadès* (Paris, 1962), *Sites et Forteresses de l'Atlas* (Paris, 1951).

Khatabi, A., and Sigilmassa, M., *The Splendours of Islamic Calligraphy* (Thames & Hudson, 1976); *Matisse in Morocco: The Paintings and Drawings, 1912–13* (National Gallery of Art, Washington DC).

MWNF (Museum With No Frontiers), *Andalusian Morocco. A Discovery in Living Art*, (Random House, 2002). An excellent introduction to this fundamental strain in Moroccan art and architecture.

Parker, R.B., *Islamic Monuments in Morocco* (Baraka Press, 1981).

Wade, D., *Pattern in Islamic Art* (London, 1976).

Islam

The Koran, trans. NJ Dawood (Penguin, 2003), or *The Qur'an* (OUP, 2008) are the most easily available of the various rival texts.

Burckhardt, Titus, *An Introduction to Sufi Doctrine* (World Wisdom, 2008).

Guillaume, Alfred, *Islam* (Penguin, 2006). First published in 1956.

Nigosian, Solomon, *Islam: The Way of Submission* (Aquarian, 1987).

Rogerson, Barnaby, *The Prophet Muhammed: A Biography* (Abacus, 2004).

Flowers, Birds and Animals

Bergier, P. and F., *A Birdwatcher's Guide to Morocco* (Prion Press, 2004). A practical site guide for the committed birder.

Haltenorth, T. and Diller., H., *A Field Guide to the Mammals of Africa* (Harper Collins, 1980).

Huxley, Anthony and Polunin, Oleg, *Flowers of the Mediterranean* (Chatto & Windus, 1990). The classic well-thumbed travelling companion, now sadly out of print.

Jonsson, Lars, *The Birds of Britain and Europe with North Africa and the Middle East* (Helm Field Guides, 1999).

Thevenot, M., Vernon, R., Bergier, P., *Birds of Morocco* (British Ornithologists Union, 2003).

Shirihai, H., Svensson, L., *Photographic Guide to the Birds of the Western Palearctic* (A&C Black, 2008). Lavishly illustrated guide.

Raine, Peter, *Rough Guide to Mediterranean Wildlife* (1990). Fine general coverage plus a detailed country chapter.

Cookery

Benkirane, Fettouma, *Secrets of Moroccan Cooking*, and *Moroccan Cooking: The Best Recipes* (Sochepress, 1996).

Carrier, Robert, *Taste of Morocco* (Arrow, 1997). An illustrated labour of love concentrating on the palace traditions.

Guinaudeau, Z., *Fez, Traditional Moroccan Cooking* (Rabat, 1957).

Roden, Claudia, *The Book of Jewish Food* (Viking, 1997). A fascinating exploration of Jewish culinary tradition, including a section on Morocco.

Stevens, Tara, *Clock Book: Recipes from the Modern Moroccan Kitchen* (33 Books, 2010). Wonderful recipes and inspiring stories from the Café Clock and the medina in Fez.

Wolfert, Paula, *Good Food from Morocco* (John Murray, 1962). All the secrets of traditional home cooking.

Language

The official language of Morocco is Arabic, though 40 per cent of the population speak one of the three Berber dialects as their first language. Moroccans have a natural linguistic ability, and in the cities they will typically speak Arabic, possibly know one of the Berber dialects, learn French or Spanish at school and also juggle with a little English, Dutch or German. In all but the most rural areas you will be understood speaking French. Spanish is understood and spoken in Spain's old colonial possessions in the far north and south, the Rif and the Western Sahara. Hotel porters, guides and hustlers can usually be relied on to know some English. In short, it is easy to travel and communicate in Morocco without learning Arabic. However, if you can learn a few phrases or greetings you will not only give great pleasure but will also earn goodwill useful in any transaction or relationship.

For useful phrases to use in a restaurant and a French menu-reader, *see* **Food and Drink**, pp.65–6.

Moroccan Arabic

Pronunciation

Classical Arabic and modern Arabic as spoken in Cairo or Mecca are very different from the official language of Morocco – Maghrebi Arabic. It is a very guttural language, but this does not mean that it should be hard sounding.

As a general rule, hard consonants should be pronounced as far back in the throat as possible, thereby softening them slightly. In particular:

'**q**' should be quite like a 'k', softened by being vocalized from farther back in the throat

'**gh**' should sound like a purring 'gr', again from the back of the throat, a hardened French 'r'

'**kh**' like a Gaelic 'ch', pronounced from the back of the throat, as in the Scottish 'loch'

'**j**' again a softer sound, like the French pronunciation of the letter, as in 'Frère Jacques'

'**ai**' should sound like the letter 'i' as you would pronounce it when reciting the alphabet

'**ay**' should sound like the letter 'a' as in the recited alphabet

Basic Phrases

Yes *Eeyeh*
No *Waha, La*
Please *Minfadlik*
Thank you *Shokran/Barakalayfik*
Good *Mizeyen*
Bad *Meshee mizeyen*

Meetings, Greetings, Conversation

Sir *Si, Sidi*
Madam *Lalla*
Hello *Labes (informal), Salam Alaykoom*
How are you? *Ooach khbar'ek?*
Fine *Labes*
Good morning *Sbah l'khir*
Good evening *Msa l'khir*
Goodbye *B'slemah*
Goodnight *Leela saieeda*
My name is... *Ismee ...*
How do you say ... in Arabic? *Keef tkoobal ... Arbia?*
I don't understand *Ma fhemshi*
I don't know *Ma arafshi*
Help! *Ateqq!*
Excuse me *Smeh lee*
Sorry *Asif*
Never mind/such is life *Maalesh*
No problem *Mush mushkillah*

Travelling and Directions

train *tren*
bus *l'kar/tobis*
car *tomobeel, sayara*
ticket *bitaka/beeyay*
left *al leeser*
right *al leemin*
When is the first/last/next ...?
  Waqtash ...loowel/l'akher/lee minbad?
Where is ...? *Fayn kayn ...?*
  a hotel *otel/fondouk*
  a restaurant *restaurant*
  a lavatory *vaysay*
  the bus station *mahata d'lkeeran*
  the train station *mahata d'ltren*
  a bank *bank*
  a post office *bousta/barid*

At a Hotel

I would like a room *B'gheet beet*
Do you have a room? *Wesh andik wahid beet?*
Can I look at it? *Wesh yimkin nshoof?*

Numbers

1 *wahed*
2 *jooj*
3 *tlata*
4 *arba*
5 *khamsa*
6 *setta*
7 *seba*
8 *tmenia*
9 *tse'ud*
10 *ashra*
20 *ashrin*
50 *khamsin*
100 *mia*
1000 *alef*

Buying and Bargaining

How much is that? *Bsh hal hadeek?*
Too expensive *Ghalee bzef*
Do you have...? *Wesh andik ...?*
larger *kebira*
smaller *seghira*
cheaper *rkhaysa*
This is no good *Hadee meshee mizeyen*
I don't want any *Mabgheet shee*
Okay! *Wakha!*

French

Despite an official Arabicization policy, French remains the language of higher education, technology, government and big business.

Pronunciation

Vowels

a/à/â between *a* in 'bat' and 'part'
é/er/ez at end of word as *a* in 'plate' but a bit shorter
e/è/ê as *e* in 'bet'
e at end of word not pronounced
e at end of syllable or in one-syllable word pronounced weakly, like *er* in 'mother'
i as *ee* in 'bee'
o as *o* in 'pot'
ô as *o* in 'go'
u/û between *oo* in 'boot' and *ee* in 'bee'

Vowel Combinations

ai as *a* in 'plate'
aî as *e* in 'bet'
ail as *i* in 'kite'
au/eau as *o* in 'go'
ei as *e* in 'bet'
eu/œu a s *er* in 'mother'
oi between *wa* in 'swam' and *wu* in 'swum'
oy as 'why'
ui as *wee* in 'twee'

Nasal Vowels

Vowels followed by an *n* or *m* have a nasal sound.
an/en as *o* in 'pot' + nasal sound
ain/ein/in as *a* in 'bat' + nasal sound
on as *aw* in 'paw' + nasal sound
un a s *u* in 'nul' + nasal sound

Consonants

Many French consonants are pronounced as in English, but there are some exceptions:
c followed by *e, i* or *y*, and *ç* as *s* in 'sit'
c followed by *a, o, u* as *c* in 'cat'
g followed by *e, i* or *y* as *s* in 'pleasure'
g followed by *a, o, u* as *g* in 'good'
gn as *ni* in 'opinion'
j as *s* in 'pleasure'
ll as *y* in 'yes'
qu as *k* in 'kite'
s between vowels as *z* in 'zebra'

13
Language

s otherwise as *s* in 'sit'

w **except in English words** as *v* in 'vest'

x **at end of word** as *s* in 'sit'

x **otherwise** as *x* in 'six'

Stress

The stress usually falls on the last syllable except when the word ends with an unaccented *e*.

Basic Phrases

Yes *Non*
No *Oui*
Please *S'il vous plaît*
Thank you *Merci*
Good *Bon*
Bad *Mauvais*

Meetings, Greetings, Conversation

Sir *Monsieur*
Madam *Madame*
Hello *Bonjour*
How are you? *Comment allez-vous?*
Fine *Ça va bien*
Good morning *Bonjour*
Good evening *Bonsoir*
Goodbye *Au revoir*
Goodnight *Bonne nuit*
My name is *Je m'appelle*
How do you say ... in French? *Comment dit-on ... en français?*
I don't understand *Je ne comprends pas*
I don't know *Je ne sais pas*
Help! *Au secours!*
Excuse me *Excusez-moi*
Sorry *Pardon*
Never mind/ such is life *C'est la vie*
No problem *Pas de problème*

Travelling and Directions

What time does it leave (arrive)?
A quelle heure part-il (arrive-t-il)?
From where does it leave? *D'où part-il?*
Do you stop at... ? *Passez-vous par... ?*
How long does the trip take?
Combien de temps dure le voyage?
A (single/return) ticket to...
un aller or aller simple/aller et retour) pour...
How much is the fare?
Combien coûte le billet?

Have a good trip! *Bon voyage!*
airport *l'aéroport*
aeroplane *l'avion*
berth *la couchelle*
bicycle *la bicyclette/le vélo*
train *train*
bus *autobus*
car *voiture*
ticket *billet*
left *à gauche*
right *à droite*
When is the firstt ... ?
A quelle heure part le premier ... ?
When is the last ... ?
A quelle heure part le dernier ... ?
When is the next ... ?
A quelle heure part le prochain ... ?
Where is ... ? *Où se trouve ... ?*
a hotel *un hôtel*
a campsite *un camping*
a restaurant *un restaurant*
a lavatory *un W.C.*
the bus station *la gare d'autobus*
the train station *la gare*
a bank *une banque*
a post office *une poste*

At a Hotel

I would like a room *Je voudrais une chambre*
Do you have a room? *Est-ce que vous avez une chambre?*
Can I look at it? *Est-ce qu'on peut la voir?*
How much is the room per day? *C'est combien la chambre par jour?*
How much is the room per week? *C'est combien la chambre parsemaine?*
a single room *une chambre pour une personne*
a twin room *une chambre à deux lits*
a double room *une chambre pour deux personnes*
... with a shower/bath *... avec douche/salle de bains*
... for one night/one week *... pour une nuit/une semaine*
bed *un lit*
blanket *une couverture*
pillow *un oreiller*
soap *du savon*
towel *une serviette*

Numbers

1 *un*
2 *deux*
3 *trois*
4 *quatre*
5 *cinq*
6 *six*
7 *sept*
8 *huit*
9 *neuf*
10 *dix*
20 *vingt*
50 *cinquante*
100 *cent*
1000 *mille*

Buying and Bargaining

How much is that? *C'est combien?*
Too expensive *Trop cher*
Do you have...? *Est-ce que vous avez des ...?*
larger *plus grand*
smaller *plus petit*
cheaper *moins cher*
This is no good *Ça ne va pas*
I don't want any *Je n'en veux pas*
Okay! *Okay!*

Index

Main page references are in **bold**. Page references to maps are in *italics*.

Acknowledgements

The editor would like to thank: the staff at the Moroccan national tourist office in London and their branches in Morocco; Tara Stevens and Mike Richardson at the Clock Café in Fez; Meredith Marshall; Elspeth Anderson; Isobel McLean; and Catherine Knight at New Holland.

2nd American edition published in 2011 by

CADOGAN GUIDES USA
An imprint of Interlink Publishing Group, Inc
46 Crosby Street, Northampton, Massachusetts 01060
www.interlinkbooks.com
www.cadoganguidesusa.com

Text Copyright © Barnaby Rogerson 2000, 2011
Copyright © 2011 New Holland Publishers (UK) Ltd

Cover and photo essay photographs: front cover © PCL Travel; back cover © Photolibrary
Photo essay photographs: © istockphoto.com, except p.15 (top): © Alamy.
Maps © Cadogan Guides, drawn by Maidenhead Cartographic Services Ltd
Publisher: Guy Hobbs
Text update: Alexander Monro
Cover design: Jason Hopper
Photo essay design: Sarah Gardner
Editor: Mary-Ann Gallagher
Proofreading: Elspeth Anderson
Indexing: Isobel McLean

Printed and bound in Italy by Legoprint
Library of Congress Cataloging-in-Publication Data available

ISBN: 978-1-56656-820-3

The author and publishers have made every effort to ensure the accuracy of the information in this book at the time of going to press. However, they cannot accept any responsibility for any loss, injury or inconvenience resulting from the use of information contained in this guide.

Please help us to keep this guide up to date. Although we have done our best to ensure that the information in this guide is correct at the time of going to press, laws and regulations are constantly changing and standards and prices fluctuate. We would be delighted to receive any comments concerning existing entries or omissions.

To request our complete full-color catalog, please call us toll free at 1-800-238-LINK, visit our website at www.interlinkbooks.com, or send us an email: info@interlinkbooks.com.